Exam Ref 70-342
Advanced Solutions of
Microsoft Exchange
Server 2013

Brian Reid
Steve Goodman

PUBLISHED BY
Microsoft Press
A Division of Microsoft Corporation
One Microsoft Way
Redmond, Washington 98052-6399

Library of Congress Control Number: 2014951932
ISBN: 978-0-7356-9741-6

Printed and bound in the United States of America.

First Printing

Microsoft Press books are available through booksellers and distributors worldwide. If you need support related to this book, email Microsoft Press Book Support at mspinput@microsoft.com. Please tell us what you think of this book at *http://aka.ms/tellpress*.

Acquisitions Editor: Karen Szall
Developmental Editor: Karen Szall
Editorial Production: Troy Mott, Ellie Volckhausen
Technical Reviewer: Andrew Higginbotham
Copyeditor: Christina Rudloff
Indexer: Julie Grady
Cover: Twist Creative • Seattle

Contents at a glance

Contents

What do you think of this book? We want to hear from you!

Microsoft is interested in hearing your feedback so we can continually improve our books and learning resources for you. To participate in a brief online survey, please visit:

www.microsoft.com/learning/booksurvey/

Chapter 2: Design, configure, and manage site resiliency 65

Chapter 4: Configure and manage compliance, archiving, and discovery solutions   203

Chapter 5: Implement and manage coexistence, hybrid scenarios, migration, and federation 279

What do you think of this book? We want to hear from you!

Microsoft is interested in hearing your feedback so we can continually improve our books and learning resources for you. To participate in a brief online survey, please visit:

www.microsoft.com/learning/booksurvey/

Introduction

Most Exchange Server books take the view of telling how to complete each task. For the designer of Exchange Server organizations, this is not sufficient. This is why there is both an exam on how to complete tasks, and also a second exam on why to complete tasks. This book covers the objective domain of Microsoft Exam 70-342, and the "why" for why you would do something in the product, as well as some of the "how" for the more in-depth features.

This book covers every exam objective, but it does not cover every exam question. Only the Microsoft exam team has access to the exam questions themselves and Microsoft regularly adds new questions to the exam, making it impossible to cover specific questions. You should consider this book a supplement to your relevant real-world experience and other study materials. If you encounter a topic in this book that you do not feel completely comfortable with, use the links you'll find in text to find more information and take the time to research and study the topic. Great information is available on MSDN, TechNet, and in blogs and forums.

Microsoft certifications

Microsoft certifications distinguish you by proving your command of a broad set of skills and experience with current Microsoft products and technologies. The exams and corresponding certifications are developed to validate your mastery of critical competencies as you design and develop, or implement and support, solutions with Microsoft products and technologies both on-premises and in the cloud. Certification brings a variety of benefits to the individual and to employers and organizations.

> **MORE INFO** **ALL MICROSOFT CERTIFICATIONS**
>
> For information about Microsoft certifications, including a full list of available certifications, go to *http://www.microsoft.com/learning/en/us/certification/cert-default.aspx*.

Acknowledgments

It is not an easy effort writing a book on Exchange Server. As you can probably guess from the scope of the chapter headings, this book for Microsoft Exam 70-342 covers a large portion of Exchange Server and Exchange Online in Office 365. It is therefore not possible to write a book that covers this data, though some of it is similar to that in Exchange Server

2010, by far a lot has changed subtly and also in detail. That is not including Office 365, and specifically here, the pieces on Exchange Online and Office 365. This appears to change daily, and although it is not that frequent, there will be bits of this book that may well work differently from between when we wrote it and when you read it—that is the effect of cloud computing.

There are many people that are involved with writing a book, not least I would like to start with thanking Steve Goodman my co-author, and Nicolas Blank my co-director at NB Consult whose idea it was that I should write this book and not the one for Exam 341! Paul Robichaux and Bhargav Shukla are writing the book for 70-341, so that at least there is a pair of these books for both exams! I would also like to thank Andrew Higginbotham for his technical review and his BBQ, Ashley Poxon for reading early chapter proofs for me, and for the help from various MVPs, including Justin Harris.

But finally, and most importantly, I would like to thank Jenny my wife, for the evenings lost writing, sorry! For your support and care, thanks! For the love you give me in modeling our savior Christ, my love back.

—Brian Reid

I'd like to mirror Brian's sentiments and thank my fellow MVPs who have supported both the writing and editing of this book, along with Microsoft Press. In particular I'd like to thank Brian Reid my co-author, Paul Robichaux for recommending me to Microsoft Press, and Karen Szall for her support and patience.

Finally, I'd like to thank my family—my wife Lisa for putting up with the many nights taken up writing, and my daughters Isabelle and Olivia for constantly reminding me of what's really important. Last but not least, I'd like to thank my father for reading every book I write cover to cover, whether he understands it or not!

—Steve Goodman

Free ebooks from Microsoft Press

From technical overviews to in-depth information on special topics, the free ebooks from Microsoft Press cover a wide range of topics. These ebooks are available in PDF, EPUB, and Mobi for Kindle formats, ready for you to download at:

http://aka.ms/mspressfree

Check back often to see what is new!

Microsoft Virtual Academy

Build your knowledge of Microsoft technologies with free expert-led online training from Microsoft Virtual Academy (MVA). MVA offers a comprehensive library of videos, live events, and more to help you learn the latest technologies and prepare for certification exams. You'll find what you need here:

http://www.microsoftvirtualacademy.com

Errata, updates, & book support

We've made every effort to ensure the accuracy of this book and its companion content. You can access updates to this book—in the form of a list of submitted errata and their related corrections—at:

http://aka.ms/ER342/errata

If you discover an error that is not already listed, please submit it to us at the same page.

If you need additional support, email Microsoft Press Book Support at mspinput@microsoft.com.

Please note that product support for Microsoft software and hardware is not offered through the previous addresses. For help with Microsoft software or hardware, go to *http://support.microsoft.com*.

We want to hear from you

At Microsoft Press, your satisfaction is our top priority, and your feedback our most valuable asset. Please tell us what you think of this book at:

http://aka.ms/tellpress

The survey is short, and we read every one of your comments and ideas. Thanks in advance for your input!

Stay in touch

Let's keep the conversation going! We're on Twitter: *http://twitter.com/MicrosoftPress*.

Preparing for the exam

Microsoft certification exams are a great way to build your resume and let the world know about your level of expertise. Certification exams validate your on-the-job experience and product knowledge. Although there is no substitute for on-the-job experience, preparation through study and hands-on practice can help you prepare for the exam. We recommend that you augment your exam preparation plan by using a combination of available study materials and courses. For example, you might use the Exam ref and another study guide for your "at home" preparation, and take a Microsoft Official Curriculum course for the classroom experience. Choose the combination that you think works best for you.

Note that this Exam Ref is based on publicly available information about the exam and the author's experience. To safeguard the integrity of the exam, authors do not have access to the live exam.

## CHAPTER 1

Configure, manage, and migrate Unified Messaging

U nified Messaging provides a voice interface in Exchange Server 2013, providing features including voicemail and audio access to individual mailboxes. The Unified Messaging features are part of the Client Access and Mailbox roles in Exchange, and are available in every Exchange 2013 deployment. This is a big change from the previous two versions of Exchange where Unified Messaging was a separate role. Both the Client Access and Mailbox Server Roles contain parts of Unified Messaging, with the former hosting the Unified Messaging Call Router service, and the latter hosting the Unified Messaging service itself.

> **IMPORTANT**
> **Have you read page xix?**
> It contains valuable information regarding the skills you need to pass the exam.

In this chapter, you explore how to configure Unified Messaging to talk to a typical Internet Protocol Private Branch Exchange (IP-PBX) using the Session Initiation Protocol (SIP). SIP is the modern phone system equivalent of the Simple Mail Transfer Protocol (SMTP) used for email. Coverage of topics that you should expect to be on the exam include understanding how to set up Unified Messaging, along with areas of consideration when designing for high availability.

This chapter also discusses managing Unified Messaging after it is in use within the organization. Tasks once deployed include managing settings and features for individual users and configuration of policies, along with managing additional language packs. Alongside the management of Unified Messaging, this chapter covers troubleshooting various aspects of a Unified Messaging deployment such as troubleshooting security settings, monitoring call statistics, or troubleshooting SIP communications.

To ensure that you are equipped with the right knowledge to perform an upgrade of Exchange where a deployment of a previous version of Unified Messaging is already in place, this chapter covers migration of Unified Messaging to Exchange 2013, including the necessary preparation, planning, and considerations for coexistence. Additionally, this chapter also covers how to move Unified Messaging enabled mailboxes, move voice services, and removing the legacy Unified Messaging environment.

Objectives in this chapter:

- Objective 1.1: Configure Unified Messaging (UM)
- Objective 1.2: Manage Unified Messaging
- Objective 1.3: Troubleshoot Unified Messaging
- Objective 1.4: Migrate Unified Messaging

Understanding Unified Messaging

Before you explore how to configure Unified Messaging in Exchange Server 2013, take a few moments to gain a better understanding of what it offers, and how it fits into the overall Exchange Server product.

Unified Messaging provides a voice interface to the Exchange Server. This forms a key tenet of integrating Exchange into a Unified Communications solution, the theory being that a single set of communications systems work together providing the user with a streamlined experience no matter how they access the system. From an administrator perspective, the Unified Messaging role provides administrators with a feature set that they would otherwise require third-party products for, allowing an organization that has chosen to implement the Microsoft stack (often referred to as a Microsoft Shop) the ability to fully function just using Microsoft products, often allowing the removal of old expensive systems.

Features provided with Unified Messaging include:

- **Voice mail** A comprehensive voice mail system using existing mailboxes as the underlying store for voice mail messages. This feature-rich voice mail includes basic functionality like enabling message waiting indicators on desk phones and integration with Microsoft Lync.

- **Transcription of voice messages** In supported locales the Exchange Server can process the audio recording and insert a transcription of the message for the recipient to read in Outlook, allowing the user to quickly triage voice mail.

- **Protected Voice Mail** When enabled, Protected Voice Mail allows private messages to be encrypted using Active Directory Rights Management Services. This provides the same enterprise-grade protection offered for Office documents and standard email messages.

- **Missed call notifications** In addition to just allowing callers to record voice mail, Unified Messaging also provides notifications when a call is missed. When a call is transferred to voicemail, but the caller neglects to leave a voicemail message, a notification is sent instead.

- **Call Answering Rules** Those familiar with rules in Outlook will find the concept of Call Answering Rules straightforward. Multiple rules can be configured specifying conditions, such as the calendar status of the call recipient, with actions to be taken. This includes diverting the call to a colleague, presenting a menu of options to the caller, or

Exchange can even attempt to reach the call recipient on alternative phone numbers before transferring to voice mail.

- **Play on phone** Outlook 2007, 2010 and Outlook 2013 along with Outlook Web App allows the voice mail recipient to choose to play the voice message on the desk phone (or another number, if allowed) rather than through the PC speakers. This functionality extends to the Outlook Web App options pages and allows the user to initiate a call from OWA to record greetings. This is a big improvement over navigating the voice mail options menus via a desk phone.

- **Outlook Voice Access** Unified Messaging is not just about providing access to voice mail in the email client. Outlook Voice Access provides functionality allowing a user to call into their mailbox from any phone and manipulate their own mailbox. The user can either via speech recognition, or using the phone keypad, request the server to read messages, reply to messages, or even adjust appointments. A great example of how this can work is if a person is running late for a meeting, they can dial into Outlook Voice Access and ask Exchange to push the meeting back 15 minutes. All attendees will receive an updated invitation.

- **Auto attendant** Most people have called a company and instead of speaking directly to a person, have been greeted by a computer presenting options to direct the call. For example, "If you are calling to open a new account, please press one; if you are calling to enquire about your bill, please press two." This functionality is called an auto attendant and is included within Unified Messaging. The Exchange auto attendant features include the common keypad-operated menus along with speech recognition. Trees of menus can be combined through the use of multiple, linked auto attendants and if enabled, callers can search the global address list and then be directed straight to the right person. Auto attendants are not necessary for a Unified Messaging implementation.

- **Inbound fax support** When Unified Messaging was first introduced within Exchange Server 2007, Unified Messaging was capable of interpreting fax messages directly and delivering them to a user mailbox. While inbound fax support is still included, Exchange 2013 requires a third-party product to be used to perform the fax conversation. This works by, after detecting a fax, Exchange performing a redirect to the fax solution.

Because Exchange Server 2013 always includes the Unified Messaging services as part of the Mailbox and Client Access Server roles, the installation is no more complicated than a standard installation of Exchange Server 2013.

During the installation of prerequisites for Exchange Server, some unusual prerequisites are required, including the Desktop Experience and the Microsoft Unified Communications Managed API Core Runtime. In the context of Unified Messaging, these prerequisites begin to make a lot of sense.

The Unified Communications Managed API Core Runtime is particularly important because this bundle provides the core software that underpins the voice functionality of Exchange 2013, including Automatic Speech Recognition and Text-to-Speech (TTS).

Objective 1.1: Configure Unified Messaging (UM)

The basic configuration of Unified Messaging is necessary to enable your Exchange infrastructure to communicate with your telephone system, and requires an understanding of both your Exchange environment and your phone system.

This objective covers how to:

- Configure an IP gateway
- Configure a UM call router
- Create and configure an auto attendant
- Configure a call answering rule
- Design Unified Messaging for high availability
- Create a dial plan

Configuring an IP gateway

In computing terms an IP gateway can mean many things. In the context of Unified Messaging, it represents the phone system's last hop before it reaches Microsoft Exchange Unified Messaging. In most cases, this will be the IP address of the IP-PBX, or if it is an analogue or IP-PBX system that is not compatible directly with the Unified Messaging service, a gateway device that translates from one phone system language to another, often called a session border controller.

The UM IP gateway object

The IP gateway is used by Exchange Server 2013 to ensure it understands the mapping between each phone system and the relevant configuration, such as dial plans in Exchange Server. Dial plans are covered later in detail later, but simply put, they are used to group extensions together.

In Figure 1-1, you see an example of a simple phone system connected to Exchange. The IP-PBX connects directly to Exchange Server and is defined as the IP gateway. Upon connection, the Exchange 2013 server will verify that it has a definition in Active Directory.

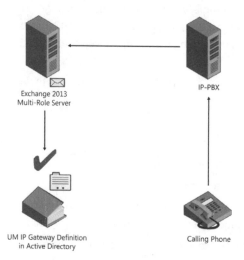

FIGURE 1-1 An example of an IP gateway connected to an Exchange 2013 server

What you need to know before configuring an IP gateway

When configuring an IP gateway in Exchange Server, you will need to know a number of details about the device before you can add it to Exchange:

- A descriptive name you will use to name the IP gateway in Exchange Unified Messaging.
- The IP address or Fully Qualified Domain Name (FQDN) of the device.
- The dial plan that the IP gateway should be associated with.
- Whether the IP gateway supports outgoing calls from Exchange Unified Messaging.
- Whether the IP gateway can process Message Waiting Indicator (MWI) notifications, used to light up or extinguish the Message Waiting lamp on IP phones.

> **IMPORTANT** **USING THE FQDN FOR THE ADDRESS OF THE IP GATEWAY**
>
> If you are using the SIP Secured or Secured encryption setting on the associated dial plan, you must use the Fully Qualified Domain Name for the address of the IP gateway. This is because a valid, matching SSL certificate is required, and the SSL certificate name must match the IP gateway address.

The IP gateway, whether it is a gateway device providing an interface between both systems, or if it is an IP-PBX, will need to be configured too. This configuration will typically include:

- The Fully Qualified Domain Name of the Exchange 2013 Client Access Servers it will route calls to, sometimes defined as another IP gateway in the IP-PBX, or a trunk.
- Definitions for the numbers that will be routed to the UM servers. These may be contact objects in the case of a Lync/Skype for business system.

- Configuration of the IP gateway can be accomplished using either the Exchange Admin Center, which is the web browser user interface for managing Exchange 2013, or via the Exchange Management Shell, which is the command line interface based upon PowerShell.

Via the Exchange Admin Center the basic settings can be configured. The settings that can be configured include:

- The name of the IP gateway.

- The address of the IP gateway.

- Whether outgoing calls are allowed through the IP gateway.

- If the Message Waiting Indicator signals are allowed.

Via the Exchange Management Shell the same settings can be configured, using the Set-UMIPGateway cmdlet, and in addition a wider range of settings are exposed for configuration:

- **Port**   This parameter specifies the port that the IP gateway is expected to listen on. By default Unified Messaging expects the IP gateway to listen on TCP port 5060. If this is not the case, a port can be specified here and Exchange Unified Messaging will attempt to contact the IP gateway on the alternative port.

- **IPAddressFamily**   This allows IP version 4 and/or IP version 6 to be used. By default, *IPv4Only* is chosen. If *IPv6* is chosen, IP version 6 will be used first, then in the event of failure, IP version 4 will be used. If *IPv6only* is chosen, the call will fail if the inbound or outbound request to or from the IP gateway does not support IP version 6.

- **ForceUpgrade**   This allows the UM IP gateway object definition to be upgraded.

- **DelayedSourcePartyInfoEnabled**   This allows the incoming call from the IP gateway to be delayed if the SIP invite request contains no calling party and diversion information.

- **Simulator**   This parameter allows an administrator to specify that client will attempt to connect to the server directly, rather than an actual IP gateway device. This is used for testing.

- **Status**   This parameter allows the IP gateway to be disabled. This is typically used to disable one of multiple gateways when it the IP-PBX team need to perform maintenance on it.

Additional IP gateway configuration cmdlets available

The Exchange Management Shell is always used under the hood by the GUI to make configuration changes to Microsoft Exchange, and in most cases only the most common actions are available via the GUI. To make complex or non-routine configuration changes, the Exchange Management Shell is usually required. In the previous section you saw an example of the range of parameters available for configuring all relevant attributes for the IP gateway definition.

As you saw, a range of cmdlets are available that expose the full range of functionality. These are as follows:

- **New-UMIPGateway**   Used to create a new IP gateway configuration object in Microsoft Exchange.

- **Remove-UMIPGateway**   Used to delete configuration settings for the IP gateway in Microsoft Exchange.

- **Disable-UMIPGateway**   Used to rapidly prevent a UM IP gateway from being available for use within Microsoft Exchange.

- **Enable-UMIPGateway**   Used to rapidly enable a UM IP gateway previously disabled.

- **Get-UMIPGateway**   Used to retrieve either all UM IP gateways configured within the Exchange organization, or examine settings for a particular gateway.

- **Set-UMIPGateway**   As described in the previous section, used to make core configuration changes to an IP gateway configuration within Microsoft Exchange, or when combined with Get-UMIPGateway can be used for making changes en-mass.

> *MORE INFO*   **THE PARAMETERS**
>
> Each gateway cmdlet listed above has a set of parameters. These can be discovered from the Exchange Management Shell using the Get-Help cmdlet followed by the cmdlet you want to know more about. Use the Online parameter with Get-Help to view the list of parameters and their descriptions, along with examples of use on the Microsoft TechNet website.

Configuring an IP gateway using the Exchange Admin Center

To create a new IP gateway, open the Exchange Admin Center, as shown in Figure 1-2, and complete the following steps:

1. Log in as an administrative user and navigate to the Unified Messaging section.

2. Select the UM IP Gateways tab.

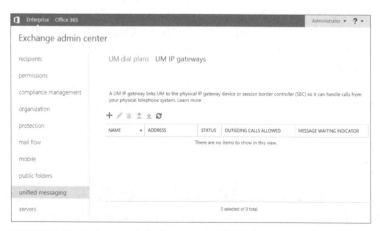

FIGURE 1-2 The Exchange Admin Center in the UM IP Gateways section with no IP gateways defined

3. To add a new UM IP gateway, choose the Add (+) button. This opens the New UM IP Gateway window, shown in Figure 1-3.

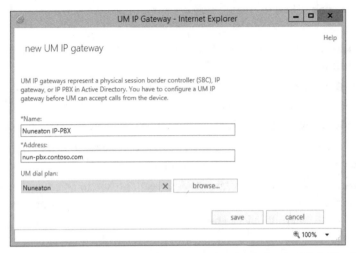

FIGURE 1-3 Creating a new UM IP gateway using the Exchange Admin Center

4. In the Name text box, enter the descriptive name chosen. This is for the administrator reference.

5. In the Address text box, enter the IP address or Fully Qualified Domain Name.

6. Select the correct UM dial plan to associate with this UM IP gateway.

After creating a UM IP gateway within the Exchange Admin Center, its properties can be altered either via the Exchange Admin Center or via the Exchange Management Shell. Before examining a UM IP gateway, it is important to understand what changes can be made.

The toolbar icons in the UM IP Gateway tab, shown in Figure 1-4, provide additional options after selecting an individual UM IP gateway. The option to Add a new IP gateway is always shown first on the left. The other options are to Edit, Delete, Disable, Enable IP gateways, followed by the ability to refresh the list. These toolbar icons correspond to being able to use the New-UMIPGateway, Set-UMIPGateway, Disable-UMIPGateway, Enable-UMIPGateway cmdlets and the refresh button calls the Get-UMIPGateway command to retrieve the full list of UM IP gateways configured.

For each UM IP gateway, a number of columns are disabled. These are based on the output of Get-UMIPGateway and represent the current attributes configured in Exchange.

NAME	ADDRESS	STATUS ▲	OUTGOING CALLS ALLOWED	MESSAGE WAITING INDICATOR
Nuneaton IP-PBX	nun-pbx.contoso.c...	Enabled	Yes	On

FIGURE 1-4 A UM IP gateway selected with toolbar icons providing access to common functionality

To make configuration changes to the attributes of an individual UM IP gateway, click the Edit button to open the properties window for the selected UM IP gateway, as shown in Figure 1-5. You can alter the basic configuration of the UM IP gateway.

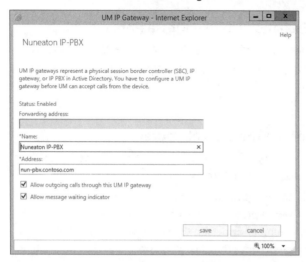

FIGURE 1-5 Editing the UM IP gateway via the Exchange Admin Center

Configuring an IP gateway using the Exchange Management Shell

To create a new IP gateway using the Exchange Management Shell, you will use the New-UMIPGateway cmdlet. In addition to defining the name, address, and associated dial plan for the UM IP gateway, you can define the IP address family settings at the time of creation if you need to change the default. This example creates a UM IP gateway with the same settings as used in the previous section.

Creating a New UM IP gateway

```
New-UMIPGateway -Name "Nuneaton IP-PBX" -Address nun-pbx.contoso.com -UMDialPlan
"Nuneaton"
```

To view the configuration of the newly defined UM IP gateway, use the following.

Get UM IP gateway configuration

```
Get-UMIPGateway -Identity "Nuneaton IP-PBX"
```

To make a configuration change, such as updating the address value, use the following.

Set UM IP gateway configuration

```
Set-UMIPGateway -Identity "Nuneaton IP-PBX" -Address nun-pbx.contoso.com
```

Configuring the UM call router

The UM call router is newly introduced with Exchange Server 2013. In previous versions of Exchange, the Unified Messaging service was responsible for dealing with and diverting calls where necessary.

Changes to the architecture of Exchange Server in Exchange 2013 mean that the UM call router service is necessary to ensure that the server hosting the active copy of the mailbox performs all relevant actions for the user.

UM Call Router role within Exchange Unified Messaging

The UM call router service runs on each server hosting the Client Access role. The Client Access role in Exchange 2013 typically is a protocol-aware proxy, or performs redirection, and this concept applies to Unified Messaging. The UM call router performs the redirection functions for traffic arriving from IP gateway devices.

Understanding call redirection via the UM call router

Understanding how this works requires a very basic understanding of the protocol used for Voice over IP (VoIP) signaling, the Session Initiation Protocol (SIP).

SIP traffic does not contain any call audio but the traffic instead is a text-based conversation between the two systems, and is used to provide some information about the call, such as the caller, and information about the number or person they are calling. Only after the initial transaction in the SIP message completes does the dialog box start, and the two systems use Session Description Protocol (SDP) within the SIP dialog box to decide what Real Time Protocol (RTP) audio codec to use for the audio streams.

The UM call router will only participate in the initial SIP message because, as the role it fulfils is to redirect, it will use the information provided about the recipient to look up the mailbox server that hosts the recipient's mailbox, and then respond with a *302 redirect message* providing the Fully Qualified Domain Name of the mailbox server and port. The conversation with the UM call router ends at this point.

Ports and addresses used by the UM call router

The ports that the UM call router can listen for communications from an IP gateway are set by default to the following ports:

- Port 5060, used for unencrypted TCP traffic.
- Port 5061, used for traffic secured by TLS.

As Unified Messaging in Exchange Server 2013 fully supports IP version 6, the UM call router is able to accept connections from IP gateway devices using either IP version 4, or IP version 6. This can be configured based on requirements.

SIP traffic can use both TCP unencrypted and be secured by the TLS protocol. The choice typically depends on your security requirements and the supported methods that your IP gateway can use. Microsoft Lync/Skype for business must use TLS, however some third-party IP-PBX systems must use TCP.

Configuring the UM call router using the Exchange Management Shell

All configuration for the UM call router service must be performed using the Exchange Management Shell. There are very few options available for configuration and most organizations will not need to change the default settings.

Because both the UM call router service and the UM service share a common history, they have similar options within each services' respective Get/Set-UMCallRouterSettings and Get/Set-UMService cmdlets. Naturally the UM service cmdlets have the vast majority of attributes available.

When making modifications to the UM call router service, the following parameters are available using the Set-UMCallRouterSettings cmdlet:

- **Server** This parameter is used to define the Client Access Server that the cmdlet will make configuration changes against.
- **SipTcpListeningPort** This parameter defines the TCP/IP port that the UM call router service will listen on for incoming requests from an IP gateway using an unencrypted protocol.
- **SipTlsListeningPort** This parameter specifies the TCP/IP port that the UM call router service listens for encrypted communications on.
- **UMStartupMode** This parameter is used to define if the UM call router service will use just the TCP mode, just the TLS mode, or startup in Dual mode where it listens on both ports.
- **Dial Plans** This parameter, when using Microsoft Lync/Skype for business, is used to list all of the Unified Messaging dial plans that this UM call router will service. It can contain multiple dial plans.
- **IPAddressFamily** and **IPAddressFamilyConfigurable** These parameters can be used to alter whether the IP address family is configurable, and if it should listen on IPv4Only, IPv6Only or Any. By default this is set to Any.

Additional parameters are available, however these are marked as reserved for Microsoft Internal Use. Usually this means they are used within Microsoft Office 365, which also runs Microsoft Exchange Unified Messaging services.

In the example below, the Set-UMCallRouterSettings cmdlet is used to change the UM Startup mode from the default TCP to Dual, then restart the UM call router service to apply the changes.

```
# Altering the UM Startup mode to Dual
Set-UMCallRouterSettings -Server LJD-E1501 -UMStartupMode Dual
Restart-Service MSExchangeUMCR
```

Creating and configuring an auto attendant

Auto attendants are used in many organizations that need to deal with volumes of inbound calls and transfer calls to the right person, or right part of the organization easily, and without requiring an operating to handle each and every call.

Features provided by auto attendants

The most common use for the auto attendant is to provide a menu to the caller offering them some high-level options. The call is then transferred either to people, or another automated system (often to another automated attendant).

The options, known as *prompts* allow up to nine options to be presented to callers. They typically match with auto attendants that are using dial pad entry rather than voice entry, and of course to avoid annoying callers more than necessary.

The attendant voice language support is tied directly to the language packs installed on the Exchange environment. Each auto attendant has a single language defined.

By default, the auto attendant will announce itself as the Microsoft Exchange auto attendant to callers; however for many customers this is not desired. The most basic feature to replace this is to define a company name, which will then be used via the Text-to-Speech (TTS) engine in Unified Messaging to read the company name instead. Many organizations will prefer to use either whoever has the most appropriate sounding voice in the company, or use a professional to record a set of custom greetings. If these are defined and uploaded, these will be used.

Auto attendants also have the ability to, based on your definition of business hours in your region, play a different set of prompts to the caller. This is useful because some departments within the organization may only operate during business hours, and sometimes a different extension will deal with enquires outside of normal hours.

For each prompt a label is defined. The label itself can be associated with a custom prompt or will be read to the caller using the TTS functionality. If the auto attendant has been configured to respond to voice commands, the labels defined will be used to match what the caller asks for. Otherwise, the caller will be expected to press a number on the dial pad of their phone.

Finally, auto attendants can provide functionality called *dial by name*. This allows access to the caller to, depending on configuration, get transferred to someone or leave a voice message. The caller can have access to the following:

- The whole Global Address List, useful for internal callers.
- People within the same dial plan as the auto attendant, which is useful for switchboard-style functionality when a caller phones a particular office.
- A particular address list, allowing curation of a list of people that callers are allowed to search through.

If people using the dial by name feature can't find who they want, the ability to transfer to an operator still exists; likewise Exchange Unified Messaging also allows callers to choose from multiple matches; for example if two people named John Smith work for the same organization.

Defining an auto attendant

An auto attendant is stored as an object in Active Directory within the Configuration partition alongside organization-wide settings for Exchange. This means that each UM auto attendant is, by design, available to all Exchange Servers within the organization.

Although each auto attendant is stored within a dedicated UM auto attendant container, logically an auto attendant is associated with a dial plan. When managing auto attendants from the Exchange Admin Center, each auto attendant appears to be stored within the configuration of a dial plan. Although this is an abstraction because the UM auto attendants are not child Active Directory objects within dial plans, it does illustrate the relationship and how they are intended to be managed.

From the Exchange Management Shell, the auto attendant related tasks are managed through dedicated auto attendant cmdlets, reflecting their nature as standalone configurations that are mapped to dial plans. However, this does not change the fact that dial plans can have many auto attendants mapped, but an individual auto attendant can only be mapped to a single dial plan.

Example auto attendant defined

In the following examples, the process to create an auto attendant is shown using both the Exchange Admin Center and using the Exchange Management Shell. Both methods will create an auto attendant with the following configuration:

- Associated with a dial plan named Nuneaton.
- Named customer services.
- Does not respond to voice commands.
- An access number of +44 1234 555 555.
- Uses the UK English for the voice interface.
- A business name of Contoso.
- Uses the default business hours and non-business hours greetings.
- No informational announcement.
- Business hours defined as 9:00 until 17:00.
- Business hours menu enabled with the following options:
  - Press 1 to speak to Sales on extension 10001.
  - Press 2 to speak to Billing on extension 10002.
  - Press 3 to speak to Customer Care on extension 10003.
- Dial by name disabled.

Creating an auto attendant using the Exchange Admin Center

In this example, you will apply the definition for a Unified Messaging auto attendant to our Exchange Server environment using the Exchange Admin Center.

You start by creating the new auto attendant object.

1. To find the user interface for creating, managing, and removing auto attendants, navigate to the Unified Messaging section of the Exchange Admin Center, and select the UM Dial Plans tab.

2. Select the dial plan for the auto attendant from the list, and then select the Edit (pencil) icon to open the Dial Plan properties, as shown in Figure 1-6.

FIGURE 1-6 The list of existing dial plans

3. On the Dial Plan properties page, scroll down to the UM Auto Attendants section. To create a new UM auto attendant shown in Figure 1-7, select Add.

FIGURE 1-7 The management UI for viewing the list of existing UM auto attendants

4. The New UM auto attendant page will open. On this page you can create the basic configuration of the auto attendant, including:

- The name of the auto attendant.

- Whether or not the auto attendant is created as enabled.

- Whether or not the auto attendant will be voice-command enabled, or whether it will require the caller to use the dial pad for navigation.

- The access numbers that will be associated with the auto attendant, for example the customer services number that the IP-PBX system will forward to Unified Messaging.

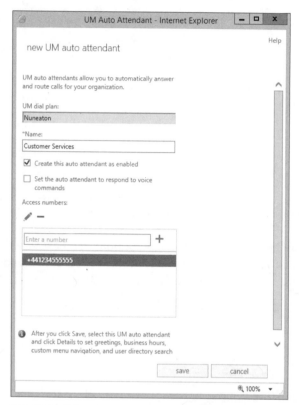

FIGURE 1-8 Using the new UM Auto Attendant Wizard to configure the basic settings

5. After entering the relevant details, choose Save.

Configuring an auto attendant using the Exchange Admin Center

The newly created auto attendant will require additional configuration after creation to meet the defined requirements. To add this information, complete the following steps:

1. Select the new auto attendant from the list of auto attendants on the opened Dial Plan page, and select Edit to open the newly defined auto attendant.

2. The first change is to define the Language and Company Name, on the General tab. Select General, and scroll down to the relevant sections. In Figure 1-9, English (United Kingdom) has been selected from the Language For Automated Voice Interface dropdown list, and the Business Name **Contoso** entered.

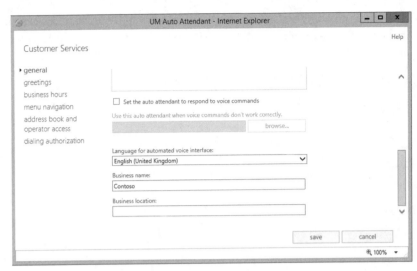

FIGURE 1-9 Configuring the General properties of the new auto attendant

3. The next settings that must be chosen are on the Business Hours tab. Select the Configure Business Hours option, and use the mouse to select the correct business hours to match the organizations' working day and working week, as shown in Figure 1-10.

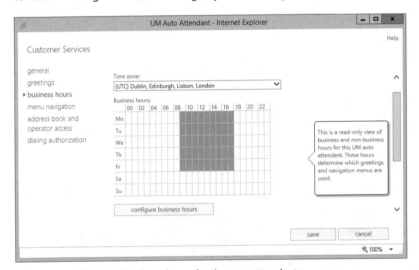

FIGURE 1-10 Editing the business hours for the auto attendant

4. The Menu Navigation tab, shown in Figure 1-11, provides the main configuration options for the auto attendant. This is the location where you define the menu structure that the user will hear. Select the Enable Business Hours Menu Navigation check box to make the menu active and enabled during the defined hours. Next, use the Add button to create each prompt to meet the specification defined.

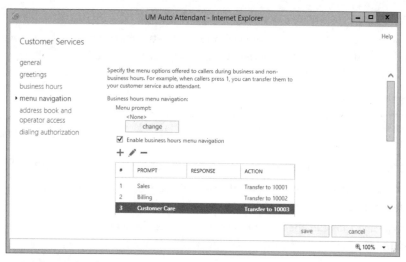

FIGURE 1-11 Using the EAC to edit the menu prompts

5. Finally, your specification has defined that inbound calls will not have the option to search the Global Address List. Therefore, you need to disable this feature within the auto attendant. To disable this feature, select the Address Book And Operator Access tab, and then clear both check boxes under Options For Contacting Users, as shown in Figure 1-12.

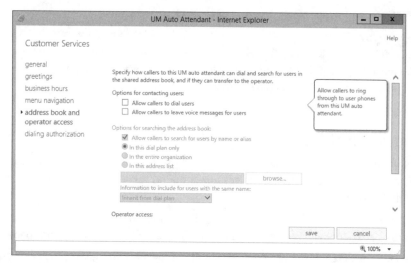

FIGURE 1-12 Functionality to enable a caller to search the GAL is disabled

Creating an auto attendant using the Exchange Management Shell

The same auto attendant can be created with the same settings using the Exchange Management Shell. To create a new auto attendant with the same settings required, the following PowerShell code can be used.

Create a new auto attendant

```
New-UMAutoAttendant -UMDialPlan 'Nuneaton' -Name 'Customer Services'
-SpeechEnabled:$false -PilotIdentifierList @('+441234555555') -Status Enabled
```

Configuring an auto attendant using the Exchange Management Shell

Because the Exchange Admin Center uses the same PowerShell commands under the hood, the same two-step approach must be used to perform post-creation configuration.

In the following example, the key mapping and business hours schedule can look complex because both use arrays to pass a list containing multiple values to a single parameter.

Configure the auto attendant

```
Set-UMAutoAttendant -Identity 'Customer Services'  -BusinessHoursKeyMapping @('1,Sales,1
0001,,,,,,,','2,Billing,10002,,,,,,,','3,Customer Care,10003,,,,,,,')
-BusinessHoursSchedule @('Mon.09:00-Mon.18:00','Tue.09:00-Tue.18:00','Wed.09:00-
Wed.18:00','Thu.09:00-Thu.18:00','Fri.09:00-Fri.18:00') -InfoAnnouncementEnabled False
-BusinessName 'Contoso' -BusinessHoursKeyMappingEnabled:$true -CallSomeoneEnabled:$false
-InfoAnnouncementFilename '' -Language 2057
```

> **TIP EXCHANGE MANAGEMENT SHELL COMMANDS**
>
> Learn how to perform complex Exchange Management Shell commands via the Exchange Admin Center. In the EAC, select the Help icon in the upper-right corner, and then select Show Command Logging. The EAC provides a line-by-line report of the equivalent commands that would be required via the Exchange Management Shell.

Configuring a call answering rule

Call answering rules are similar to rules used in Outlook to automatically move messages and give users the ability to decide for themselves how inbound callers who are transferred to voice mail should be dealt with.

Although call answering rules can be configured by administrators using PowerShell, call answering rules are generally managed by a user in the Outlook Web App options page.

Just like Outlook Rules, a user can configure multiple rules within their mailbox and, based on a number of parameters, perform a different action rather than just send the caller to voice mail.

The flow for call answering rules is simple. If a call answering rule is defined, and the conditions match the incoming call, the rule will be used. Otherwise the call will go to voice mail. A call answering rule can use the following conditions when determining if it should be triggered, including:

- If the user has Out of Office set.

- If the user's calendar is set to Free, Busy, Tentative, or Out of Office.

- In the case that the user has multiple extensions, perform an action based on the extension that the call was received by.

- The time window that the call fits into.

- Who is calling.

- Or a catch-all to trigger on all incoming voicemails.

Once a condition has been met, a number of actions can be performed against the inbound call including:

- Transfer of the call to an extension.

- Transfer of the call to an external number, if allowed by administrator policy.

- Automatically attempt to ring a number of alternative numbers and if answered, transfer the call (an automatic "Find me" option).

- Present an auto-attendant style menu to the caller.

Self-service configuration as a user

The primary method for configuring call answering rules is via the Outlook Web App options pages, and where possible users should manage their own call answering rules to avoid unnecessary administrator intervention.

The interface for call answering rule management is located within the Phone section of OWA options, underneath the Voice Mail tab. As shown in Figure 1-13, users are provided a list of call answering rules underneath a toolbar providing the ability to Add, Edit, Delete, and change the rule order.

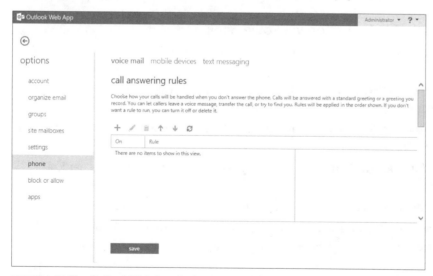

FIGURE 1-13 The Outlook Web App Options pages with the Call Answering Rules panel selected

The interface to create a new call answering rule, shown in Figure 1-14, will look familiar to users who have created Outlook rules, and administrators who have used the Exchange Admin Center to create transport rules. In the following example, a new call answering rule is created by a user. This rule will only be active when the user has their Out of Office message enabled and will give the caller the option to leave a message as normal, or transfer to the Sales team to have their query dealt with immediately.

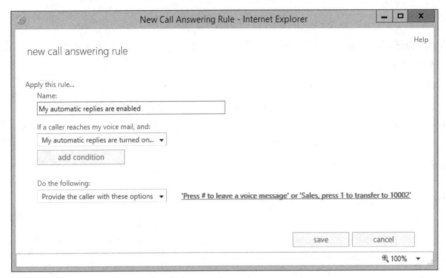

FIGURE 1-14 Creating a new call answering rule

Although the GUI interface is aimed squarely at users, administrators can access the UI as the user by assigning themselves the Helpdesk role via the RBAC Permissions management.

Administrator configuration via PowerShell

A range of cmdlets are available for managing call answering rules as an administrator via PowerShell:

- **New-UMCallAnsweringRule**   Used to add a new UM call answering rule to an individual user's mailbox.
- **Remove-UMCallAnsweringRule**   Used to delete unwanted UM call answering rules on behalf of users.
- **Get-UMCallAnsweringRule**   Used to list UM call answering rules for a particular mailbox.
- **Set-UMCallAnsweringRule**   Used to alter an existing UM call answering rule.
- **Enable-UMCallAnsweringRule** and **Disable-UMCallAnsweringRule**   Used to switch on and switch off UM call answering rules respectively.

In the following example, you use the Set-UMCallAnsweringRule cmdlet to alter the call answering rule you created. You will add an additional option, giving callers the option to be transferred to the billing department as well as sales.

```
# Configure UM call answering rules
Set-UMCallAnsweringRule  -Name 'My automatic replies are enabled' -Mailbox 'John Smith'
-KeyMappings "4,10,,,0,,0,,","1,1,Sales,,0,,0,10002,","1,2,Billing,,0,,0,10003,"
```

Designing Unified Messaging for high availability

High availability within Exchange is typically implemented by ensuring that there are multiple servers available within an Exchange environment that can take over operations if a single server fails. This ensures that the availability of the Exchange system meets the business requirements that mandated high availability.

The exact level of availability required often depends on the defined service level agreement (SLA), recovery time objective (RTO), and recovery point objective (RPO). Exchange Server 2013 has a fairly well defined method for implementing high availability through the use of multi-role servers, Database Availability Groups (DAGs), and multiple database copies. This often allows the architect of an Exchange solution to exceed the business requirements at no extra cost.

In Exchange 2013 the software that interacts with a user's mailbox are all contained within the Mailbox role, including the ability to render Outlook Web App, send and receive mail, mount and read the mailbox database, and (as you might imagine) perform Unified Messaging related tasks.

Unified Messaging high availability

As mentioned in the UM call router section earlier on, the Client Access role acts as a proxy or redirector, and helps with high availability by allowing an IP gateway to contact one of many Client Access Servers, and then be redirected to the Mailbox server currently hosting the recipient's mailbox. The overall concept is often described as, "Every server is an island." This makes the concept of UM high availability simple because there will always be a UM server within close proximity of a user mailbox. The UM server will be on the same server.

When designing architecture for Exchange 2013 and sizing various roles, bear in mind that because each Mailbox server is in effect running multiple roles, you cannot perform a sizing exercise for Unified Messaging in isolation. Instead, it must follow resulting guidelines from the overall sizing exercise for Exchange. Therefore, an Exchange 2013 server sized for mailboxes according to Microsoft recommendations will provide the following capacity:

- A limit of 100 concurrent Unified Messaging calls per server.
- A requirement of one free CPU core per voice mail transcription, otherwise the voice mail transcription will be skipped.

These limits impact the capacity planning for Exchange if you are looking to scale up, and host a very large number of mailboxes per server. In a large organization with (for example) a few thousand mailboxes per server, it would be unusual to receive over 100 concurrent voice mail messages at the same time.

If voice mail transcription is important to your organization though, and you do not expect to have enough free CPU cores, you may need to scale out rather than scaling up.

> **MORE INFO** **PREFERRED ARCHITECTURE**
>
> Microsoft provides the preferred architecture (PA) blueprint for deploying a highly available Exchange Server 2013 environment in a scalable and cost efficient manner. The resulting deployment is in line with the way the product is designed and takes into account high availability for Unified Messaging. Read more about preferred architecture at *http://blogs. technet.com/b/exchange/archive/2014/04/21/the-preferred-architecture.aspx*.

UM-specific considerations

In addition to normal design considerations for high availability of Exchange Server 2013, such as mailbox placement in relation to clients, you also need to consider the overall impact of your design for the organization's voice traffic. In particular, consider how a highly available environment with mailboxes distributed across a large number of Exchange servers will impact the way UM IP gateway devices interact with Exchange. This is particularly relevant if your design is multi-site. The following scenarios must be considered:

- If a mailbox becomes active in a different site to the IP gateway that will forward the call to voicemail, the UM call router will redirect the SIP traffic to the server with the active mailbox. Ensure that:
  - The Wide Area Network (WAN) links across sites have sufficient bandwidth for the number of concurrent calls expected.
  - Quality of Service (QoS) is in place across both the local network and the WAN link to ensure that voice traffic has a high priority.
  - Latency across the WAN link is not high. In general, if you are replicating a Database Availability Group across the WAN it should be sized accordingly and be a good, reliable link. However, many organizations segment replication traffic, but the voice traffic may traverse the normal LAN.
- Networks used by IP-PBX systems are often restricted with a firewall to prevent traffic from the LAN accessing the voice networks. Ensure that IP gateway devices like IP-PBX systems can access all possible Exchange Client Access Servers running the UM call router service and all possible Exchange Mailbox Servers hosting UM mailboxes in the same dial plan. Also ensure the Exchange servers can connect to the IP gateway devices.
- Most IP gateway devices will use secured SIP communications. This means that a valid SSL certificate will need to be in place on each server. Many deployments for Exchange 2013 will use a third-party SSL certificate for HTTPS access using a public DNS name. For Unified Messaging you are likely to need valid certificates issued by an internal

CA, with each server having a certificate with the Fully Qualified Domain Name of the Exchange Server itself.

By following these design considerations, it should be possible to implement a reliable Exchange 2013 Unified Messaging infrastructure that provides high availability.

Create a dial plan

Dial plans are the telephony equivalent of site objects in Active Directory. A dial plan usually contains the block of numbers available for a logical or physical building or campus, and is associated with many other Unified Messaging related configuration objects.

You've already seen in section one that each IP gateway is associated with a dial plan and an auto attendant is associated with a dial plan. In addition, each mailbox enabled for Unified Messaging is associated with a dial plan so you can see that without at least one dial plan it is not possible to configure Exchange Unified Messaging. It is the building block of configuration that most other configuration rests on.

The relationship between a UM dial plan and an IP-PBX dial plan

UM dial plans can map directly to the dial plans defined on your IP-PBX. They typically represent the same information, such as a block of numbers for the site.

If you have a complicated IP-PBX set up, for example a number of dial plans that break up number blocks within the same site, such as one dial plan using 1000-1050 and a second dial plan using 1051-1100, you may want to consider defining a single Unified Messaging dial plan that encompasses both IP-PBX dial plans. The simpler you can make the configuration, the better.

Other relevant information needs to be collected from your IP-PBX to allow you to create a dial plan with the correct settings. This information includes:

- The extension length or number of digits.
- The type of dial plan.
- The VoIP security mode, either SIP-secured or unsecured.
- The audio language to match the users of the IP-PBX dial plan.
- The region code, for example 44 to represent the United Kingdom of Great Britain and Northern Ireland.

Types of UM dial plan

Defining the UM dial plan with the correct type is critical if you want to ensure the UM IP gateway or IP-PBX sending calls to Unified Messaging will be understood. There are three key types of UM dial plan available:

- **Telephone Extension** This is expected in the same extension format length defined in the dial plan, for example a five-digit extension such as 10001.

- **SIP Uniform Resource Identifier (URI)**   This is typically used on more modern systems and looks like a user principal name or email address, for example *john.smith@ contoso.com*.

- **E.164 number**   E.164 is a standard for phone numbers and works internationally. A + symbol prefixes the country/region code, then the full number is quoted, for example +44 1234 510 001.

Determining the correct dial plan type will depend entirely on the configuration of your IP-PBX. For example, Lync/Skype for business uses the SIP URI format.

Creating a dial plan using the Exchange Admin Center

In this example you create a new dial plan for another site, Oxford. A different dial plan will be chosen to demonstrate that each dial plan could perhaps relate to a different IP-PBX. Many organizations have a multitude of systems.

To create a new dial plan, navigate to the Unified Messaging section of the Exchange Admin Center and select the UM Dial Plans tab. A list of existing UM dial plans will be shown. In Figure 1-15, you see the Nuneaton dial plan listed. Select the Add option from the toolbar.

FIGURE 1-15 The list of UM dial plans is shown in the EAC

The new UM Dial Plan page, shown in Figure 1-16, is displayed. The core settings will be entered, including:

- The Name: Oxford.
- The extension digits for the site, which in this case is five digits and would be suitable for extensions, such as 10001.

- A dial plan type of telephone extension is selected. This will mean the IP-PBX or UM IP gateway is not Lync/Skype for business and instead is probably a third-party IP-PBX.

- The VoIP Security Mode of unsecured is selected. This indicates that the IP-PBX will attempt to contact the UM call router and UM service via unencrypted channels; you will need to ensure that the UM Startup mode for each server reflects this.

- Because Oxford is a site in the United Kingdom of Great Britain and Northern Ireland, the Audio Language English (United Kingdom) is selected, and Country/Region Code of **44** is entered.

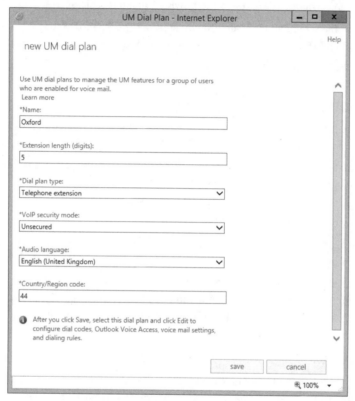

FIGURE 1-16 Creating a new UM dial plan

Creating a dial plan using the Exchange Management Shell

Creating the new dial plan using PowerShell is straightforward. Using the same options shown previously, you can specify parameters to match each chosen option, as shown here.

Create a new Dial Plan

```
New-UMDialPlan -Name 'Oxford' -URIType 'TelExtn' -NumberOfDigitsInExtension 5
-VoIPSecurity 'Unsecured' -DefaultLanguage en-GB -CountryOrRegionCode '44'
```

Thought experiment
Providing a menu to inbound callers

In this thought experiment, apply what you've learned about this objective. You can find answers to these questions in the "Answers" section at the end of this chapter.

Your manager at Contoso has asked if you can configure the system so that callers will receive a menu when they call a particular extension, and also if they try calling the Finance Manager's voice mail.

1. Which feature in Exchange will allow you to provide a menu to callers?

2. Should you use the same feature when someone reaches the Finance Manager's voice mail? If not, which feature would be most appropriate and how would you configure it as an administrator?

Objective summary

- A dial plan is very similar to an Active Directory site and usually represents the number range used, and is configured to match the IP-PBX on site at the same location.
- IP gateways are either the IP-PBX, or a device that bridges communications between Exchange UM and the PBX system.
- The call router redirects SIP traffic from the IP gateway to the Mailbox server hosting the Active copy of the Mailbox.
- Auto attendants are tied to dial plans and can be configured to provide a menu to inbound callers or access to the GAL.
- Call answering rules are similar to Outlook rules and allow users to decide what happens to inbound voicemail calls based on a number of conditions, like if they are Out of Office, and then perform actions like present a menu, or transfer a call.

Objective review

Answer the following questions to test your knowledge of the information in this objective. You can find the answers to these questions and explanations of why each answer choice is correct or incorrect in the "Answers" section at the end of this chapter.

1. You configure a new IP gateway for TLS-secured communications using the IP address 192.168.1.1 and port 5061. You are unable to receive voice mail messages. Why is this?

   A. The IP address configured is incorrect.

   B. The FQDN of the IP gateway should have been specified instead.

   C. A firewall is configured in between the IP gateway and the UM server.

   D. The port chosen is not suitable for secured communications.

2. Which types of UM dial plan must be associated with one or more Exchange 2013 servers?

A. SIP

B. E.164

C. Extension

D. All types

3. A call is forwarded from the UM IP gateway to Exchange Server 2013, and reaches the UM call router. What is the next step before the voice mail reaches the user mailbox?

A. The UM call router establishes an audio connection with the IP gateway.

B. The UM call router proxies the connection to a Mailbox Server.

C. The UM call router always redirects the call to the UM service on the same server, regardless of where the Mailbox is located.

D. The UM call router redirects the inbound call to the UM service on the server where the Mailbox is located.

Objective 1.2: Manage Unified Messaging

Configuration of core Unified Messaging features does not enable any functionality for users within an Exchange environment. To allow calls received by Unified Messaging to be directed to user mailboxes, users must have configuration settings applied. This configuration often requires updating and modification as needs change or users move within an organization.

> **This objective covers how to:**
> - Assign a dial plan to a user.
> - Move users between dial plans.
> - Enable and disable UM features for a user.
> - Set up protected voice mail.
> - Configure UM mailbox policy
> - Manage UM language packs

Assigning a dial plan to a user

In the same way that an IP gateway is assigned to a dial plan, a dial plan must be assigned to users. This provides the configuration link between an IP-PBX and the eventual user who receives a voice mail.

A user mailbox can only be assigned to a single dial plan at any one time. Dial plans are not assigned directly to a user but are assigned by associating a user with a UM mailbox policy. Each dial plan has at least one UM mailbox policy, because a default UM mailbox policy is created for each dial plan when the dial plan is created.

From one day to the next, a user is not likely to change dial plans. A dial plan for a user will be assigned in a number of circumstances:

- The user starts with the organization and is assigned a new AD account, mailbox, and phone extension.
- The user moves and is assigned a different phone extension, typically in circumstances like moving office or changing job roles within the organization.
- A new IP-PBX system is installed and users are being migrated from the old IP-PBX to the new IP-PBX.

The assignment of a dial plan is therefore performed when you move a user between dial plans, and when you enable Unified Messaging features.

Moving users between dial plans

The first example of assigning a dial plan is when a user who already has a Unified Messaging enabled mailbox, needs to change to a new dial plan.

In an example scenario, John Smith, will be moving from the Nuneaton office, which uses a third-party IP-PBX to the Oxford office, which uses a Lync/Skype for business IP-PBX.

To move a user between the two dial plans, you must perform the following steps:

1. Disable Unified Messaging for the user in Exchange.
2. Enable the user on the new IP-PBX system's dial plan and ensure the new details, such as telephone extension, are recorded.
3. Enable Unified Messaging for the user in Exchange, selecting a new UM dial plan and UM mailbox policy.
4. Disable the user on the old IP-PBX system's dial plan, if required.

The move between dial plans is not transparent and does have impact on the user. During the move between dial plans, the user will be unable to receive new voicemail or use features like play on phone.

Because messages are stored in the mailbox for the user, existing voice mail messages will not be impacted, along with customizations like custom greetings. However, when re-enabling Unified Messaging, the user will receive a new PIN number for UM access.

> *NOTE* **A SECONDARY DIAL PLAN**
>
> To maintain consistency during a migration between IP-PBX systems, or when a user changes offices, a secondary dial plan may be assigned to the user. This prevents the need to remove Unified Messaging and re-enable it. The following Microsoft TechNet article explains how to assign a secondary dial plan and can be found at *http://technet.microsoft.com/en-us/library/ff629383(v=exchg.150).aspx*.

Enabling and disabling UM features for a user

Whether it is the first time you are assigning a dial plan to a user, or you are moving a user between dial plans, you will need to use the same set of features to perform this configuration. For each user you make these changes to, you will need to know some basic information.

When a call within a particular dial plan reaches Exchange Unified Messaging, it still needs to know which mailbox within the dial plan to forward the call to, and what kind of features the user should be allowed to access or configure.

Therefore, you will need to know some basic information including:

- The UM mailbox policy to assign to the user, along with the associated UM dial plan.
- The user's telephone extension number.
- Whether to create a new, randomly generated PIN number, or whether to set a PIN manually. Regardless of which option is chosen, the user will be sent an email with the new PIN.
- Whether the user must reset the PIN number on first login.

The use of Unified Messaging also has licensing implications. Each UM-enabled user requires an Enterprise Client Access License (or equivalent).

Enabling Unified Messaging for a user via the Exchange Admin Center

To enable Unified Messaging for an individual user, complete the following steps:

1. Navigate to the Exchange Admin Center and choose the Recipients section.
2. Select the Mailboxes tab, and select the user that must be enabled for Unified Messaging.
3. As shown in Figure 1-17, the action pane on the right side of the Exchange Admin Center will show a range of tasks applicable for the selected user. Within the Phone And Voice Features section, Unified Messaging will be shown as Disabled. Choose the Enable link.

FIGURE 1-17 Enabling phone and voice

4. The Enable UM Mailbox Wizard opens in a new window as shown in Figure 1-18. The
    first page requires that you select an appropriate UM mailbox policy. Choose Browse
    to select a UM mailbox policy, and then select Next.

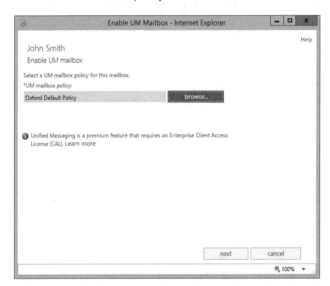

FIGURE 1-18 Selecting a UM mailbox policy for a newly enabled UM mailbox

5. The last page of the Enable UM Mailbox Wizard, shown in Figure 1-19, requires
    entry of unique information for the user and must match the dial plan that the user

is assigned to. For example, a dial plan expecting five-digit extensions will require a five-digit extension entered into the wizard. Enter the extension number, and choose appropriate PIN settings.

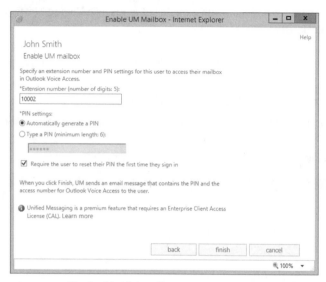

FIGURE 1-19 The Enable UM Mailbox Wizard allows the extension and PIN to be entered

6. Click Finish. After completing the wizard, the mailbox should be enabled for Unified Messaging.

Enabling Unified Messaging for a user via the Exchange Management Shell

PowerShell is especially useful in cases where many users must have mailboxes enabled for Unified Messaging at once. This is a common scenario where UM is being enabled after Exchange mailboxes are in use within the organization.

The following PowerShell command enables the mailbox for John Smith to use Unified Messaging with the same settings used in the Exchange Admin Center.

```
Enable-UMMailbox -Identity 'John Smith' -UMMailboxPolicy 'Oxford Default Policy'
-Extensions '10002' -PinExpired:$true
```

Disabling Unified Messaging for a user via the Exchange Admin Center

Removing Unified Messaging from a user mailbox is straightforward and does not affect their ability to use other Exchange functionality. For example, disabling Unified Messaging will not prevent them from using ActiveSync or Outlook, and the user can still access previously received voice mail messages. They simply do not have a link to the phone system any longer.

> **IMPORTANT** **A POSSIBLE BUSINESS IMPACT**
>
> When moving users between dial plans, it is worth reiterating that during the disable and subsequent re-enable, the user will be unable to receive voice mail. This could have a business impact as unanswered calls will be met with a call failed tone while Unified Messaging is disabled for that particular user.

To perform the action of disabling Unified Messaging for a user via the Exchange Admin Center:

1. Navigate to Recipients, and then select the Mailboxes tab.

2. Select the user to disable Unified Messaging for and then, underneath Phone And Voice features, select Disable next to Unified Messaging. As shown in Figure 1-20, a warning will be displayed asking the administrator to confirm the action.

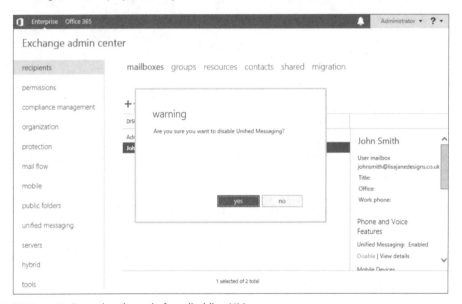

FIGURE 1-20 A warning shown before disabling UM

3. Click Yes to confirm the action. Unified Messaging will be immediately disabled for the user.

Disabling Unified Messaging for a user via the Exchange Management Shell

Disabling Unified Messaging via PowerShell is simple and requires no additional options. The following Disable-UMMailbox cmdlet with the mailbox name specified will, after confirmation, disable UM features for the user.

```
Disable-UMMailbox -Identity 'John Smith'
```

Setting up protected voice mail

Protected voice mail allows voice mail messages to be marked as private so that a voice mail message can only be opened by the intended recipient. This functionality uses core Windows Server technology to ensure compatibility across a range of supported clients, and offers a wide range of functionality, more than most users need.

The foundation of protected voice mail is the Windows Server Information Rights Management (RIM) features. IRM in Windows provides the facility to protect content so that only the right people can see the content, and because it is deeply integrated into Windows and Microsoft Office, it provides a high degree of control over what people can do with the content. Because it is deeply integrated with Windows and makes use of the existing identity foundation within Active Directory, it is near transparent to users of the systems.

IRM is made available to Exchange 2013 either via on-premises servers running Active Directory Rights Management Services, or in the cloud via Azure Active Directory Rights Management Services. IRM can be used elsewhere in Exchange, either server-side in transport rules that protect content based on certain criteria, or by users applying IRM templates within Outlook or Outlook Web App.

When used with Exchange Unified Messaging, IRM provides the following functionality:

- Voice mail messages marked as Private stored in Exchange are encrypted.
- Voice mail messages can only be opened by the intended recipient using their Active Directory credentials.
- The recipient of a voice mail message cannot save the voice mail message or attached audio file.
- The recipient of a voice mail message cannot forward the voice mail message or audio.
- Voice messages are protected, but fax messages and other types of message created via Outlook Voice Access, such as email or calendar appointments, will not be protected.

Before Protected Voice Mail can be used, the IRM functionality must already be installed and configured. A minimal on-premises deployment requires the following:

- A Windows Server 2008 R2, 2012, or 2012 R2 server with the Active Directory Rights Management Services server role.
- A SQL Database server to support the Active Directory Rights Management Services role.
- The Active Directory Rights Management Services client installed on workstations. The AD RMS client is included with Windows 7, Windows 8 and Windows 8.1.

Protected voice mail settings

Settings for protected voice mail can be configured either using the Exchange Admin Center or Exchange Management Shell. Settings are stored within UM mailbox policies, which means that different groups of users within each dial plan can have different protected voice mail settings enabled.

The following configuration settings are available:

- **Protect Authenticated Voice Mail**   Allows users logged into Outlook Voice Access to send protected messages to other UM users by marking the message as Private, or optionally ensure all authenticated voice mail is protected.

- **Protect Unauthenticated Voice Mail**   Allows callers to mark a message as Private, or protect all unauthenticated voice mail.

- **Require Play On Phone**   Prevents voice mail messages from being played via the PC and instead enforces the use of play on phone, where the UM server initiates a call to the user's phone number to play the voice mail message.

- **Allow Voice Responses To Email And Calendar Items**   Allows a protected voice message to be sent as a reply via Outlook Voice Access.

- **Protected Voice Mail Text**   Specifies the text to add to the voice mail email message when a voice mail has been protected.

Setup of protected voice mail using the Exchange Admin Center

Configuration for protected voice mail is within UM mailbox policies, meaning that different groups of users within a single UM dial plan can have different settings applied.

In this example, you will use the Exchange Admin Center to protect messages marked as Private by unauthenticated callers, and mark all authenticated callers messages as protected. You will ensure that protected messages are played on the phone, allow protected voice responses via Outlook Web App, and add a simple message stating that the user must have a supported client to listen to protected voice mail.

To change the protected voice mail setting:

1. Open the UM dial plan within Unified Messaging's UM Dial Plans tab, and then open the Default UM mailbox policy for the dial plan, as shown in Figure 1-21.

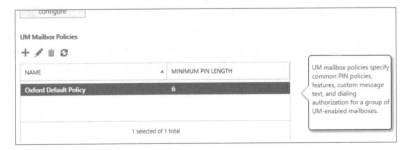

FIGURE 1-21 A list of UM mailbox policies is shown

2. Navigate to the Protected Voice Mail tab, shown in Figure 1-22. Select Private from the Protect Voice Messages From Unauthenticated Callers drop-down list.

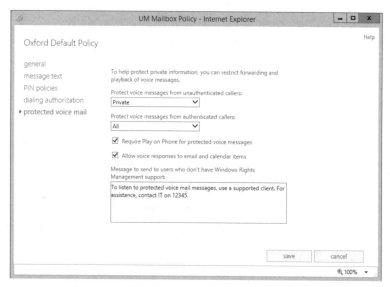

FIGURE 1-22 The Protected Voice Mail tab of the UM Mailbox Policy is shown

3. From the Protect Voice Messages From Authenticate Callers drop-down list, select All.

4. Ensure both Require Play On Phone For Protected Voice Messages and Allow Voice Responses To Email And Calendar Items check boxes are selected.

5. Enter an appropriate message of less than 512 characters within the Message To Send To Users Who Don't Have Window Rights Management Support text box.

Setup of protected voice mail using the Exchange Management Shell

To perform the same configuration from Exchange Management Shell, use the Set-UMMailboxPolicy cmdlet, as shown in the following example.

```
Set-UMMailboxPolicy -Identity 'Oxford Default Policy'
-ProtectUnauthenticatedVoiceMail 'Private' -ProtectAuthenticatedVoiceMail 'All'
-AllowVoiceResponseToOtherMessageTypes:$true -RequireProtectedPlayOnPhone:$true
-ProtectedVoiceMailText 'To listen to protected voice mail messages, use a supported
client. For assistance, contact IT on 12345.'
```

In both examples, the configuration will only be applied and usable if IRM is already setup and configured within the organization.

Configuring UM mailbox policy

The purpose of a UM mailbox policy is to enable different features to groups of users within a single UM dial plan. A UM dial plan can contain multiple UM mailbox policies, and a UM mailbox policy can be assigned to multiple users.

A user can only be assigned a single UM mailbox policy; and a UM mailbox policy can only be associated with a single dial plan.

UM features that can be controlled via UM mailbox policies

A wide range of features are controlled by UM mailbox policies, from the user features that are enabled, PIN policies in place, text provided to new UM users, where calls can be placed and the aforementioned protected voice mail settings.

The settings available include:

- The name of the UM mailbox policy.

- The time limit allowed for the personal greeting, which is heard by callers to voice mail.

- User features, such as:

    - Whether voice mail preview is enabled.

    - Whether users can configure their own call answering rules.

    - If the Message Waiting Indicator lamp will be controlled on behalf of the user.

    - If the user is allowed to access Outlook Voice Access.

    - Whether missed call notifications will be sent as email messages to the user.

    - Whether or not the Play on Phone functionality is available.

    - If inbound faxes are enabled, along with a fax server URI.

- Whether or not Microsoft analysis of voice mail messages is enabled, a feature that allows Microsoft to randomly analyze voice mails for the purpose of improving language packs.

- Message text for the following notifications:

    - When a user is enabled for Unified Messaging.

    - When a user's UM PIN is reset.

    - When a new voice mail is received.

    - When a new fax message is received.

- PIN policies including:

    - The minimum PIN length in digits.

    - How often a PIN can be re-used (PIN recycle count).

    - Whether common PIN patterns, like 1234 are allowed.

    - The enforced PIN lifetime in days before the PIN must be changed.

    - The number of PIN failures before the PIN must be reset.

    - The number of PIN failures before Outlook Voice Access is locked out.

- Whether or not a user can make or transfer calls to other numbers within the same dial plan from within Unified Messaging.

- Whether a user can make or transfer calls to any internal extension from Unified Messaging.

- The rules for allowed in-country/region external calls that can be transferred or initiated from Unified Messaging.

- The rules for allowed international calls that can be transferred or initiated from Unified Messaging.

Configuring a UM mailbox policy using the Exchange Admin Center

In this example, you'll examine the needs of a typical organization and how these needs might be met using UM mailbox policies. A dial plan is configured within Unified Messaging named Nuneaton. This dial plan contains all users at the Nuneaton site who are UM-enabled.

There are two types of users as far as Unified Messaging is concerned. The majority of users have a fairly relaxed configuration and are allowed to access all standard Unified Messaging features. It has been decided that some users must not be able to access all Unified Messaging features; therefore a new UM mailbox policy has been added within the configuration for the UM dial plan, named Nuneaton Restricted Policy, shown in Figure 1-23.

FIGURE 1-23 The UM mailbox policy list shows both of the policies for the Nuneaton UM dial plan

To meet the organization requirements, the UM mailbox policy must be amended to prevent access to Voice Mail Preview, Call Answering Rules, and Outlook Voice Access. Additionally, the default setting to disable inbound fax messages must remain disabled.

Open the UM mailbox policy in the Exchange Admin Center, and select the General tab, as shown in Figure 1-24. Then, within the User Features section, make the configuration changes.

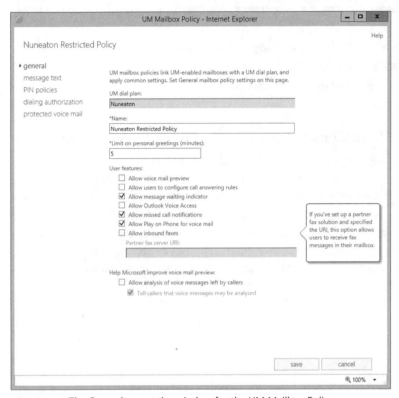

FIGURE 1-24 The General properties window for the UM Mailbox Policy

Managing UM language packs

The purpose of Unified Messaging language packs is to allow Exchange 2013 to speak and understand the language throughout the global different regional differences. For example, the built-in United States language pack will not speak in a way that audiences in the United Kingdom will prefer, nor will the US language pack understand the regional twang of a resident of Birmingham, UK with much accuracy. The built-in US language pack will stand even less chance of understanding the Polish or German language and certainly cannot interact with callers in either language.

Therefore, to extend the functionality of Unified Messaging, add-on language packs must be installed onto Exchange 2013 servers.

Where to install UM language packs

There are two basic deployment strategies for Unified Messaging language packs:

- Install the UM language packs required on all servers that host UM-enabled mailboxes.
- Install the UM language packs that match the regions the servers and associated dial plans reside in.

The first strategy usually works the best because it removes the possibility that a mailbox moved between regions will move to a server that does not have the correct language pack installed.

A full list of available language packs, the country/region and culture ID is available at the following page on TechNet: *http://technet.microsoft.com/en-us/library/bb124728(v=exchg.150).aspx*. Additionally, each individual UM language pack can be obtained from *http://go.microsoft.com/fwlink/p/?linkId=266542*.

Viewing installed UM language packs

The list of installed UM language packs can be viewed via the Exchange Admin Center by navigating to the Servers main tab. Select the Exchange Server that you want to view the list of language packs, then choose to view the properties for the server.

In the Server properties window, select the Unified Messaging tab, as shown in Figure 1-25. The installed languages will be shown under the Prompt Languages heading.

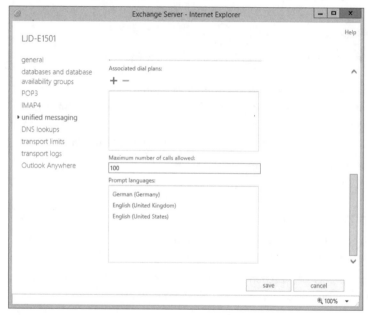

FIGURE 1-25 Prompt Languages for the UM server listed

The same information can be obtained using the Exchange Management Shell. Execute the following PowerShell cmdlet.

```
Get-UMService -identity <Server Name>
```

The PowerShell output will show the installed language packs.

Installing a UM language pack

There are two ways to install a Unified Messaging language pack. The easiest way, if the intention is to install on a single server, is to run the downloaded executable. For example, to install the Australian English language pack download UMLanguagePack.en-AU.exe from the Microsoft website. After downloading, run the file as an elevated user. On the Setup Progress page, the Exchange Server GUI setup will be shown on a progress bar, as shown in Figure 1-26, and the UM language pack will install.

FIGURE 1-26 The Exchange Server Setup program installs the UM Language Pack via the GUI

If multiple language packs must be installed it is often faster and more accurate to install the language packs via the command line, using the Exchange Server Setup.exe. Use Setup. exe with the /AddUmLanguagePack switch, specifying the languages to install, the location of the downloaded language packs, and confirm that the license terms are accepted.

```
setup.exe /AddUmLanguagePack:en-AU,en-GB /s:C:\Exchange\UMLanguagePacks /
IAcceptExchangeServerLicenseTerms
```

Removing a UM language pack

Language packs might need to be removed and reinstalled during the life of an Exchange Server install, for example when a newer version of a UM language pack is released.

To remove a UM language pack, the Exchange Server command line Setup.exe must be used, with the /RemoveUMLanguagePack switch. The following is an example.

```
setup.exe /RemoveUmLanguagePack:en-AU
```

This removes the installed language pack from the server. Before attempting this procedure, ensure that the language pack is not used by the server in any UM dial plans bound to the UM service, or bound to the UM call router service.

> ## *Thought experiment*
> ### New office opens in Poland
>
> In this thought experiment, apply what you've learned about this objective. You can find answers to these questions in the "Answers" section at the end of this chapter.
>
> The organization you manage Exchange for opens a new office in Poland. They will continue to use the existing Lync/Skype for business phone system that is in place globally and already has working Unified Messaging dial plans in place. Your Exchange organization consists of two Database Availability Groups with the UM dial plans already assigned to all Exchange Servers, and the users for the office in Poland will have mailboxes on the first DAG.
>
> 1. What is the minimum you need to do to ensure that Polish users can interact with Outlook Voice Access in their native language?
>
> 2. What steps might you perform if you want to set the default prompt language and limit the number of servers that require the Polish language pack installed?

Objective summary

- A dial plan is the equivalent of an Active Directory site and usually maps to a logical location within an organization, or at the very minimum an IP-PBX system.

- Moving users between UM dial plans requires the user to have UM disabled and then re-enabled on their mailbox.

- Protected Voice Mail uses IRM to prevent unauthorized users from accessing private voice mail messages, and requires a working AD RMS infrastructure in place.

- UM mailbox policies contain user specific settings, and one user can be assigned one UM mailbox policy.

- A UM mailbox policy must be assigned to a single dial plan, and a dial plan can contain multiple UM mailbox policies.

- Language packs contain voice prompts and the diction to understand a caller speaking the associated language and are installed as an add-on to Exchange Server deployments.

Objective review

Answer the following questions to test your knowledge of the information in this objective. You can find the answers to these questions and explanations of why each answer choice is correct or incorrect in the "Answers" section at the end of this chapter.

1. Two groups of users within the same dial plan need different features enabled; the first group requires access to voice preview, whereas the second group must not have voice preview enabled. How should you accomplish this?

A. Create a new UM dial plan with voice preview disabled. Edit the dial plan settings for the second group of users and assign them to the new UM dial plan. Disable voice preview within the dial plan.

B. Create a new UM mailbox policy with voice preview disabled. Assign the new UM mailbox policy to a new UM dial plan, and update the UM dial plan for each user in the second group.

C. Create a new UM mailbox policy with voice preview disabled within the original UM dial plan. Update the UM mailbox policy for the second group of users.

D. Create a new UM dial plan with voice preview disabled. Disable Unified Messaging for the second group of users and re-enable UM with the new dial plan.

2. A user often visits two different offices and has an extension at both offices. Each office has a different PBX system with different UM dial plans. What is the correct way for an administrator to allow the user to receive voice mail to calls received at either office?

A. Configure the user account so that a secondary dial plan and telephone extension is specified.

B. Set up the PBX system so that instead of sending calls to voice mail the call is forwarded to the other office extension.

C. Request the user contact the helpdesk when arriving at each office so that the dial plan can be altered.

D. Assign the additional extension to the UM mailbox.

Objective 1.3: Troubleshoot Unified Messaging

Sometimes things go wrong, both during and after implementation. Therefore, from time to time, it is necessary to perform troubleshooting steps to help understand the root cause of the issue.

This objective covers how to:

- Troubleshoot and configure mutual Transport Layer Security (MTLS).
- Monitor calls and call statistics.
- Troubleshoot and configure Quality of Service (QoS).
- Troubleshoot SIP communication.

Troubleshooting and configuring mutual Transport Layer Security (MTLS)

Communications between servers rely on mutual TLS to help ensure the connection between both systems is secure. This means that when one server acts as a client, not only does the responding server need to present a valid SSL certificate, but the server acting as the client must participate in the certificate Exchange.

In this scenario, one side of the conversation will be the UM IP gateway and the other side of the communication will be an Exchange Server. Not only do both the UM IP gateway and Exchange server need to have SSL certificates installed, but the SSL certificates need to be configured with the correct names, typically the Fully Qualified Domain Name of each server. They also must both use certificates from certificate authorities both sides trust.

A typical deployment of Exchange Unified Messaging and an IP-PBX relies on a common internal certificate authority (CA) to issue certificates for VoIP use. There are often many SSL certificates issued for various parts of an IP-PBX system to ensure communications are properly secured. Third-party SSL certificates are also used typically with Exchange for standard client communications and within the IP-PBX solution for communication with mobile and external users or partners.

The most common Exchange misconfiguration for Unified Messaging relates to the SSL certificate names. For general client communications, a subject alternative name (SAN) certificate, sometimes known as a Unified Communications Certificate, is used and issued by a third-party certificate authority.

This certificate does not usually contain the actual Fully Qualified Domain Name of each individual Exchange Server and does not require it for client access, therefore an additional SSL certificate is often required.

View installed SSL certificates

As a first step to troubleshoot whether the Exchange configuration for MTLS are set up correctly, you will examine the installed SSL certificates on relevant Exchange Servers. This will tell you a number of key configuration settings:

- Certificate issuer
- Certificate principal name and subject alternative names
- Certificate assigned services

Complete the following steps:

1. Start by opening the Exchange Admin Center and navigating to Servers.

2. Select the Certificates tab. The Certificates tab allows you to examine all Exchange Server certificates in use within the Exchange organization, including those used for Exchange server to Exchange server communications, TLS communications for SMTP, HTTPS, POP3, IMAP4, and of course Unified Messaging.

3. From the Select Server drop-down list, select the server that appears to have issues establishing a MTLS connection. After selecting a server, the list of Exchange Server certificates should be displayed.

4. Upon selecting each certificate from the list, the Issuer will be displayed in the right-side action column. In the example in Figure 1-27, there is an obvious initial issue with the certificate selected if it will be used for Unified Messaging. The certificate is a self-signed certificate, issued by the Exchange Server itself.

5. For the certificate to be valid for MTLS use, the issuer will need to be one that both the Exchange Server and the UM IP gateway trust as a certificate authority. For certificates used externally, this is usually a third-party certificate authority, and for internal use, such as an internal UM IP gateway, an Enterprise certificate authority is often sufficient.

6. To further examine the selected certificate, choose the Edit (pencil) icon from the tool-bar to open the Exchange Certificate properties window.

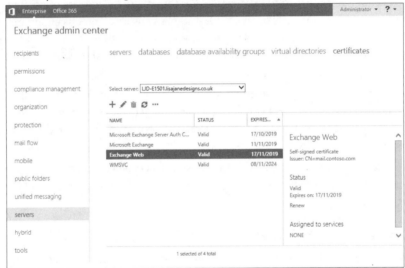

FIGURE 1-27 The list of installed SSL certificates on the Exchange Server is shown

The Exchange Certificates properties window is composed of two tabs. The first tab, General, allows examination of the certificate principal name and subject alternative names. The full list of names is within the Subject Alternative Names list box. In Figure 1-28, the list of names does not include the Fully Qualified Domain Name of the Exchange Server itself. This is not unusual for the certificate used for client access because this will usually be a single SSL certificate installed on all Exchange Servers sharing the common HTTPS names.

For Unified Messaging though, expect a certificate from a valid issuer that includes the FQDN for the server itself.

FIGURE 1-28 Subject alternatives names for the installed SSL certificate are shown

The second tab is named Services. This tab, shown in Figure 1-29, shows the services that the SSL certificate is currently enabled for use with. For the purposes of Unified Messaging, the following services are relevant:

- Microsoft Exchange Unified Messaging, used by the Mailbox role.
- Unified Messaging Call Router, used by the Client Access role.

If the certificate is from a valid issuer, and has valid names but is not enabled for the UM-related services, it will not be available for MTLS use, and in combination with adjusting the UM services startup mode to Dual or SIP Secure must be set before use.

FIGURE 1-29 Assigned services for the SSL certificate

Creating a replacement SSL certificate for secured SIP communications

In the previous example, the certificates installed and available on the Exchange Server were not valid for Unified Communications use, nor enabled. To remediate this issue, a new certificate must be created with the correct issuer and options, and then enabled correctly.

To perform these steps via the Exchange Admin Center:

1. Navigate to Servers and the Certificates tab, and then choose New Certificate. On the first page of the New Exchange Certificate Wizard, the following options will be presented:

   - Create A New Request For A Certificate From A Certificate Authority
   - Create A Self-Signed Certificate

2. For a UM-compatible certificate, choose to create a new request for a certificate from a certificate authority, then choose Next.

3. On the second page of the wizard, you must enter a friendly name for the certificate. The friendly name has no effect on the operation of the certificate and helps the administrator of Exchange understand the purpose and use. Select a friendly name and then continue through the wizard.

> **NOTE** **CERTIFICATE MANAGEMENT FOR A LARGE NUMBER OF SERVERS**
>
> When managing a large number of Exchange Servers, certificate management can take time. To assist with easy identification, always select a descriptive name for the certificate friendly name that is consistent across servers and services. A UM certificate could have a name like Enterprise CA Exchange UM (server.contoso.com), whereas the third-party SSL certificate used across all servers for Client Access could have a name like Third-Party Exchange Web (mail.contoso.com).

4. On the next page of the wizard, a prompt asks you to Specify The Servers You Want To Apply This Certificate To. Add and Remove buttons allow the administrator to select Exchange Servers within the organization. Select the servers that will have the certificate applied to.

5. If issuing a UM certificate from an internal CA, for simplicity create a single certificate for each UM server. This process involves creating a single UM certificate for each individual server.

6. On the final input page of the wizard, the domains to be used for the certificate are shown. Default input from the wizard includes the domain name; for example, contoso.com and service name for HTTPS servers. Add a new name for the FQDN of the server, for example **server01.contoso.com**. Set the server name as the default, and then remove the service names like autodiscover.contoso.com that you will not use for Unified Messaging.

7. After completing the certificate request, a Base 64 encoded certificate request will be generated with the file extension REQ. The request file is plain text and can be pasted into a certificate authority request form, or uploaded when prompted. The resulting public certificate file, usually with the extension CRT is imported via the Exchange Admin Center and matches up with the Private Key stored on the Exchange Server to make up the complete private and public parts of the SSL certificate.

If multiple certificates must be created, it is faster to use the Exchange Management Shell to make multiple requests. The New-ExchangeCertificate cmdlet is used to create a new SSL certificate request and performs the same underlying actions that the New Exchange Certificate Wizard does. In the following example, a new certificate request is created with the same options and stored in the $Request string variable, then exported to a file. The Import-ExchangeCertificate cmdlet is then used to import the certificate file that is provided later on by the certificate authority.

```
$Request = New-ExchangeCertificate -GenerateRequest -FriendlyName 'Exchange UM
(server01.contoso.com)' -SubjectName 'C=GB, O=Contoso, CN=server01.contoso.com'
-DomainName server01.contoso.com -Server 'server01' -KeySize '2048'
-PrivateKeyExportable:$true
Set-Content -path 'C:\Certificates\ExchangeUM.REQ' -Value $Request

Import-ExchangeCertificate -FileData ([Byte[]]$(Get-Content -Path C:\Certificates\
ExchangeUM.CRT -Encoding byte -ReadCount 0))
```

Ensuring the SSL certificate is enabled for UM use

Just creating a new SSL certificate and correctly importing it onto the right servers on its own is not enough to ensure it can, and will be, used for Exchange Unified Messaging. An Exchange Server can have a large number of SSL certificates, valid and otherwise, however only the SSL certificates that have been assigned to specific services will be used.

The procedure within the Exchange Admin Center to assign the newly create certificate for use is similar to the procedure used to view the services that the certificate is being used for.

1. Navigate to the Exchange Admin Center, and select the Servers section.

2. Select the Certificates tab. The newly created SSL certificate should be listed by its friendly name.

3. Choose to Edit the certificate, which opens the Exchange Certificate properties window. Select the Services tab. Under Specify The Services You Want To Assign This Certificate To, select the check boxes that are appropriate for your server's role:

   - For a client access server, select Unified Messaging Call Router.

   - For a mailbox server, select Microsoft Exchange Unified Messaging.

   - For a multi-role server, select both Unified Messaging Call Router and Microsoft Exchange Unified Messaging.

4. Choose Save to apply the settings. If you haven't already, ensure that the Startup Type for Unified Messaging is set to Dual or SIP Secured before assigning the SSL certificate.

If the new SSL certificate, or multiple SSL certificates are being applied to multiple servers, or the preferred approach is to use the Exchange Management Shell, the same task can be accomplished using the Enable-ExchangeCertificate cmdlet. This cmdlet uses the thumbprint of the SSL certificate rather than its name to ensure that the correct certificate is chosen, so the Get-ExchangeCertificate cmdlet must be run first to retrieve a list of installed SSL certificates on the relevant server. After recording the correct certificate thumbprint, the services to enable must be chosen. Short acronyms are used to choose the relevant services to enable. UM relates to the mailbox role and the UMCallRouter relates to the client access role. The example below enables the SSL certificate on a multi-role server.

```
Get-ExchangeCertificate
Enable-ExchangeCertificate -Services 'UM,UMCallRouter' -Identity '<Certificate
Thumbprint>'
```

Monitoring calls and call statistics

Typically the team that manages the organization's phone system and the team that manages the Exchange infrastructure are different teams, which can make understanding who is accessing Unified Messaging, and how often they access the system, hard to gauge without the right tools. Exchange Unified Messaging includes two tools to provide this information to Exchange administrators. If UM administrators and PBX administrators are in the same team, or work closely together, a clear picture of calls and call statistics can be built.

Reasons to monitor calls and call statistics

The sizing for Exchange Server 2013 assumes a certain maximum load of 100 concurrent calls. Therefore, for larger organizations that move mailboxes and databases between servers for other reasons, it is important to keep abreast of the overall load Unified Messaging places on the Exchange infrastructure.

Incoming calls that have issues are not likely to be reported directly to the Exchange administrators, if at all. For example, if an auto attendant is failing or has issues with audio quality, new business may be missed and customers may not be able to reach representatives at the organization. Callers who cannot get through to the person they intended to call and wish to leave a voicemail, could be seeing occasional dropped calls. These will not be apparent immediately because the person initiating the call is not an employee and has no way of logging a service request with the help desk. They may simply call the next company on their list.

It might instead be that an executive in your organization is unsure if the system was available over a specific period of time; perhaps the person they were expecting to leave a message with lost their cell signal during that period and made the suggestion that the organization's system was at fault. Using the monitoring capabilities within Exchange, an administrator can use the records to verify that Exchange wasn't (or maybe was) at fault.

Tools available for call monitoring and statistics

Unified Messaging includes three tools for monitoring Unified Messaging; call statistics, call logs, and current active calls. The last 90 days of call statistics and call logs are kept, and monthly statistics are kept for a default of 12 months.

Viewing call statistics

The Exchange Admin Center provides a user interface to select the information you want to view by different categories and then display it on-screen immediately. The following options are available when viewing call statistics through the EAC:

- Show one of the following:
    - Daily statistics for the last 90 days.
    - The monthly statistics, covering up to the last 12 months.
    - All statistics available.
- All UM dial plans, or statistics from a particular UM dial plan.
- Statistics from all UM IP gateways or statistics from just one UM IP gateway.

To view call statistics, navigate to the Exchange Admin Center and select the Unified Messaging section. Choose the UM Dial Plans tab, and select the More button from the tool bar. On the drop-down menu, shown in Figure 1-30, select Call Statistics.

FIGURE 1-30 The menu option for Call Statistics and User Call Logs

The Call Statistics window will open. This provides the opportunity to select the data based on the parameters and extract data to view. The columns returned include:

- The date for the row shown
- Total calls received that day
- Voice messages received
- Missed calls
- Outlook Voice Access calls
- Outgoing calls placed
- Auto attendant calls received
- Inbound fax calls.

- Other unclassified calls.
- Failed or rejected calls.
- Statistics for audio quality.

For each row of data, additional information can be shown, such as audio quality details for a particular day, or an export of all call logs for a day (row) shown, which can then be imported for further analysis into Microsoft Excel.

The same statistics can be retrieved via the Exchange Management Shell. This is useful in a scenario such as automated retrieval of statistics. The equivalent cmdlet for retrieving call statistics is Get-UMCallSummaryReport. In the example below, the daily call statistics are retrieved for the Nuneaton UM dial plan.

```
Get-UMCallSummaryReport -GroupBy Day -UMDialplan Nuneaton
```

Viewing call logs

Unified Messaging call logs provide the ability to view information about calls to and from a particular UM-enabled mailbox. Call logs for each user are stored for up to 90 days. Call logs are also available for view via the Exchange Admin Center in the same More drop-down list on the UM Dial Plans tab of the Unified Messaging section that call statistics is found.

After selecting user call logs from the menu, the Unified Messaging Reports window will open. This provides a single option, which is to select a user. Only UM-enabled users will be shown and can be selected. After selecting a user mailbox, a list of all call records will be shown, with the following columns:

- Date and time of the call.
- Duration of the call.
- The type of the call, such as:
  - **Call Answering** Where the call was received by UM and a voice mail was recorded.
  - **Call Answering Missed Call** Where the call was received by UM, but the caller did not record a voice mail.
  - **Subscriber Access** Where the user called into Outlook Voice Access.
  - **Auto Attendant** If the call was answered by an auto attendant.
  - **Play On Phone** When the user chose to initiate playback of the voice mail from Outlook or OWA to a phone extension or phone number.
  - **Find Me** When a call answering rule was configured to attempt to call one or more additional numbers and forward the call to the user at one of those numbers if answered.
  - **Unauthenticated Pilot Number** A failed attempt to access Outlook Voice Access.
  - **Greetings Recording** When the user updates or records their greetings messages.
  - **None** Other types of undefined call.
- The Calling Number attempting to reach the user.

- The number the caller dialed, the Called Number.
- The UM IP gateway that passed the call to Microsoft Exchange.
- Audio quality statistics.

The entire set of rows can be exported and for each row, the audio quality can be examined in detail by selecting the Audio Quality Details button. The same data can be extracted by using the Exchange Management Shell. The following is an example.

```
Get-UMCallDataRecord -Mailbox John.Smith@contoso.com
```

Viewing active calls

In some circumstances, for example before failing over a server, or to gain a snapshot of how many calls are active while troubleshooting an active issue, you might want to view a point-in-time snapshot of the active UM calls on an Exchange Server.

This cannot be accomplished using the Exchange Admin Center, but can be accomplished using the Exchange Management Shell, or by using the Windows Performance Console. The Performance Console uses the current calls counter for the object MSExchangeUMGeneral to display a tracking view of active calls.

To view the current active calls using the Exchange Management Shell, use the Get-UMActiveCalls cmdlet. The Server, IPGateway, and DialPlan parameters allow the information returned to be scoped to relevant information. The following is an example.

```
Get-UMActiveCalls -Server Server01
```

Troubleshooting and configuring Quality of Service

By configuring Quality of Service, Unified Messaging can play its part in ensuring that network packets for voice traffic are guaranteed delivery, and best efforts are provided to maintain transmission quality. To utilize Quality of Service within an organization, each device that passes traffic must participate, including the IP-PBX, UM IP gateway, network routers, and switches, and of course the Exchange Servers.

Differentiated Services Code Point (DSCP) marking is used to mark values on packets to ensure that each hop along the data path understand the importance of the traffic and treat the traffic accordingly.

Controls to set DSCP marking for Quality of Service are not built directly into Exchange Server but are built into the foundation products that support UM and Exchange. The first cornerstone of QoS is built into Windows Server itself, via the QoS Packet Scheduler, which switches the ability to use QoS on or off. The second cornerstone of QoS is built into one of the prerequisite packages for Exchange Server, the Microsoft Unified Communications Managed API (UCMA).

Configuring Quality of Service for Unified Messaging

Quality of Service for Unified Messaging is configured on Exchange Servers by using a combination of the Registry Editor and Group Policy editor to create a new policy that applies to all relevant Exchange Servers; or by editing the local policy on an individual server.

To create the Registry settings, open the Registry Editor, and navigate to the following key: HKEY_LOCAL_MACHINE\Software\Microsoft\RTC\Transport. Create a new DWORD entry named **QoSEnabled**, and set the value to 1.

To configure the Group Policy for the local server:

1. Open the GPEDIT.MSC tool while logged into the server using an account that is a member of the local Administrators group.

2. Expand Computer Configuration, and then within Policies, expand Administrative Templates, Network, QoS Packet Scheduler, DSCP.

3. Within DSCP, first select Controlled Load Service Type, and open its properties window. Choose Enable, and enter a DSCP Value of **24**.

4. Select Guaranteed Service Type, and open its properties window. Select Enable, and enter a DSCP value of **40**.

5. To complete the configuration, restart the Unified Messaging Services.

> *IMPORTANT* **CHECK WITH YOUR VENDOR**
>
> Check with your UM IP gateway, IP-PBX or networking vendor as to their preferred value for the Guaranteed Service Type. Although Microsoft Lync expects 40, some vendors expect audio traffic to be marked as 46.

Troubleshooting Quality of Service

To verify that QoS is enabled end-to-end throughout the path that the packets will take between the UM server and an endpoint, you must have visibility into all relevant areas of the network.

For an Exchange Admin, there are two key tasks to perform to verify if QoS is correctly configured on a Unified Messaging server, and traffic is being transmitted with the correct DSCP marking.

To verify that QoS is correctly configured on an Exchange Unified Messaging server:

1. Log into the server and open the Registry Editor.

2. Open HKEY_LOCAL_MACHINE and expand the Software\Policies\Microsoft\Windows\Psched\DiffservByteMappingConforming key.

3. Locate the following two values:

   - SERVICETYPE_GUARANTEED (DSCP 40, 0x28)
   - SERVICETYPE_CONTROLLEDLOAD (DSCP 24, 0x18)

   If both values are set, the Unified Messaging server will attempt to tag traffic according to the QoS policy set.

The second task to perform to verify that Unified Messaging related packets are being transmitted with the required DSCP markers is to monitor traffic between endpoints using a packet monitor. Microsoft provides a monitoring tool for sniffing local network traffic, called Microsoft Message Analyzer. This supersedes the older NetMon tool and provides a wider range of templates.

Microsoft Message Analyzer can be downloaded and installed from the Microsoft Download website.

Troubleshooting SIP communication

Session Initiation Protocol (SIP) is the text-based communications protocol used by Voice over IP (VoIP) communications in Exchange UM to set up communications between VoIP endpoints.

If SIP communication cannot function, no Unified Messaging calls will be received. It is therefore important to understand where to check when things do not go as planned.

Key ports to check

SIP communication uses (unless you reconfigure the UM service and UM call router service) the following ports for communication, and subsequent Real Time Protocol (RTP) communications.

Service	Port	PURPOSE
UM call router	5060	SIP unsecured
UM call router	5061	SIP secured
UM service	5062	SIP unsecured
UM service	5063	SIP secured
UM service worker processes	5065 and 5067	SIP unsecured
UM service worker processes	5066 and 5068	SIP secured
UM service	1000 – 65535 (negotiated during SIP session)	RTP audio steam port

Ensure that the Windows Firewall configuration allows incoming traffic on these ports. The installation of Exchange Server 2013 will add these exclusions, however security conscious administrators, or security teams who have implemented Group Policies to control firewall rules may have made changes, particularly to the ranges used for the RTP audio streams.

Additionally, although it is not supported to implement firewall devices with rules other than Any/Any (effectively the same as no firewall) between Exchange Servers, it is supported to implement firewall rules between the UM IP gateway and the Exchange UM servers.

Verify that the firewall devices along the path between both UM servers and UM call routers and the UM IP gateways allow traffic to these ports, and the respective ports that the UM service will place outbound calls to.

Tools available for troubleshooting SIP communications

Microsoft provides a number of tools to use when attempting to troubleshoot traffic between the Exchange UM-related servers and the UM IP gateway devices. The primary tool to utilize on the Exchange UM server is the Microsoft Message Analyzer, available from the Microsoft Download website.

The Microsoft Message Analyzer captures and decodes the SIP traffic if the communications are not MTLS secured. This typically means that for Lync/Skype for business servers, troubleshooting should be initiated from the IP-PBX side.

Lync/Skype for business includes a VoIP-focused traffic logging tool that can record and display a SIP conversation and allow troubleshooting to be conducted. Part of the Lync Server Resource Kit, the Lync Logging Tool in combination with Snooper will allow the specified types of communication (for example, SIP traffic) to be captured.

Thought experiment
Providing reports to management

In this thought experiment, apply what you've learned about this objective. You can find answers to these questions in the "Answers" section at the end of this chapter.

You have been asked to provide a regular report to management showing the number of UM calls received each month and provide access to the phone team so they can match up voice mails received to inbound phone calls.

1. What solution will allow you to automate exporting reports without needing to generate the reports manually?

2. The user call logs will provide the information that the phone team needs. Apart from giving Organization Admin access, what role could you grant to the phone team?

Objective summary

- The most common issues with Unified Messaging usually relate to network communications.
- SSL certificates must be trusted and configured correctly on both the UM IP gateway and each Exchange 2013 server participating in UM communications.
- Call statistics provide a summary of the organizations calls. Call logs provide information about calls to and from a user mailbox.
- Quality of Service requires network and IP-PBX systems to be configured, as well as the UM server, and ensures voice traffic is given appropriate priority.
- SIP communications are the key to setup of traffic between servers and require specific ports to be open on the UM servers, UM call routers, and the UM IP gateway.

Objective review

Answer the following questions to test your knowledge of the information in this objective. You can find the answers to these questions and explanations of why each answer choice is correct or incorrect in the "Answers" section at the end of this chapter.

1. You need to verify if the installed SSL certificate for server01.contoso.com will work with your Lync/Skype for business system with MTLS. Which certificates are valid? (Choose all that apply.)

   A. Self-signed certificate with the FQDN of the server.

   B. Certificate issued by an internal Enterprise CA including the FQDN of the server.

   C. Certificate issued by a third-party including the HTTPS name (mail.contoso.com).

   D. Third-party certificate including the FQDN of the server.

2. SIP secured communications appear to fail. You ask the networking team to check that the correct ports are open. Which port is not required for SIP secured communications?

   A. 5060

   B. 5061

   C. 5063

   D. 5068

Objective 1.4: Migrate Unified Messaging

When an organization moves from an older version of Exchange Server and already uses Unified Messaging, much of the key configuration will already be in place and working. In such scenarios a properly executed migration will be required to ensure that users do not experience downtime during the Exchange upgrade.

> **This objective covers how to:**
> - Prepare to migrate.
> - Plan a migration strategy.
> - Plan a coexistence strategy.
> - Move UM mailboxes between sites.
> - Redirect the SIP gateway to Exchange.
> - Decommission the legacy system.

Prepare to migrate

The deployment of and migration to Exchange Server 2013 includes UM software within both the Client Access and Mailbox roles. This means the foundation for the migration will be in place before the migration of UM-enabled mailboxes takes place. This differs to older versions of Exchange Server, as in Exchange 2007 and Exchange 2010 organizations would typically use standalone Exchange Unified Messaging servers. Therefore, from 2007 to 2010 many organizations would continue to deploy these as standalone roles.

Preparation for the migration is instead based on understanding the services in use within the organization, and ensuring the new Exchange 2013 servers are configured correctly to allow a smooth migration. The specifics of implementing certificates, UM dial plans, and other core configuration objects have already been covered in depth earlier in this chapter so the focus here is solely on the high level areas that must be taken into account, along with the order of proceedings for success.

In preparation for migration, look to collect information about the following areas within the existing Exchange 2007 or Exchange 2010 Unified Messaging services:

- Is SIP secured (MTLS) in use on the existing UM services? Record the startup mode configured on each server.

- Record the Unified Messaging related SSL certificates that are currently in place, including the names in use and each certificate issuer. For example, is the SSL certificate issued by a third-party, issued by an internal/Enterprise certificate authority, or even a self-signed certificate?

- Check with the administrators responsible for the network and firewalls. Are custom firewall rules in place to allow traffic between UM IP gateway devices and Exchange UM servers? What are the rules?

- Have custom ports been configured for SIP use, rather than standard ports such as 5060 and 5061? If custom ports have been configured for the UM service, investigate if there is a need for this configuration, or if it was an arbitrary choice.

- If upgrading from Exchange 2007, are fax services in use? Exchange 2010 and above require a fax provider instead, so if the organization uses this functionality and will continue to do so, preparation will include selecting a compatible third-party solution to integrate with Exchange 2013.

- If upgrading from Exchange 2010 and fax services are in use, ensure that the current third-party solution supports Exchange 2013. If an upgrade is required, take time to understand the steps to perform (and at which point to perform the steps) during the upgrade.

- What dial plans are in use within the organizations and what Exchange UM servers is each dial plan assigned to? E.164 and extension-based dial plans will not be bound to any Exchange 2013 server; but SIP-based dial plans will need to be bound to particular Exchange 2013 UM servers.

- Record each UM IP gateway and associated Hunt Groups that are configured on the existing Exchange 2007 or 2010 systems. Ensure that the system is supported with Exchange 2013 before attempting to migrate. Many IP-PBX systems require updates.

- Any auto attendant will also need recording to ensure that functionality is tested before and after migration.

- Finally, use the current UM-enabled mailbox count and call statistics as input to Exchange sizing.

As part of the preparation for the Unified Messaging migration, the core Exchange Server 2013 implementation must take place. For UM migration this will require that both the Client Access and Mailbox server roles installed within the organization to ensure the UM call router and UM service is available.

Planning a migration strategy

A migration to Exchange 2013 Unified Messaging will usually be an intra-forest migration. An intra-forest migration is when the new version of Exchange is installed into the same forest as the old version of Exchange.

The benefit of an intra-forest migration is that most configuration is stored in Active Directory rather than on individual Exchange Unified Messaging servers. Therefore, UM dial plans and UM-enabled mailboxes (and other configuration) are available and ready for the Exchange 2013 servers to consume. Mailboxes moved as part of an intra-forest migration will not need re-enabling for Unified Messaging.

Other organizations, particularly those that are consolidating forests after a merger or acquisition, will perform a cross-forest migration. A cross-forest migration requires re-creation of the same UM dial plans, UM mailbox properties, auto attendants, UM IP gateways, and other associated configuration before mailboxes can be migrated cross-forest. A mailbox moved as part of a cross-forest migration will need to have Unified Messaging re-enabled after the mailbox move successfully completes.

Migrations from earlier versions of Exchange, to Exchange Server 2013 Unified Messaging, follow standard upgrade and migration procedures. Mailboxes are moved using the latest version of the tools, either in the Exchange Admin Center or via the Exchange Management Shell. This allows administrators to either use Move Requests, or new with Exchange 2013, Migration Batches.

As with all mailbox moves, the same standard considerations apply. A mailbox move will consume approximately the same amount of disk space in log files as the mailbox size; therefore moving 50 mailboxes that are 10 GB in size in a single operation will consume at least 500 GB of log space, in addition to at least 500 GB of space in the mailbox databases. This space is not permanently used and will be reclaimed after the next time the database is backed up or (in the case of Exchange Native Protection with circular logging) as soon as the logs are replayed on other nodes. The potential log space requirements during migration often require administrators to factor in a longer period of coexistence as part of the migration strategy.

In addition to moving user mailboxes, include migrating system mailboxes as part of the migration strategy from Exchange 2010. These are often hidden from view but available when using Get-Mailbox with the Arbitration parameter. The system mailbox is used for the storage of UM prompts, announcements, and auto attendant menus.

Planning a coexistence strategy

When mailboxes will continue to function as normal from a user perspective on both the old and new versions of Exchange, the organization is in a period of coexistence. This requires that software that communicates with Exchange server is capable of working correctly with both the older version and Exchange Server 2013.

For many organizations, the IP-PBX system, fax system or other third-party device, such as a dedicated session border controller (SBC) will require software updates to ensure compatibility with Exchange 2013. It is the responsibility of the administrator planning for coexistence to examine the matrixes from third-party vendors to understand their requirements when implementing coexistence. This may require devices are upgraded to an interim software version, or implementing side-by-side systems during this period. The configuration of the IP-PBX software and how it can coexist can be worthy of its own book, so to help meet this challenge, a dedicated gateway device may come to the rescue.

During the coexistence period, IP gateways that communicate with Exchange will remain configured to initially communicate with the legacy version of Exchange. The same SIP redirect messages issued by the UM call router are used by the UM services to redirect the IP gateway to the correct Exchange server version capable of receiving the call and directing it to the correct mailbox.

Where possible, coexistence is preferred to a cutover migration because it allows staged moves of users and rollback of any changes. A smaller initial pilot group of users can be migrated to Exchange 2013 for user acceptance testing purposes before migrating larger groups.

Moving UM mailboxes between sites

With previous versions of Exchange, the endpoint for the UM IP gateway would always be the configured UM server matching the dial plan and Exchange Server version. This relationship between dedicated UM server roles and UM IP gateways, allowed mailbox migrations throughout the organization to take place without affecting UM services. An inbound call to a user mailbox would reach the UM server where the call would be answered and the voice message received.

In Exchange Server 2013, the UM call router will redirect the inbound call to the server hosting the active copy of the user's mailbox. This requires careful planning of UM dial plan server assignments for SIP-based dial plans, but also can have unexpected effects on call quality. Moving a UM mailbox between sites will mean that the SIP traffic between the IP gateway and the Exchange mailbox server will need to traverse the WAN link.

When planning for UM mailbox moves between sites, ensure that consideration has been taken for the effect on the underlying WAN, and appropriate measures have been put into place before attempting the mailbox moves. These measures including enabling Quality of Service, bandwidth planning, latency testing, and ensuring firewall devices are configured correctly.

Redirecting the SIP gateway to Exchange

After successfully migrating mailboxes from the legacy version of Exchange, to Exchange 2013, existing UM IP gateways will need to be reconfigured. During coexistence SIP gateway traffic will have been redirected automatically to Exchange 2013 servers, therefore the networking software has been tried and tested.

The SIP gateway will however need to be updated so that the Exchange 2013 Unified Messaging servers will be the new endpoint. Before making the configuration change, ensure that the UM dial plans are correctly associated with both the UM call router and the UM services.

Decommissioning the legacy system

Before removing old versions of Unified Messaging from the organization, ensure that supporting Exchange migration steps have taken place, including migrating all UM-enabled mailboxes to Exchange Server 2013. For example, if the UM server is also an Exchange 2010 transport server, all related transport migration must be performed according to relevant guidance for that role.

After ensuring that calls are not being received by the legacy Exchange 2007 or 2010 server, the following steps must be taken to correctly decommission the legacy system:

1. Using the Exchange Management Console, navigate to Servers, Unified Messaging, and select the UM server to decommission. In the Actions pane, disable all incoming calls to the server.

2. With the incoming calls disabled, the server can now be removed for the existing Unified Messaging dial plan (or multiple dial plans) it was associated with. Use the Exchange Server 2013 management tools to remove the UM server from the dial plan.

3. Uninstall all Unified Messaging language packs currently installed on the Exchange UM server, before proceeding with the full uninstallation of Microsoft Exchange.

Always ensure that a Unified Messaging server that is no longer in use is properly decommissioned and uninstalled. As with all Exchange Servers, not only is the server installed onto the Windows Server but it is installed into Active Directory. Following the correct procedure for uninstallation ensures clean removal and is the only supported way to remove the server from the Exchange organization.

Thought experiment
Exchange Server consolidation

In this thought experiment, apply what you've learned about this objective. You can find answers to these questions in the "Answers" section at the end of this chapter.

You are planning a migration from Exchange 2007 to Exchange 2013, and as part of the design a centralized Exchange infrastructure will be implemented at your main datacenter, rather than Exchange 2007 servers at every site. The existing environment has a 1-to-1 relationship between IP gateways and UM servers, whereas the new environment will use a single Database Availability Group with eight multi-role servers.

1. What impact could this have on audio quality and how might you mitigate this?

2. What network areas should you investigate if you want to ensure that communications between IP-PBX systems and the new Exchange 2013 servers will succeed?

Objective summary

- Exchange 2013 Unified Messaging is always installed with Exchange, so your preparation may include installation of the new UM version.
- Use the information available in the legacy Exchange environment to help you plan your new implementation. Use UM mailbox counts and statistics to aid sizing.
- Most migrations involve a degree of coexistence, so ensure you co-ordinate upgrades to dependencies carefully.
- Move SIP gateway configuration to Exchange 2013 last.

Objective review

Answer the following questions to test your knowledge of the information in this objective. You can find the answers to these questions and explanations of why each answer choice is correct or incorrect in the "Answers" section at the end of this chapter.

1. The IP gateway is configured to connect to Exchange 2007 using an IP address. When a user is migrated to Exchange 2013, the calls to UM never reach the UM call router service on an Exchange 2013 server. Firewall rules are correct. Which of the following is a possible resolution?

   A. Reconfigure the IP gateway to use the IP address of the Exchange 2013 server instead of the Exchange 2007 server.

   B. Reconfigure the IP gateway so it can use DNS resolution.

   C. Update the settings on the IP gateway to use the DNS name of the Exchange 2007 server.

   D. Verify that the SSL certificates are correctly configured on the Exchange 2013 servers.

2. The final mailbox has been migrated to Exchange 2013 and your colleague switches off the final Exchange 2010 UM servers without uninstallation. What issues may an administrator see if the servers are not uninstalled correctly? (Choose all that apply.)

   A. No issues, this is the correct way to decommission the server.

   B. The UM servers may still appear in Exchange management tools and cause time-outs.

   C. A future upgrade to a newer Exchange version may not be possible without remediation.

   D. SSL certificate generation will fail.

Answers

This section contains the solutions to the thought experiments and answers to the objective review questions in this chapter.

Objective 1.1: Thought experiment

1. Use the auto attendant feature to provide a menu to inbound callers.

2. Call answering rules can be used to provide a menu on an individual user's voice mail. The helpdesk role can allow an administrator to configure this or this action can be performed using PowerShell.

Objective 1.1: Review

1. **Correct answer:** B

   A. **Incorrect:** The underlying IP address must be correct, however the MTLS session will not be able to begin using an IP address.

   B. **Correct:** MTLS will use a FQDN of a server or device with a matching SSL certificate.

   C. **Incorrect:** While a firewall may cause problems with establishing communications, the FQDN of the server should be specified first before further troubleshooting.

   D. **Incorrect:** The port chosen, 5061 is suitable for MTLS communications. 5060 is used for unsecured communications.

2. **Correct answer:** A

   A. **Correct:** SIP dial plans must be associated with Exchange 2013 Servers.

   B. **Incorrect:** E.164 dial plans cannot be associated with an Exchange 2013 Server.

   C. **Incorrect:** Extension dial plans cannot be associated with an Exchange 2013 Server.

   D. **Incorrect:** Only SIP dial plans can be associated with Exchange 2013 Servers.

3. **Correct answer:** D

   A. **Incorrect:** The SIP protocol does not initiate audio, and the UM Call Router will redirect the traffic rather than initiate an audio call.

   B. **Incorrect:** Although some traffic is proxied by a Client Access server, UM traffic is redirected.

   C. **Incorrect:** While in the scenario where the UM call router answering the call is the same server as the one hosting the active copy of the mailbox being called, this is not always going to be true in larger organizations.

   D. **Correct:** The UM call router will lookup the location of the active copy of the user mailbox and redirect the SIP call to the Mailbox server.

Objective 1.2: Thought experiment

1. Install the Polish language pack on all Exchange Servers in both Database Availability Groups and allow users to select their preferred language

2. Install the Polish language pack on the DAG nodes that will host mailboxes for the Polish users. Create a new UM dial plan and set the default language to Polish, and assign the UM dial plan to the same DAG nodes and the Polish user mailboxes.

Objective 1.2: Review

1. **Correct answer:** C

   A. **Incorrect:** The Voice Preview setting is configured via the UM mailbox policy, not a UM dial plan. Additionally, to switch UM dial plans, the user must have UM disabled and re-enabled.

   B. **Incorrect:** The Voice Preview setting is indeed configured via a UM mailbox policy but a new UM dial plan is not required.

   C. **Correct:** A new UM mailbox policy can be added to the existing UM dial plan with Voice Preview disabled, and users can simply be switched to use the new UM mailbox policy.

   D. **Incorrect:** The Voice Preview setting is configured via the UM mailbox policy, not a UM dial plan.

2. **Correct answer:** A

   A. **Correct:** A secondary dial plan allows the user to receive voice mail from two separate IP-PBX systems.

   B. **Incorrect:** Although this technique may work, it may involve additional expense to route calls externally between systems or introduce complex troubleshooting.

   C. **Incorrect:** The user will only be able to receive voice mail for one number at a time using this approach, and it increases the user and IT team workload.

   D. **Incorrect:** Adding the extension alone will not allow the user to receive voice mail. They must also have a matching dial plan.

Objective 1.3: Thought experiment

1. You can use the Exchange Management Shell to generate reports. Any task that can be performed via the Exchange Admin Shell can be contained within a script and then automated as a scheduled task.

2. The UM Management role group will provide access to the UM features within Exchange Server without providing the phone team full access to Exchange.

Objective 1.3: Review

1. **Correct answers:** B and D

    A. **Incorrect:** A self-signed SSL certificate cannot be used for MTLS with Lync/Skype for business.

    B. **Correct:** An Enterprise CA trusted by both systems with the FQDN of the server is valid.

    C. **Incorrect:** The UM services will use a FQDN rather than the defined HTTPS URLs and the communication will fail.

    D. **Correct:** A third-party CA trusted by both systems including the FQDN of the server is valid.

2. **Correct answer:** A

    A. **Correct:** This port is used for unsecured SIP communications by the UM call router service.

    B. **Incorrect:** This port is used for SIP secured communications by the UM call router service.

    C. **Incorrect:** This port is used for SIP secured communications by the UM service.

    D. **Incorrect:** This port is used for SIP secured communications by the UM worker process.

Objective 1.4: Thought experiment

1. Audio quality may suffer when the WAN links between sites are congested. Consider implementing Quality of Service before your migration begins.

2. IP-PBX systems will now need to communicate over WAN links to the central datacenter. Ensure that routing rules and firewall rules allow traffic to flow both ways, and the correct ports are open.

Objective 1.4: Review

1. **Correct answer:** B

    A. **Incorrect:** This may allow the UM call to succeed for the user migrated, but is likely to break UM for Exchange 2007 users.

    B. **Correct:** The redirect from the Exchange 2007 server will refer the IP gateway to a FQDN and port number of an Exchange 2013 UM call router.

    C. **Incorrect:** As the issue appeared to be the DNS-based redirection, this change may break communications with the Exchange 2007 UM server as well.

    D. **Incorrect:** As the IP gateway is using an IP address to communicate with the Exchange 2007 server, MTLS is not configured and working.

2. **Correct answers:** B and C

   A. **Incorrect:** The issues described in B and C are one of numerous issues that may occur.

   B. **Correct:** The list of Exchange servers returned by management tools will include the switched off UM servers and the tools may attempt to contact and interrogate the servers, causing timeouts and error messages.

   C. **Correct:** Just like Exchange 2013 cannot be installed into an organization that still has Exchange 2003 servers, the UM servers that have not been uninstalled properly will still appear to exist within the organization. This may prevent a future upgrade.

   D. **Incorrect:** SSL certificate generation does not depend on the availability of existing servers.

## CHAPTER 2

Design, configure, and manage site resiliency

Email services are typically mission critical to most businesses, so knowing how to design, configure, and manage Exchange Server 2013 for redundancy across multiple locations is a key requirement of the Exchange Server "IT Pro" type of administrator. Getting the design correct is of the first consideration, because you will have issues in the configuration and management of the service across multiple sites if it is not designed correctly.

This chapter discusses the features and roles of Exchange Server 2013 that are utilized in a resilient site design so that you can be sure you have a solid understanding of the requirements of the software, and so that your network, servers, and processes will work as required.

Objectives in this chapter:

- Objective 2.1: Manage a site-resilient Database Availability Group (DAG)
- Objective 2.2: Design, deploy, and manage a site-resilient CAS solution
- Objective 2.3: Design, deploy, and manage site resilience for transport
- Objective 2.4: Troubleshoot site-resiliency issues

Objective 2.1: Manage a site-resilient Database Availability Group (DAG)

The Database Availability Group is a collection of up to 16 Exchange Server 2013 servers with the Mailbox Role installed that may or may not also have the Client Access Server (CAS) role installed. The mailbox database located on any one of these servers can be replicated onto one or more other remaining servers.

Understanding DAGs is a key requirement of the IT pro in designing Exchange Server solutions, and it is a key objective of this exam. This exam will concentrate its questions on the site-resiliency aspect of DAGs, and not the initial configuration of a DAG or its mailbox databases since that is covered in exam 70-341.

Planning and implementing Datacenter Activation Coordination (DAC)

Datacenter Activation Coordination (DAC) mode is a setting that you make on a DAG's configuration that is designed to prevent split-brain conditions at the database level, in a scenario in which you're restoring service to a primary datacenter after a datacenter switchover has been performed.

A split-brain condition is where a single DAG is operating in two (or more) locations, is not communicating across a shared link, and has mounted the same database in both locations. In both locations, Exchange Server is making changes to the mailboxes in the database. It could be that the owner of the mailbox has successfully logged in and is sending emails on one active copy, or it could be that the server has mounted the database in the site where emails from the internet arrive and so is adding new emails to the same mailbox, but in a different active copy of the same database.

There can only be one active copy of a mailbox database at any given time within a DAG. Typically the database is active in the primary site for the DAG, and there are passive copies in the primary site and in any secondary site. Changes that happen to a given database are logged into the same database's transaction logs, and these logs are copied to the other servers where they are replayed into the passive database. When all is operating correctly, the changes are happening on only one database, the active database, and these same changes are identically repeated on all passive copies.

In a split-brain scenario both databases are making independent changes to their copy of the database, and the only way to resolve this is to delete one or more copies, leaving only one active database and any database that remained in a passive state. Any database, that also though it was active, will need to be removed. This removed copy will need to be re-added & re-seeded; making it a passive copy once again. Seeding a database is heavy on a network link and can be time consuming. This entire process will result in the loss of any changes/additions of data that occurred on this unintentionally activated copy. Therefore, it is important to avoid a split-brain condition.

To ensure that only one copy of a database will be mounted, and avoid split brain, Exchange Server uses the Datacenter Activation Coordination Protocol (DACP) as a way to communicate with other Exchange Servers in the DAG, and to determine if each server has the rights to mount its databases or not regardless of whether the rules of cluster quorum would determine that it has majority.

DAG scenario without Datacenter Activation Coordination enabled

The DAC property is not enabled by default, so consider this scenario where you have two servers in the primary datacenter and the witness server (a total of three votes in the primary datacenter), and a second datacenter that contains two other servers. In the event of a full outage at the primary datacenter, the two DAG members and the witness server go offline. The IT department restores service in the secondary datacenter (by forcing quorum on the surviving nodes in the cluster), and the databases are mounted in the secondary datacenter.

The reason for the outage in the primary datacenter goes away and the servers restart. All three servers (two DAG members and the witness server) come online, but the WAN to the secondary datacenter does not come up (as is typical in outages involving power loss). In the primary datacenter the Exchange Servers see that they have quorum (three votes out of five voting members) and so mount their databases. But the databases in the secondary datacenter are also mounted, and so changes can occur to two copies of the same database (split-brain).

DAG scenario with Datacenter Activation Coordination enabled

Though the DAC property of the DAG is not enabled by default, it should be enabled for all DAGs with two or more members that use continuous replication. DAC mode shouldn't be enabled for DAGs that use third-party replication mode unless specified by the third-party vendor.

When the DAC property is set, split-brain conditions are avoided. Even though a server is located in a site that has quorum, it will not mount its databases until it receives the okay from a server that has already mounted its databases.

Consider the above scenario again, this time in a DAG that has DAC enabled. Power has been lost to the primary datacenter, and the secondary datacenter has been activated for service. Power is restored to the primary location though initially the WAN is not back online. The Exchange Servers and the witness server all come back online and the site has quorum, but as no Exchange Server in that site can contact any Exchange Server in the DAG that has already mounted its databases, they do not mount their own databases. Service remains active in the secondary datacenter.

Later the WAN is restored and the Exchange Servers in the primary site can contact the Exchange Servers in the secondary site. The cluster is updated with the latest configuration of the cluster from the secondary site, and the servers in the primary site learn they were evicted from the cluster. Therefore, the cluster service stops on these machines. At no time did these primary datacenter servers communicate with a member of the DAG that had already mounted its databases.

Once the primary datacenter servers are added back into the cluster and are members of the DAG again, they will see that they are passive servers and that they can resume transaction log copying from the changes made in the secondary datacenter. With regards to being able to mount their databases, they will be able to communicate with another member of the

DAG (in the secondary datacenter) that has already mounted its databases, and so will receive permission to mount its own copies of the databases if required to.

Finally, to fully restore service and move the active copy back to the primary site, the active copy of the database is moved and successfully mounted without data loss, on to a server in the primary site.

How DAC mode works

To avoid the split-brain condition, in Exchange Server 2013 a mailbox server will not mount its databases until it has confirmation from another server in the DAG that it is allowed to mount its databases. In a scenario where the entire site is down and then comes back online, each Exchange Server will boot into a mode where it is not allowed to mount databases. All of the servers in the primary site will communicate with each other, but as no server has the right to mount databases they will all not mount their databases. Once the WAN is restored and connectivity resumed to the secondary datacenter, the servers in the primary site can communicate with servers that have mounted databases, and so are allowed to mount their own databases if required.

DAC mode is managed by the Active Manager, the process that mounts databases on a server, storing a bit in memory that reads either 0 or 1. On booting, an Exchange Server always has this bit set to 0. It will never mount databases whilst the value of the bit is 0, and it will never change the value to 1 unless it can communicate with another server in the DAG that already has the value set to 1.

This communication of the value of the DAC mode bit is known as the Datacenter Activation Coordination Protocol (DACP).

Enabling DAC mode

To enable a DAG with two or more nodes to utilize the DACP protocol, set the DatacenterActivationMode property of the DAG to DagOnly.

```
# Enables DAC mode
Set-DatabaseAvailabilityGroup "DAGName" -DatacenterActivationMode DagOnly
```

To determine if a DAG is running in DAC mode use either of the following.

```
# A value of DagOnly means DAC mode is operational for the named DAG.
(Get-DatabaseAvailabilityGroup DAGName).DatacenterActivationMode
Get-DatabaseAvailabilityGroup DAGName | FL DatacenterActivationMode
```

If you use the Exchange 2013 Server Role Requirements Calculator (*http://aka.ms/E2013Calc*) and use the scripts that you can export from the Distribution tab of this workbook, you are given the option of enabling DAC mode as part of this export (see Figure 2-1). As long as you have configured values such as server names and other DAG settings in the calculator, the script export process will create a CSV file called DAGInfo.csv that will be used by the CreateD-AG.ps1 script. When you are ready to create the DAG in your Exchange Server deployment, and your disks are configured as required by the Diskpart.ps1 script (also from the calculator), then the CreateDAG.ps1 script will make the DAG and set the settings on it for you. These settings include the maximum mounted databases, witness shares, and server names.

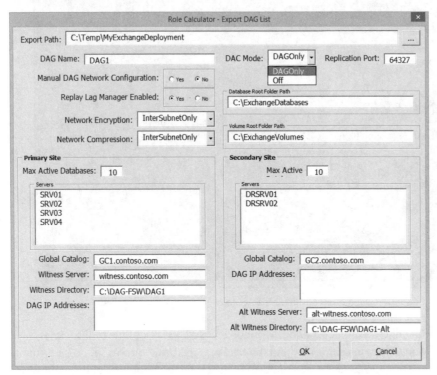

FIGURE 2-1 The Export DAG List dialog box showing the DAC Mode drop-down list with DAGOnly selected

Other scripts that can be exported from the calculator will create the databases and the database replicas for you across all of the servers in the recommended distribution.

DAC mode for DAGs with two members

In a DAG with just two members you need to take into account special considerations when enabling DAC mode because the DACP bit is not enough to protect against split-brain scenarios.

> **NOTE** You cannot enable the DatabaseActivationMode setting on DAGs that have only a single member (see Figure 2-2).

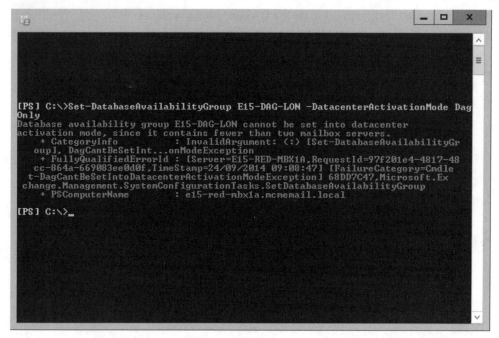

```
[PS] C:\>Set-DatabaseAvailabilityGroup E15-DAG-LON -DatacenterActivationMode Dag
Only
Database availability group E15-DAG-LON cannot be set into datacenter
activation mode, since it contains fewer than two mailbox servers.
    + CategoryInfo          : InvalidArgument: (:) [Set-DatabaseAvailabilityGr
   oup], DagCantBeSetInt...onModeException
    + FullyQualifiedErrorId : [Server=E15-RED-MBX1A,RequestId=97f201e4-4817-48
   cc-864a-669083ee0d0f,TimeStamp=24/09/2014 09:08:47] [FailureCategory=Cmdle
   t-DagCantBeSetIntoDatacenterActivationModeException] 68DD7C47,Microsoft.Ex
change.Management.SystemConfigurationTasks.SetDatabaseAvailabilityGroup
    + PSComputerName         : e15-red-mbx1a.mcmemail.local

[PS] C:\>_
```

FIGURE 2-2 Error displayed when attempting to set DACMode on a single member DAG

In a DAG with only two members and DAC mode enabled, the boot time of the witness server (which would be in the same site) and the time that the DACP bit was set to 1 are compared. If the time that the DACP bit was set to 1 is earlier than the boot time of the witness server, it is assumed that all of the servers in the site were rebooted, and thus an event has occurred across the site to cause a site-wide outage.

If the DACP bit was set at a time later than the witness server's boot time, it is assumed that the DAG member had a reboot event that was not related to a site outage.

If the reboot event is not related to a site outage (in other words, the time the DACP bit was set is later than the witness server boot time), the DAG member is allowed to mount databases.

> *IMPORTANT* **REBOOT TIME AND CLUSTERS**
>
> The boot time of the witness server is used to help distinguish the type of reboot event that has occurred, so you should never reboot the witness server and the sole DAG member at the same time. If they are rebooted at the same time, the sole DAG member will not be allowed to mount databases. If this happens, you need to run the Restore-DatabaseAvailabilityGroup cmdlet to reset the DACP bit and permit the DAG member to mount databases.

Other benefits of DAC mode

As well as preventing split-brain condition in a DAG, the DAC mode setting allows the use of Exchange Server cmdlets to perform datacenter switchovers. The cmdlets that can be used include the following:

- **Stop-DatabaseAvailabilityGroup**   This cmdlet is used to remove a member from the DAG or to remove an entire site from a DAG; like when you need to switch service over to the secondary datacenter. This cmdlet can be run only when the DAG is configured with a *DatacenterActivationMode* value of DagOnly. In the event of server or site failure (rather than planned switchover), you must use the ConfigurationOnly switch to update the state of the DAG members in the Active Directory when the actual servers are unavailable.

- **Restore-DatabaseAvailabilityGroup**   This cmdlet brings the DAG online in a switchover event. You need to mention the site name (-ActiveDirectorySite) and optionally the alternative witness server and directory if these were not already configured as part of the DAG. In the event of a site outage, this cmdlet would be used after a failed site is removed from the DAG using Stop-DatabaseAvailabilityGroup. This cmdlet forcibly evicts from the DAG those servers on the StoppedMailboxServers list and thus resets the requirements for quorum. This allows the remaining DAG members to establish quorum, mount databases, and provide service. If there is an even number of surviving DAG members, or if there is only one surviving DAG member, then this cmdlet configures the DAG to use the alternative file share witness. A file share witness is required when the cluster has an even number of nodes (to provide a tie-breaking 3rd vote).

- **Start-DatabaseAvailabilityGroup**   This cmdlet is used to restore service in a recovered datacenter after the datacenter switchover to the secondary datacenter has occurred, and now the recovered datacenter is ready to take part in providing service again. After running this cmdlet, the servers that had been evicted from the cluster by the Restore-DatabaseAvailabilityGroup cmdlet can be restored to service either by bringing all of the servers in a DAG in a given site online, or by specifically mentioning the server to bring online, should not all of the servers in the site be ready and available to resume service.

- **Move-ActiveMailboxDatabase**   This cmdlet is used to bring the active database from one server to another. In the scenario of site recovery it would be used to move the databases that are active in the secondary datacenter back to being active in the primary datacenter. It is used to finish recovery of Exchange Server following the resumption of service in the restored primary datacenter.

- **Update-MailboxDatabaseCopy**   This cmdlet is used to resume replication between the active and a selected passive copy after the service has been restored. Note that this cmdlet can also be used to initially seed a new database copy and is not just used when restoring service after an outage.

Given customer node requirements, recommend quorum options

Quorum is a feature of the cluster service in Windows Server. The cluster service is used to provide the server-up/server-down management of the Exchange Database Availability Group (DAG). At a simple level of description, the cluster nodes all communicate with each other and share a configuration that they all store, called the quorum database. One cluster member is deemed the owner of this database in the case of conflicting information in the copies of the quorum database.

Exchange Server uses a configuration of the cluster service known as Node and File Share Majority. In this configuration the quorum database is stored on all servers and replicated from the server with the writable copy of the quorum to all of the other servers in the cluster. The cluster can remain up and running and providing service if a majority of nodes of the cluster are available. The majority is calculated by taking the number of nodes in the cluster, halving this number, and adding 1 to the result. Because a DAG can have up to 16 nodes, the number of nodes in the cluster determines how many nodes need to be running for the cluster to be available for service. In the case of Exchange Server, if the cluster has majority it can mount databases and service requests to the data in the mailboxes from the other services within Exchange (such as transport and client access).

Table 2-1 shows you how many nodes need to be up in a cluster based upon the total number of nodes in the cluster. If this or more nodes are online, it is said that the cluster has majority, or it can also be said that the cluster has quorum.

TABLE 2-1 Number of nodes that need to be up to have majority

Nodes in cluster	1	2	3	4	5	6	7	8	9	10	11	12	13	14	15	16
NEEDED FOR MAJORITY	1	2	2	3	3	4	4	5	5	6	6	7	7	8	8	9

You can see from Table 2-1 that as you increase your node count, the number of servers that you need to keep online does not increase to the same pattern. Thus if you had a DAG with three servers in it and added a fourth, you would not have increased your resilience because you could still only sustain a single node failure

The file share witness

To avoid this issue of even numbers of nodes having the same resiliency as one less server in the cluster, Exchange Server changes the quorum type depending upon the number of nodes. When you have an even number of nodes in the cluster, the cluster is running Node and File Share Majority, and when you have an odd number of nodes in the cluster, the quorum type is Node Majority.

You can see the type of quorum your DAG is running by using Get-Cluster DAGName | Get-ClusterQuorum | Format-List in PowerShell, as shown in Figure 2-3. The same figure shows the output of Get-DatabaseAvailabilityGroup E15-DAG-RED | Format-List Servers, which shows that the DAG has three nodes in it and therefore the cluster reports that it's QuorumType is NodeMajority.

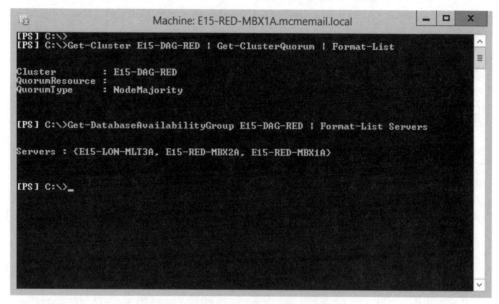

FIGURE 2-3 PowerShell output showing DAG and cluster properties

When you have an even number of Exchange Servers in the DAG, Exchange Server changes the QuorumType to NodeAndFileShareMajority, and an additional server that hosts a file share votes on the majority of the cluster. Note that the role of the file share in terms of voting only comes into play when there is not enough servers online in the cluster to provide majority on their own. Thus if you had a four node DAG and all four nodes where online, though you would be in a Node and File Share Majority cluster, you would not need the vote of the file share to see if you have quorum. If two of the servers in this four node DAG were offline or unavailable (the other side of a disconnected WAN for example), the vote of the file share witness server would come into play.

The file share witness is any Windows Server computer that can host a file share that is in the same forest as the DAG, though the recommendation is a server running the CAS role because all of the correct permissions are already in place for Exchange to create the folder, share, access, and lock a file inside the share when it needs to.

The file share witness (and an alternative file share witness in another site for when you have site failover) are set when you create the Database Availability Group. For example, the following cmdlets create a DAG called DAG1 with both the file share witness and alternative file share witness set.

```
// Creating a Database Availability Group and specifying all of the witness servers
New-DatabaseAvailabilityGroup DAG1 -WitnessServer FS1 -WitnessDirectory C:\DAG\DAG1
Set-DatabaseAvailabilityGroup DAG1 -AlternateWitnessServer DRFS1
-DatacenterActivationMode DagOnly
```

The WitnessServer and WitnessDirectory parameters are valid in the New-DatabaseAvailabilityGroup cmdlet and in the Set-DatabaseAvailabilityGroup cmdlet. The AlternateWitnessServer parameter can only be set in the Set-DatabaseAvailabilityGroup cmdlet.

You are not required to pick a witness server, and if you do not, a CAS server in the same site that you are running the New-DatabaseAvailabilityGroup cmdlet in will be selected. This CAS server, if it coexists with a mailbox role server, cannot be a member of the DAG. If you have an Exchange Server design that leads to a single DAG and co-located server roles, you need to pick your own file share that is not one of the Exchange Servers in your deployment. Exchange Server will not auto-select an alternative witness server.

> **NOTE** **CHOICE OF FILE SHARE WITNESS SERVER**
>
> Microsoft recommends that you use a client access server running on Microsoft Exchange Server 2013 in the Active Directory site containing the DAG, but not a member of the DAG. This allows the witness server and directory to remain under the control of an Exchange administrator.

If you need to pick a file server that is not an Exchange Server, you need to add the Exchange Trusted Subsystem (ETS) universal security group into the local administrators group of that server. If the file server is also a domain controller, you need to add the Exchange Trusted Subsystem universal security group into the BUILTIN\Administrators group on any domain controller in the domain, and wait for replication to complete. The Exchange Trusted Subsystem group can be found in the Microsoft Exchange Security Groups OU in the root domain of the forest.

Once the file server is selected from an available CAS, or you specify the server during the creation of the DAG,1 or when you change the DAG settings, Exchange Server creates the directory specified or uses the default directory path and shares this folder. Multiple DAGs can use the same witness server, but they must use a different path for the witness directory.

The file share witness is used when the cluster needs to determine if it has quorum and there are not enough nodes online to achieve this. The cluster name owner, or the Primary Active Manager (PAM) in the DAG, will attempt to lock a file on the file share witness. If they are able to, this counts as an additional vote, and so in the case of an even number of servers in the DAG, when half the servers are online the locking of the file share witness means the site that contains the PAM will have an additional vote. Typically this means that they will achieve majority.

Figure 2-4 shows a four node DAG across two sites. The file share witness is located in the primary site, and all four servers are up and have mounted databases.

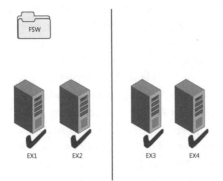

FIGURE 2-4 Four node DAG with all servers online

In Figure 2-5, the file share witness vote means that one side of the cluster can reach majority and mount databases. The other side of the DAG in the secondary datacenter cannot reach majority, and so the cluster service stops and the databases dismount.

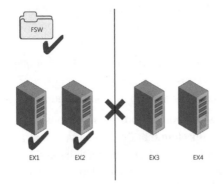

FIGURE 2-5 Four node DAG after a WAN outage

Cluster features in the operating system

Exchange Server 2013 can run on Windows Server 2008 R2, Windows Server 2012, and Windows Server 2012 R2. For the two 2012 versions of Windows Server, the Standard Edition is sufficient as this contains the failover clustering feature. For Windows Server 2008 R2, a DAG requires Enterprise Edition because the Standard Edition does not contain the failover clustering role.

EXAM TIP

Exchange Server 2013 SP1 or later is required when using Windows Server 2012 R2 as the operating system.

In Windows Server 2012, support has been added for dynamic quorum and dynamic witness. In Windows Server 2012 R2, these features are enabled by default.

Dynamic quorum is a feature where the node count for determining majority is not fixed to the number of nodes in the cluster, but the number of nodes that were online at the point of calculating quorum. In Windows Server 2008 R2, the number of nodes that are part of the quorum calculation are as described in the previous section, which means that the number of nodes for quorum equals the number of servers in the cluster. In Windows Server 2012, a cluster node loses its vote if it goes offline and regains it when it comes online. Therefore, a DAG with three nodes on Windows 2008 R2 has to have two nodes up to keep majority. The file share witness is not used because there is an odd number of nodes. But the same DAG running on Windows Server 2012 or 2012 R2 can sustain the loss of two nodes one after the other and keep majority. It does this via dynamic quorum. The loss of one server majority is recalculated and the DAG becomes a two node DAG with file share witness. That is three votes, and as long as either two nodes, or the witness server and the single DAG node are up, Exchange can keep mounting databases. Simply put, if the cluster experiences a failure that allows it to remain up and maintain quorum, then dynamic quorum can recalculate the quorum. This allows the cluster to survive additional failures and maintain quorum (more than it could without dynamic quorum). However, if your initial failure is widespread enough to cause quorum loss, the cluster will go down. So dynamic quorum really helps when you have cascading failures.

Dynamic quorum does not help in a scenario where you would lose quorum. For example, in a single site DAG with three nodes and you lose two nodes at the same time, you go from three votes (no file share witness) to one vote. One vote is not enough to maintain quorum.

This allows for a scenario called *last man standing* where you can progressively loose nodes and thus votes until you have one server remaining. Note that this one server might not host all of the databases or be sized to host the load of all the user connections, and so even though the cluster is up and one Exchange Server is up, not all of your databases might be up.

> **IMPORTANT CONSIDERING DYNAMIC QUORUM**
>
> Do not design your DAG to take into account dynamic quorum. That means do not design every server in the DAG to hold a replica of every database, and size each server to support all of the users in the event of last man standing.

If you have two nodes left, dynamic quorum removes the vote from one node. One node will have a vote and one node will not. Use Get-ClusterNode ClusterName | Format-Table Name, DynamicWeight, State to determine which node has the vote, and do not shut that node down. If you do, the other node's cluster service will go offline as it does not have a vote. The cmdlet will report DynamicWeight = 1 for the server that has the vote.

Quorum scenarios

Now that you have an understanding of the different scenarios where a file share witness will come into play, and that having quorum (or majority) is vital to maintaining service, we will look at some customer scenarios and best choices.

We will look at the following four scenarios:

- Coho Winery has two servers at their vineyard and no other locations to host offsite servers.
- Blue Yonder Airlines has a six node DAG with two of the servers in a secondary data-center for high availability and site resiliency purposes.
- Northwind Electric Cars has a well-connected office and factory located in different cities with users at both locations.
- Humongous Insurance has 32,000 employees and need to have automatic failover to the secondary datacenter in the event of an outage in their primary New York data-center.

Coho Winery single site two node   This customer only has a single site but needs to ensure their email server is always available because they use it to receive orders from their suppliers. Therefore, they have a two node DAG. Their file share witness is located on their file server. They are running Windows Server 2012 R2 as their operating system for Exchange Server and so dynamic quorum comes into the equation when they need to shut down a server for maintenance, and they need to ensure they move the voting node and then keep that server online.

Blue Yonder Airlines   This is a midsized regional airline company that has centralized all of its email in its head office in London. They have a disaster recovery datacenter near Oxford. They have a six node DAG supporting 4000 mailboxes with two of the nodes in the disaster recovery datacenter. All active mailbox databases are replicated to two other servers, one at the HQ for initial failover, and one at the DR site for second failover. They can lose one server and all of the mailbox databases remain on servers in the head office. At the loss of a second server in London, most mailboxes are activated on the two remaining servers in London but a small handful are activated in the secondary datacenter. The loss of two servers in London is acceptable because cross-site failover of mailbox databases is allowed. However, because they are running Exchange Server 2013 on Windows Server 2008 R2 they cannot use dynamic quorum. Therefore, because the cluster is a six-node cluster, it will make use of the file share witness. This means that with the loss of two servers in the primary site majority is main-tained, or the loss of one server in the event that the WAN should also fail.

When two servers fail, but the WAN is online, there are four reachable servers. Four is a majority of six. When three servers fail, the file share witness vote becomes important because there are now three servers online (which is not a majority of six), but the extra vote from the file share witness means there are four votes. These votes are a majority, and so the cluster remains running. As long as the three failed servers are not the only servers a given database was replicated to, all mail databases remain online. If the WAN to the DR site goes offline, the two servers near Oxford will go offline (because they do not have majority). IT pros in the primary site must ensure that three Exchange Servers and the file share witness remain online while the WAN is offline.

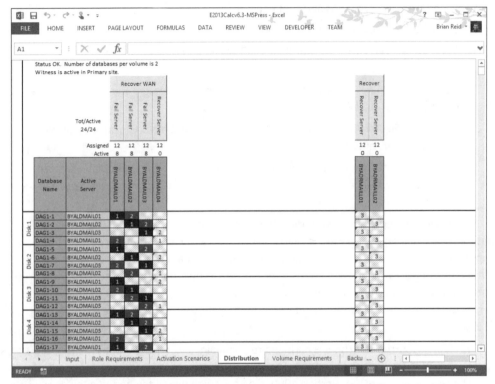

FIGURE 2-6 Exchange 2013 Storage Calculator used to model WAN and server failure scenarios

Exchange Server Role Calculator for Exchange 2013 is a great tool for modeling these scenarios. For example, in Figure 2-6, you can see this six-server node with the WAN failed between sites (the WAN buttons reads, "Recover WAN"), and thus the two servers in the secondary datacenter are offline, and one server in the primary site has also failed. Even though Blue Yonder Airlines has lost the resources of half of their Exchange Servers, they are still able to maintain quorum and service email to their employees.

Northwind Electric Cars This customer has 2,000 staff, with 1,500 in the main office and 500 on the assembly line. There is good WAN connectivity between the sites even though they are located in different cities. Therefore they opted for two DAGs and a file share witness server located in each site (one for each DAG). The user mailboxes are located in the DAG that is in the majority at the local site. Quorum is maintained per DAG, and so each office is a separate failure domain.

If the WAN fails, the Exchange Servers that are in the secondary site for each DAG go offline. This results in some Exchange Servers in each location going offline, but because these servers are just passive copies and not used for transport shadow redundancy from the other servers in the site, there is no immediate impact to the users.

When a site fails, the mailboxes for that site could be activated in the other site if recovery of the primary site would exceed any required SLA. The other site and its servers would not be affected by the outage in the first site.

Humongous Insurance This customer is planning a migration to Exchange Server 2013 from Exchange Server 2007. As part of the migration, Humongous Insurance will make use of new technologies such as 8 TB SATA drives to reduce their storage costs in a JBOD deployment that is an eight node DAG across two datacenters. They will locate their file share witness in a third datacenter that has MPLS networking links to both the primary and secondary datacenters. Figure 2-7 shows the Distribution tab of the Exchange Server 2013 storage calculator with four servers in each site, and the file share witness in a third datacenter. The WAN in the primary datacenter has failed. The MPLS links that they have in place from the various user locations remain working, as does the link to the file share witness site and the secondary site. On the WAN failing, the secondary site can reach the file share witness and therefore is able to have five votes from a DAG of eight nodes. It is therefore able to keep majority even though the primary servers are all unreachable. The Exchange mailbox databases all mount in the secondary site automatically, and because the primary site is not able to reach the file share witness, it is only able to acquire four votes. Therefore, the cluster service in the primary datacenter does not get majority, and the databases dismount.

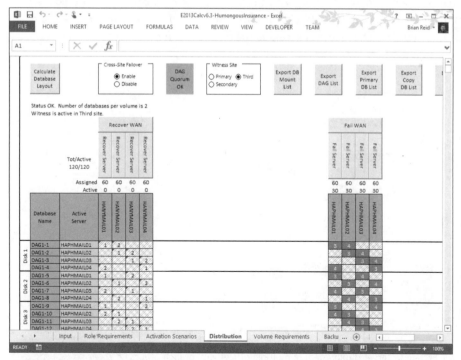

FIGURE 2-7 Modeling a WAN failure and automatic failover with a third site file share witness

Planning cross-site DAG configuration and configuring DAG networks

When you have a DAG that crosses a WAN boundary, there are a number of additional items to consider in your configuration. These are:

- The number of DAGs you need
- DAG IP addressing considerations
- Configuring DAG networks and rediscovering DAG networks
- Network compression

How many Database Availability Groups do you need?

There are a number of aspects to the question regarding the number of DAGs that you need. The most important aspect to consider is the location of your user population.

If you take a simple Exchange Server scenario like the one shown in Figure 2-8, you will see that there are users in a number of network locations. You will also see that their nearest network is Paris or Berlin, depending on their location. There are also users at each main office in Paris and Berlin. The servers are kept at the main office.

In the scenario in Figure 2-8, there are users located in both Paris and Berlin. Each user connects to their mailbox which is located in the main office. If the four Exchange Servers in the scenario were placed into a single DAG, an outage of the Paris-Berlin WAN would result in all of the mailboxes being mounted in Paris because that is the location of the file share witness. This would result in a loss of access to their mailboxes for the users in Berlin, and the sites connected to it.

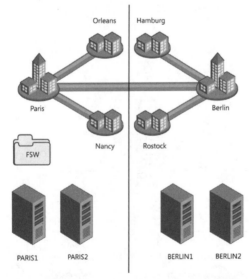

FIGURE 2-8 Exchange Server deployment in multiple offices with branch offices

If the network topology for this company is such that direct connections from, for example Rostock, reached Paris by way of Berlin, then when the Paris-Berlin WAN goes offline Rostock cannot reach Paris. Even though their mailbox is online, they cannot access it from the office. Therefore, this scenario needs two DAGs. A Paris DAG with one or two servers in Paris depending upon load, sizing, and availability requirements, with a site-resilient copy in Berlin. This DAG would have a file share witness in Paris and a Berlin-homed DAG with the file share witness in Berlin. When the WAN fails, the Paris DAG will mount its databases in Paris, and the Berlin DAG will mount its databases in Berlin. This is known as an Active/Active (Multiple DAG) model and can be seen in Figure 2-9. This model avoids the WAN link between the two sites being a potential single point of failure, though it does require more servers than a single DAG for the same user count and mailbox size. If the WAN can be a resilient WAN, an Active/Active (Single DAG) model can be deployed where there are active mailbox databases mounted in each site. Because the WAN is resilient, an outage of part of the WAN results in an alternative route being used, and the mailbox databases staying online in their desired locations.

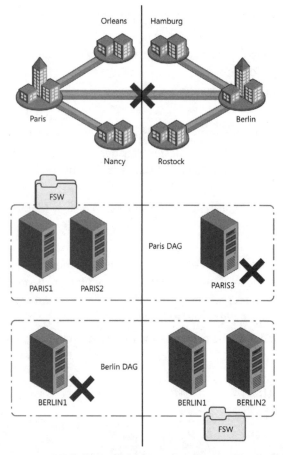

FIGURE 2-9 A two datacenter design where users are located at or networked to each datacenter

DAG IP addressing considerations

In a Windows Server 2008 R2 or Windows Server 2012 cluster, you need to have an IP address assigned to the DAG for each site that the DAG can operate in. You can either assign an IP address manually when creating the DAG in Exchange Management Shell, or allow DHCP to assign an IP address to the DAG. For auto assignment of IP addresses, you obviously need to have a DHCP server running in each site that the DAG is in, and available IP addresses at the time of failover. If you do not have a DHCP server or servers that can supply IP addresses to each site, or you cannot guarantee available IP addresses in the DHCP pool when failover occurs, you should manually assign a valid IP address for each site and ensure that nothing else uses that address by removing it from the DHCP pool or updating your documentation on available addresses.

In a Windows Server 2012 R2 cluster with Exchange Server 2013 SP1 or later, you can create a DAG that does not have an underlying cluster name or IP address requirement. This is known as a DAG without a cluster administrative access point. DAGs without administrative access points have the following features:

- There is no IP address assigned to the cluster/DAG, and therefore no IP address resource in the cluster core resource group.

- There is no network name assigned to the cluster, and therefore no network name resource in the cluster core resource group

- The name of the cluster/DAG is not registered in DNS, and it is not resolvable on the network.

- It is not required to pre-create the cluster name object (CNO) in the Active Directory.

- The cluster cannot be managed using the Failover Cluster Management tool. It must be managed using Windows PowerShell, and the PowerShell cmdlets must be run against individual cluster members.

- There is no computer object that needs to be created in the Active Directory for the cluster. This avoids a series of administrative tasks and removes potential issues if the object is accidently deleted.

Each of these features will impact the way you interact with the cluster, most notably in terms of the management tools used. But the features that remove the need for a network name (CNO) and IP address reduce the resources required by the cluster service, and therefore reduce the items that if they fail will cause the cluster to failover or go offline.

To create a DAG without an administrative access point, use the following in the Exchange Management Shell.

```
New-DatabaseAvailabilityGroup -Name DAG1 -WitnessServer EX4
-DatabaseAvailabilityGroupIPAddresses ([System.Net.IPAddress])::None
```

> **IMPORTANT BACKUP SOFTWARE CONSIDERATIONS**
>
> Some third-party backup software that connects to the cluster using the DAG name will not work with a DAG that has been created without an administrative access point.

Configuring DAG networks and rediscovering DAG networks

The cluster that underlies the DAG requires at least one network that all the nodes share and that the clients of the DAG can use to reach the mailbox databases. Optionally you can have a second network in the cluster that Exchange will use for transaction log replication. Clients do not connect to the DAG via the replication network and so it is dedicated to the role of replicating transaction logs as fast as the network will allow.

It is important to consider if you need a replication network at all. In a cross-site DAG, the most likely configuration for the WAN between the sites is that you have a single WAN. Therefore, all cross-site communication is on this single connection even though you have two network cards in each server. Splitting the client and replication traffic onto separate networks in the LAN at each end, only to combine them on the WAN, means that in reality you have a single network that the replication traffic will cross.

If you do have two WAN links, a large enough user population, or dedicated network switching and trunking such that you really can take the replication traffic off of the network that the clients are on, then it is worth doing. For smaller networks or networks with capacity beyond their requirements and sufficient switching capacity, it is probably easier to keep the administration of Exchange Server simple, and keep to a single client and replication network.

If you have a second network for replication, it must be configured correctly. For Exchange Server this network should be configured as follows:

- **Not registered in DNS** It is not reachable by clients, and so clients should not resolve this server on this network. This setting can be seen in Figure 2-10.

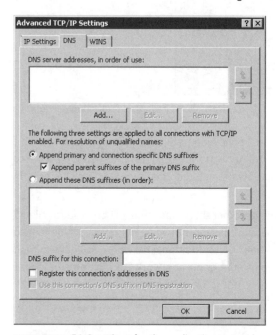

FIGURE 2-10 DNS settings for the replication network

- **Not having a default gateway** You should have one default gateway on the server and this should be on the network card that all unknown routes use (the client network in our example). The replication network should have manual routes configured so that you can reach the replication network in the other sites.

- **The client or MAPI network is listed above the replication network in the network binding order** The binding order can be changed from the Network Connections window. Press ALT to see the menu and then choose Advanced, and Advanced Settings. The Advanced Settings dialog box is shown in Figure 2-11. Note that Microsoft recommends that IPv6 is not disabled (see *http://support.microsoft.com/kb/929852*).

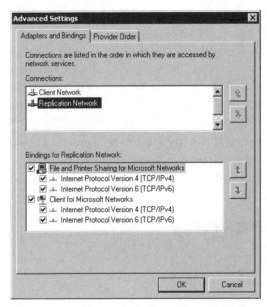

FIGURE 2-11 Setting the network binding correctly for a dedicated replication network

If you get the network card and client/replication network configuration correct, Exchange Server 2013 will auto-configure your DAG networks for you. The DAG networks are a configuration that helps Exchange understand how the network is configured. They are not physical networks or settings on the network card.

If your Exchange Servers have networks other than those that will be used for clients and replication, you will need to disable them in the DAG network. Examples include management networks and backup networks. If you have these additional networks you have to manually configure your DAG networks and then use the -ignorenetwork $true parameter in Exchange Management Shell to mark the network as not to be used by the DAG.

Network compression

When a DAG is created, Exchange Server will by default compress network traffic between the nodes when they go cross-site, but by default network traffic is not compressed within the site. Compression takes a little additional CPU to complete at each end, but reduces the traffic considerably. In places where you have limited bandwidth the extra CPU impact is acceptable as you usually have capacity, whereas you might not have capacity on the WAN.

There is typically not much point enabling compression on a LAN as the capacity is available for uncompressed traffic.

Compression is set as a property of the DAG and not the underlying DAG network. To check the compression of your DAG, use the following Exchange Management Shell cmdlet.

```
Get-DatabaseAvailabilityGroup E15-DAG-RED | Format-List NetworkCompression
```

The possible values for network compression are:

- **Disabled**   All intra-DAG traffic is not compressed regardless of DAG node location.
- **Enabled**   All intra-DAG traffic, including replication and database seeding is compressed.
- **InterSubnetOnly**   All DAG replication traffic (not seeding traffic) is replicated between subnets. Replication within the LAN is not compressed.
- **SeedOnly**   Only database seeding traffic is compressed.

Compression generates a saving of about 30 percent over uncompressed traffic and should be used inter-subnet unless you have WAN optimizers that can do a better job. Given that all of the traffic is typically unique, WAN optimizers are unlikely to achieve this and should be turned off for traffic on the replication port of TCP 64327.

> **NOTE   CHANGING THE TCP PORT**
>
> The replication port of TCP 64327 can be changed. If it is, firewalls on the Exchange Server need to be updated to allow the new port and network inspection devices should be configured to ignore the traffic on this new port.

Creating a DAG on Windows Server 2012 and 2012 R2 Servers

A cluster name object (CNO) is automatically created in the Active Directory by cluster service on Windows Server 2008 R2 when the DAG is created. This does not happen automatically on Windows Server 2012 or 2012 R2 and needs to be created manually. If you are making a DAG without an administrative access point, you do not need to pre-create a CNO because this type of DAG does not need one.

Thought experiment
Patching Exchange Servers

In this thought experiment, apply what you've learned about this objective. You can find answers to these questions in the "Answers" section at the end of this chapter.

1. You are the network administrator of Fabrikam Inc and you have six Exchange 2013 SP1 servers distributed across two sites. Your operating system is Windows Server 2012 R2. There are four servers in your primary site and two servers in the disaster recovery site. DAG Mode is set to DAGOnly. Your file share witness is located in the primary site. Each database has four copies and is therefore replicated three times from the active copy. This replication is twice in the primary site and once more to the DR site.

2. How many servers can you switch off at a given time and ensure quorum is maintained and service stays online for users? Cross-site failover of databases is allowed.

3. In the event of a WAN outage, what does the maximum number of servers that you can patch at a single time reduce to?

Objective summary

- Datacenter Activation Coordination (or the DatacenterActivationMode parameter) is recommended when you have more than two servers in the DAG.
- Ensure that you understand that two servers in a DAG should still have Datacenter Activation Coordination enabled, but be aware of the implications of restarting the file share witness at the same time as restarting a DAG member.
- DAC mode allows you to use the Exchange cmdlets only to switch or failover to a secondary datacenter and to switch back again upon resumption of service without the risk of split-brain condition occurring in the cluster.
- Quorum is both the database in the cluster that stores the cluster settings (it is the cluster hive in the registry), and a term that indicates that the cluster has majority.
- Exchange Server manages the cluster type, changing it from NodeMajority to NodeAndFileShareMajority depending upon the number of servers in the cluster. NodeAndFileShareMajority is used when the cluster has an even number of nodes.

- The file share witness is used to provide an extra vote to determine quorum in the event that only half of the nodes are reachable in an even numbered cluster. The file share witness contains a file called Witness.log that one Exchange Server, the Primary Active Manager (PAM), which is the server that owns the cluster resources, attempts to lock to ensure majority. Therefore, ensure that the PAM and the file share witness are both located in the primary site unless the witness server is in a third site.

- It is recommended to keep your Exchange Server deployment simple as that reduces the risk of human error from causing a site or server outage. Therefore a single network for DAG replication and client traffic is recommended.

Objective review

Answer the following questions to test your knowledge of the information in this objective. You can find the answers to these questions and explanations of why each answer choice is correct or incorrect in the "Answers" section at the end of this chapter.

1. One winter's day a supplier-level power failure occurs impacting the primary site. Staff are sent home and your requirement is to bring Exchange Server online in the disaster recovery site. What are the steps to do this when the file share witness is located in the primary site and DatacenterActivationMode is set to DAGOnly? The alternative witness server had been configured when the DAG was originally set up.

   A. Stop-DatabaseAvailabilityGroup -ActiveDirectorySite <PrimarySite> followed by Resume-DatabaseAvailabilityGroup -ActiveDirectorySite <SecondarySite>

   B. Stop-DatabaseAvailabilityGroup -ActiveDirectorySite <PrimarySite> followed by Start-DatabaseAvailabilityGroup -ActiveDirectorySite <SecondarySite> -WitnessServer FS1

   C. Stop-DatabaseAvailabilityGroup -ActiveDirectorySite <PrimarySite> followed by Restore-DatabaseAvailabilityGroup -ActiveDirectorySite <SecondarySite>

   D. Stop-DatabaseAvailabilityGroup -ActiveDirectorySite <PrimarySite> followed by Restore-DatabaseAvailabilityGroup -ActiveDirectorySite <SecondarySite> -WitnessServer FS1

2. You need to design a DAG layout for a company with 5000 staff located around the world. The company has three datacenters, one located in San Francisco, one in Madrid, and one in Tokyo. Mailbox sizes mean that one server in each site is sufficient to store the data and a second server is needed for high availability. The network infrastructure of the company allows all users to access all parts of the network via an MPLS cloud network, but the fastest links are to the geographically closest datacenter. If the MPLS network links fail, cross-site connectivity will be broken. What will this Database Availability Group (or groups) configuration look like to ensure a working solution in both active and failure scenarios?

   A. Create a single DAG with two servers in each datacenter as members of this DAG with the file share witness in Madrid.

B. Create two DAGs, one with the PAM and file share witness in San Francisco and the other with the PAM and FSW in Tokyo. Add one server in Madrid to the San Francisco DAG, and the other server to the Tokyo DAG.

C. Create three DAGs, one for each datacenter and expand the DAG to the nearest other datacenter where an additional server will be placed for site resilience for that primary datacenter of the DAG.

D. Create four DAGs. One in each datacenter with two servers in it, and then a fourth DAG that holds the replica servers and is distributed geographically across all of the datacenters.

Objective 2.2: Design, deploy, and manage a site-resilient CAS solution

As well as ensuring that your databases are resilient across different mailbox servers, it is also important to ensure that the client access layer is redundantly available as well. Clients all connect to their mailbox layer via the client access server (CAS) layer. Unlike earlier versions of Exchange Server, there is no client connectivity direct to the mailbox database.

This objective covers how to:

- Plan site-resilient namespaces
- Configure site-resilient namespace URLs
- Perform steps for site rollover
- Plan certificate requirements for site failovers
- Predict client behavior during a rollover

Planning site-resilient namespaces

In Exchange Server 2010, failover to a second site of the client access layer involved a change in the namespace. The namespace is what users and clients need to connect to Exchange to reach their mailboxes. For example, mail.contoso.com would be a namespace for the Contoso Pharmaceuticals email service and dr-mail.contoso.com might be a namespace needed when mailboxes are moved to the DR site. If you used protocol specific namespaces such as smtp.contoso.com for transport and owa.contoso.com then you would need disaster recovery/second datacenter versions of the primary URLs as well.

In the event of a full site failover, it is possible to update DNS and move the entire namespace to the secondary site. But while some databases are on the primary site and others on the secondary site, and the client access layer is operational at both sites. This meant that in Exchange 2010 you needed two namespaces. The primary driver for this was that connectivity between the CAS layer and the mailbox databases was RPC based which required a fast network with low latency between the tiers and so performance issues could occur if the CAS tier was in a separate site from the mailbox database. That is, your mailbox was on a database in the secondary datacenter but you were using a CAS server at the primary datacenter. In Exchange 2010, cross-site access could be disabled and then CAS connectivity would failover to the remote site, but a namespace change would occur.

In Exchange 2013, all connectivity between Exchange Servers has been moved to the HTTP protocol (and SMTP for transport, and IMAP or POP3 if using an older client). There is no cross-server RPC connectivity. This means that the client connection is ultimately made to the server that contains the active mailbox database for that user's mailbox and that all connectivity happens to and from that server. Exchange Server 2013 provides a proxy layer, known as the CAS role. This proxy layer ensures that user connections are made to the correct mailbox server. Therefore a user or client can connect to any CAS role server, authenticate to prove who they are, and then the CAS role proxies their connections to the mailbox role server that holds their active mailbox database. This is shown in Figure 2-12.

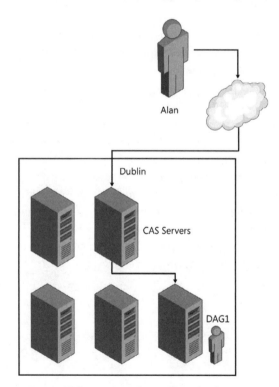

FIGURE 2-12 CAS proxy to active mailbox database

In Figure 2-12, it does not matter if the user connects to either of the two CAS servers shown because both of them will proxy the user to the same mailbox server, the one that is active for their mailbox.

When Exchange Server 2013 is installed into more than one datacenter, and some or all of these datacenters have an inbound Internet connection, it is possible to use different technologies to direct the user at a specific datacenter. For example, this could be a technology that routes the user's connection to their geographically closest datacenter rather than the datacenter that holds their active mailbox.

The Exchange CAS layer will then direct the traffic using the same protocol that the user connected with, and which is a protocol that is capable of dealing with lower latency links, i.e. HTTP, to the mailbox server that is active for that user's mailbox.

This can be seen in Figure 2-13, which is an expansion of the network shown in Figure 2-12. If in this figure the user has a mailbox in Ireland but was travelling in the United States (US), they would be directed to the San Antonio datacenter as that is closer to them over the Internet. When on the private network of the company, the endpoint the user has connected to in San Antonio is then connected to the location of the mailbox server in Dublin. The user receives fast Internet connectivity rather than a high latency connection to another part of the world over the public Internet, and the performance they see from Exchange Server is quick. This is similar to the model that Office 365 uses with the Exchange Online service, and importantly for namespace simplicity, allows the user to use a single namespace regardless of their location or the location of their mailbox. In this example, if this was Contoso, all users throughout the world would use *mail.contoso.com* to access Exchange Server.

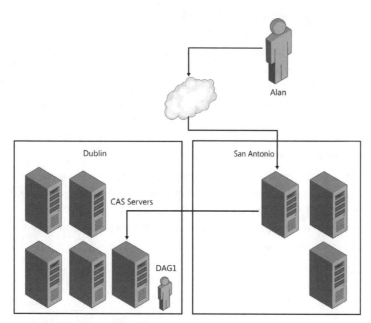

FIGURE 2-13 Single namespace design with multiple datacenters

MORE INFO   **USING THE LAB ENVIRONMENT**

MVP Paul Cunningham has written a blog post at *http://exchangeserverpro.com/exchange-2013-client-access-server-high-availability/* which shows how to configure the Outlook Anywhere namespace for high availability and quick failover times in a lab environment using DNS round robin.

This is an excellent scenario to test in a lab as it introduces you to the concepts of load balancing without the layout of a load balancer, though for real world experience we recommend downloading a trial virtual load balancer from one of the vendors listed at *http://technet.microsoft.com/en-us/office/dn756394*.

In past examples, we have used both bound and unbound namespace models. A bound namespace is where the name is specifically targeted to a single datacenter and an unbound model is where the namespace works regardless of which datacenter you connect to.

Configuring site-resilient namespace URLs

Once you have decided upon the type of namespace that you will have with Exchange Server 2013, and the domain name that you will use for the namespace, you need to configure the InternalURL and ExternalURL of a series of web services and the hostname value for Outlook Anywhere. These URLs and hostnames will direct clients to the correct servers by the client resolving that server via DNS.

The majority of clients obtain their settings via the AutoDiscover service. This service returns to the client the InternalURL and ExternalURL for each web service, and the hostnames for Outlook Anywhere based on the site that the user's mailbox is active in. The Autodiscover namespace is the first namespace value that you need for Exchange. The Autodiscover namespace is always the SMTP domain name (such as *contoso.com*) or Autodiscover and then the SMTP domain name (for example *autodiscover.contoso.com*). This namespace is unbound, that means it is the same regardless of where users are located. It only changes where you have more than one SMTP namespace (for example *contoso.com* and *contoso.co.uk*), and then Autodiscover is based upon the user's SMTP domain in their email address.

If you want your users to connect through a single namespace, such as *mail.contoso.com* for all Internet facing sites as described above, then every web service in Exchange Server will have the same URL regardless of site. If you take a look at the example in Figure 2-14, you can see that though there are three sites, two of which are accessible via the Internet, the URL used for each service in each site will be *mail.contoso.com*.

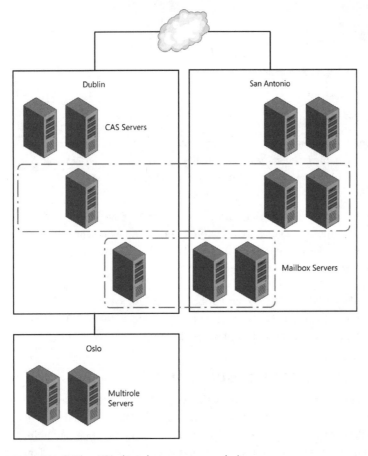

FIGURE 2-14 Setting URLs based on namespace design

For the URLs in a single namespace model, as shown in Figure 2-14, it does not matter if an ExternalURL is set for each service in Oslo, as the namespace is the same in all sites. If Figure 2-14 represented a company with multiple namespaces, the following could be an example that would be needed for the ExternalURLs

- Dublin: ie-*mail.contoso.com*
- San Antonio: *us-mail.contoso.com*
- Oslo: No external namespace

In the event of a failover, the single namespace model would require no additional configuration as a device such as a geo load-balancer or IP AnyCast would direct traffic to any working datacenter. The working datacenter is either capable of hosting mailbox databases from the DAG that was active in the failed datacenter, or being able to reach the datacenter that is hosting the databases.

In the event of a failure with a bound namespace model, where different URLs are bound to servers per datacenter, things work differently. If have an outage in Dublin (based on Figure 2-14), and *ie-mail.contoso.com* namespace becomes unreachable, you will need to either wait for the outage to resolve itself. Alternatively you could manually update DNS to point *ie-mail.contoso.com* to the same IP address as *us-mail.contoso.com*. Connections will now either connect back to Dublin over the WAN (if it is still up and it was an Internet connection outage only), or you will need to failover the databases to the DAG's secondary datacenter in San Antonio. Of course technology like DNS-based geo-load balancing can be used to swap the DNS records to the working datacenter for you rather than doing it manually.

Setting the namespace URLs in Exchange Server

The steps to configure the site resilient namespace are to set the ExternalURL for the following services using either ECP or Exchange Management Shell:

- **Outlook Web App** *https://mail.contoso.com/owa*
- **Exchange Control Panel** *https://mail.contoso.com/ecp*
- **Outlook Address Book** *https://mail.contoso.com/OAB*
- **ActiveSync** *https://mail.contoso.com/Microsoft-Server-ActiveSync*
- **Exchange Web Services** *https://mail.contoso.com/ews/exchange.asmx*
- **Outlook Anywhere** *mail.contoso.com* (note that this is the ExternalHostname property and not ExternalURL)

In sites that are not Internet connected, such as Oslo in Figure 2-14, you need to leave the ExternalURL blank (or set it to $null). The InternalURL is often set the same as the ExternalURL because that makes connectivity for users easier to manage, regardless of where the user is, if the URL is the same. If the InternalURL is different it should be set the same for every server in the site.

An example of setting the Outlook Web App URL for the multi-namespace example in Figure 2-14 is as follows.

```
Set-OwaVirtualDirectory <ServerNameInDublin> -InternalUrl https://ie-mail.contoso.com/
owa -ExternalUrl https://ie-mail.contoso.com/owa

Set-OwaVirtualDirectory <ServerNameInSanAntonio> -InternalUrl https://us-mail.contoso.
com/owa -ExternalUrl https://us-mail.contoso.com/owa

Set-OwaVirtualDirectory <ServerNameInOslo> -InternalUrl https://mail.contoso.no/owa
-ExternalUrl $null
```

> **NOTE PROTOCOL SPECIFIC LOAD BALANCING**
>
> With a layer 7 load balancer in front of Exchange Server, it is possible to use protocol specific URLs. When a protocol fails, the load balancer will automatically connect you to a different server for just that protocol. You can find out more how URLs such as *https://owa.contoso.com/owa* and *https://phone.contoso.com/microsoft-server-activesync* can work at *http://blogs.technet.com/b/exchange/archive/2014/03/05/load-balancing-in-exchange-2013.aspx*.

Performing steps for site rollover

In the event of a site outage, the steps that you need to take to failover the DAG depend upon the type of namespace model you have in place, as well as other technologies such as Anycast DNS or geo-load balancing. For simplicity, these steps assume that technologies such as those mentioned are not in use, and manual DNS changes will need to be made.

1. Failover mailbox databases to the secondary site. This involves Stop-DatabaseAvailabilityGroup and Restore-DatabaseAvailabilityGroup if using DAC Mode as a multi-site DAG should be (though it is not the default).

2. Changing DNS both internally and externally to point to the IP associated with the load balancer virtual IP in the secondary datacenter.

Planning certificate requirements for site failovers

As Exchange 2013 uses Internet protocols for all client connectivity, every name used by Exchange Server in client connectivity should be listed on a single digital certificate. This means that a certificate used by Exchange should include *autodiscover.domain.com*. It should also include the namespace used for the primary site, as well as each protocol if using protocol independent namespaces and the secondary site namespaces.

The same certificate should be used on all servers because the HTTP authentication cookie that CAS generates when the user first logins is generated using the certificate on the server. When the load balancer directs that user connection to a different CAS server, as stateful connections are not required, the authentication cookie can be read as the same digital certificate is installed, and so the user is not required to authenticate again. Also, digital certificates are not licensed per server, and so the purchase of one certificate can be exported, with the private key, from the machine it is created on. It can then be imported onto all of the other Exchange CAS servers. Any Exchange mailbox only server role can use the self-generated certificate because clients do not connect directly to the mailbox role services. The same is true of certificates on the Exchange Back End website on a multi-role server as this website correlates to the mailbox server role. Whereas, the Default Web Site correlates to the CAS role and will require a trusted certificate bound to it.

Therefore, if you have a network such as that shown in Figure 2-15, you would generate the following certificate:

- *autodiscover.contoso.com*
- *newyork.contoso.com*
- *dallas.contoso.com*

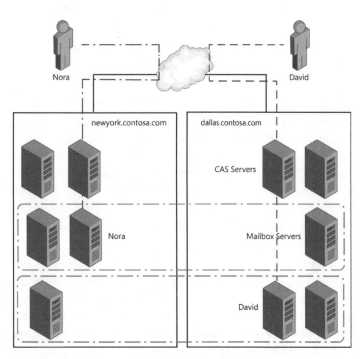

FIGURE 2-15 A bound namespace model with multiple datacenters and sites where users connect to their local namespace

Compare the above with a network that supports a single namespace and a file share witness in a third site. This would need a certificate with either:

- *autodiscover.contoso.com*
- *mail.contoso.com*

Or, if using per-protocol load balancer checks:

- *autodiscover.contoso.com*
- *mail.contoso.com*
- *ecp.contoso.com*
- *oa.contoso.com*
- *eas.contoso.com*
- *oab.contoso.com*
- *mapi.contoso.com*
- *ews.contoso.com*

Predicting client behavior during a rollover

The exact behavior of any given client during planned switchover or unexpected failover can be determined by valid testing of the client. This testing should take into consideration the firmware or software version of the client because different products and versions will respond in different ways (specifically ActiveSync clients).

Let us consider some points of interest that will help predict what you should expect to see during rollover of the service to a secondary site, so that testing with real hardware and software is likely to validate your decisions.

DNS caching   As all connectivity to Exchange Server is over IP protocols, and these protocols are reached by the way of a DNS hosted FQDN, the longer a client caches an out of date IP address for a given domain name, the longer the client will fail to connect. In the event of a failure where you are using DNS round robin for availability (not recommended as there is no service awareness with DNS round robin), if the client caches a single IP address for a given DNS FQDN and that IP goes offline, the duration of the cache impacts the clients time without connectivity. If the client caches all of the DNS addresses returned to it, as do the majority of modern clients, loss of connectivity to one IP means a second IP can be used without downtime.

DNS round robin load balancing   Clients that support multiple record caching or very short DNS caching work with DNS round robin based load balancing. The only problem with DNS round robin is that servers that are not responding correctly at the application layer (even though they are responding to ping etc. at the TCP layer) will still be connected to the client, and so the client needs to be aware of what constitutes correct service. If the client sees a valid TCP connection but invalid data at the protocol layer, they need to discard that IP address and try another one. This requires intelligence built into the client. The latest versions of web browsers and Outlook will do this to the TCP layer, but not to the application layer.

Layer four load balancers   When the client is connected to Exchange Server by the way of a layer four load balancer, and when a server goes offline, the load balancer stops connecting users to it. From a DNS perspective there is only one IP address for a namespace, and it becomes the load balancers responsibility to keep clients connected. When a server fails the user is abstracted from this because the connection from the client to the load balancer stays up. From the perspective of the load balancer, the loss of a TCP session to the real server that it is load balancing constitutes a loss of service. There is no intelligence in the higher layers of the TCP protocol stack.

> **NOTE** **HEALTH CHECKS**
>
> Some load balancers will use the health checks discussed in the next section with layer four, TCP-only services. If the single check that they implement to a real server goes offline at the application layer (layer seven), they disconnect the server at layer four (the TCP layer) and seamlessly direct users to a working real server.

Layer seven load balancers   Some load balancing products that sit between the client and the real server can also operate at the application layer. This allows them to understand the application request and deal with it appropriately. From an Exchange Server viewpoint this typically means forwarding the Exchange URLs to Exchange Server and blocking requests to the servers that would be invalid.

Exchange Server 2013 supports a health checking service that load balancers can make use of to ensure that they are connecting their clients to real servers that are actually working. In the case of Exchange Server 2013, each HTTP protocol has a URL called Healthcheck.htm that returns a 200 response code when the checked service is operating correctly. Status code 200 means that all is okay for HTTP. A single load balancer can be configured to check the status for multiple endpoints and make a decision on whether or not the real server that it is load balancing is available. For example, if the managed availability service of Exchange Server for Outlook Web App determines that OWA is not functioning properly on a given server, then /owa/healthcheck.htm on that server will not respond with 200 OK. When the load balancer sees this response it will take the server or maybe just requests that attempt to go to /owa away from the client. The load balancer will continue to check the health of the real server and when it comes back online again will add it back to the load balancing pool. Figures 2-16 and 2-17 show two different load balancing products and their user interfaces for setting the monitoring options.

FIGURE 2-16 Setting OWA health checks on a Kemp load balancer

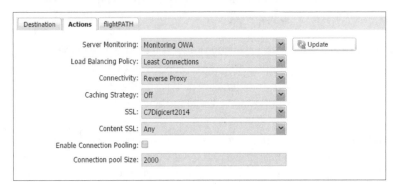

FIGURE 2-17 Setting OWA health checks on a JetNEXUS load balancer

Redundant load balancers The aim of both layer four and layer seven load balancers is to abstract from the client the state of the real server they are connecting to, and to ensure that loss of a server does not result in loss of a client's ability to connect to the real server. But what happens when the load balancer fails, or as load balancers are typically available as virtual machines, what happens when the host machine fails and takes down the load balancer? Typically you would install two load balancers as a failover pair. One load balancer is active for the IP addresses that Exchange is being published across, and the other in the pair is passive. The two load balancers check the state of the other frequently, and the passive load balancer takes ownership of the virtual IP in the event of failure of the primary. Configuration within the load balancer says what happens when the passive comes back online. The virtual IP is represented at the network layer with a mac address that moves between the devices as required. As long as the switch in front of the load balancer can cope in a timely fashion to the switching of the mac address from one port to another, the client is not impacted during load balancing failover.

Geographically redundant load balancing   When your datacenters are geographically separate you need to ensure that the load balancing devices are able to take ownership of the shared virtual IP in the event of an outage. In the case of geo-load balancing, if the primary load balancing pair go offline, as the datacenter is offline, the secondary load balancer sees this by way of a shared communication and updates the DNS record to point to their virtual IP. The load balancers are configured to provide DNS resolution for requests by the client. In a geo configuration, for say mail.contoso.com, either a new zone called "mail" is created within "contoso.com" and that zone is delegated to the load balancer cluster, or the record mail.contoso.com is a CNAME for a record in the zone hosted by the load balancer such as mail.geo.contoso.com, where geo.contoso.com is a zone that is delegated to the IP address of the load balancer (as shown in Figure 2-18). Then the IP address for mail.geo.contoso.com is the virtual IP from the working load balancer. When the working environment fails, the mail.geo.contoso.com record becomes the virtual IP of the load balancer in the second datacenter.

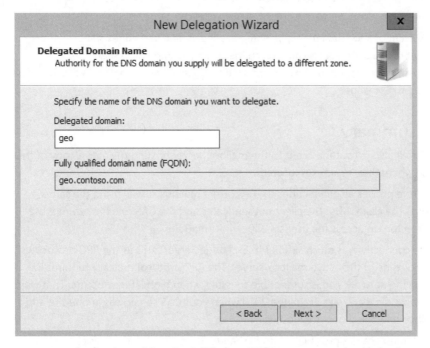

FIGURE 2-18   Configuring a delegation in Windows DNS to support geo-load balancing

Thought experiment

Patching Exchange Servers

In this thought experiment, apply what you've learned about this objective. You can find answers to these questions in the "Answers" section at the end of this chapter.

You are the network administrator of Contoso Pharmaceuticals and you have Exchange 2013 servers distributed across four sites. Each site has its own disaster recovery datacenter that office staff would relocate to in the event of their site becoming unavailable. Each database has four copies, two in the primary site and two in the DR site. The file share witness is located in a datacenter in a different region.

1. In the event of a single server failing, no databases become active in the DR site. But in the event of two servers failing at the same time, some databases become active in the DR site. What namespace do you need to have on your External-URL for servers in the DR site to ensure that users can connect to their database without issue?

2. In the event of a full site outage, planning has shown that Exchange can be brought online before users could reach the DR site to start work. Therefore, what namespace considerations do you need to make to ensure that users can connect to Exchange?

Objective summary

- The CAS role always routes a client to the mailbox server hosting the active copy of the database where their mailbox is located.
- The CAS role proxies all connections to the correct mailbox server, using the same protocol as the client, after the client authenticates and the CAS role has queried the Active Directory to access the user's mailbox information.
- Cross-site connectivity is much simpler in Exchange Server 2013 as the RPC protocol is not used outside of the active mailbox server. The RPC protocol typically requires low latency on the network and is susceptible to issues when high latency occurs. That was always a possible issue with Exchange 2010 when your CAS server was in one site and the mailbox had failed over to another.
- A single namespace is a possibility with Exchange Server 2013 due to this change in protocols used between servers.
- Options for site resilience need to take into consideration the namespace used, that is, if it is bound to a given datacenter or unbound (where the same namespace is used everywhere).
- It is recommended to use the same certificate across all CAS role servers (or multirole servers, where you are setting the certificate on the CAS role specifically).

Objective review

Answer the following questions to test your knowledge of the information in this objective. You can find the answers to these questions and explanations of why each answer choice is correct or incorrect in the "Answers" section at the end of this chapter.

1. You need to request and install a digital certificate for the four client access servers that will be used in your Exchange Server 2013 deployment. (Choose all that apply.)

    A. Run New-ExchangeCertificate on each CAS server

    B. From the Exchange Admin Center generate a new certificate request for autodiscover.yourdomain.com

    C. From the Exchange Admin Center generate a new certificate request for autodiscover.yourdomain.com and all of the names used by all of the CAS servers in all of the datacenters

    D. Purchase a UCC digital certificate from a trusted third-party certificate authority

    E. Delete the default certificate configured by the Exchange installation

2. You are creating a plan to ensure that if an Internet link failure occurs at your primary datacenter, and you successfully move your mailboxes over to the DR site, that all users will be able to connect. You want to do this with the least IT management tasks required. (Choose all that apply.)

    A. Ensure that all ExternalURLs for all protocols are *mail.contoso.com*.

    B. Ensure that OWA has its ExternalURL set to *mail.contoso.com* but that all other protocols have ExternalURL set to null.

    C. Configure your internal DNS server to have an A record for each CAS server in both sites listed with their own IP address.

    D. Configure your internal DNS server to have an A record for *mail.contoso.com* that has the IP address of your load balancer that load balances Exchange Servers in the primary datacenter as the IP address of this A record.

    E. Configure your external DNS server to have an A record for each CAS server in both sites listed with their own IP address.

    F. Configure your external DNS server to have the externally NATed IP address of your load balancer that load balances Exchange Servers in the primary datacenter.

Objective 2.3: Design, deploy, and manage site resilience for transport

So far in this chapter, you have considered site resiliency for mailbox databases with database availability groups, and client access servers by using consistent URLs and load balancers. The final service to consider is the transport services, or more specifically the SMTP protocol.

In Exchange 2010, the transport service was a role that you could co-exist with other roles or, though it was not recommended, install as a dedicated role. In Exchange 2013, as server hardware is at a point where installing the roles all on the same server is better, the transport role has disappeared as an installation option, but still exists on both the CAS role and the mailbox role. Because it is a role within Exchange Server 2013, we need to consider it for site-resiliency.

This objective covers how to:

- Configure MX records for failover scenarios
- Manage resubmission and reroute queues
- Plan and configure send/receive connectors for site resiliency
- Perform steps for transport rollover

Configuring MX records for failover scenarios

Email delivery in Exchange Server uses a number of different configuration options such as send connectors to deliver email away from a server or receive connectors to accept email onto a server. For both of these connectors, and for inbound and outbound connectors in Office 365 (which is covered in a later chapter), mail exchanger (or MX) resource records play an important part.

When an email is being sent from the Internet to Exchange Server (or any other email system), you either need a configuration known as a smarthost or MX records in public DNS. A smarthost value is the name or IP address of the server that you want to send the email to. This is controlling mail flow directly. To avoid managing how everyone on the Internet wants to send you email on an individual basis, if you publish in your public DNS zone an MX record that ultimately resolves to the IP address of your inbound email server, users on the Internet can email your users easily.

When you create an MX record in DNS you need to provide the following:

- You need to provide an A record in DNS that resolves to the external IP address of the system that receives email for your domain from the Internet. If you have a spam and virus filtering service in front of your Exchange Server, the IP address will be the external IP address of this device. If you have a cloud hosted spam and virus filtering service that you have subscribed to, you do not need to create the A record as the filtering company will have created it already, but you will need to know the name of this A record.

- You need to provide an MX record created in your domain, typically with no host name, that uses the A record created above. If you have a spam and virus filtering cloud service in use, they will provide you with the A record.

- You also need to provide a priority value. This is a number that you allocated to each MX record and which control the order that multiple records, if you have them, are used.

In Figure 2-19 you can see the MX record creation dialog box from a Windows DNS server. This dialog box shows that the MX record for *contoso.com* has a priority of 10 and points to the Microsoft cloud hosted spam and virus filtering service called Exchange Online Protection (EOP). The value for the MX record in this case is provided by EOP to the Contoso administrators.

FIGURE 2-19 Adding an MX record in DNS

Different public DNS providers will have different ways for you to add MX records, but they will all require these three pieces of information. If you are hosting your own mail server or SMTP filtering service on premises it is important to note that the A record that the MX record refers to must be an A record (or AAAA for IPv6 records) and cannot be a CNAME record.

When a sending SMTP server wants to deliver to your domain, they look up the MX record in public DNS for your domain, resolve this to the IP address of the A record, and then connect to that IP address. This can be tested using the command line with Nslookup. The command line to type is **nslookup -q=mx domain.com**. Figure 2-20 shows you an example output.

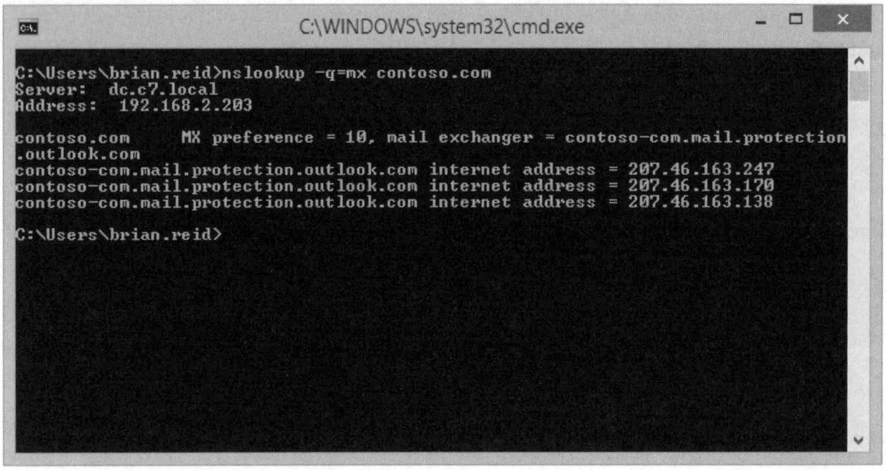

FIGURE 2-20 Nslookup output for an MX record query

You can see from this figure that there is an MX record of priority 10 and that resolves to three A records each with a different IP address. This is only one way to do high availability of SMTP services, because an SMTP server will automatically pick one A record from the list (usually the first one) and connect to that server. If that server does not respond, the next record on the list will be used. Within an Active Directory site, Exchange Servers use the same technique to connect to other servers. They resolve the IP addresses of all the Exchange mailbox servers in the site and then connect to one of them, and if that fails, connect to another. You do not need MX records within the Active Directory site, but the principle of connection is the same.

Behind each of the multiple IP addresses that this example MX record points to could be an SMTP server, or it could be a load balancer and a considerable number of servers. As SMTP manages its own load balancing you can publish a single IP per server on your external firewall direct to each inbound SMTP server that is able to receive from the Internet. If you are short of available IP addresses, you would use a load balancer. A load balancer can be used to remove connections from a server that is not responding, or to keep the number of connections across all of your servers about the same, but with SMTP it has its own retry functionality built into the protocol, so it is not always required.

In addition to having multiple A records behind a single MX record, you can have multiple MX records each pointing to a different SMTP host. If these records all have the same priority value, they will be used equally by the sending SMTP server. Imagine for example a domain with three MX records, all with priority 10, with the following hosts:

- *mail-us.contoso.com*   A   131.107.2.200
- *mail-gb.contoso.com*   A   131.107.6.150
- *mail-hk.contoso.com*   A   131.107.9.99

When this domain is queried for its MX records using Nslookup, this would result in the answer shown in Figure 2-21.

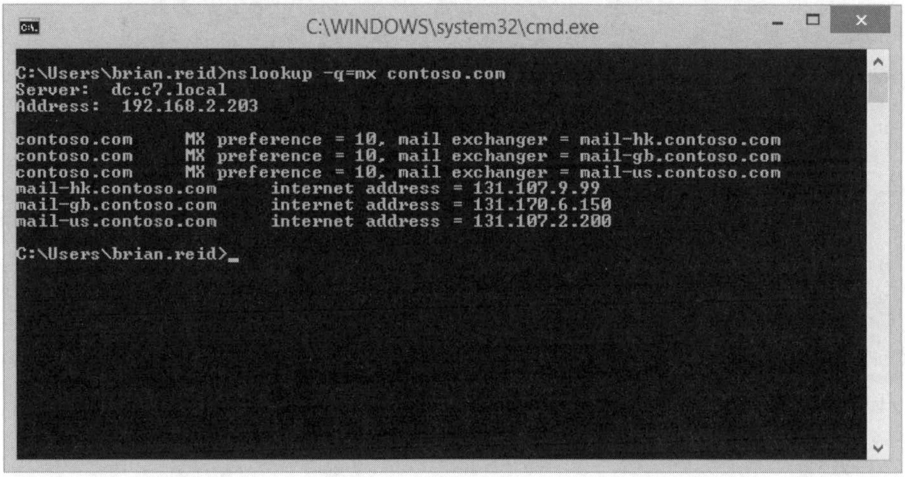

```
C:\WINDOWS\system32\cmd.exe                                    -  □  ×

C:\Users\brian.reid>nslookup -q=mx contoso.com
Server:   dc.c7.local
Address:  192.168.2.203

contoso.com       MX preference = 10, mail exchanger = mail-hk.contoso.com
contoso.com       MX preference = 10, mail exchanger = mail-gb.contoso.com
contoso.com       MX preference = 10, mail exchanger = mail-us.contoso.com
mail-hk.contoso.com     internet address = 131.107.9.99
mail-gb.contoso.com     internet address = 131.170.6.150
mail-us.contoso.com     internet address = 131.107.2.200

C:\Users\brian.reid>_
```

FIGURE 2-21 Nslookup response to an MX query with more than one MX record

You can see from Figure 2-21 that each MX record is shown, and each A record IP address is shown. As DNS in this example is a DNS server that supports round robin, each A record and associated IP address will be returned in a different order each time. Therefore, each querying SMTP server would connect to the first returned IP address and send its email. Though as you can see from the example, this would mean that inbound emails would be distributed across the world irrespective of the sending server or the recipient because the first IP address returned to the sending SMTP server is done by DNS and is irrespective of the source or destination of the email.

Taking the above example, if the Hong Kong office was the primary office and the London and New York offices were to be used to receive email if the Hong Kong office went offline, you would either give *mail-hk.contoso.com* a higher priority than the other two records, or decrease the priority of the other two records. When talking of MX records, the lower the priority value, the higher the priority of the server. This means that an MX record with a priority of 10 will be connected to before any MX record with a priority of 20. The MX server with a priority of 20 will only be connected to when the 10 priority server does not respond. This can be seen in Figure 2-22. In this figure the Hong Kong office has a priority of 10 and the other two offices have decreasing priority (i.e. the numbers increase). Therefore, inbound email via MX record lookup will always go via *mail-hk.contoso.com*.

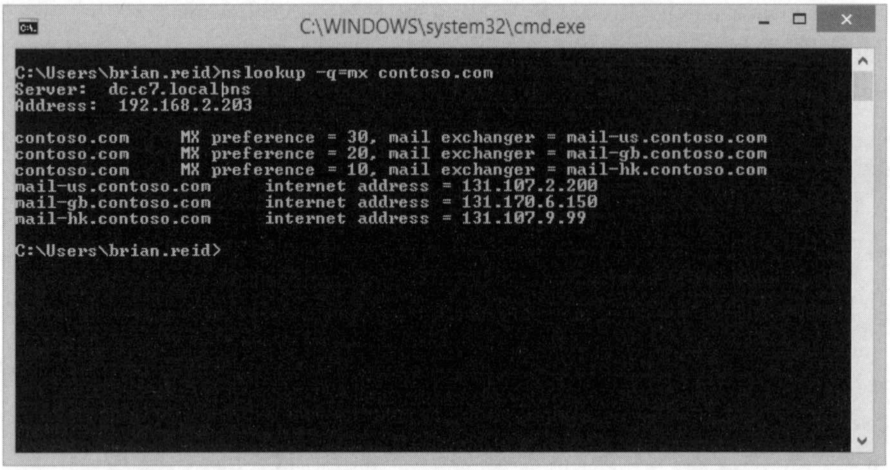

```
C:\WINDOWS\system32\cmd.exe                                        _ □ ×

C:\Users\brian.reid>nslookup -q=mx contoso.com
Server:   dc.c7.localbns
Address:  192.168.2.203

contoso.com      MX preference = 30, mail exchanger = mail-us.contoso.com
contoso.com      MX preference = 20, mail exchanger = mail-gb.contoso.com
contoso.com      MX preference = 10, mail exchanger = mail-hk.contoso.com
mail-us.contoso.com      internet address = 131.107.2.200
mail-gb.contoso.com      internet address = 131.170.6.150
mail-hk.contoso.com      internet address = 131.107.9.99

C:\Users\brian.reid>
```

FIGURE 2-22 Nslookup showing different priority results for an MX record lookup

---

NOTE MX PRIORITY AND SPAM FILTERING

It is a common theory that spam generating malware and the like, lookup the lowest priority MX record and deliver to that server on the premise that there might be less rigorous
filtering, if any, on the server that is used for mail flow backup.

There is also a theory that a way to reduce your inbound spam is to publish an invalid
server as your first MX record. Real SMTP servers will fail to connect and move onto the
next lower priority server, but malware-generating spam will move onto another recipient.

Both of these theories are the opposite of each other and both will probably reduce inbound spam to some degree, but a good quality spam and virus filtering service is a must
for any company.

Therefore, for inbound site resilient email delivery, you should have multiple MX records
each of different priorities with the highest priority/lowest value being the A record to the
primary server.

When you use a spam and virus-filtering service, there are different techniques to direct
email to your preferred server after they have been sent through the filter, and to automatically use a secondary server in the event that the first becomes unavailable. The exact
configuration will depend on the vendor of the server, but adding multiple smarthosts or IP
addresses with a priority similar to that used in MX records is a common implementation.

Microsoft Exchange Online Protection uses a different technique for emails that clear
the filter and are due to be delivered onward to an on-premises server. In Exchange Online
Protection the outbound connector is used and the smarthosts value used to determine the
IP address of the target server. If the smarthosts value is a name (and not an IP address), this
name will first be looked up as an MX record, and then secondly resolved as an A record. This
means that you can add a single smarthosts value that can be priority based. This is done by

creating multiple MX records for inbound email that are different than the MX record for your domain (as that needs to point to Exchange Online Protection) either by creating an MX record for a hostname in your domain, or for a separate domain. In Figure 2-23 you can see the output from two Nslookup commands, the first for the domain and the second for *onprem. contoso.com*. The MX for *contoso.com* goes to EOP and the MX for *onprem.contoso.com* goes to *mail-hk.contoso.com* with a priority of 10, and if that is offline *mail-gb.contoso.com* as that record has a lower priority. In EOP the smarthosts value for the outbound connector would be *onprem.contoso.com*.

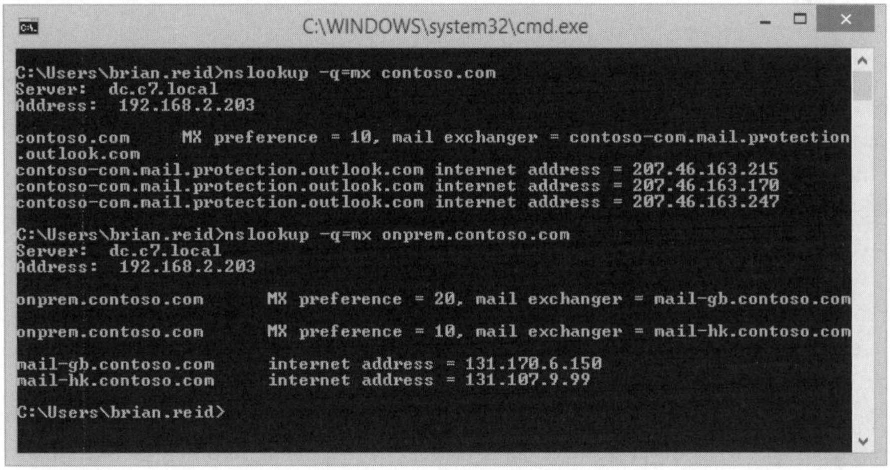

```
C:\WINDOWS\system32\cmd.exe                                  _  □  ✕

C:\Users\brian.reid>nslookup -q=mx contoso.com
Server:  dc.c7.local
Address:  192.168.2.203

contoso.com        MX preference = 10, mail exchanger = contoso-com.mail.protection
.outlook.com
contoso-com.mail.protection.outlook.com  internet address = 207.46.163.215
contoso-com.mail.protection.outlook.com  internet address = 207.46.163.170
contoso-com.mail.protection.outlook.com  internet address = 207.46.163.247

C:\Users\brian.reid>nslookup -q=mx onprem.contoso.com
Server:  dc.c7.local
Address:  192.168.2.203

onprem.contoso.com        MX preference = 20, mail exchanger = mail-gb.contoso.com

onprem.contoso.com        MX preference = 10, mail exchanger = mail-hk.contoso.com

mail-gb.contoso.com        internet address = 131.170.6.150
mail-hk.contoso.com        internet address = 131.107.9.99

C:\Users\brian.reid>
```

FIGURE 2-23 MX records for EOP and a site resilient EOP smarthost

In this example, EOP will deliver all filtered email to 131.107.9.99 (*mail-hk.contoso.com*) as the smarthost value in the connector reads *onprem.contoso.com*. If mail-hk goes offline, it will automatically use *mail-gb.contoso.com*, but while the mail-hk host is online it will never use the mail-gb host.

Managing resubmission and reroute queues

Within Exchange Server 2013, MX records are not used to deliver email between DAGs, sites, and servers. Instead a list of all the mailbox servers in the target DAG, or if not DAG, the target Active Directory site are used in a round robin fashion for connecting to. Each connection that a given transport server makes is logged into the connectivity log files. There is a connectivity log file for each transport service including FrontEndTransport on the CAS and Hub and Mailbox Transport on the mailbox role. An example of a connectivity log file can be found at C:\Program Files\Microsoft\Exchange Server\V15\TransportRoles\Logs\Hub\ Connectivity for the transport service on the mailbox role. If a server is not responding and it is selected as a target for SMTP connections, this will be logged in the connectivity log as an attempt to connect. Because the connection will fail, the source server will pick another server, if there is another available, and connect to it. Therefore, for very simple and easy site and cross-site resiliency in Exchange Server, you should have more than one mailbox role (or multi-role) server per Active Directory site that you have Exchange Servers located in.

EXAM TIP

It is always a good idea to have an understanding of least cost routing. Exchange Server only uses the least cost route to deliver messages, and so understanding the impact and where messages are likely to queue is a good candidate for an exam question. More information on least cost routing can be found at *http://technet.microsoft.com/en-us/library/aa998825.aspx.*

In the event that all the target servers in a DAG or site are offline, or the target network is unavailable, Exchange Server will attempt delivery to the nearest server to the point of failure. This is done by taking the Active Directory site link costs to the target site, or to the site that contains the nearest member of the target DAG, and connecting to the first available server along that least cost path. An example of this is shown in Figure 2-24. In this figure you can see five sites for a European company where the faster network, and therefore the Active Directory replication links, go through Paris. For fault tolerance, there are slower backup links direct to some regional offices, but with more costly Active Directory site links, they are not used unless the lower cost link is unavailable. The Zurich site is down so the Exchange Server in Zurich is unreachable. A user in London sends an email to a recipient whose mailbox is on the Zurich server. The least cost path for this email to take is London to Paris to Zurich, which would have a cost of 20. All other possible routes would have costs of 50 or higher and so Exchange Server will not use them because it only uses the least cost route. Remember that though the least cost route is calculated, Exchange Server will still attempt to connect directly to the target server in the destination site or DAG before any server on the route.

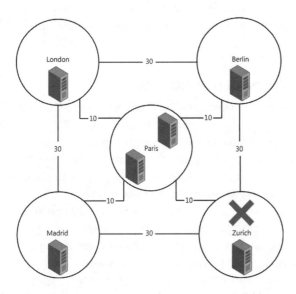

FIGURE 2-24 Least cost routing when a site is unavailable

Therefore, with Zurich being offline, the connection from London direct to Zurich will fail and so the Exchange Server in London will connect to one of the two Exchange Servers in Paris. If the Zurich site remains offline for a while, further emails from London to Zurich will begin to queue approximately evenly across both servers in Paris. Emails from Madrid and Berlin will also take the least cost route, which for them is the route via Paris. This means that emails from Berlin and Madrid senders will also queue in Paris. The direct links from Berlin and also from Madrid to Zurich are more expensive than the links via Paris, and so are not used.

On the Paris servers, the messages will queue and the queue will be retried every minute for five minutes, and then every 10 minutes until the messages time out at two days. Once the Zurich site is back online and the Exchange Server in Zurich is able to receive connections from Paris and the other sites, mail flow will resume within the retry time of 10 minutes.

Using Exchange Management Shell and the Retry-Queue cmdlet, a retry can be forced rather than waiting for the next retry interval. The next retry interval can be determined by using the Get-Queue cmdlet.

Considering Figure 2-24, imagine a scenario where the link from Paris to Zurich is unavailable, but the site is up and the separate links from Berlin and Madrid are online. In this scenario, email from London will still queue in Paris, but email from Madrid and Berlin will connect successfully. This is because although the least cost route from, for example, Madrid is Madrid to Paris to Zurich as a cost of 20, the Exchange Server in Madrid will make a direct connection to the server in Zurich and successfully connect.

The only way to get the emails queued on the Paris servers (from Paris and London senders) to Zurich while the link is down, would be to either change the cost of the Paris-Zurich link to more than 40 (so that the cost of the Paris to Berlin to Zurich link is less expensive), or to remove the Paris-Zurich link.

If you remove the link rather than increase the cost, note the following:

- The Paris, Madrid, Zurich link, which also has a cost of 40, will not be used because the Paris, Berlin, Zurich link will be chosen as the least cost route. This is because both Paris, Berlin, Zurich and Paris, Madrid, Zurich cost 40. Therefore, the hop count is used to choose the least cost route. In this example though, both routes have two hops and so a single least cost route has not been determined. When more than one route has the same least cost, and as there is still more than one route with the same hop count, the route that has the lowest alphabetical site name will be chosen. Therefore, in this example Paris, Berlin, Zurich will always be the least cost route over Paris, Madrid, Zurich given the above costs and hop count because Berlin is lower alphabetically than Madrid.

- When any link cost or other factor that is used to determine least cost route is changed, only new messages are automatically evaluated for these changes. Existing messages already queued on a server have passed through the routing stage of the server and are waiting to connect to the determined next server. Their route will not automatically be recalculated.

- The IP networking and routing is the same as the Active Directory site links. London does not have a direct site link to Zurich and so cannot connect to Zurich directly. There is no valid route from London, but there is a valid route to the other sites, and so Paris can be connected to.

To fix this issue without fixing the problem with the Paris-Zurich routers and link, the Paris-Zurich connector could be increased in cost from 10 to 100 (Set-ADSiteLink Paris-Zurich-ExchangeCost 100). If this was to happen, new emails from London would go London to Berlin to Zurich at a cost of 60, and emails from Paris would go Paris to Berlin to Zurich at a cost of 40. The London server would still attempt to connect directly to the Zurich server, but as it does not have connectivity, it would now connect to Berlin as that is the hop before Zurich on the least cost route, unlike Paris which was the previous hop when the link costs were lower. Once queued at Berlin, it would connect successfully to Zurich and bypass the broken connection between Paris and Zurich.

If London had IP connectivity direct to Zurich, there would be no need to change the costs as the messages would not queue in Paris.

In the above scenario where messages from London and Paris are queued on the Paris server and the cost of the Paris-Zurich link is changed to 100, you will also need to force the emails in the queue to be recalculated for routing so that they can be sent to Berlin. To do this, you would use the Retry-Queue –Resubmit $true cmdlet. For example, if you ran Get-Queue you might see 100 emails queued for the Zurich Active Directory site with a Queue ID of PARIS1\1234, where PARIS1 is the server name and 1234 is the queue ID. In this case, you would change the cost of the Paris-Zurich connector and then run Retry-Queue PARIS1\1234 –Resubmit $true. In the example shown in Figure 2-24, you would need to repeat this cmdlet, with the correct queue ID on PARIS2 as well (for example Retry-Queue PARIS2\554 -Resubmit $true where 554 is the queue ID on server PARIS2). This can be seen in Figure 2-25.

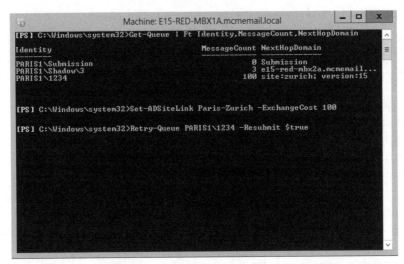

FIGURE 2-25 Resubmitting messages that are queued after site link costs changed

In the event that there are messages queued on a server, and you need to take that server down for maintenance, in Exchange Server 2013 there is the Redirect-Message cmdlet. This cmdlet will actively move messages from one Mailbox server (that is where the transport queue lives) to another server. To use Redirect-Message, you need to stop the server receiving inbound messages; otherwise, when the redirection is complete, it will be able to accept new messages again. Once the redirection is complete, you can run the required maintenance on the server knowing that the server will not be a valid target for incoming messages.

There are two cmdlets needed to take a server into maintenance from a transport perspective. These are:

- Set-ServerComponentState <SourceServerName> -Component HubTransport -State Draining -Requester Maintenance
- Redirect-Message -Server <SourceServerName> -Target <TargetServerName>

Shadow and poison queues are never redirected to the other server. Therefore, for site resiliency, ensure that any server that is taken down for maintenance is back online as soon as possible. That server might contain shadow messages for other servers in the delivery group that, in the event of loss of those other servers or lagged copy rollback, this server might be needed for. Shadow messages are always stored on another server in the same delivery group as the receiving server. The delivery group is either other servers in the Active Directory site (if the server is not a member of a DAG), or other members of the DAG, or if the DAG has members on more than one site, the members of the DAG in the other site. For more details on shadow redundancy, see later in this chapter.

Planning and configuring send/receive connectors for site resiliency

As you have seen in the previous sections, you add additional MX records or IP addresses for the same host that the MX record uses to provide site resiliency for inbound email from the Internet. Within Exchange Server, you just need to have more than one mailbox role server to receive email from other Exchange Servers.

On the Exchange Server itself there are numerous receive connectors to accept the inbound email. The default receive connectors are as follows:

- Client Access Role:
  - Default Frontend Servername
  - Outbound Proxy Frontend Servername
  - Client Frontend Servername
- Mailbox role:
  - Default Servername
  - Client Proxy Servername

Unlike Exchange 2010, there is no requirement to configure any settings to receive anonymous emails that are destined for your Exchange organization This requirement isn't needed because the Default Frontend Servername receive connector accepts anonymous connections by default.

As each client access role server has a receive connector that accepts anonymous connections, configuring inbound mail flow for site failover scenarios comes down to load balancer or MX, server name or IP address configuration. For inbound email from the Internet, you need to have a way to ensure that when a site goes offline, that the standby site can take over emails easily. This is best done with two or more MX records of differing priority as discussed earlier, though geo-load balancers can be used as well for larger deployments.

For internal mail flow that starts outside the Exchange organization, for example application servers and devices that generate email notification and reports, these need to be configured with the IP address of an Exchange client access role server because these servers have the frontend transport service and anonymous submission should you need it. The problem with configuring applications and devices with an IP address is that you need to change it on all of the applications and devices when failover occurs, or when you upgrade to a newer version of Exchange, or add new servers. Therefore, the best way to control mail flow within the network inbound to Exchange is to use an MX record and an A record pointing to multiple IP addresses, and to use an FQDN that resolves to this MX or A record within the applications and devices.

This FQDN allows the IP to be changed in the event of a failure in the current target server, or to have multiple IP addresses and to make use of the native load balancing within the SMTP protocol. If you have applications or devices that can only take an IP address, or if you have multiple IP addresses in an A record and this negatively impacts these applications, you should use a load balancer to distribute the load and to allow simple failover to a different server or site in the event of an outage, or when it comes time to migrate to a new server.

Performing steps for transport rollover

In the event of an outage of either a CAS or mailbox role server, there may be impacts to message delivery that will need resolving, or impacts to messages that were in the queue on the server that failed.

In the event of server failure, any technology that directs connections to an alternative server will be sufficient. As discussed in previous sections of this book, this can include load balancers, or for inbound emails, more than one MX record or more than one IP for the MX or A record being used. In scenarios where you have one or more of these systems in place, new connections made after the time of failure will fail to connect to the box suffering outage, but will succeed in connecting to alternative servers.

If a message was currently in transit, a different scenario needs to be looked at first. All mail flow into Exchange Server 2013 should go via a client access server, and receive connectors on mailbox servers should not be modified to receive external traffic. When an email is received by the frontend transport service on a CAS role server, listening on TCP port 25, the initial connection is made and the SMTP headers accepted. Upon receiving the RCPT TO header, the frontend transport service queries the Active Directory to determine the mailbox database of these recipients. If these recipients are mailboxes, the frontend transport service makes a connection to the DAG or site (if the mailbox is not in a DAG) that contains the active mailbox copy. If there is more than one recipient, an evaluation of up to the first 20 recipients is made to determine which DAG or site should be used for the majority of these first 20 recipients. If the recipients are distribution lists or other mail objects (mail users, and so on), a connection is made to a mailbox role server in the same site as the CAS server.

Once this connection is made, the body of the message is passed through the CAS frontend transport service without further modification or inspection. It is passed to the selected mailbox role server and the transport service on that server.

Upon being received by this transport service on the mailbox role server, and before the sending server in front of the CAS role has received any acknowledgement of receipt, the transport service connects to another transport service in the same delivery group. That is, if this is a cross-site DAG member, it will attempt to connect to a member of the same DAG in a remote site. If the DAG is not cross-site, or there is no response from up to four remote DAG members, it will connect to a DAG member in the same DAG and same site. If the mailbox server is not a DAG member, it will attempt to connect to up to two servers in the local Active Directory site. These values for cross-site and local site retries can be configured via Set-TransportConfig and can be seen in Figure 2-26.

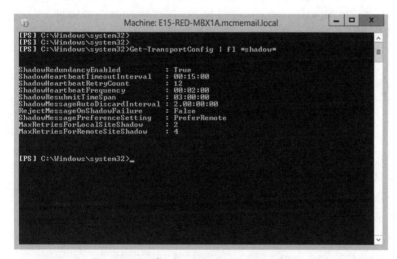

FIGURE 2-26 Get-TransportConfig showing shadow redundancy related settings

Once connected to a second transport service on another mailbox server in the same delivery group, a copy of the message, the shadow message, will be sent to this server to be kept for two days (or the ShadowMessageAutoDiscardInterval from Get-TransportConfig if this has been changed). The second transport server acknowledges the first for successful receipt of the shadow message. The first transport server acknowledges the frontend transport proxy service of successful receipt of the message and then, and only then (unless connections time out), does the frontend transport service acknowledge the sending SMTP server.

This sequence of events means that should a server fail during receipt of a message or receipt of the shadow, the preceding server will reconnect automatically to redeliver.

Once the transport service has the message in its queue, it will connect to the mailbox transport service on the server containing the active copy of the mailbox. The message is handed to the mailbox transport service over SMTP to port TCP 475 on the actual server holding the active mailbox. If this server should fail during delivery, the holding transport server can redeliver. If the holding transport server should fail while queuing this message, the shadow holder will promote its copy of the message to the primary copy and deliver it should it not receive acknowledgement of successful delivery from the primary transport service after three hours. Three hours is the ShadowHeartbeatTimeoutInterval x ShadowHeartbeatRetryCount, or 12 x 15 minutes = 3 hours.

Both the transport service holding the primary copy of the message, and the shadow copy of the message persist the message in the mail queue database for two days. This persistence of the mail queue database is known as the Safety Net. In the event of delivery failing to the database, or the database failing over to a passive copy of the database and suffering loss of log files, and therefore loss of messages, the copy of the message in the transport mail queue database (the Safety Net) can be redelivered automatically.

In the event of a lagged database copy being mounted without being replayed, for example in the case of logical database corruption such as an active deletion of data or virus outbreak, the mail queue database can replay up to its stored duration and so result in minimal data loss even though the database has been rolled back in time. Therefore, it is important that the duration of time that the mail queue database stores messages, which is two days by default, equals or exceeds the ReplayLagTime value on a mailbox database copy. The SafetyNetHoldTime parameter on Set-TransportConfig defaults to two days and can be increased as the ReplayLagTime can be up to 14 days.

Thought experiment
Configuring send connectors

In this thought experiment, apply what you've learned about this objective. You can find answers to these questions in the "Answers" section at the end of this chapter.

You are the network administrator of Northwind Traders Inc. and you have a CRM and sales application that sends invoices and receipts by email following an online purchase.

1. How would you configure any connectors in Exchange to ensure all invoices and receipts are journaled before onward delivery, and that a single server outage does not stop the delivery of these invoices and receipts?

2. What permissions would you need to set on the connector to allow relay of messages to the Internet? (There are three possible answers here.)

Objective summary

- Use a single MX record and multiple A records if you have a single site and multiple servers. If you have more than a handful of servers, a load balancer is usually a better option and a single IP address on the MX record.

- For smarthost values use a FQDN rather than an IP address because it is easier to manage change in the longer term.

- For multiple sites with inbound SMTP connectivity, either use a cloud hosted filtering service that can direct users's email to the correct site, for example using conditional routing in EOP. If there is no facility in the cloud filtering service, or a cloud filtering service is not an option, use the highest priority MX record for the primary site.

- For message resubmission, remember least cost routing. Understanding this will help you determine the servers that will queue messages given specific site, network, and server failures.

- Use the -Resubmit parameter of Retry-Queue in the event that you want queuing emails to be reevaluated for new routes if changes have been made that will change the least cost route to a target site or DAG.

- Take a look at *http://vanhybrid.com/2013/11/28/script-putting-exchange-server-2013-into-maintenance-mode/* for a script that will help you place a server into maintenance mode.

- Exchange Server 2013 should have no requirement to modify receive connectors for anonymous submission. For authenticated client submission, the recommendation is to use port 587 and not 25. Authentication on port 587 will allow relay if the authentication is successful.

- Set-TransportConfig is used to configure the shadow redundancy timeouts and settings such as whether to use a cross-site DAG or only to use the same site (regardless of DAG node location).

- Ensure that any lagged database has a ReplayLagTime of less than or equal to the SafetyNetHoldTime.

Objective review

Answer the following questions to test your knowledge of the information in this objective. You can find the answers to these questions and explanations of why each answer choice is correct or incorrect in the "Answers" section at the end of this chapter.

1. Contoso wants to have a 7 day lagged database copy and wants to ensure that their SafetyNet duration is set to the same value. What command would they use?

    A. Get-TransportService | Set-TransportService -SafetyNetHoldTime 7Days

    B. Get-TransportService | Set-TransportService -SafetyNetHoldTime 7:00.00

    C. Set-TransportConfig -SafetyNetHoldTime 7Days

    D. Set-TransportConfig -SafetyNetHoldTime 7:00:00

2. Which of the following accepted domains can be included in an email address policy?

    A. Authoritative

    B. InternalRelay

    C. OpenRelay

    D. External Relay

3. Contoso and Fabrikam are two divisions of the same company. Both were historically separate entities and remain so for email due to compliance reasons. Both organizations have an Exchange Server 2013 deployment in two different datacenters and they use rack space at the partner company's datacenter to host passive DAG nodes. They would also like to use the Internet connection of the partner in the event of an outage with their own connection for inbound mail flow. What do they need to configure in addition to the records pointing to the primary datacenter?

    A. Create the following DNS records:
       contoso.com MX 5 mail.fabrikam.com
       fabrikam.com MX 5 mail.contoso.com

    B. Create the following DNS records:
       contoso.com MX 10 mail.fabrikam.com
       fabrikam.com MX 10 mail.contoso.com

    C. Create the following DNS records:
       contoso.com MX 20 mail.fabrikam.com
       fabrikam.com MX 20 mail.contoso.com

    D. For each organization, create an internal relay accepted domain and a send connector with the matching address space as the accepted domain.

    E. For each organization, create an external relay accepted domain and a send connector with the matching address space as the accepted domain.

Objective 2.4: Troubleshoot site-resiliency issues

This objective of the site resiliency chapter looks at different troubleshooting options to consider for diagnosing and finding faults within the items that we have looked at throughout this chapter.

> **This objective covers how to:**
>
> - Resolve quorum issues
> - Troubleshoot proxy and redirection issues
> - Troubleshoot client connectivity
> - Troubleshoot mail flow
> - Troubleshoot datacenter activation
> - Troubleshoot DAG replication

Resolving quorum issues

For your database availability group to be online and able to mount databases it must have quorum. That is to say it must have a majority of servers in the cluster online. If it does have exactly the minimum number of servers required to reach majority, then the file share witness will have a file locked on it to add an additional vote and maintain quorum. This ensures that should the DAG drop to an equal number of nodes online and offline (or unreachable), the DAG will stay online in the primary site. With the file share witness it means you will always have one datacenter in a multi-site DAG that should be able to reach quorum and the other site would fail to reach quorum. Datacenter Activation Coordination (DAC) mode is an additional check within a DAG to ensure that not only does a majority need to be present but nodes must contact another node with their DACP bit set to 1 before being able to mount their databases. DAC mode is disabled by default but should be enabled on all DAGs with two or more servers.

When you have an outage that takes away a single DAG node, you are taken closer to not having quorum. When quorum is lost, all the databases in the cluster dismount. Therefore, it is important to understand quorum and ensure that network outages and maintenance events would not place you in a position of losing quorum. In Windows Server 2008 R2, quorum is calculated as a majority of the total number of nodes in the cluster and unless you evict nodes from the cluster (as you do in a failover event with Restore-DatabaseAvailability-Group) your majority is always calculated from the total number of nodes in the cluster that are online or offline. In Windows Server 2012 R2, as individual servers go offline, the total node count for majority is recalculated and therefore majority can remain with fewer nodes online. Note that this feature, called *dynamic quorum*, is enabled by default in 2012 R2 but is available in Windows Server 2012.

Troubleshooting quorum is therefore a knowledge of the operating system in use under Exchange Server, the total or online number of nodes and what half + 1 of this count is because half + 1 is the majority.

To find out your cluster configuration in the DAG you can use PowerShell commands such as Get-Cluster, Get-ClusterNode, and Get-ClusterQuorum. Some of these are shown in Figure 2-27.

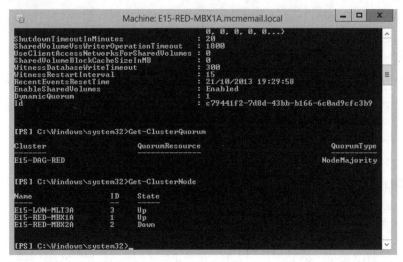

FIGURE 2-27 Cluster reports via Windows PowerShell

Troubleshooting proxy and redirection issues

All client connectivity to an Exchange 2013 mailbox happens through the Client Access Server role. The CAS role is an intelligent proxy server for Exchange Server clients. It authenticates the client or determines the recipient of the mail message and forwards the network traffic to the server that is active for that mailbox (the server that's hosting the active/mounted copy of the database with the user's mailbox in it). Therefore, if client connectivity to a 2013 mailbox is failing there are two places to consider. The first is the CAS role and the second is the mailbox server that is active for that user's mailbox. If you have multiple CAS role servers, the first step to troubleshoot is to use a different server. If you have a load balancer make sure that it is configured to detect individual protocol health issues and redirect clients when Exchange managed availability updates the Healthcheck.htm file for each protocol.

If the CAS servers are working okay and are able to proxy the connection to a mailbox server, but there is still no connectivity, you would troubleshoot issues with opening the actual mailbox. Also consider using various protocols to see if it was protocol specific. Exchange Server can quarantine mailboxes that introduce performance issues to the server and a mailbox in quarantine would be unavailable, whereas other mailboxes on the same database would be working fine.

> **MORE INFO** **MAILBOX QUARANTINE**
>
> More details on mailbox quarantine can be found at *http://technet.microsoft.com/en-us/library/jj218650(v=exchg.150).aspx.*

When the mailbox is located on a legacy Exchange Server and the client connects to a CAS 2013 server, the CAS 2013 server will prefer to proxy the connection to the target Exchange version unless the connection is to OWA on an Exchange 2007 server, or to OWA or ECP on an Exchange 2010 server with the External URL set. In these two cases the CAS 2013 server will redirect to the legacy URL for OWA 2007, and the External URL for OWA/ECP 2010. Exchange 2013, apart from the two cases above, will proxy to the FQDN of the 2007 or 2010 Exchange Server. Therefore, for legacy Exchange connectivity each Exchange Server needs to be able to connect directly to the FQDN of each legacy server in the organization. It is worth pointing out that firewalls between Exchange Servers and other Exchange Servers and domain controllers are not supported.

> **MORE INFO** **PROXY AND REDIRECTION**
>
> Much more detail on proxy and redirection can be found in the Exchange Team blog at *http://blogs.technet.com/b/exchange/archive/2014/03/12/client-connectivity-in-an-exchange-2013-coexistence-environment.aspx.*

Troubleshooting client connectivity

When you have client connectivity issues, the first piece of troubleshooting is to see the scope of the issue. Does it affect everyone, or one person, or somewhere in between? Once you have a scope to the issue you can look for something that might be common between all of the users. For example, are they all in the same database or site or something that would allow you to tie the connection issue to something you can go and investigate?

For client connectivity, another great tool is the ability to use multiple client types to connect to Exchange Server. For example, if Outlook is having an issue, do you get the same with OWA? If SMTP is having an issue, what about IMAP or POP3, if you are using a client that uses these protocols? If you can limit connectivity issues to a given client type, that will help. For issues where clients cannot connect, but you are able to open a web browser and login to OWA, start troubleshooting at any recent changes and consider settings and configuration such as AutoDiscover as part of client troubleshooting because OWA does not need AutoDiscover (unless you are using OWA for Devices on the iPhone/iPad or Android phone because AutoDiscover is used by these apps).

Once you have a scope of the issue, and a client that the problem is exhibited in, you are a good way to looking for an answer. Always examine the event viewer logs on a server to see if an issue is caused by something that might be surfaced in the logs, and always be very careful about making changes to fix issues without a good understanding of the issue first, as a change could compound the problem.

Troubleshooting mail flow

To understand and troubleshoot mail flow is to understand the SMTP protocol, which Exchange Server services do what, and what the connectors and other configuration items are used for.

Troubleshooting connectors

Receive connectors in Exchange Server are the SMTP server. To send email into and across an Exchange Server organization, email is accepted by a receive connector. When there is more than one receive connector on a target machine, the connectors need to be configured so that they either listen on a unique IP address or port (the connectors binding) or that they answer for specific ranges of IP addresses. Troubleshooting for specific bindings is easy. As long as you can make a connection to the binding IP and port, you know connectivity is working. But how can you tell if you have connected to the right receive connector when the connector is supposed to answer you based on your source IP address? The easiest way to do this is to configure the banner property of the receive connector. The banner is the message that starts with 220 that you receive when you connect to a receive connector. If you set each receive connector on a server to a unique value, you can clearly tell which receive connector you have reached when you connect to it on its listening IP address and port.

Once you have made a successful connection to the listening IP address and port, it is also useful to be able to enter the commonly expected SMTP verbs by way of a telnet session. To open a session using the telnet client to a remote Exchange Server, use telnet remote_IP_address port. If you were trying to connect to server 131.107.2.200, you would type **telnet 131.107.2.200 25** and you would expect to see 220 and the configured banner, or if it's the default banner, you would expect to see 220 and the server name and date/time. Once you have connected, use the EHLO domain.com command to say hello to the remote server and to tell it your domain name. It should respond with 250 OK or 250-SomeSMTPVerbs and then 250 VERB. The last line will read 250 space verb. All of the other lines will read 250 hyphen verb.

After the supported verbs are returned, try MAIL FROM: *email.address@domain.com* and then RCPT TO: *valid.address@recipient.domain.com*. When telnetting into Exchange Server on port 25, you cannot enter an external email address unless you are connecting to a receive connector that allows for relay.

The DATA command follows the successful entry of the MAIL FROM and RCPT TO commands. You can have one MAIL FROM and one or more RCPT TO commands. One DATA command ends the message envelope and moves onto the message body.

In the message body, enter To:, From:, and Subject: all with valid values after the colon and each on their own line. After Subject: have a blank line to end the headers, and then type the message body. Finish the message with a period on a line on its own followed by QUIT.

If in any of the verbs typed previously, you do not get the expected response, (for example the response shown in Figure 2-28), you have further troubleshooting to do. The most common reason why an anonymous connection will fail to an Exchange Server is if the server is out of resources such as disk space or memory and is known to be in a state called *backpressure*. A look in the event logs will give the reason. When this is resolved, mail flow will automatically resume.

Telnet 192.168.5.126

```
220 E15-RED-CAS.mcmemail.local Microsoft ESMTP MAIL Service ready at Tue, 7 Oct
2014 20:06:03 +0100
ehlo contoso.com
250-E15-RED-CAS.mcmemail.local Hello [192.168.5.39]
250-SIZE 37748736
250-PIPELINING
250-DSN
250-ENHANCEDSTATUSCODES
250-STARTTLS
250-X-ANONYMOUSTLS
250-AUTH NTLM
250-X-EXPS GSSAPI NTLM
250-8BITMIME
250-BINARYMIME
250-CHUNKING
250 XRDST
mail from: brian@contoso.com
250 2.1.0 Sender OK
rcpt to: jenny@mcmemail.co.uk
250 2.1.5 Recipient OK
data
354 Start mail input; end with <CRLF>.<CRLF>
```

FIGURE 2-28 Using telnet client to successfully connect to an Exchange Server receive connector

> **MORE INFO EVENT LOGS AND BACKPRESSURE**
>
> The website at *http://technet.microsoft.com/en-us/library/bb201658(v=exchg.150).aspx*
> covers more details on the entries found in the event log during backpressure.

Outbound connectors, or send connectors on the transport service, will queue messages that cannot be delivered. All of the other send connectors on other services are stateless and do not queue messages. Therefore, if there is a problem with a send connector that uses a Frontend CAS to proxy through, it will queue in the transport service. If the destination is offline or otherwise unavailable, the message will queue in the transport server that holds the send connector to that destination. If the transport service is offline, the mailbox transport submission service, which delivers messages between the mailbox and the transport service, will not queue and the message will stay in the outbox in the client.

> **EXAM TIP**
>
> Different clients will use different folders to send email from. They will not always use the Outbox. Messages that are being sent from OWA will stay in Drafts until they are sent and messages in Outlook cached mode will use Sent Items to send the email from (unless you are disconnected). Outlook in online mode uses the Outbox as its delivery folder.

When messages are queued on the transport service you can use Get-Queue or Get-QueueDigest to review the queue on a given machine, or across all of the machines in the DAG or site. Get-Queue | Format-List LastError will return the last error on any given queue. Sometimes you will not get an error on a queue, but will get errors on the messages in the queue, and for this you need to use Get-Message | Format-List LastError instead.

Troubleshooting transport services

In Exchange Server 2013, there are a number of transport services. These are as follows (with the process name in brackets) and the role the service runs on listed as well:

- Mailbox server role

  - Transport (EdgeTransport.exe)

  - Mailbox transport delivery service (MSExchangeDelivery.exe)

  - Mailbox transport submission service (MSExchangeSubmission.exe)

- Client Access Server role

  - Frontend transport (MSExchangeFrontendTransport.exe)

The frontend transport and the two mailbox transport services are stateless, that is they proxy messages and do not store them on disk. Frontend transport finds the correct mailbox server to proxy the message to, that is it will deliver the message to any server in the same DAG or site (if not a DAG member) as the active mailbox and to any local mailbox server in the same site for messages going to legacy servers or distribution groups.

If frontend transport is not running, TCP port 25 will not be listening on the CAS server. The transport service on the mailbox server will listen on TCP 25 if it is a mailbox only role server, but on TCP 2525 if it is co-located with a CAS role server, so that CAS only listens on TCP 25. You cannot have two services listening on the same port, though in Exchange 2013 it is possible to build receive connectors on the transport service that listen on port 25 when CAS is also listening on that port. This can cause lots of issues, so ensure on all co-located servers that you always bind receive connectors to frontend transport service.

The mailbox transport services send messages to databases (mailbox delivery) and receive from the mailbox databases (mailbox submission). If either of these services are offline then sending or receiving from the database will not occur.

> *NOTE* **HEALTH MANAGER**
>
> Exchange 2013 comes with the Health Manager service. The job of the Health Manager is to check the health of Exchange, such as can it log into OWA, or send and receive emails, and so on, and if not, to fix the issue. Often this will involve restarting services and can involve blue screening the server to force a reboot (in the event that the disks are not responding). Therefore, it can be the case that the issue is gone by the time you get a report about it, because the Health Manager will have started or restarted the service for you.

Therefore, look up maintenance mode for Exchange Server because that is how you tell the Health Manager not to restart stuff or attempt to fix stuff if you have the server offline or partially offline on purpose.

Troubleshooting transport-related configuration

Change is usually the biggest cause of outages in IT systems. For example, someone has changed something and now something is broken. For transport, the objects that you need to configure to ensure valid mail flow typically work until something changes in them or the send to or receive from targets change, such as a smarthost of firewall rule changes and now the smarthost is unreachable.

Always have change control and keep a record of all configurations before they are changed and after they are changed. In Exchange Management Shell (and Windows PowerShell in general), this is easy to implement with the use of Start-Transcript and then at the end Stop-Transcript. This records everything you do to a log file. Therefore before you make changes, for example to an Accepted Domain, you would run Get-AcceptedDomain | fl to write to the screen and also to the transcript log file, the configuration you have in place at this time. Then make your changes. If you need to role these changes back, you have what you need to role it back to.

If you use ECP to make changes, remember that the admin audit log can be queried to show you what you have changed, but it will not show you what it was before the change was made!

Troubleshoot datacenter activation

If you have a site failover and you need to activate passive copy databases in your secondary datacenter, you need to ensure that you use the Stop-DatabaseAvailabilityGroup and the Restore-DatabaseAvailabilityGroup cmdlets. This adds the servers that are part of the cluster in the failed site (Stop-DatabaseAvailabilityGroup -ActiveDirectorySite PrimarySiteName) to the DAG stopped servers list, and then the Restore cmdlet evicts them from the cluster and reduces the node count so that majority can be obtained in the secondary/surviving datacenter.

Unless you have the file share witness in a third site that the secondary datacenter can access and the primary cannot, you must do manual processes like the one described here to perform a failover to the other site. With a file share witness in the third site that both sites have independent access to, you can have automatic failover as long as both sites hold an even number of cluster nodes and at the point of failure, the primary site goes down, but the third site with the file share witness does not then automatic failover occurs as majority is maintained.

If you do not have DAC mode enabled, which you should on a two or mode node DAG, then you need to use cluster commands to assist in the failover process. With DAC mode, as well as stopping split-brain scenarios, this allows you to use Exchange cmdlets only to manage the DAG instead of needing to know the additional cluster commands as well.

Troubleshooting DAG replication

Unless it is otherwise changed, DAG replication occurs over port 64327.Therefore, this port should be open for connectivity between nodes of the same DAG, though of course it is not supported to have any firewall between any Exchange Server and it can generate unexpected results.

For the Database Availability Group, replication happens on the replication network if one has been designated. Ports need to be open for this connectivity on the network that Exchange expects it to be on.

To see the state of the replication of your DAG, use Get-DatabaseAvailabilityGroup to find the DAG settings. Use Get-MailboxDatabaseCopyStatus to find the state of the replication and which servers are active for which databases, such as. which server the database is mounted on. The copy and replay queue lengths, described below, should ideally be low (<10) unless you are looking at a lagged database, which will have a high replay queue but should still have a low copy queue.

The Get-MailboxDatabaseCopyStatus cmdlet will return the database status of the local machine and show the health of the database. One server in the DAG should have the database Mounted, and other servers should have the database Healthy. Disconnected and other states should be investigated. From Figure 2-29, you can see Get-MailboxDatabaseCopyStatus run against the local server (with no additional parameters) and against a remote server (Get-MailboxDatabaseCopyStatus -Server servername).

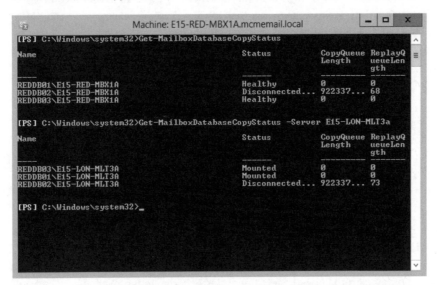

FIGURE 2-29 Get-MailboxDatabaseCopyStatus against two servers in the same DAG

Figure 2-29 shows that the databases that are working are mounted on the second server in the output and healthy on the first with no copy queue or replay queue. One database is offline and has an unreachable source database, hence the large number of items to copy, - which is actually showing an error rather than real count of logs outstanding.

Using Get-MailboxDatabaseCopyStatus, you can find out the count of transaction logs that are created on the server that holds the mounted, or active, copy of the database and that need to be shipped to all the other copies of the database. They are copied from the active copy to each passive copy. There is no passive-to-passive copying. It is important to note that if you have multiple passive copies of a database on the far side of a WAN link, the logs will be copied once per passive copy and will require double or more bandwidth.

Use Get-MailboxDatabaseCopyStatus on each passive copy to see the log copy status. If a server is behind on its log copy, it will have a higher than expected value. You should trouble-shoot the log replication process from the active to that passive server.

Once logs arrive on the passive server, they are inspected for integrity and copied again if they fail the inspection. They are then written into the passive database replica. If there are issues writing the log into the database, for example on a disk with poor write speeds, the replay log count will increase. On a lagged database copy, there will always be a replay queue length of the number of transaction logs generated in the time window that the database is lagged by. On a server with a generally consistent level of activity and mail flow, this number will generally be the same from one day to the next at the same time of day. It will fluctuate over the day and week because the active copy will change in terms of its activity levels. For a lagged database copy, consider the values of the replay queue length that you expect and ensure that these are not massively over your expectations.

If you have a large copy queue length or a large replay queue length on a passive server, you will need the disk space to store these logs. For a large copy queue length, it will mean the logs are not removed from the active copy even if the active copy is backed up. Always attempt to fix the copy or replay issue rather than manually deleting log files. If you delete a log file that is required by a passive copy of that database, you will most likely have to reseed the entire database.

Thought experiment
Planning namespaces

In this thought experiment, apply what you've learned about this objective. You can find answers to these questions in the "Answers" section at the end of this chapter.

You are the network administrator of Alpine Ski School. An avalanche has hit your office and it is now destroyed. You want to recover Exchange Server in your DR site down the mountain. The top-of-the-mountain Active Directory site is called Moun-tainTop and the DR site is called Basecamp. What do you need to do?

Objective summary

- A DAG needs to maintain quorum for databases to remain mounted in it. You looked at ensuring that maintenance, patching, etc. do not cause an entire DAG outage due to less than the majority of the DAG nodes remaining online.

- Unexpected failures can happen. Do not actively shutdown servers for maintenance that will bring you close to losing majority.

- If you evict servers from a cluster and therefore from the DAG, you will need to copy the entire database back to that server when you add it back into the DAG unless all of the log files containing all of the changes are still available on the active node. Do not remove servers from clusters unless there is a site failover or the end of the server's role within the DAG.

- For the most part, Exchange will proxy connections through the CAS role to the active mailbox server or to a legacy server in the same Active Directory site as the mailbox. There are only a few occasions where a redirection occurs and these are for OWA 2007, where the user is redirected to the legacy namespace (which is required), and OWA 2010 where the user is redirected to the ExternalURL if one is set.

- In the case of redirecting from Exchange 2013 to Exchange 2010 with an ExternalURL set, you will need to authenticate again if you are running a lower cumulative update release.

- Use the Health Manager service and Managed Availability to try to ensure that Exchange Server remains functional and healthy, and to failover databases and restart services/servers to try and resolve issues.

- Use the Get-MailboxDatabaseCopyStatus cmdlet to know the copy status of your databases and to help ensure your databases remain with their replicas up to date.

Objective review

Answer the following questions to test your knowledge of the information in this objective. You can find the answers to these questions and explanations of why each answer choice is correct or Incorrect in the "Answers" section at the end of this chapter.

1. Which of the following Windows PowerShell commands will return the list of servers and the state of the servers in a cluster?

   A. Get-ClusterNode

   B. Get-ClusterServer

   C. Get-Cluster <Name> | FL *node*

   D. Cluster.exe Node

2. You notice that when using Get-MailboxDatabaseCopyStatus on a server that hosts only passive database copies, you have a large copy queue length of over 10,000 logs

for one of these databases. Which of the following could be the potential impacts of this issue?

A. Backups will not truncate log files.

B. Disk space for logs might run out.

C. The active database might dismount.

D. The transaction logs on the lagged copy will auto play forward.

3. What does the RCPT SMTP verb do?

A. It tells the SMTP server to send a read receipt.

B. It tells the SMTP client to send a read receipt.

C. It tells the SMTP client that the email has been received.

D. It tells the SMTP server the email address of the recipients of the email.

Answers

This section contains the solutions to the thought experiments and answers to the objective review questions in this chapter.

Objective 2.1: Thought experiment

1. You can switch off three servers in the primary site or one server in the primary site and both servers in the secondary site.

2. To prevent outage in the event of a non-resilient WAN failure during server maintenance, a single node can be successfully taken offline at a time. If any server in the secondary site in unavailable, you are limited to a single server in the primary site. Different combinations of answers are available based on the number of servers that are online at any given time, and the Mailbox Role Calculator is a great tool for helping you understand these numbers for a given scenario.

Objective 2.1: Review

1. **Correct answer:** C

   A. **Incorrect:** Resume-DatabaseAvailabilityGroup is not a valid cmdlet.

   B. **Incorrect:** Start-DatabaseAvailabilityGroup is used to restart the DAG in the failed site that is back online again. It is not used to reduce the DAG to just the secondary site and bring the DAG online in the event of a failure.

   C. **Correct:** The correct commands are Stop-DatabaseAvailabilityGroup followed by Restore-DatabaseAvailabilityGroup.

   D. **Incorrect:** The question says the alternative witness server has already been set so it is not needed to be set again, but if it was needed it would be set as a property of the DAG with Set-DatabaseAvailabilityGroup –AlternateWitnessServer.

2. **Correct answer:** C

   A. **Incorrect:** This answer does not meet the requirement for a failure scenario because all of the databases would go online in Madrid in the event of a site outage.

   B. **Incorrect:** This answer would result in an outage of servers or sites failing to Tokyo or San Francisco. If the failure was a network failure that isolated Madrid mailboxes, these users would come online in the other data centers and not where the users are located.

   C. **Correct:** Each user population needs a DAG that in the event of failure comes online in their nearest datacenter. If a failure occurred in any of the other answers there would be a scenario where some users' mailboxes would come online in a site that the user could not access.

   D. **Incorrect:** This is not a valid DAG design. All servers that hold a replica of a database must be in the same DAG.

Objective 2.2: Thought experiment

1. As each site with its associated DR site is geographically separate you can use the bound namespace model and bind a namespace to each region. For example, the UK region would be *mail-uk.contoso.com* and the US region *mail-us.contoso.com*. The unbound model would work (*mail.contoso.com* for everyone) though this would depend upon factors not described in the question. As Exchange 2013 does not have an RCP connection between servers you can connect to a CAS proxy in the primary site and successfully reach a server in the remote site. The ExternalURL in the DR site should be the same in the primary site.

2. Because you have the files share witness in a third site, you can bring Exchange online in the DR site automatically. You only need to make sure that the DNS A record for the namespace points to the load balancer in the DR site. If you have a geo-load balancing solution, this would happen automatically; if not, you would need to change the IP address once for that region's namespace.

Objective 2.2: Review

1. **Correct answers:** C and D

    A. **Incorrect:** This will create a self-signed certificate on the server that contains the servers name only and will not be trusted.

    B. **Incorrect:** This answer does not include all of the names that the certificate needs to have.

    C. **Correct:** This answer is the first part of the answer. The certificate will be used on all CAS servers and so this one certificate needs to have all of the names used by Exchange on it.

    D. **Correct:** This answer is the second part of the answer. A trusted certificate needs to be purchased and the request created in C will be used to create this certificate.

2. **Correct answers:** A, D, and F

    A. **Correct:** Using a single ExternalURL means only two names needed in the certificates. That will be *mail.contoso.com* and *autodiscover.contoso.com*.

    B. **Incorrect:** If this were done, only OWA would be available externally. Other protocols like Outlook Anywhere and Exchange Web Services would not be available externally.

    C. **Incorrect:** Each CAS server needs to be registered in DNS for management purposes, but for client connectivity you would need to add the Exchange namespace record to DNS as well.

    D. **Correct:** This answer ensures that internal users connect to Exchange via the load balancer and not directly or individually to one server via its FQDN.

E. **Incorrect:** This will result in DNS round robin load balancing, which means removing the records manually from DNS when servers stop responding. This requires a lot of hands-on management.

F. **Correct:** This answer ensures that external users connect to the load balancer serving the Exchange Server via the IP address that they can reach from outside of the network.

Objective 2.3: Thought experiment

1. The business has a requirement to journal the invoices and receipts; they are sent through Exchange Server rather than directly using an SMTP relay. Therefore, you would need a receive connector configured, preferably on more than one server and either round robin DNS records to list the IPs of these multiple servers and use the FQDN of this A record in the CRM and sales application, or you could use a load balancer in front of Exchange with a virtual IP for TCP 25 that connects to an available Exchange Server. To ensure journaling of all email, you would create a journal rule and not use the journaling property on a mailbox database.

2. There are three possible ways to do this:

   A. Configure the application to have a username and password of an account in the Active Directory that has a mailbox and then connect to TCP port 587 to send email. This will require an authenticated connection but relay is already available on this connection.

   B. Create a new receive connector with Externally Secured permissions on the frontend transport service on a few CAS servers. Ensure that the RemoteIPRange parameter of the connector is set to the IP addresses of the CRM and sales application. And finally ensure that relay permissions (accept any recipient) are granted to the connector.

   C. Create a new receive connector with anonymous permissions on the frontend transport service on a few CAS servers. Ensure that the RemoteIPRange parameter of the connector is set to the IP addresses of the CRM and sales application. And finally ensure that relay permissions (accept any recipient) are granted to the connector.

Objective 2.3: Review

1. **Correct answer:** D

   A. **Incorrect:** SafetyNet duration is a global setting and not set per server. The value for the SafetyNetHoldTime parameter is also incorrect.

   B. **Incorrect:** SafetyNet duration is a global setting and not set per server.

C. **Incorrect:** The value of SafetyNetHoldTime is written as a timespan value. Timespan values are Days:Hours:Minutes. This answer uses a string value and so is incorrect.

D. **Correct:** SafetyNet duration is a global setting and not set per server or database. Therefore Set-TransportConfig is used.

2. **Correct answers:** A and B

A. **Correct:** Authoritative domains can be included in an email address policy.

B. **Correct:** Internal relay domains can be included in an email address policy.

C. **Incorrect:** OpenRelay is not a valid accepted domain type.

D. **Incorrect:** External Relay domains cannot be included in an email address policy.

3. **Correct answers:** C and E

A. **Incorrect:** This answer would route all emails during normal working times to the wrong datacenter.

B. **Incorrect:** This answer would distribute emails across both datacenters all the time.

C. **Correct:** This answer adds a lower priority MX record that would only be used when the higher priority record server has gone offline.

D. **Incorrect:** As the question covers two different organizations there is a choice of which accepted domain to include. The internal relay allows the email address of the other company to be added to email address lists and email addresses in the other domain given to users in the first domain. This is not required by the scenario and so this is not the best answer given the options.

E. **Correct:** This answer allows for emails to be accepted by the other partner and forwarded to the first partner, queued if necessary, but without accidently opening the possibility of having an email address list with this domain listed on it.

Objective 2.4: Thought experiment

1. Check the copy queue length on the passive databases. This will give you an idea of possible data loss.

2. Remove the cluster nodes in the office that is out of use. You can do this using Stop-DatabaseAvailabilityGroup -ActiveDirectorySite MountainTop -ConfigurationOnly. This will not connect to the servers in the MountainTop site (as they are unreachable) but write to the local domain controller that they are out of the cluster should they ever come back online again.

3. Then you would run Restore-DatabaseAvailabilityGroup to evict the nodes in the MountainTop site from the cluster and reduce the cluster node count to just the servers in the Basecamp site (that is, the other site).

4. If the number of outstanding transaction logs is 12 or less, the databases will mount. If it is more than 12, you will need to issue the Mount-Database database_name command. On the databases mounting, any time window of lost logs will be requested from the SafetyNet database automatically to attempt to reduce data loss. The transport service database (mail.que) in the Basecamp site will have a copy of all the recent messages as shadow redundancy defaults to ensuring messages are shadowed to the other site the DAG is located in.

Objective 2.4: Review

1. **Correct answer:** A

   A. **Correct:** Get-ClusterNode returns the nodes in the cluster and their status with regard to being up or down.

   B. **Incorrect:** This PowerShell cmdlet is not a valid cmdlet.

   C. **Incorrect:** This PowerShell cmdlet does not contain information about the cluster nodes.

   D. **Incorrect:** This is a cmd prompt executable and not a PowerShell cmdlet. It does return the same information as the correct answer and the exe can be run in a PowerShell window, but it is not a PowerShell cmdlet as required by the question.

2. **Correct answers:** A, B, and C

   A. **Correct:** As there will be log files that have not been copied to a passive copy they cannot be truncated by backup. This is expected behavior when you have a copy queue length that exceeds 100 logs.

   B. **Correct:** This is also correct. You should have enough disk space on the server with the active copy to store enough logs to cover your largest expected network outage - which is the most likely reason for a large copy queue length.

   C. **Correct:** If you run out of disk space on the active log folder then if the active database shares that drive, you run out of disk space for the database too, which will cause the database to shutdown.

   D. **Incorrect:** The playing forward of any lagged copy happens when the lagged copy disk space runs out and not when the active copy is short on disk space.

3. **Correct answer:** D

   A. **Incorrect:** The Notify verb is used for receipts.

   B. **Incorrect:** SMTP verbs are sent from the client to the server.

   C. **Incorrect:** The SMTP server tells the SMTP client that the message has been received with a 250 response to the data termination period or the BDAT verb.

   D. **Correct:** RCPT is the recipient verb in SMTP.

## CHAPTER 3

Design, configure, and manage advanced security

This chapter looks at the various security features of both Exchange Server and the underlying operating system. You will look at these security features from the viewpoint of the IT professional and consider the impact of them to the user. It is a well-known adage that if security is difficult to implement, the user will not use it, or will work around it. You will also see how some of these security features can be implemented on behalf of the user so that Exchange Server, for example, encrypts messages automatically.

In this chapter you look at how to implement these different security features, looking at the best designs for them first, and then how to manage them in a live Exchange Server 2013 environment.

Objectives in this chapter:

- Objective 3.1: Select an appropriate security strategy
- Objective 3.2: Deploy and manage IRM with Active Directory Rights Management Services (AD RMS)
- Objective 3.3: Configure and interpret mailbox and administrative auditing
- Objective 3.4: Troubleshoot security-related issues

Objective 3.1: Select an appropriate security strategy

The first and most important thing to consider when selecting a security feature from either Exchange Server or the operating system is to pick the right one for your needs, and then to select it at the right time. This objective looks at the features of each of the different security features in the following list, discuss its pros and cons, what it can do and cannot do (or should not be used for), and when is the best time to consider implementing the feature.

Understanding security and related options is a key requirement in designing Exchange Server solutions, so it is a key objective of this exam.

Evaluating role-based access control (RBAC)

Role-based access control (RBAC) is the method of granting or removing access to various parts of Exchange Server for administrators and users. RBAC was introduced in Exchange Server 2010 and works the same way in Exchange Server 2013, however, the user interface to allow manipulation of RBAC has been improved in the latest version.

A good introduction to RBAC can be found at *http://blogs.technet.com/b/exchange/archive/2009/11/16/3408825.aspx*, which discusses the RBAC triangle of power. Even though this is an Exchange Server 2010 document, it is still valid for Exchange Server 2013. The concept with RBAC is that you want to change permissions on where someone can administer, what -someone can administer, and who that someone is. This is the "where", "what," and "who," and this comprises the three parts of RBAC. Figure 3-1 shows this "triangle of power."

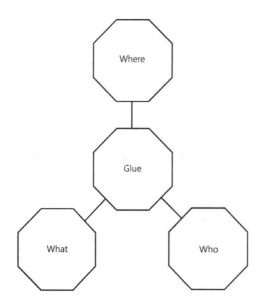

FIGURE 3-1 The RBAC "triangle of power"

The "where" is where you want your permissions to apply. This can be an OU, or a database, or a group of servers. By default, new RBAC roles apply to the parent scope, which is all objects. If you want to apply a role to a subset of the objects, you either define the scope as part of the role, or you create a new scope first with New-ManagementScope, and then use this scope against multiple roles.

The "what" is what your role is able to do. This is, at its simplest level, a list of the Exchange Management Shell cmdlets and the parameters of those cmdlets that you are allowed to run. From the Exchange Management Shell, if you are restricted by RBAC so that a cmdlet is not available to you, the cmdlet does not appear in the shell. If you are using Exchange Control Panel, the areas that you cannot modify are not shown, or they are shown as read only.

The "who" is who will be able to perform the operation. This is either a user or a group. It is best practice to assume that even though you might want to grant the permissions to a single user now, you should apply the permissions to a group that contains that one member, and then adjust the group membership later rather than creating a second RBAC configuration for an additional user. A group for RBAC is known as a *role group*, and a role group is just a standard universal security group flagged for use by RBAC.

Finally, once you have the where, what, and who, you need to glue them all together. This is the *Management Role Assignment*. A Management Role Assignment is a one-to-one mapping of each where, what, and who. Once you have an assignment in place, the users affected by that assignment receive those permissions. RBAC permissions are cumulative, that is they are not the most restrictive takes precedence like in Active Directory and file shares. If you don't want someone to have permission, do not add them.

RBAC "where"

Where you can work with an RBAC permission is the target that you are going to apply the permission to. In terms of RBAC language, this is the ManagementScope. To look up existing scopes, use Get-ManagementScope. To create new ones, use New-ManagementScope.

An example of a management scope is to give the users in the Birmingham office help desk the rights to modify only the users in the Birmingham OU. An Exchange Management Shell cmdlet such as the following could be used to create this scope.

```
New-ManagementScope -Name "Birmingham Users" -RecipientRoot "contoso.com\Birmingham"
```

For a scope, you can use the following to control the "where":

- **ServerList**   A list of servers, for example New-ManagementScope <name> -ServerList "MBX1,MBX2."

- **RecipientRoot**   An OU and all objects under that OU, for example New-ManagementScope <name> -RecipientRoot "domain.local\ParentOU\ChildOU."

- **DatabaseList**   A list of mailbox databases such as New-ManagementScope <name> -DatabaseList "DB01,DB02,DB03."

For more advanced control and to avoid having to update lists in the scope all of the time, you can create queries. If the object you need to administer is covered by the query result you get to do the administration. Some example filters are:

- **ServerRestrictionFilter** Servers that meet a given criteria such as partial name or AD site location, for example New-ManagementScope <name> -ServerRestrictionFilter {ServerSite -eq "CN=Redmond,CN=Sites,CN=Configuration,DC=contoso,DC=com"}.

- **RecipientRestrictionFilter** Users who meet a given criteria such as an Active Directory property or other description. An example is New-ManagementScope <name> -RecipientRestrictionFilter { Title -Like "*VP*" }.

- **DatabaseRestrictionFilter** Databases that match a criteria such as the database name, for example New-ManagementScope <name> -DatabaseRestrictionFilter {Name -Like "SEA*" }.

Finally, for the scope, or the "where," there can be exclusive scopes. If you have an exclusive scope set (using -Exclusive on the cmdlet), only users assigned to your scope or other exclusive scopes can administer the covered object. It cannot be administered by any other standard RBAC scope. Exclusive scopes allow you to lock down permission assignment to selected users or databases, for example to a given discrete group of administrators.

RBAC "what"

The ManagementRole is the "what" in RBAC. All ManagementRoles that you create are based on an existing management role. This means that you take an existing management role (Get-ManagementRole) and make it work for you. For example, if you find a management role that does close to but more than what you need to do, you can remove any extra cmdlets and parameters that you do not want this ManagementRole to have. Always leave the Get- cmdlets for any Set- cmdlets that you are planning on keeping; you will always want to be able to get the current values before you change them with a Set- cmdlet.

Here is an example of a new management role.

```
New-ManagementRole -Name "VIP Editor" -Parent "Mail Recipients"
```

This creates a new management role called VIP Editor. Notice that the name describes what it will do. You can immediately see that it is going to have something to do with mail recipients because the parent management role is Mail Recipients.

Once the role is created, you need to remove the permissions that are in excess on this role. Remember that you cannot add cmdlets that do not exist on the parent role. An example here that would allow VIP Editors to modify just a few settings on the target user would be to remove all of the cmdlets except for one (you have to leave at least one).

```
Get-ManagementRoleEntry "VIP Editor\*" | Where {$_.name -ne "Get-User"} | Remove-
ManagementRoleEntry
```

The above removed all of the cmdlets from the VIP Editor management role except for Get-User. Get-User is a useful one to leave because it will get user information that the role holder will need.

Finally, we need to add back in the cmdlets and parameters that the role holder will be able to call. We can do this with the following example.

```
Add-ManagementRoleEntry "VIP Editor\Set-User" -Parameters Office,Phone,Mobilephone,
Department,Manager
```

This adds in the Set-User cmdlet, and only the listed parameters. Now that you have the "where," and the "what," it is time for the "who."

RBAC "who"

The "who" is the users or group that get designated these rights. The "who" is the RoleGroup, and behind the scenes the ManagementRoleAssignment. Once you create a RoleGroup, you say who, what, and the where, and join them together. The three pieces that you created are glued together and this is why you make the ManagementRoleEntry (the "what") and the ManagementScope (the "where") before you create the RoleGroup.

For example, if you are creating a group of administrators to have only the ability to modify some settings for the VIP users of Contoso, you would create something like the following.

```
New-RoleGroup "VIP Editors" -Roles "VIP Editor" -CustomRecipientWriteScope "VIP Users"
```

If you take all of the examples here that made the ManagementRoleEntry and the ManagementScope, you have the following Exchange Management Shell cmdlets.

Restricting permissions for VIP Users

```
New-ManagementScope -name "VIP Users" -RecipientRestrictionFilter {memberofgroup -eq "cn
=VIPs,ou=VIP,dc=domain,dc=com"}
New-ManagementRole -Name "VIP Editor" -Parent "Mail Recipients"
Get-ManagementRoleEntry "VIP Editor\*" | Where {$_.name -ne "Get-User"} | Remove-
ManagementRoleEntry
Add-ManagementRoleEntry "VIP Editor\Set-User" -Parameters Office,Phone,Mobilephone,
Department,Manager
New-RoleGroup "VIP Editors" -Roles "VIP Editor" -CustomRecipientWriteScope "VIP Users"
```

Before running these cmdlets in your test lab, ensure that this OU actually exists in your environment and that it has users in it. Then change the New-ManagementScope line so that the dc= values are correct. If you make the scope without making these changes, you need to use Set-ManagementScope to correct the filter.

Finally, add a user to the VIP Editor group (located in Microsoft Exchange Security Groups OU) and log in as that user to Exchange Control Panel, or run Exchange Management Shell as that user. In ECP you should be able to modify only the Office, Phone, Mobilephone, Department, or Manager properties. The effect this has on ECP can be seen in Figure 3-2 where the Phone property and the Mobilephone property can be set but the other values in this dialog box cannot be set.

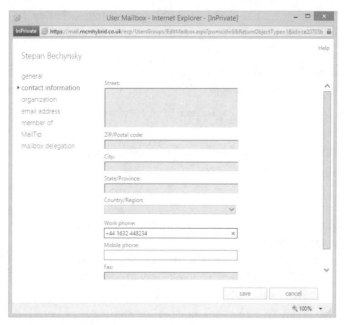

FIGURE 3-2 Restricted rights applied via RBAC and seen in Exchange Control Panel

Evaluating BitLocker

Some Microsoft Windows editions since Windows Vista have shipped with a product called BitLocker Drive Encryption. It is commonly known as BitLocker. It was available in Windows Vista, Windows 7 Enterprise and Ultimate editions, and in Windows 8 it is available in the Pro and Enterprise editions. It is available on all editions of Windows 8.1, though the feature BitLocker and its ability to modify and configure it is only available in the Pro and Enterprise editions. RT and home editions support a device encryption feature based on BitLocker. The matching Windows Server editions since Windows Server 2008 also support BitLocker.

BitLocker is a logical disk encryption system that can encrypt both the system and data partitions, and in Windows 7 and Windows Server 2008 R2 and later also supports removable drives with BitLocker To Go. Because it is a logical disk encryption system, you can protect volumes that are part of a physical disk or volumes that span multiple disks. It is supported with Exchange Server and because the BitLocker encryption/decryption process has an overhead of only a single digit percentage, it does not add additional disk I/O.

BitLocker requires two NTFS formatted volumes to allow for encryption of the operating system, a boot volume of at least 100 MB, and then the operating system volume, which is usually the C drive . Since Windows 7, the installation program has made these partitions for you automatically so that you do not need to rebuild the operating system if should you want to turn on BitLocker at a later date. Therefore, from an Exchange Server viewpoint, it can be enabled later in the life of the server, though the best time to enable it is before any data is written to the server's disks because the encryption process is a background task that encrypts every sector of the volume. Once the volume is protected, the encryption keys are protected and then all future writes to the volume and reads from the volume pass through a low level encryption/decryption device driver. To the higher level drivers and applications such as Exchange Server, the disk does not appear to be encrypted and the data appears to be unmodified in any way from what the application would have expected.

To allow for encryption of any data volume, you do not require the 100 MB volume that the operating system requires. This 100 MB volume contains the operating system boot code that needs to be unencrypted to allow for the loading of the operating system from a protected volume. Therefore for Exchange Server, you could choose to protect your Exchange databases and transaction logs only if you wanted, but remember that the default installation location for Exchange Server is the operating system partition. It is to the installation location that the initial mailbox database is created, as well as considerable amounts of log files, the binaries, and the transport databases.

In addition to encrypting the entire volume, BitLocker uses a variety of combinations of authentication mechanisms. These ensure that the disk cannot be read when it is outside the server in which it was created unless a recovery key is available. Therefore BitLocker can be used to protect data stored to the disk, should the risk of the disk ever falling into the wrong hands be considered a possibility. For example, even though the security of the Office 365 data centers is considerable, the Exchange Online service uses BitLocker on the servers that they use for their customers' data.

The options that exist for BitLocker authentication include both on server and off server choices. Any off server choice means that the authentication key, either manually entered (a PIN) or by the use of a removable hardware device (a USB key), will need to be present when the server is rebooted. Therefore, it is likely that any Exchange Server implementation that uses BitLocker will require a Trusted Platform Module (or TPM) chip as part of the hardware. The TPM can hold the BitLocker key in its secure cryptographic store and provide it as needed during the boot process. The TPM can be combined with off server authentication systems such as PIN entry or USB key as mentioned earlier, but again this would require operator intervention at reboot. The use of a DAG allows you to have an Exchange Server running and holding your active databases while potentially another copy of those databases is on an Exchange Server that has rebooted and is waiting authentication for BitLocker. This requires additional management and personal access to the physical location where the servers are stored. Therefore, you would typically not use a DAG unless the site security conditions so required it and the impact to Exchange Server operations has been planned well in advance.

> *NOTE* **NETWORK UNLOCK**
>
> BitLocker Network Unlock is a feature that was introduced in Windows 8 and Windows Server 2012 as a way to unlock operating system volumes protected with BitLocker. Network Unlock enables easier management for BitLocker enabled desktops and servers in a domain environment by providing automatic unlock of operating system volumes at system reboot when connected to a wired corporate network. This feature requires the client hardware to have a DHCP driver implemented in its UEFI firmware.

Computers that incorporate a TPM can also create a key that has not only been wrapped, but also tied to specific hardware or software conditions. This is called *sealing* a key. When a sealed key is first created, the TPM records a snapshot of the configuration values and file hashes. A sealed key is only *unsealed* or released when those current system values match the ones in the snapshot. BitLocker uses sealed keys to detect attacks against the integrity of the Windows operating system.

When BitLocker is used without a TPM, the required encryption keys are stored on a USB flash drive that must be presented to unlock the data stored on a volume. When BitLocker is used with just a TPM chip, the drives cannot be read if they become separated from their host server.

Microsoft does not support BitLocker in a virtual machine, but does support BitLocker on Hyper-V on the host operating system.

When implementing BitLocker, the operating system will go through the checks required to make sure the system can be protected. This means that it will look for a TPM chip or the Allow BitLocker With A Compatible TPM Group Policy option. If the system cannot support BitLocker because it does not have a TPM chip you can choose the alternative key options as appropriate.

To enable BitLocker on Windows Server, you need to install the BitLocker Drive Encryption feature as shown in Figure 3-3.

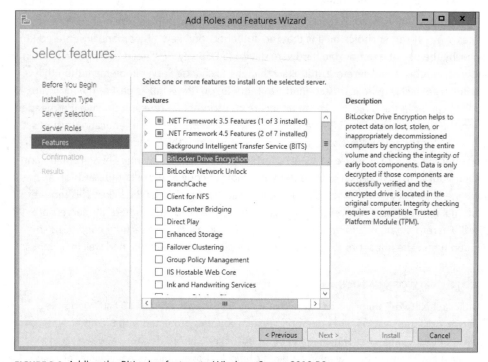

FIGURE 3-3 Adding the BitLocker feature to Windows Server 2012 R2

Once the feature is installed, BitLocker can be enabled (Figure 3-4) on either the system volume or any data volume as required. The installation will make recommendations to the storing of a recovery key. If the operating system is being protected, this defaults to the TPM chip that would need to be present in the server and enabled in the BIOS. If a data partition is being protected, you can use the TPM, apassword, or a smart card to store the encryption key.

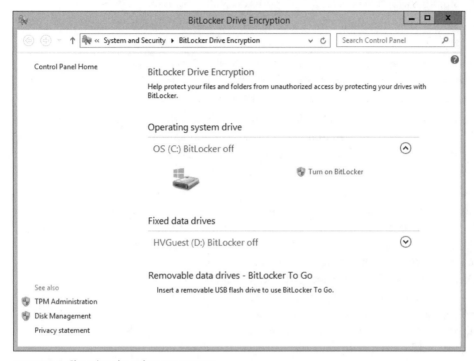

FIGURE 3-4 Choosing the volume to protect

In addition to the TPM, smartcard, or removable USB device you can also add additional protection of a password, but for Exchange Servers and especially those stored in remote data centers from the administrators, this option would prove problematic.

Finally, you get to save a recovery key. This can be printed out or saved to a file or USB key. This recovery key should be saved somewhere safe and far away from the server to which it belongs. In Windows Server 2012 and 2012 R2, it can be saved to your Microsoft Account where you can access the key later from *https://onedrive.live.com/recoverykey*.

> ***IMPORTANT*** **BITLOCKER AND WINDOWS SERVER 2008 R2**
>
> When the operating system is Windows Server 2008 R2, a security patch is required to en-
> able BitLocker on the Exchange Server mailbox role server that is part of a DAG. BitLocker
> incorrectly identifies the non-shared disks that would be used in a DAG as being shared
> disks, and shared disks are not supported for BitLocker.

Evaluating smart cards

Smart cards are typically credit card sized cryptographic devices that are easy to carry and can additionally be integrated with door entry and photo identification systems. From the viewpoint of the Exchange Server administrator, smart cards have two purposes:

1. Storing encryption keys for the purposes of S/MIME by users.

2. Storing login information for the purposes of authenticating administrator login to servers.

You will note that both of these features are actually operating system features that Exchange Server, or in the case of S/MIME, the Outlook client, make use of. That is also true for the preceding BitLocker discussion and all of the remaining items in this objective.

Smart cards store cryptographic information in such a way that it can be written to the chip on the card, but cannot be read from the chip. Any cryptographic function that the computer needs to do, such as encrypting an email or logging into a server, requires that the smart card is present or the computer will not be able to access the cryptographic information.

Specifically, the smart cards used by Windows store the private key from a public and private key encryption system on them. Public and private keys are covered in the "Evaluating S/MIME" section later in this chapter. Because the private key should only be held by the key holder, placing the private key on a write-only media such as a smart card ensures that even if the private key is lost, the actual key cannot be read. Also it is probable to assume the PIN number needed to access the smart card, and which is needed to use the key, is probably not lost as well. Additionally, when cryptographic functions need to take place, the microprocessor on the card does the encryption and decryption. The keys to do this work are never given to the host computer, but the host computer will hand the encrypted data to the card and get back the clear text data.

Smart cards are tamper proof, and it is impossible to read the private key and other information from the card. The disadvantage of a smart card, apart from having to have it with you wherever you need to use the keys on the card (which is of course an advantage as well), is that you also need the correct hardware to read the card. Over time different smart card hardware has been available, and over the last fifteen or so years, these have included serial connected hardware, smart card readers inside laptops, USB readers, and keyboards with smart card readers included. Figure 3-5 shows a current smart card reader and a card inside the reader.

FIGURE 3-5 A USB smart card reader and a smart card

For login to the Exchange Server for administrative purposes, it is possible to significantly increase the protection of these elevated network credentials because the login details do not cross the network. The PIN used to authorize use of the smart card is used on the device with the smart card reader and no further. If the user enters the correct PIN, and the stored credentials on the card are valid, the user has logged in.

With password based authentication, the security is based on the complexity of the password. The shorter or more predictable the password, the easier it is to determine. Passwords can be learned by way of social engineering, however, the PIN is typically of no use without the card. Passwords are also susceptible to brute force attacks, where repeated attempts are made to guess the password or to read that data from the network packets that contain the password as it is sent across the wire. If a smart card is obtained from the user, a brute force attack might be used in an attempt to learn the PIN,, but the device will stop working and lock the card after a low number of invalid PINs are used. Meanwhile, the user requests that the card be invalidated and a new one issued.

For Exchange Server 2013 it is important to remember that you can use Exchange Control Panel and login to do administration using a web browser or Remote PowerShell. Both of these can be started from a session that is not smart card protected and so other means need to be used to either limit administration to certain controlled workstations, or the servers themselves, where a smart card must be used. An example of using a smart card to login to Remote PowerShell is shown in Figure 3-6.

FIGURE 3-6 Using a smart card to login to Windows PowerShell

New to Windows 8 and Windows Server 2012 R2 are virtual smart cards. These get around the infrastructure requirements of typical smart cards by using the TPM chip on some laptops, tablets, and phones to replace the smart card and the reader. Virtual smart cards appear in Windows as a smart card that is always inserted. More information on virtual smart cards can be found at *http://technet.microsoft.com/en-gb/library/dn593708.aspx*.

Evaluating Information Rights Management (IRM)

Information Rights Management (IRM) (or sometimes referred to in the context of Windows as RMS after the server role, Rights Management Services) is a way to ensure that the rights to use a document or email remain with the document or email for its life. Rights Management is used in a lot of digital media, most notably in the protection of music and videos that have been downloaded where a license needs to be acquired to play the media on every device that you would use.

From the viewpoint of the Exchange administrator, IRM is an optional feature that requires the use of both the Exchange Enterprise CAL and the RMS CAL for Windows. These CALs can be assigned to the users who would encrypt or view the documents, and emails that are protected with the RMS server.

Microsoft released Azure RMS in Office 365 in early 2014 and has added functionality to that product since its release. For Azure RMS licensing, you need an Office 365 E3 or E4 license to create content, and you do not need a license to consume protected content. Azure RMS can be added to some other Office 365 licenses as an additional license if E3 or E4 licenses are not used.

Because RMS protection stays with the document or email, it is used to set policy on the document or email that is being protected. From the viewpoint of the user, when they protect any document, they choose the policy. From the viewpoint of the Exchange administrator, they can set up transport rules to protect emails that meet certain criteria.

The next objective in this book looks at the steps to deploy and manage RMS. In brief, you need to install an AD RMS cluster, which is one or more servers running the AD RMS role and configured as a group of servers that work with the same key. You do not install failover clustering to make this cluster, although as AD RMS is a web service, it is a good candidate for a load balancer if you have more than one server. Once the AD RMS server is in place, you then configure Exchange Server to use AD RMS to protect emails and the attachments inside emails (if they can be protected as an individual document). This protection can happen in Outlook Web App and Outlook if you have installed an Office ProPlus edition. Protection can also happen when using transport rules, journaling rules and the evaluation of protected documents as they travel through the Exchange Server.

The disadvantage of RMS is that it is complex to share this protection outside of the boundary of your Active Directory forest. Therefore, it has typically been used in large companies to protect internal-only content.

The aim of Azure RMS is to make the sharing of protected content outside of your company via shared storage and any device a reality.

> **MORE INFO**   **AZURE RMS**
>
> For your information, there is a series of articles starting at *http://www.c7solutions.com/ 2013/11/the-new-rights-management-service*, which cover Exchange Server, SharePoint, and the Azure RMS product. The Azure RMS product is not included on the exam, but it is important to know as the technology develops in this direction.

Evaluating S/MIME

Secure/Multipurpose Internet Mail Extensions (*S/MIME*) is a protocol for the sending of signed and encrypted messages by email. It requires a digital certificate per user, and it also requires that the certificate have the email address of the sender as its subject name. The holder of the digital certificate needs the private key for that certificate to be available as well.

The benefit of S/MIME is that the recipient can be certain that what they receive is what the sender sent, and that the sender really was the sender who sent it. S/MIME also allows for the message to be encrypted so that it is readable only to the recipients and not anyone else.

The disadvantage of S/MIME is that the onus on the use of the certificate and the interpretation of the received message is on the user. Exchange Server 2013 Service Pack 1 and later can make use of certificates stored in the Active Directory so that Outlook Web App can send and receive S/MIME protected emails. The user needs to have the certificate (although this can be centrally issued from an internal certificate authority) and the user needs to decide which emails to sign and encrypt.

S/MIME comes with a series of terminologies that are important to understand. They also make for good exam questions! The first of the two terminologies previously introduced is *digital signing*. This is analogous to signing a letter. Your signature authenticates the letter as being from you, and indicates that the words of the letter are your words. The second term mentioned previously is *message encryption*, and from an S/MIME viewpoint this is taking a clear text email and encrypting it in such a way that only the recipient can view it. To understand these terms, you need to look at how digital certificates are used for digital signing and encryption.

How digital certificates are used for security

To be able to understand S/MIME and evaluate it well, you need a good understanding of the PKI. A *PKI*, or Private Key Infrastructure, is the system in place for the creation validation, distribution, and evaluation of digital certificates. If you are going to use S/MIME to sign and encrypt emails sent outside your organization, you need to use an external PKI that both the sender and the recipient trust. This external PKI has a certificate authority at its root that both the sender and the recipient will use to validate the certificates used for signing or encrypting the messages. If you only use S/MIME for internal recipients, you can use a PKI that has a certificate authority at its root that is available internal to your company only.

A certificate authority is a fundamental element of message security. Messages are secured using keys and though these keys are created on the users own computer, they are validated as belonging to the user by the certificate authority. If the user loses their keys, the certificate authority marks them as revoked, and so any emails received from the sender with those keys after that revocation date are to be considered suspect. Therefore it is very important to trust the certificate authority at the heart of the PKI.

To sign or encrypt messages, the user will use a certificate. The exact certificate used will vary, and this is covered more in later sections of this chapter, but the certificate contains a key, the certificate has an owner, and the certificate has been validated as belonging to that owner by the certificate authority.

In S/MIME, as with technologies such as smart cards, TLS, and SSL, there are two keys. These are known as the *public key* and the *private key*. The key pair is mathematically related, but if you hold only one of the keys, you cannot calculate the other key. It is theoretically possible to use brute force to guess a key and so when you are looking at S/MIME and the keys you will see reference to key length. The longer the key the harder it will be to guess the other key in the pair, and the longer it takes to sign and encrypt data with these keys.

S/MIME uses these two keys to allow for the following two features, each of which has some benefits associated with them:

- Signing Emails:
    - **Authentication**   You know who the sender is.
    - **Message integrity**   The message has not changed since it was sent.
    - **Non-repudiation**   The sender cannot claim they did not send it.
- Encrypting Emails:
    - **Privacy**   The message can only be read by the recipient.
    - **Message integrity**   The message has not changed since it was sent.

You will look at these terms and how they work with S/MIME in the next section.

S/MIME terminology

Private key   Of the two keys that are used in S/MIME, one is designated the private key. The user keeps the private key. Smart cards can be used to further protect the storage of the private key off of the user's computer, but typically it is stored in the user's profile and accessible only via the Microsoft Crypto API. If this key falls into the wrong hands, or can be used by anyone other than the key holder, the key should be revoked at the certificate authority. If the private key encrypts anything, it can only be decrypted by the user's public key. The same key cannot be used to encrypt and decrypt the same message.

Public key   This is the other related, but asymmetric, key created at the same time as the private key. Unlike the private key that never leaves the computer, the public key is distributed and can be stored in a central area for access such as in the Active Directory or via a website that the certificate authority manages. The public key is stored with the user's digital certificate. If the public key encrypts anything, it can only be decrypted by the user's private key. The same key cannot be used to encrypt and decrypt the same message.

Digital certificate   This is the user's public key that is validated as belonging to the user by the certificate authority. The certificate contains information pertaining to the user and the public key. The certificate is generated by the user's computer and then sent to a certificate authority. The certificate authority takes a hash of the data in the certificate and signs it with the certificate authority's private key. This signed hash is stored with the certificate and returned to the user. When a recipient wants to validate that the certificate comes from the user and has not been tampered with, they too hash the certificate as did the certificate authority, and then they compare the hash they generated with the hash the certificate authority signed and placed on the certificate. The signed hash cannot be modified without breaking the signature. Therefore, if the hashes match the certificate, the certificate is unmodified and therefore came from the user who claims to have sent it.

Hash   A mathematical function that takes a given input and generates a unique number from that input. There should be no possibility of two different inputs generating the same hash. Common hash algorithms are MD5, SHA1, and SHA256. Of these, the recommendation at the time of writing is to use SHA256 for digital certificates.

Authentication   The digital signature validates the identity of the user. Because only the sender holds the key used to sign the email, it must have been the sender who sent that email. By default, there is no authentication of email and so there is no way to know if a user really sent that email. S/MIME authentication in the digital signature solves this issue because there is only one person who holds the private key.

Non-repudiation   Because the signature used to sign the message is unique, the sender cannot say that their signature was not used. As S/MIME provides authentication so that you know whom the sender is, it can then additionally provide non-repudiation. Without authentication, non-repudiation is impossible to provide.

Message integrity   When a message is digitally signed the data that makes up the message body is hashed and the sender signs that hash with their private key. The hash is attached to the message and the message sent. On receipt, a S/MIME aware client will take the signed hash and generate a hash from the message body. If both hashes are the same, the message must be the same as it was at the time the sender sent it. Note that the message envelope is not included in the hash, The message envelope can change throughout the transfer of the message by, most commonly, the addition of multiple received headers as the message is transferred through different SMTP servers. Both digital signatures and data encryption provide message integrity.

Privacy   This is where the message is encrypted by the recipient's public key. As the message is now protected with the public key that belongs to the intended recipient, it can only be read by someone holding the recipient's private key, which should be the recipient.

> *NOTE* **PRIVACY AND DIGITAL SIGNATURES**
>
> Though digital signatures provide message integrity, they do not provide privacy. Messages with only a digital signature on them still contain a clear text copy of the message, as do normal SMTP messages. They can be read by anyone with access to the network or storage where the email travels through or ends up on. Some S/MIME clients provide for opaque-signed, where Base 64 encodes the clear text message to obfuscate it, but because Base 64 is not an encryption method, it can easily be decoded and read.

S/MIME digital signing

Now that you have looked at the terminology, take a look at how it works so that you can evaluate S/MIME for your Exchange Server mailboxes.

First, you need to obtain an S/MIME digital certificate either from your internal company certificate authority or from a trusted third-party certificate authority. A trusted certificate authority, either internal or external, is one whose public key is stored in the certificate store on your computer and on all of your recipients' computers. The S/MIME certificate needs to be valid for your email address. In the Outlook Trust Center, there is a Get A Digital ID button that will give you a list of current S/MIME certificate providers.

The exact process for getting your certificate will vary depending on the provider. After you have downloaded your digital certificate to your computer, you need to configure Outlook to use that certificate for S/MIME. This is done (in Outlook 2013) by clicking File, Options, Trust Center, Trust Center Settings, E-mail Security, Settings. This can be seen in Figure 3-7.

FIGURE 3-7 S/MIME Settings in Outlook

In the Change Security Settings dialog box, click each of the Choose buttons to select your signing certificate and then your encryption certificate. You might have one certificate that does both signing and encryption, or you might have two. If you have one certificate you would select the same one for both choices. If you have multiple email accounts in Outlook and have different certificates in both, you create a new Security Settings Name for each, then when you are sending emails you can pick which S/MIME profile to use.

On the E-Mail Security tab in the Trust Center, shown in Figure 3-8, you can select whether you want to encrypt or sign all of your outgoing emails, or both, and if you would like an S/MIME read receipt for each. You can also choose to opaque-sign messages. To enable this setting, clear the Send Clear Text Signed Message When Sending Signed Messages check box.

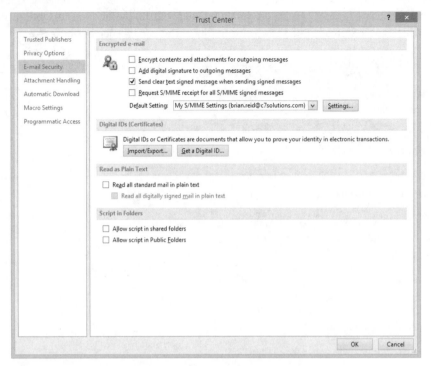

FIGURE 3-8 Encrypted email options in the Outlook 2013 Trust Center

When you have your certificate configured in Outlook, you can send and receive signed and also encrypted emails (which is covered in the next section). To sign an email, start by composing a new email, clicking the Sign button on the Permissions area of the Options tab, and then clicking Send when ready. This can be seen in Figure 3-9. If you have any certificate issues, such as not having a certificate for the sending email address you are using, you will be prompted and given an opportunity to go to the Trust Center to fix the issue.

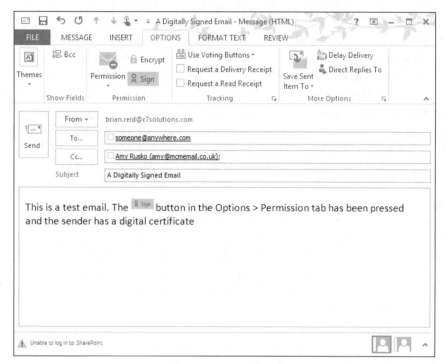

FIGURE 3-9 The Sign button is selected in an Outlook 2013 email

When you click Send, Outlook will take the message and run it through the hash algorithm that is selected for the certificate in the Trust Center. This generates a unique hash for the email, and this hash is then encrypted with the sender's private key. Note the hash is encrypted here and not the email body. This hash is typically smaller than the email body and therefore it is quicker to encrypt the hash than the entire email. The encrypted hash and the email body in clear text are sent to the recipient. Typically the sender's public key is also sent with the message.

On receipt, the recipient's client will validate the encrypted hash by generating a new hash of the email body as received. The client also takes the sender's public key and uses that to decrypt the encrypted hash that came with the email. This gives the client two hash values to compare.

If the two hashes match, the email has not been tampered with (message integrity). It must have been signed by the sender (non-repudiation) and it must have come from that sender (authentication).

S/MIME message encryption

To encrypt a message, you need to have the recipient's public key. Note that this is different from signing, where you do not need anything from the recipient. When you encrypt a message you need to encrypt it with the recipient's public key so that the recipient, with his or her own private key, can decrypt it.

The easiest way to get the recipient's public key is for them to send you a signed email. You can then reply with an encrypted email or you can save the public key for the user with their contact information in your address book for future use. You can also publish keys to the Active Directory, which can then be retrieved automatically by Outlook for users inside your organization, or contacts outside that have been added to the Active Directory.

Because each user has a different public/private key pair, when you encrypt emails to more than one user you need to have the public key for each user. Also, odd though it seems, you also need to have your own public/private key pair. The reason for this is that Outlook encrypts the message using your own keys and saves it to Sent Items. The copy in Sent Items is not the one you actually send to the recipient, as you could never open that again, but instead is a copy effectively sent to yourself. Therefore, to encrypt emails in Outlook you need your own public/private key as well.

Once you have the public key from the recipient and your keys configured for encryption, you can click the Encrypt button on the Options tab. This can be seen in Figure 3-10. If you do not have the recipient's public key, you will get the error shown in Figure 3-11.

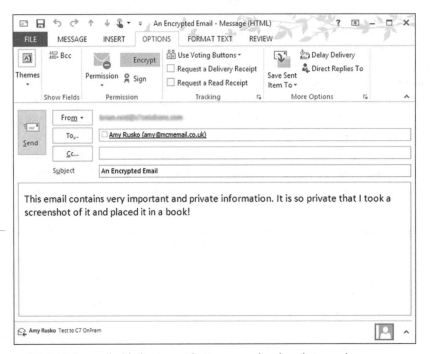

FIGURE 3-10 An email with the encrypt button pressed and ready to send

FIGURE 3-11 Encryption Problems dialog box when sending to users whose public key you do not have

The dialog box shown in Figure 3-12 contains the message you receive if you do not have your own encryption certificate. Outlook when it sends an encrypted message to someone else will store a copy of the message in the Send Items folder. This copy needs to be encrypted so that only the sender can read it. To encrypt a message to yourself, the sender, Outlook needs to encrypt the message using the senders public key so that it can be opened only by the sender from the Sent Items folder.

FIGURE 3-12 The Invalid Certificate error when you do not have your own encryption certificate

Finally, note that only message integrity is available with signed or encrypted emails. Therefore if you want an encrypted but authenticated email, an encrypted email that can be nonrepudiated, you need to sign and encrypt the email which means clicking both buttons in Outlook.

When you send the email, the client generates a *session key*. This is a key that will encrypt the email quickly because public/private keys take a long time to do this. The session key is used to encrypt the message body, and then the client takes the session key and the public key of the recipient and encrypts the session key so that only the recipient can read it. This process is repeated for each recipient and a copy that contains the encrypted message body and the encrypted session key for that recipient is sent to each recipient.

Upon receipt of the encrypted email, the client decrypts the session key using their private key and once they have the session key they can decrypt the message body. If the message is also signed, validation of the signature can also happen as previously described. Upon opening the email, the client will see the encryption icon, which can be clicked to show the certificate and sender information. An example dialog box showing the message's security properties can be seen in Figure 3-13.

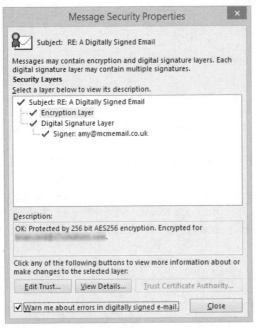

FIGURE 3-13 Message Security Properties dialog, reached by clicking the Encrypted or Signed icon in the recipients email

> **MORE INFO** **S/MIME**
>
> Further information on S/MIME can be found on TechNet at *http://technet.microsoft.com/ en-us/library/aa995740.aspx.*

S/MIME and Outlook Web App

To use S/MIME with Outlook Web App, you need two things in addition to Exchange Server 2013 Service Pack 1 or later. To read signed or encrypted emails, you need the S/MIME control running in Internet Explorer and the digital certificate needs to be available to the server via the Active Directory, or if you are using Exchange Online, via Azure Active Directory DirSync. More information on S/MIME in OWA can be read from the Office Blogs site at *http://blogs.office.com/2014/02/26/smime-encryption-now-in-office-365/.* Though the title says Office 365, it is valid for both on-premises Exchange 2013 Service Pack 1 and Exchange Online.

To configure Exchange Server 2013 to support S/MIME in OWA, you use the Set-Smime-Config Exchange Management Shell cmdlet. With this cmdlet, you can let users choose their signing certificate if they have more than one, set the encryption algorithms, and set timeout values to retrieve certificates from the Active Directory.

Evaluating Domain Secure/TLS

Domain Secure is a feature of Exchange Server 2010 that shows users when a message was guaranteed encrypted from end-to-end between two organizations. In Exchange Server 2013, you can still use Domain Secure, but the icon that appears in Outlook does not appear. Therefore, although the user does not get confirmation of the fact that the message was secure for the entire network session, the concept can still be used because messages will not flow between the configured domains if any of the domain secure configuration is not working.

Domain Secure is also known as mutual TLS. TLS, or Transport Layer Security, is the encryption protocol used to protect messages as they travel between Exchange Servers in your organization and optionally when traveling outside your organization. For email transport, Exchange Server 2013 will always use TLS between Exchange Servers within the organization unless it has been actively turned off. It is usually only turned off when a WAN optimizer device is used between two sites and the WAN optimization cannot take place because the traffic is encrypted. Therefore, for most organizations, the mail flow within an Exchange organization is encrypted on the network with TLS.

Between Exchange organizations, or between Exchange and any other SMTP system, TLS is negotiated during the SMTP communication. Exchange will default to using Enhanced SMTP, and will issue the EHLO SMTP verb on connection (rather than the HELO verb). If the SMTP server that is being connected to supports Enhanced SMTP, it will respond to the EHLO with 250-XXX where XXX is a list of the verbs that the server supports. If the receiving server has a digital certificate installed and the private key is available to that server, it will offer the STARTTLS verb. If Exchange Server receives 250-STARTTLS, it will swap certificates and then encrypt all communication to the other server using the public key received from that server. The other server will encrypt all communication to the sending server with the sending server's public key. Only the respective holders of the private key can decrypt this traffic.

> **IMPORTANT   SESSION KEYS**
>
> In reality, the public and private keys are not actually used to encrypt and decrypt the entire message, though it is easier to describe it that way as is have done in the preceding paragraph. In reality, the public and private keys are used to encrypt a uniquely generated key, known as the session key, and the session key is used to encrypt and decrypt the message content. Each SMTP session will use a different session key.

If the receiving SMTP server does not offer to start a TLS session, Exchange will automatically send the content in clear text. This means that if TLS is possible it will be used, but if not, it will not generate an error. This is known as opportunistic TLS. Opportunistic TLS will also not care if the certificate that is presented that contains the public key is valid. As long as the receiving server has the private key for the offered public key, Exchange Server will encrypt the data. That is, if the certificate is invalid because it does not contain the SMTP domain in the certificate subject, or if the expiry dates on the certificate are in the past, or the valid from date is in the future, or the certificate is revoked, it will still be used by Exchange. All Exchange Server is doing is using the key pair to do encryption.

If you want to guarantee that email is going to a valid server, you can. This is where Domain Secure was useful in Exchange Server 2010, and a range of settings are valid in Exchange Server 2013. Domain Secure will guarantee that the presented certificate was valid and matched the SMTP domain name of the recipient, as well as ensuring that your certificate was valid for your domain name and the issuing date is before the current date and time, and the expiry date is after the current date and time. Typically if anything is wrong with your certificate, Domain Secure will fail, and unlike opportunistic TLS, it will not fail over to clear text but instead queue the message for sending later.

In Exchange Server 2013, there are new options that are easier to use than Domain Secure. They are easier to implement because they do not have the requirement that the certificate must contain the SMTP domain as its subject name. These options are based around configuring the send connector or writing transport rules.

Mutual TLS with Domain Secure

The steps needed to configure mutual TLS with Domain Secure between two Exchange Server organizations are as follows. Note that there can be no other SMTP server between the two servers that are involved in the inter-organization communication because this would break the mutual TLS negotiation. Therefore, Domain Secure only works for domains where the MX record is published direct to the Exchange Server mailbox server or Edge server, and not to an intermediary smarthost or anti-spam filtering service. This scenario is not common and, therefore, it is not common to find Domain Secure actually in use between two companies. You might see this scenario if the two companies host alternative DNS zones rather than the public DNS zone so that they can deliver via MX delivery but not to the same smarthost server that all other Internet senders would connect to.

To configure Domain Secure, you need the following:

- End-to-end connection between the send connector you will create and the receive connector your partner organization will create.
- Create a send connector for the address space of the domain. This connector must not use the CAS server nor must it use any smarthost. It must reach the target domain using MX or DNS lookup. The CAS server or smarthost is not the endpoint that the message is going to. Domain Secure is end-to-end encryption, and the message cannot be viewed or processed by any intermediate server.
- Ensure that you can send emails at this time to the target domain. If you cannot, you need to resolve the issues now. Domain Secure settings will make it harder to resolve simple issues so, before you turn on Domain Secure, ensure that mail flow is working.
- Run Get-TransportConfig and look for the TLSReceiveDomainSecureList and the TLS-SendDomainSecureList. Set both of these values to all of the domains that you will do

Domain Secure to. Each domain will be listed on both parameters. Your own domain is not listed here. This can be seen in Figure 3-14.

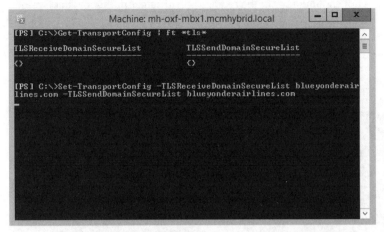

FIGURE 3-14 Setting TLSReceiveDomainSecureList and TLSSendDomainSecureList

- Mutual Auth TLS must be enabled for the send connector you created previously. This can be done in ECP or with Set-SendConnector <name> –DomainSecureEnabled $true as seen in Figure 3-15.

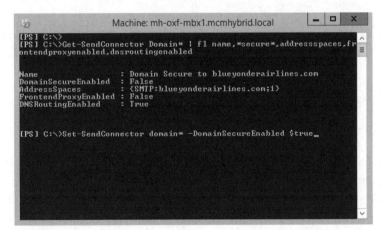

FIGURE 3-15 Viewing and setting DomainSecureEnabled

- Ensure that Domain Secure (mutual TLS) is enabled on the default receive connector at the recipient organization.
- Ensure that you have a certificate that contains your SMTP domain as a valid subject of the certificate and that the receiving Exchange Server has the same for their domain. Ensure these certificates are installed in the Local Computer store so that Exchange can use them.

- Send emails and ensure they are received. If they queue, use Get-Queue | FL LastError to see what the error is. Figure 3-16 shows the Certificate Validation Failure error when the recipient is not configured with the required certificate. Another common reason for a failure is the inability to lookup the Certificate Revocation List (CRL) from the certificate authority (over TCP port 80) due to proxies or firewalls blocking Internet access from this server.

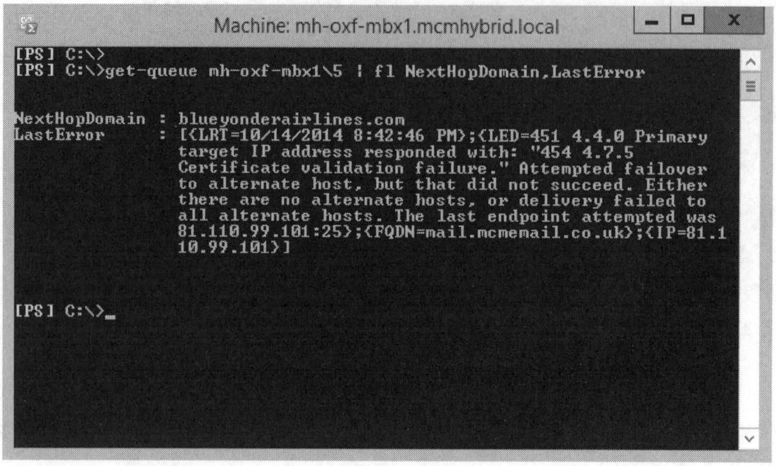

FIGURE 3-16 Domain Secure errors exposed in with Get-Queue

- Unlike Exchange 2010 you will not see the green tick icon that you used to get with Domain Secure in Outlook 2010 when using Domain Secure with Exchange Server 2013.

TLS with Send Connectors

With Exchange Server 2010 Service Pack 1 and later, you can override the default behavior of Exchange using any certificate for TLS and then not doing TLS if no certificate is presented. In other words, you can override opportunistic TLS and require a certificate or a certificate with certain values to be in place or the email will queue and not get delivered.

To configure a send connector to ensure that it will only send if TLS is used, you need to set the TlsAuthLevel parameter and then the TlsCertificateName and TlsDomain if the TlsAuthLevel requires it. TlsAuthLevel is used for hybrid mail flow with Office 365.

TlsAuthLevel has three values that it can be set to. These are EncryptionOnly, CertificateValidation, or DomainValidation. EncryptionOnly tells the sending Exchange Server to use TLS and not to downgrade to clear text but not to consider the validity of the certificate that is used by the receiving server. EncryptionOnly will allow the use of any certificate, expired or not, self signed or issued by a non-trusted certificate authority, with any subject name. The detail on the certificate does not matter for EncryptionOnly, all that is used is the public key that is part of the certificate for encrypting email to the recipient server.

CertificateValidation is one level higher than EncryptionOnly. Here the certificate must be a valid and trusted certificate that is in date and not revoked. A trusted certificate authority must issue it, but it does not need to have the SMTP domain on the certificate.

Finally, DomainValidation allows you to tell the send connector the subject name of the certificate that it will receive from the recipient system. If no domain is specified in the TlsDomain parameter, the subject on the certificate is compared with the recipient's domain. If the subject name does not match the domain specified in the TlsDomain parameter (or if blank, the recipient's domain), the message will queue until the issue is resolved. DomainValidation is useful when sending to a company that has a smarthost in front of it. Setting the TlsAuthLevel to DomainValidation can be seen in Figure 3-17. Unlike Domain Secure that does not work with smarthosts, TlsAuthLevel = DomainValidation means you can set values such as *mail.spamfilter-company.com* for the TlsDomain when you are really sending to *contoso.com*.

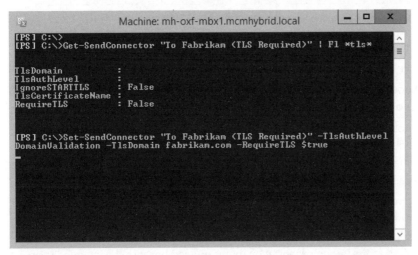

FIGURE 3-17 Setting the TlsAuthLevel and TlsDomain parameters on a send connector

DomainValidation is the highest level of protection for the TlsAuthLevel parameter. Like CertificateValidation, DomainValidation requires the certificate to be valid.

For any of the three TlsAuthLevel settings, if the receiving server is unable to do TLS, the message will queue and will never be sent clear text.

To enable a send connector to require TLS follow these steps:

- Create a send connector for the address space that you want to ensure TLS is used with. The recipient server for this address space must have a digital certificate bound to SMTP and if you "telnet <their_server> 25" and type **EHLO** they must respond 250-STARTTLS. This can be seen in Figure 3-18.

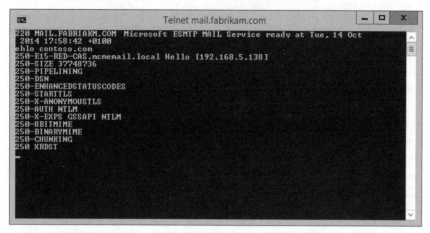

FIGURE 3-18 Testing a send connector target for the STARTTLS verb

- In Exchange Management Shell use Set-SendConnector <name> -TlsAuthLevel <EncryptionOnly | CertificateValidation | DomainValidation>.

- If you choose EncryptionOnly for TlsAuthLevel, the recipient's server needs a digital certificate and private key installed, but it does not need to be trusted or valid.

- If you choose DomainValidation for TlsAuthLevel, also use -TlsDomain <subject_name_of_recipients_certificate>. This certificate subject name does not need to match the SMTP domain you are sending to, but it must be on the certificate and the certificate must be valid and trusted.

- Send an email to that domain and check the queues for errors if it does not arrive. You can view the queues for errors with Get-Queue <queue_id> | FL LastError. Figure 3-19 shows an example error when the wrong smarthost has been used, so the email could end up going to the wrong organization, but is queued because the intended recipient server does not have the correct certificate.

FIGURE 3-19 Viewing the transport queues for TLS sending errors

TLS with Transport Rules

New to Exchange Server 2013 is the RouteMessageOutboundRequireTls transport rule action. If a transport rule is created with this action it will require the message to use TLS for its onward communication from that server.

This action can be set using the Exchange Management Shell with New-TransportRule <name> -RouteMessageOutboundRequireTls $true (as well as the other conditions, actions, and exceptions you want the rule to enforce). If you are using ECP to set the rule, you need to click the More Options link and choose Modify The Message Security and Require TLS Encryption, as shown in Figure 3-20.

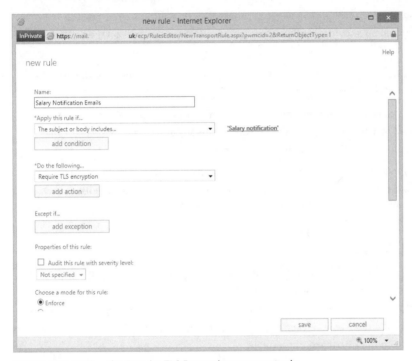

FIGURE 3-20 Setting the Require TLS Encryption transport rule

Then, when any message falls into the scope of this rule, the message will get a flag set on it internal to Exchange Server 2013 that means when it leaves this server it must use TLS. Note that for an external message to reach the recipient it must leave Exchange Server via a send connector. If that send connector is not hosted on the same machine that processes the rule, the message is sent to the site or server that hosts the send connector over TLS because it is first an internal server-to-server delivery. This first delivery meets the criteria of TLS delivery and so the action of the rule is met. Therefore every server needs to have a send connector hosted on it for this rule to work.

Using Transport Rules for TLS allows you to set conditions that are not based on the domain. For example, you could ensure that all emails with the subject "Salary notification" are protected regardless of the recipient.

Thought experiment
Consistent security configuration

In this thought experiment, apply what you've learned about this objective. You can find answers to these questions in the "Answers" section at the end of this chapter.

You manage a wide variety of servers for Contoso Pharmaceuticals. You need to ensure a consistent security configuration for your data both at rest on the server and in transit.

1. What different options could you evaluate that are already included with your Windows Server license?

2. You want to ensure that the servers on which you host Exchange Server, which are stored in a private cloud at your hosting company are physically secure. What steps could you take to make sure this happens?

3. You communicate frequently with Fabrikam Packaging Ltd who makes your boxes and other packaging materials for your products. How can you ensure that email communications to this company are enforced?

Objective summary

- RBAC is the only way in Exchange Server 2013 to assign both user and administrator rights that are not in the product by default.

- BitLocker is full volume encryption that is built into the Windows product. The encryption key is best stored in a TPM chip on the motherboard of the PC/Server so that disks separated from their host are unreadable.

- Smart cards are removable credit card sized devices that are able to store a user's private key on the cryptographic chip on the card. The use of the card requires a PIN number, so the private key cannot be used without both the card and the knowledge of the PIN. Therefore it is something you know and something you have, which is two-factor authentication compared to password-based authentication, which is just something you know.

- Protection of data at rest is encryption of the data when it is kept on its storage medium. Some protection methods do not travel with the data and so once the data is moved from its location its protection level changes. IRM is a protection and policy method that stays with the data for the life of the data.

- S/MIME is a feature of email that allows the message to be signed, to prove who sent it, and encrypted, so that only the intended recipient can view it.

- Transport Layer Security is encryption of data in transit. It is based on the HTTPS/SSL protocol but is used for more than just HTTP. For Exchange, the option to do encryption exists but can do clear text though options exist to stop communications if this is forbidden at the send or receive connector.

Objective review

Answer the following questions to test your knowledge of the information in this objective. You can find the answers to these questions and explanations of why each answer choice is correct or incorrect in the "Answers" section at the end of this chapter.

1. Over a period of time you have sent a number of S/MIME protected messages using Outlook. You did not keep a backup of your digital certificate and you have accidently deleted this certificate. Which of the following will you not be able to do going forward? (Choose all that apply.)

   A. You will not be able to sign emails.

   B. You will not be able to encrypt emails.

   C. You will not be able to read signed emails from others.

   D. You will not be able to read encrypted emails from others.

   E. You will not be able to read signed emails you have sent that are in your Sent Items folder.

   F. You will not be able to read encrypted emails you have sent to others that are in your Sent Items folder.

2. Over a period of time you have sent a number of S/MIME protected messages. Your private key is stored on a smart card and you have forgotten the PIN number. You do not have a backup of the private key. Your IT department has issued you a new certificate and updated your smart card to use the new certificate. Which of the following will you not be able to do going forward? (Choose two.)

   A. You will not be able to sign emails.

   B. You will not be able to encrypt emails.

   C. You will not be able to read signed emails from others.

   D. You will not be able to read encrypted emails from others that use your previous public key.

   E. You will not be able to read signed emails you have sent that are in your Sent Items folder.

   F. You will not be able to read encrypted emails you have sent to others that are in your Sent Items folder.

3. You need to ensure that emails to Fabrikam Bank are guaranteed to be encrypted to and from that organization. You know that the bank uses a cloud hosted anti-spam

filtering product and so direct access to their Exchange Servers is not available. What option do you need to look at first?

A. S/MIME

B. Domain Secure

C. Opportunistic TLS

D. Send connectors with TlsAuthLevel set to DomainValidation

Objective 3.2: Deploy and manage IRM with Active Directory Rights Management Services (AD RMS)

As mentioned in the previous objective on evaluating Information Rights Management, the Microsoft Active Directory Rights Management Service (or AD RMS) is the software used to configure IRM within Exchange Server and also within SharePoint, Office, and Windows File Servers. Here we will concentrate on configuring an AD RMS cluster to work with Exchange Server 2013 and configuring Exchange Server 2013 to use the AD RMS service.

For a series of videos on installing the AD RMS product and then configuring it for Exchange Server see *http://www.c7solutions.com/2012/09/installing-and-configuring-ad-rms-and-html*. This video series comes from a session at the Microsoft Exchange Conference in 2012 and looks at RMS on Windows Server 2008 R2. AD RMS on Windows Server 2012 and 2012 R2 are also compatible with Exchange Server 2013 and are configured in an almost identical way to that shown in the video. Linking Exchange Server 2013 to AD RMS is slightly different than with Exchange Server 2010, but not with any significant differences.

Figure 3-21 shows the Specify Cryptographic Mode configuration dialog box that is new to the installation since Windows Server 2008 R2 Service Pack 1, and added to the AD RMS initial configuration wizard in Windows Server 2012 and Windows Server 2012 R2. If you are creating a new cluster, you should choose Cryptographic Mode 2, though you should check the server and client requirements before doing this as Windows Vista and earlier will not support this mode and updates are required for Windows 7 and Exchange Server 2010. See more on this at *http://technet.microsoft.com/en-us/library/hh867439(v=ws.10).aspx*.

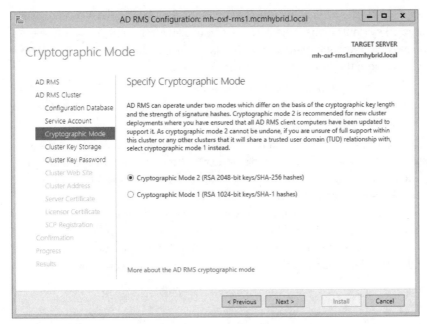

FIGURE 3-21 Enabling Cryptographic Mode 2 during AD RMS installation

Once you have AD RMS configured and Exchange Server 2013 able to use AD RMS then the following objectives can be studied in advance of completing the exam.

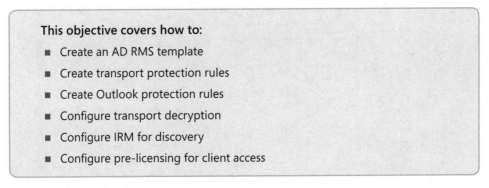

This objective covers how to:

- Create an AD RMS template
- Create transport protection rules
- Create Outlook protection rules
- Configure transport decryption
- Configure IRM for discovery
- Configure pre-licensing for client access

Creating an AD RMS template

An AD RMS template is the configuration created on the RMS server that users or Exchange Servers select when they are protecting content. For example, imagine your CEO wanted to send a confidential email to all the staff of the company and ensure that no one outside of the company's staff could read the email, and that the email was read only and could not be edited or printed.

To do this the CEO has two options. The first is using Outlook and when composing the email to set the recipients and the rights granted to the email. The second is to choose a pre-created set of rights. This pre-created set of rights is the template. For any email or other document protected by rights management, the template allows repeated and consistent use of the same settings. Note though that because the client displays the templates, it is recommended not to have more than 10 of them to select from.

To create RMS templates you need to login to the AD RMS console. You do not create RMS templates in Exchange, but Exchange Server will use them when creating rules, etc., or when users are protecting content in Outlook.

From the AD RMS console (shown in Figure 3-22) expand the server name and click Rights Policy Templates. From here you can create a distributed rights policy template or manage archived policy templates. Distributed rights policy templates are those that are in use and can have content actively protected with them. Archived templates are those that existing protected content can be opened with (they were protected with the template when the template was a distributed template), but as they are now archived they cannot be used to create new protected content. Never delete a template because you will not be able to open content protected with that template again (unless that is your intention to protect some content).

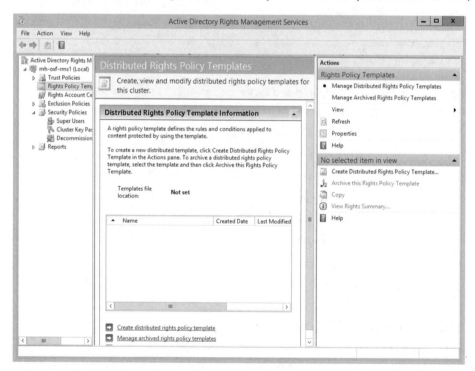

FIGURE 3-22 The AD RMS console open to the templates area

From the Rights Policy Template node of the AD RMS console click the Create Distributed Rights Policy Template link at the bottom of the screen. Add at least one language and give the template a name and a description. If you add multiple languages, the RMS client will show the template name and description that matches their application's language or Windows installation language.

Once you have given a name and description, click Next, and then click Add to add either anyone or specific users who can access the protected content. The creator of the content can always access his or her own content though this can be disabled in the template policy. Finally and optionally, enter a URL that users can click that will show them the template rights. This URL needs to be created and is not automatically made. This can be seen in Figure 3-23.

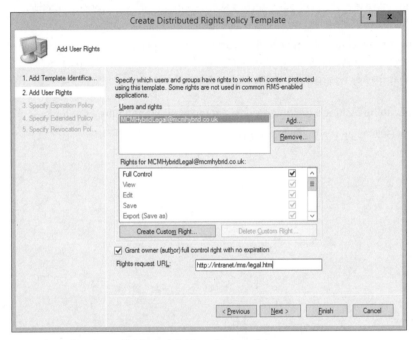

FIGURE 3-23 Creating a distributed rights policy template

When content is protected with a template, the consumer of the content needs to connect to the RMS server to get a license to access the content. The template settings, on the second page of the rights creation process, control the expiration policy. A template can be set to never expire, or to expire all content on a given date or after a certain duration from when the content was created. After this time the content cannot be accessed unless the owner updates the content with a new template, or with the same template again for a new expiry time.

Additionally, the user on retrieving the license from the RMS server is allowed to access the content without returning to the RMS server for that license again for 365 days. During the template creation process this caching of the license can be limited so that the user needs to return to the server to get a new license on a regular basis.

The rights that can be assigned to content from a template by default are as follows:

- Full Control (selects all the following rights)
- View
- Edit
- Save
- Export (Save As)
- Print
- Forward
- Reply
- Reply All
- Extract
- Allow Macros
- View Rights
- Edit Rights

Finally, if you have a template that you want to stop it being used to protect content, you need to archive it. In the Rights Policy Template screen for AD RMS you can right-click a template and archive it. If you delete it, users will not be able to get a license to access content that was created with that template and so unless they already have a cached license (if that is allowed by the template) they will not be able to access the content.

The default cache period of one year can be changed globally from the Rights Account Certificate Policies screen.

Creating transport protection rules

Once you have templates created in AD RMS you can login to an Exchange Server and ensure that Exchange can communicate with the AD RMS cluster. This is a pre-requisite to configuring any of the following Exchange IRM pieces.

To configure Exchange Server 2013 to speak to AD RMS you need to have the AD RMS URL, or if you have published the AD RMS server to Active Directory and created its SCP in the Active Directory, Exchange can look up that value and connect directly to the RMS server. You can set and change the SCP value from the Properties dialog box of the RMS server as shown in Figure 3-24. Once the SCP is set and the correct permissions granted in RMS for Exchange Server, you need to enable IRM in Exchange.

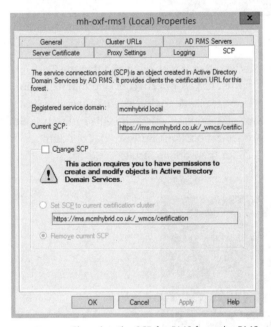

FIGURE 3-24 Changing the SCP for RMS from the RMS server properties dialog

You run the Set-IRMConfiguration cmdlet to turn on Exchange IRM. This is the full cmdlet.

```
//Enable IRM in Exchange Server
Set-IRMConfiguration -InternalLicensingEnabled $true
```

Exchange will look up the SCP endpoint, or you can use the Set-IRMConfiguration cmdlet to specify this manually if RMS is only going to be used by Exchange Server. Once found, the Exchange Server uses the value in the SCP to connect to the RMS server and then to download the licenses and certificates it needs to be able to use RMS. This cmdlet, and the enabling of the Super Users group as an Exchange Server distribution group (to give it an email address as required by RMS) can be seen in Figure 3-25.

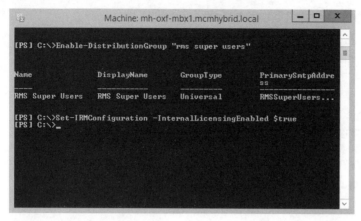

FIGURE 3-25 Set-IrmConfiguration

Once IRM is configured it is always worth checking that it is working and that the Exchange Server is able to reach the RMS server cluster. It is also worth checking that it can obtain licenses for the users and that the templates are available to download. To test that IRM is working use Test-IRMConfiguration -Sender <email@address> where the email address is an internal user with a mailbox in your Exchange organization. Running Test-IRMConfiguration should show a long list of passes. See Figure 3-26 for the working results.

FIGURE 3-26 Test-IRMConfiguration showing a full bill of health

The Sender parameter of Test-IRMConfiguration specifies the SMTP address of the sender to be tested. The cmdlet tests prelicensing and journal report decryption for the sender. The Recipient parameter specifies the SMTP address of one or more recipients. The cmdlet tests prelicensing for the specified recipients. You can specify multiple recipient addresses separated by commas. If no recipient is specified, the sender address is used as the recipient.

To obtain a list of valid templates you can use Get-RMSTemplate. Again, this will not work if the Exchange Server is not configured to connect to the RMS server.

Once the Exchange Server is able to connect to the RMS server cluster you can start to create rules to protect content. Transport rules, if you have an Exchange Enterprise CAL, can be configured to protect content based on whatever predicates you look for in the rule. Protection with an RMS template will be done as long as the template is distributed (not archived) and as long as the Exchange Server can reach the RMS server to get the licenses to create the content (or it already has the licenses cached).

To create a transport rule to protect content, login to ECP, and under Rules click the plus icon and choose Apply Rights Protection To Messages. Figure 3-27 shows a rule being created called Protect Legal Sensitive Emails. This rule will apply the Legal Department Only template to any message that is marked as having the Legal Sensitive classification. This classification was made with the New-MessageClassification cmdlet.

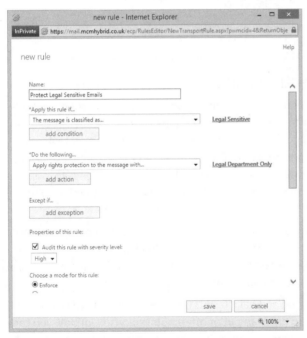

FIGURE 3-27 Creating a transport rule for RMS protection

Once this message classification and then transport rule are created the user can go into Outlook Web App and compose a new email selecting the Legal Sensitive message classification from the message properties ellipsis in OWA, as shown in Figure 3-28.

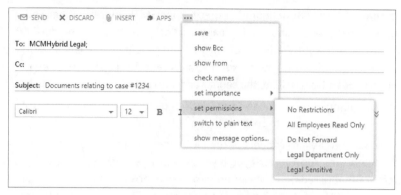

FIGURE 3-28 Setting a message classification on an email in OWA

Upon receipt of this email you should see that it has been protected with the selected RMS template as set in the transport rule. Figure 3-29 shows the email in the message pane in OWA.

FIGURE 3-29 A protected email in OWA

Creating Outlook protection rules

Though the templates in RMS allow users to protect their own content using the Office ProPlus application, this requires the user to remember to protect the content themselves before sending it. And though transport rules can protect content as seen above, the content is not protected until it arrives at the transport service of Exchange Server. The email that remains in the Sent Items folder is not protected with the template. Therefore a way needs to exist for messages to be protected from the time of leaving Outlook. The way to do this is to use Outlook Protection Rules.

Outlook Protection Rules are created on the Exchange Server, not the Outlook client, and are downloaded to the client via Exchange Web Services (EWS). The Outlook client therefore needs AutoDiscover working to reach a valid EWS endpoint so that Outlook can see there are protection rules to download, and to download them.

Once you have AutoDiscover working and have tested your EWS endpoint, which is best done by verifying that you can turn on or off an out of office notification in Outlook, you can create a protection rule which will be downloaded to Outlook the next time it starts up.

To create a protection rule you need to use the New-OutlookProtectionRule cmdlet. Figure 3-30 shows an example that sets of emails are sent to a group to get RMS protection automatically.

Outlook Protection Rules are limited on the predicates that you can set on the rules. You can only use this type of rule to protect messages that come from a user with a given department value in the Active Directory (the FromDepartment predicate), are sent to a given email address (the SentTo predicate), or are sent inside the organization or everyone (the SentToScope). You can use more than one of these predicates on a single rule, for example you could protect all messages sent from the Compliance department to users internal to the company. An example of this rule could be as follows.

Outlook Protection Rule - Compliance Department

```
New-OutlookProtectionRule "Sent By Compliance Dept." -FromDepartment Compliance
-SentToScope InOrganization -ApplyRightsProtectionTemplate "Do Not Forward"
-UserCanOverride $True
```

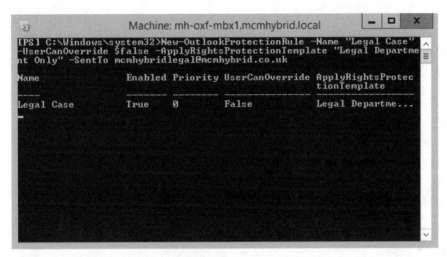

FIGURE 3-30 Setting an Outlook Protection Rule

The Outlook Protection Rules are downloaded via Exchange Web Services once every 24 hours. Changes to the rules can therefore take time to appear on client machines. To speed up the process in a lab or test environment you need to delete the PB4S-Configuration-user@ domain.com.xml file that you can find in the %appdata%\Microsoft\Outlook folder and then restart Outlook. The rules will be downloaded shortly after restarting Outlook and as long as Outlook is in the same forest, or a trusted forest as the RMS Server, it will be able to download the RMS templates and apply them.

Once Outlook Protection Rules are downloaded, the message is protected as soon as the conditions for the protection are met. In the case of SentTo for example, as soon as the valid recipient's address is added to any of the recipient fields in Outlook the message gets protected and a banner confirming that is shown. This can be seen in Figure 3-31, where just the recipient was added and nothing else.

FIGURE 3-31 Outlook Protection Rules taking effect on the predicate being met

Configuring transport decryption

When you run Get-IRMConfiguration you will see a number of different settings. The only one we have set so far is InternalLicensingEnabled to turn on RMS inside the organization. To implement AD RMS (not Azure RMS) in Exchange Online and part of Office 365 you would use ExternalLicensingEnabled and a few other settings. But the remaining settings that are valid for Exchange Server 2013 on-premises are as described below:

- **JournalReportDecryptionEnabled** This is set to True by default. It ensures that if you journal a rights-protected message, a second copy of the message, with the rights removed, is added to the journal report.

- **ClientAccessServerEnabled** This setting, which is True by default, enabled RMS in Outlook Web App. To enable IRM in Outlook Web App, you must add the Federation mailbox, a system mailbox created by Exchange 2013 Setup, to the super users group in AD RMS.

- **SearchEnabled** This allows users to search for RMS protected content using Outlook Web App or Outlook in online mode. It is True by default and requires RMS Super User rights for the Exchange Server federation account.

- **TransportDecryptionSetting** This is the main point of this section of the book. If Transport Decryption should fail, what happens? By default the setting is Optional, which means the message is processed through transport even though it is not readable. Other options are Disabled, so that transport decryption does not happen or Mandatory so that it does, and if it fails, an NDR is generated.

- **EDiscoverySuperUserEnabled** This setting is True by default. It allows members of the Discovery Management role group to view IRM protected messages when they are in a discovery mailbox. Super User rights for Exchange Server federation account are needed for this feature to work.

- **ServiceLocation** If the Exchange Server does not use the SCP to lookup the RMS server's endpoint, it can be hardcoded here. If this value is blank, the SCP in the Active Directory will be used.

- **LicensingLocation**   This is an optional array of RMS licensing URLs that are needed if you have a cross-forest RMS deployment on-premises.

The setting of TransportDecryptionSetting in the preceding list is set to Optional by default. This setting controls whether or not the transport service can decrypt and re-encrypt messages as they go through the transport service.

If you consider some of the purposes of the transport service you will see why decryption of protected content, and then encrypting it again at the end of the transport service, can be desirable. For example, in Exchange Server 2013 there is a built in anti-malware engine as well as transport rules engine, journaling, pipeline tracing, and the Data Loss Prevention feature. Each of these items has the possibility of scanning and maybe modifying the message body. If the message body is encrypted they cannot be scanned (and modified if needed). Take the anti-malware agent. If you had an Outlook Protection Rule that protected all messages sent to the Legal Team and someone picked up a computer virus and emailed that to a member of that team. The malware agent in Exchange would not see this virus and not remove it. Or take for example a more common scenario of adding disclaimers. If the message is encrypted, the disclaimer cannot be added.

Transport Decryption occurs at the start of the transport pipeline and everything in the pipeline can then process a message that is in the clear and not encrypted. As the message leaves the transport pipeline it is encrypted again as it was before, but with the modifications made to the message.

You can see the Transport Pipeline using Get-TransportPipeline, and the output from an Exchange Server 2013 Cumulative Update 5 server can be seen in Figure 3-32.

FIGURE 3-32 Get-TransportPipeline

In the pipeline output you can see the different transport agents that run at different parts of the SMTP configuration and transport routing feature. Not every transport agent is listed, but the RMS ones are. Here you can see that the RMS Decryption Agent runs in OnSubmittedMessage and the RMS Encryption Agent at OnRoutedMessage. This means that agents such as the transport rules agent (at OnResolvedMessage) will see a message in clear text and so be able to query and modify it if needed.

Configuring IRM for discovery

When discovery managers issue searches across mailboxes they might come across content that is protected with IRM. The content would be found by the search because by default the SearchEnabled property of Get-IRMConfiguration is set to true, though this also requires Exchange Server to have RMS Super User rights to work. Therefore if Exchange Server has Super User rights and SearchEnabled is at its default position of True, the discovery managers may find content in the results that the search feature was able to see inside (as it was able to decrypt it with Super User rights) but that the discovery manager is unable to see inside. Therefore in the event of a compliance search issue where content needs to be found and studied, the Discovery Management role group members will find that there are matching results, but they can view them no further as they are not Super User themselves.

Therefore to avoid this issue an additional feature was added in Exchange Server 2010 Service Pack 1 and it carries forward to Exchange Server 2013 which, if enabled, allows Discovery Managers to view the contents of IRM protected messages that they would not normally have the rights to view when they are viewing the contents of the discovery mailbox via Outlook Web App. If they export the search results to another mailbox or PST file, the right to view the IRM content does not follow. By default the EDiscoverySuperUserEnabled property is set to True.

Figure 3-33 shows the OWA search preview open for a member of the Discovery Management role group. To grant a user Discovery Management rights, add them to the Discovery Management group in the Microsoft Exchange Security Groups OU. The protected message shown in Figure 3-33 is the same as the one sent in Figure 3-28. The results preview shows that the message is protected and marked with a classification and who sent it, but it is readable by the discovery manager during eDiscovery.

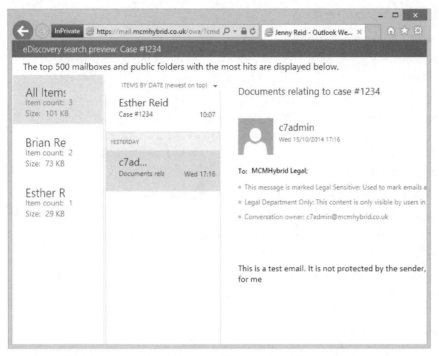

FIGURE 3-33 Search results in the discovery mailbox showing IRM protected content

Configuring pre-licensing for client access

Pre-licensing is the process whereby the client access server gets a license on behalf of the user from the RMS server and associates the license with the message. This means that users in OWA who are just viewing their email rendered in HTML are able to read RMS protected content because the client access server obtains the license for them and opens the protected message and renders the message in the web browser for them. The user, who could be remote from the RMS server and without a VPN open to the RMS server does not need to be able to reach the RMS server because Exchange will get licenses for the content on behalf of the user.

Pre-licensing is enabled by default and its current setting can be determined with Get-IRMConfiguration and looking at the ClientAccessServerEnabled setting. Prelicensing allows for offline use of RMS because the user's license is provided with the message rather than the user needing to have access to RMS server directly. This means that as well as OWA clients consuming protected content, so can RPC/HTTP or MAPI/HTTP (Outlook Anywhere) clients, and ActiveSync clients. For ActiveSync clients, the mobile phone device needs to be able to process RMS content and use the license, and most ActiveSync devices do not do this.

Thought experiment

Securing business content

In this thought experiment, apply what you've learned about this objective. You can find answers to these questions in the "Answers" section at the end of this chapter.

You work for a national football team as their IT administrator. Discussions happen frequently regarding the potential purchase and sale of players from and to competitive clubs. The team management saw in the news the other day rumors about the potential sale of a player between two other clubs and wants to ensure their email discussions are private.

1. What options would you suggest to assist with this business requirement?

2. Assuming that Microsoft AD RMS appears on the list of possible solutions, how would you ensure that your anti-virus product installed with Exchange Server and your transport rules remained working?

3. Given a choice between S/MIME and AD RMS, which would you think would be best for your business?

Objective summary

- AD RMS is the Microsoft on-premises server for IRM protection of files, SharePoint libraries, and emails. Azure RMS is the Microsoft cloud-based IRM product.

- RMS templates are created to allow users to easily pick permissions to apply to their content or for Exchange Server to easily protect content with Outlook Protection Rules or Transport Rules.

- Distributed templates are available for users to use. Archived templates are available for viewing existing protected content. Never delete a template unless you want to lock out all access to all of the content created with it.

- Exchange Server determines the location of the RMS cluster by querying a Service Connection Point (SCP) from the Active Directory that is placed there during RMS installation.

- Outlook Protection Rules use Exchange Web Services to download rules to the Outlook client to ensure that messages are RMS protected at the point of sending.

- Exchange Server can act as a RMS Super User. This means it has the rights to decrypt content that it is not the owner of, or have rights to open, and to protect content as if someone else protected it. The Exchange Server uses this right to do RMS on behalf of the user in Transport Rules, and to open content up so it can be indexed, modified, scanned, and pre-licensed.

Objective review

Answer the following questions to test your knowledge of the information in this objective. You can find the answers to these questions and explanations of why each answer choice is correct or incorrect in the "Answers" section at the end of this chapter.

1. You have installed AD RMS and have integrated it with Exchange Server. Which of the following cmdlets would you use to check that the integration with the IRM service is working? (Choose two.)

   A. Get-RMSConfiguration

   B. Get-IRMConfiguration

   C. Test-RMSConfiguration -Sender dean@contoso.com

   D. Test-IRMConfiguration -Sender dean@contoso.com

   E. .Test-RMSConfiguration -Mailbox "Halstead, Dean"

   F. Test-IRMConfiguration -Mailbox "Halstead, Dean"

2. Which of the following cmdlets will create a valid Outlook Protection Rule?

   A. New-OutlookProtectionRule "Sent By Compliance Dept." -FromDepartment Compliance -SentToScope Internal -ApplyRightsProtectionTemplate "Do Not Forward" -UserCanOverride $True

   B. New-RMSProtectionRule "Sent By Compliance Dept." -FromDepartment Compliance -SentToScope Internal -ApplyRightsProtectionTemplate "Do Not Forward" -UserCanOverride $True

   C. New-RMSProtectionRule "Sent By Compliance Dept." -FromDepartment Compliance -SentToScope InOrganization -ApplyRightsProtectionTemplate "Do Not Forward" -UserCanOverride $True

   D. New-OutlookProtectionRule "Sent By Compliance Dept." -FromDepartment Compliance -SentToScope InOrganization -ApplyRightsProtectionTemplate "Do Not Forward" -UserCanOverride $True

3. Which of the following Exchange mailboxes needs to be added to the RMS Super Users group?

   A. SystemMailbox{1f05a927-ee95-41ba-b053-4623ffd69772}

   B. SystemMailbox{e0dc1c29-89c3-4034-b678-e6c29d823ed9}

   C. FederatedEmail.4c1f4d8b-8179-4148-93bf-00a95fa1e042

   D. Migration.8f3e7716-2011-43e4-96b1-aba62d229136

Objective 3.3: Configure and interpret mailbox and administrative auditing

Exchange Server 2013 contains a number of features to record the activity of both administrators and users. The type of activity that can be recorded are actions performed by an administrator in Exchange Management Shell, or ECP, which just runs shell cmdlets for you as well as access requests to mailboxes that are not by the owner.

Both of these features will ensure that you can meet security and compliance requirements that require you to show the activity on a mailbox by users other than the mailbox owner themselves, and what and who made changes to the Exchange Servers or Exchange Online.

This objective covers how to:

- Configure mailbox audit logging
- Configure administrative audit logging
- Interpret all audit logs

EXAM TIP

The Objective Domain for the exam includes "Configure mailbox access logging," which is apparently a mistake and you shouldn't expect any questions on it on the exam because this is not a feature of Exchange Server.

Configuring mailbox audit logging

Mailbox audit logging allows the administrator or anyone with permission to view them to see the non-owner activity reports on the mailbox. By default mailbox audit logging is disabled and if a report is run against a mailbox that does not have audit logging enabled, a blank report will be returned.

When a mailbox is enabled for audit logging, all activity that is done by a user who is not the owner of the mailbox is stored in a hidden folder in the mailbox. This information stores who accessed the mailbox and when they accessed it. Because this information is stored in the mailbox, mailbox moves will result in the audit log staying with the mailbox. By default, audit logs are kept for 90 days. Entries older than 90 days are deleted. It is possible to change this duration in Exchange Server on-premises but not in Exchange Online.

When you search for entries in a mailbox audit log, Microsoft Exchange queries the mailbox audit log and exports the information. These results are then collated as an XML file and attached to an email message that is sent to the person requesting the audit log report.

To enable audit logging on a mailbox, you need to run the Set-Mailbox <Identity> -AuditEnabled $true.

By default the Update, Move, MoveToDeletedItems, SoftDelete, HardDelete, FolderBind, SendAs, and SendOnBehalf actions performed by those with rights to the target mailbox are logged. It is possible to change these audit actions and also include Update, Copy, Move, SendOnBehalf, and MessageBind actions as well as to remove some or all of the default actions. You need to use the AuditAdmin property to control these actions, and the None action is used to turn them all off again. Note that you need AuditEnabled set to $true before any of the previous activities are logged.

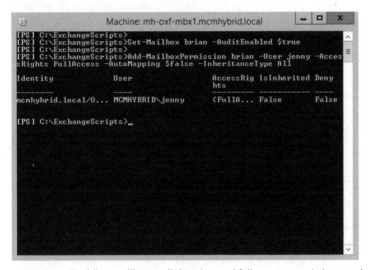

FIGURE 3-34 Enabling mailbox audit logging and full access permissions to the same mailbox.

Figure 3-34 shows setting the mailbox audit on Brian's mailbox. It also shows that the permissions have been granted to Jenny to open this mailbox.

Configuring administrative audit logging

This type of audit logging is automatically enabled. The data is stored in Exchange Server arbitration mailbox known as SystemMailbox{e0dc1c29-89c3-4034-b678-e6c29d823ed9}. This mailbox is made on the first Exchange Server 2010 database created in an organization, or if there was no Exchange Server 2010 installation on the first Exchange Server 2013 database in an organization.

In the event of upgrading from Exchange Server 2010 to 2013, one of the first things to do once your newly installed environment is stable is to move this system mailbox. This mailbox needs to be on Exchange Server 2013 to be able to record the audit logs for Exchange Server

2013 and 2010. If the mailbox still resides on Exchange Server 2010, activities on Exchange Server 2013 will not be recorded.

To check the location of all the system, or arbitration, mailboxes use the following cmdlet.

```
Get-Mailbox -Arbitration | FL Name,DisplayName,ServerName,Database,AdminDisplayVersion
```

You are looking for the AdminDisplayVersion property of the SystemMailbox{e0dc1c29-89c3-4034-b678-e6c29d823ed9} mailbox. If the version is 15.x, the mailbox has been moved to Exchange Server 2013. If the mailbox is less than version 15.0 it remains on Exchange Server 2010 and needs to be moved. You can move it with this.

```
Get-Mailbox "SystemMailbox{e0dc1c29*" -Arbitration | New-MoveRequest
```

By default, audit log entries are kept for 90 days. When an entry is older than 90 days, it's deleted. This setting can't be changed in a cloud-based organization. However, it can be changed in an on-premises Exchange organization by using the Set-AdminAuditLog cmdlet.

Cmdlets that are run in Exchange Management Shell that make changes to Exchange Server are audited. Cmdlets that query or read settings are not audited. The Exchange Control Panel runs PowerShell cmdlets for you when you make changes in ECP; therefore these changes are also audited by way of the cmdlet that is run. The work of auditing the cmdlets is done with the Admin Audit Log Agent. This is an extensibility agent that is bound to all cmdlets in Exchange 2010 and 2013 that make changes. If changes are made in any other tool and do not call an Exchange Management Shell cmdlet they are not audited, as are cmdlets run in Exchange 2007. Test- cmdlets are also not logged, though you can enable the logging of these cmdlets, it is recommended that you only do Test- cmdlets for a short period of time only due to the amount of Test- cmdlets that run in the background.

EXAM TIP

A command may take up to 15 minutes after it's run to appear in audit log search results. This is because audit log entries must be indexed before they can be searched. If a command doesn't appear in the administrator audit log, wait a few minutes and run the search again.

If you do not want every cmdlet that modifies Exchange Server logged, you can use the Set-AdminAuditLogConfig cmdlet to make changes on what to include. Any changes that affect Set-AdminAuditLogConfig are always logged regardless of other settings. We recommend that you grant permissions to configure the audit log age limit only to highly trusted users.

Interpreting all audit logs

This section looks at understanding and reading the two different audit logs that Exchange Server stores.

Mailbox audit logs

In the previous section about mailbox auditing, Jenny was granted the ability to have full access to Brian's mailbox. To search the logs or run reports to get this information, you access Exchange Control Panel (Figure 3-35).

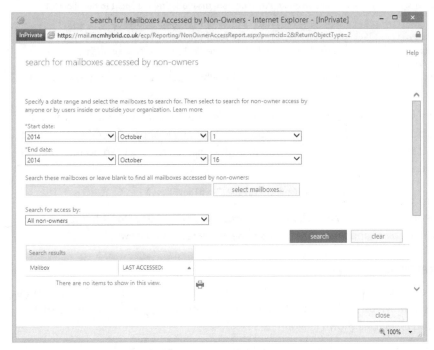

FIGURE 3-35 The ECP search for a non-owner audit log

The audit log will show this activity. To request the audit log, you need either to be an Exchange administrator or have been given access to one of two role groups. The two role groups are:

- Audit Logs
- View Only Audit Logs

The second of these two roles allows the log to be viewed in Exchange Control Panel, but not exported.

To add a user to view audit logs, you need to run the following cmdlet using the View Only Audit Logs role if you want that right instead.

```
New-ManagementRoleAssignment -Role "Audit Logs" -User <Identity>
```

Audit logs can be viewed in Exchange Control Panel via the Compliance Management section and the Auditing tab. To view an audit log report, run the Run A Non-Owner Mailbox Access Report.3-36.

If you have the Audit Logs role, you can export an audit log. Exporting audit logs will get them emailed to a selected person as an XML file. If you are using Outlook Web App, you will not be able to view XML attachments unless you configure OWA to support XML files. This can be done with the following cmdlets.

```
//These cmdlets remove the .xml file extension and MIME type from the block lists and add it to the allow list:
Get-OwaMailboxPolicy | Set-OwaMailboxPolicy -BlockedFileTypes @{Remove = ".xml"}
Get-OwaMailboxPolicy | Set-OwaMailboxPolicy -AllowedFileTypes @{Add = ".xml"}
Get-OwaMailboxPolicy | Set-OwaMailboxPolicy -BlockedMimeTypes @{Remove = "text/xml",
"application/xml"}
Get-OwaMailboxPolicy | Set-OwaMailboxPolicy -AllowedMimeTypes @{Add = "text/xml",
"application/xml"}
```

Note that this cmdlet resets the AllowedFileTypes for the Default OWA mailbox policy. If you have multiple policies, you need to change each. If you have already modified the extensions on this list, you need to ensure that you add the .xml file type. You can do this using the following syntax.

```
@{Add="<value1>","<value2>"...; Remove="<value1>","<value2>"...}
```

Audit logs are generated by a background process, and can take up to 24 hours to arrive in the target mailbox or appear on the results pane in the search window.

Administrator audit logs

To query the actions of the administrators on the Exchange Server, you can use the Exchange Control Panel as previously discussed with the mailbox auditing, or you can run the Search-AdminAuditLog cmdlet, as shown in Figure 3-36

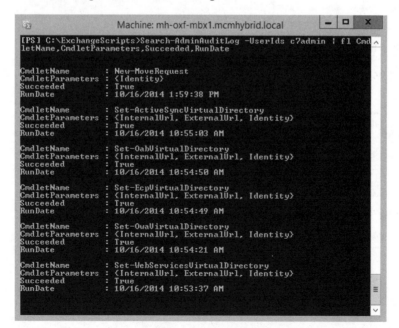

FIGURE 3-36 Running Search-AdminAuditLog to get information on a particular administrator

By default, only the first 1,000 log entries that match the criteria you specify are returned. However, you can override this default and return more or fewer entries using the ResultSize parameter. You can specify a value of Unlimited with the ResultSize parameter to return all log entries that match the specified criteria.

To email an admin audit report, you can use New-AdminAuditLogSearch rather than Search-AdminAuditLog. The following example uses this cmdlet to get the same results as the example shown in Figure 3-36:

```
New-AdminAuditLogSearch -UserId c7admin -StatusMailRecipients jenny@mcmhybrid.co.uk
-StartDate 10/1/14 -EndDate 10/16/14
```

Results can take up to 15 minutes to arrive and will not exceed 10 MB. The structure of the returned XML is described at *http://technet.microsoft.com/en-us/library/ff459251.aspx*.

Thought experiment

Searching for admin changes

In this thought experiment, apply what you've learned about this objective. You can find answers to these questions in the "Answers" section at the end of this chapter.

You are an external consultant to Tailspin Toys. Your client is seeing non-deliverable email messages being attached to suspect outbound spam messages. The issue is that these suspect spam messages are getting sent to eop@tailspin.com. Exchange Online Protection allows suspect spam to be sent to a mailbox so that it can be evaluated; however, there is no mailbox with the address eop@tailspin.com. Users are starting to get non-deliverable messages for a mailbox they did not address the email to. This problem only started in the last week and Tailspin Toys has called you to help work out the cause of the issue.

Using admin auditing, how would you go about solving the issue?

Objective summary

- Exchange Server includes administrator cmdlet auditing by default. All cmdlets that change content are audited by default.
- Mailbox auditing is disabled by default and can be enabled on selected or all mailboxes as your business needs require.
- Auditing stores 90 days of data by default, though this can be changed with the Set-AdminAuditLog cmdlet.
- To view the XML files in OWA you need to remove the .xml block and MIME type block and add it to the allowed file types list.
- You need to be an administrator to view audit logs unless the Audit Logs or View Only Audit Logs roles are granted to your mailbox.

Objective review

Answer the following questions to test your knowledge of the information in this objective. You can find the answers to these questions and explanations of why each answer choice is correct or incorrect in the "Answers" section at the end of this chapter.

1. You configure exporting of audit logs to your compliance manager but she reports back that she is having difficulty viewing them in OWA. What do you need to do? (Choose two.)

    A. Create a new OWA mailbox policy.

    B. Remove the compliance officer from the Default OWA mailbox policy.

    C. Add the .xml file type to the allowed file types and the text/xml and application/xml MIME types to allowed MIME types on the mailbox policy used by the compliance officer.

    D. Remove the .xml file type from the blocked file types and the text/xml and application/xml MIME types from the blocked MIME types parameter on the mailbox policy used by the compliance officer.

2. After upgrading Exchange Server 2010 to 2013, you notice that admin audit logs are returning empty search results. Which of the following arbitration mailboxes needs to be moved to an Exchange Server 2013 database?

    A. SystemMailbox{1f05a927-ee95-41ba-b053-4623ffd69772}

    B. SystemMailbox{e0dc1c29-89c3-4034-b678-e6c29d823ed9}

    C. FederatedEmail.4c1f4d8b-8179-4148-93bf-00a95fa1e042

    D. Migration.8f3e7716-2011-43e4-96b1-aba62d229136

Objective 3.4: Troubleshoot security-related issues

The final objective of the Advanced Security topic of the 70-342 Exchange Server 2013 Microsoft IT Pro exam is troubleshooting the items that you have looked at in this chapter. Apart from the troubleshooting items mentioned with respect to installing a feature, in this section you'll look at some of the more common and exam worthy issues that can occur with security in Windows Server as it relates to Exchange Server.

> **This objective covers how to:**
> - Determine certificate validity
> - Ensure proper Certificate Revocation List (CRL) access and placement
> - Ensure private key availability
> - Troubleshoot failed IRM protection
> - Troubleshoot RBAC

Determining certificate validity

Certificates must be trusted by both you and the recipient to be valid. In addition to validity dates, you should be able to trust the issuer and the subject name such match the server name or email address of the owner of the certificate.

Each certificate is valid for a range of time. This range can be seen in the certificate's properties. Of course this date range is compared to both the date and time on the sender's computer and the date and time on any recipient's computer. Therefore it is important to ensure that both the sending party and the receiving party in a signing or an encryption transfer are both using a range of time on the client that are the same or very close to being the same.

The best way to achieve this is to ensure that non-domain joined PCs or computing devices get their time from a reliable Network Time Protocol (NTP) server and that as domain joined Windows PCs get their time from a domain controller in their domain, and the domain controllers ultimately get time from the PDC emulator domain controller in the root domain. It is important to ensure that the PDC emulator domain controller in the root domain is able to get time from a reliable time source.

There are generally two time sources that are considered useful. One is a radio beacon that is available in some countries. A device that gets time from this beacon is connected to the PDC emulator domain controller in the root domain or you allow UDP port 123 outbound to your choice of a reliable time source. How reliable you need to be depends on the data that you are encrypting. Financial markets for example need to be very reliable due to the speed of the trades, but for most organizations, an Internet time source such as *pool.ntp.org* is sufficient. The Windows default timeserver of *time.windows.com* is typically not reliable enough.

To see the dates of a certificate, open the certificate from whichever application presents it to you, or open Internet Explorer, Internet Options, and the Content tab. Click Certificates to see your certificates and those you hold from other people (for example sent to you via an S/MIME conversation). This can be seen in Figure 3-37.

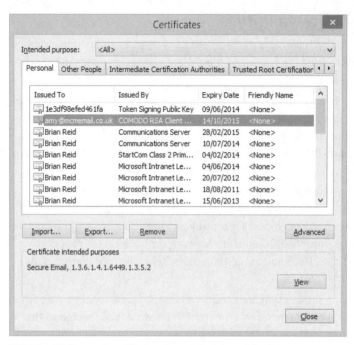

FIGURE 3-37 Personal certificates viewed via Internet Explorer

The expiry date of a certificate can be seen in the dialog box shown in Figure 3-37. Double-click any certificate to see the Valid From date as well (Figure 3-38). If you have a certificate that is not yet valid, you will not trust it either. Because certificates are considered secure until they expire or have been revoked, it is becoming called for that certificates have short validation periods. For example during the writing of this book (Oct 2014), Google announced that they would stop supporting the SHA1 hash used in SSL communications in their web browser. Microsoft has already announced that they will stop support for SHA1 in 2017. To that end, if you visit *https://www.google.com* during this time period, they have SSL certificates with a three-month validity period. This is so that by the time their web browser starts generating alerts for SHA1 hashed certificates with long validation periods, they will not be affected by it. It may well be that in a few years' time, a one-year certificate is considered too long!

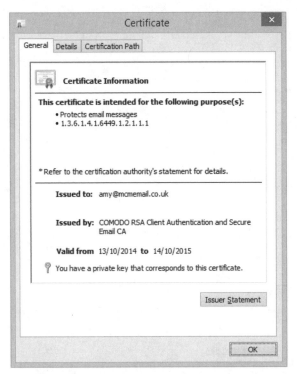

FIGURE 3-38 A certificate showing the validation dates and other information

Ensuring proper Certificate Revocation List (CRL) access and placement

In addition to validating the validity dates of a certificate, be sure that Certificate Revocation Checking is enabled in Internet Explorer, This ensures that even though the certificate is valid for its dates, it is not invalid because it has been revoked.

> **IMPORTANT   CONFIGURING REVOCATION SETTINGS**
>
> Though you configure revocation checking in Internet Explorer, it is the Internet Settings dialog box that you are viewing, which affects most applications and not just Internet Explorer. You can access the Internet Settings dialog box from Control Panel as well.

Figure 3-39 shows the Internet Settings dialog box with the revocation settings option highlighted. Notice that changes here require a restart of the operating system as they are affecting more than just the web browser.

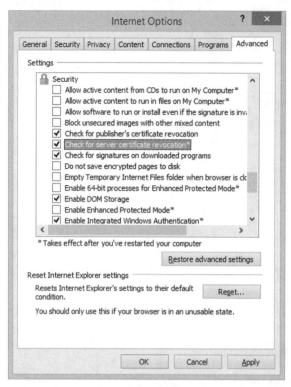

FIGURE 3-39 Internet security settings in Windows showing revocation settings

When certificate revocation checking is enabled, Windows will check with the certificate issuer that the certificate was not cancelled, or revoked, since it was issued.

Revocation checking is a process that runs over the HTTP protocol and requires a connection to the certificate authority's certificate revocation list, or CRL, location. Each certificate has the CRL location stored as part of the certificate.

To view the CRL publishing location of a certificate, you need to view the certificate properties and change to the Details tab. On the Details tab, locate the CRL Distribution Points value. This can be seen in Figure 3-40 as an example from an internally issued certificate. Notice from the figure that the URL for the certificate revocation list is via LDAP as it is stored in the Active Directory. If you have an internal certificate authority that is used by non-domain joined members, you typically ensure that it is also reachable via a HTTP endpoint as well.

To see the contents of a CRL you can copy the HTTP URL and paste it into a browser. The CRL will have a cache property and so may be stored in your web browsers cache for a while, but as long as you have HTTP Internet access (direct or via a proxy server) you should be able to see the CRL.

FIGURE 3-40 Viewing the CRL location on a certificate

For example the CRL for a Comodo free digital certificate that is used for S/MIME is *http:// crl.comodoca.com/COMODORSAClientAuthenticationandSecureEmailCA.crl.* This is always reached over HTTP and never HTTPS, because you would need to check the CRL for the SSL feature of the encrypted connection to get the CRL and so could end up in loop, so all CRL lookups are over HTTP.

CRLs typically have a short lifespan. For example the one seen in Figure 3-41 is four days. If the CRL that you download is past its update period, it is considered invalid and the source certificate that you are trying to validate will fail validation. Therefore it is important that any proxy server between the client or server and the CRL distribution point either does not cache CRL files, or caches them for as small a time as possible. Exchange Server requires access to the listed CRL of any certificate that it uses and so it requires either unauthenticated Internet access through a proxy server, or direct access via a router or firewall to the CRL endpoint. When opening OWA or Exchange Control Panel, a delay of 30 seconds is a typical indicator that the CRL is not reachable.

FIGURE 3-41 A certificate revocation list

To troubleshoot CRL lookup issues, use the CRLUtil tool from Microsoft. This tool will run in the context of the current user, which is important for checking the content of services and the computer itself. Microsoft has a wiki on how to check revocation at *http://social.technet. microsoft.com/wiki/contents/articles/certificate-status-and-revocation-checking.aspx.* Though this article applies to Windows XP, there is a link on this page for later Windows versions and a plan to merge the content to this page.

Ensuring private key availability

If you lose your private key, you cannot sign content for other users and you cannot read anything that has been sent to you that was encrypted with your key, even if you had previously opened it. Therefore, it is important to have a backup of your key, which you can password protect to keep it secure. When your key expires, it is also import to keep your key around so that you can decrypt data sent to you when the key was valid.

When you backup a certificate, you get the option to back up the private key. You must select this option to enable it; it is not the default. Depending on how you installed the certificate, the private key might not be exportable. This is the case if the private key was not marked as exportable when the certificate was imported to that computer. Therefore it is important that, as you copy certificates between machines, you keep a note of which computer you can export the private key from.

Figure 3-42 shows the Certificate Export Wizard on Windows 8.1. The exact look of the wizard differs in different versions of Windows.

FIGURE 3-42 Exporting a digital certificate with the private key

Following the wizard, you can choose to export all of the certificates in the path that this digital certificate requires. Each certificate, unless self-signed, is signed by a parent certificate authority, which in and of itself might be signed by a grandparent certificate authority, and so on. To trust the certificate you are exporting, should you import it to another computer, this chain of certificate authorities will be needed. Therefore, exporting with the chain makes it easier to import a certificate in the future and get the full trust working immediately. Also, during export you have the option to delete the private key andto set a password. This password will be needed during later import processes. If you are exporting the certificate using Windows 8.1/Windows Server 2012 R2, you can allocate a group that you need to be a member of to open the certificate in the future rather than or in addition to setting a password. The use of groups makes it easier for management purposes when you are exporting and importing certificates across servers within a team, for example, within the IT department. If you export with a password and restricted to specific group membership, you need to know the password as well as be a member of the group before the digital certificate and private key can be imported.

If you have used Active Directory Certificate Services (AD CS) as your certificate authority, you can configure the certificate authority to archive the private key during the issuing process. This allows the AD CS administrators to recover keys in the event the user loses them or they need to recover protected data. It is not possible to archive private keys for certificates that you have already issued, so this should be part of the planning for the certificate authority when you are planning for its installation.

To be able to archive keys for users, you need to enable the key recovery agent on the Recovery Agents tab of the properties of the certificate authority. When key recovery is enabled, you need to add the certificate of the administrators allowed to do key recovery. This is because these administrators will need to be available during the recovery process. You can set how many key recovery agents you want to use for key recovery. For example, if this is set to two, and you add four key recovery agent certificates to the authority, then two of those four certificates holders are needed to recover a private key. Adding more than one key recovery agent means that private key recovery can be protected by a policy rather than reliant on one individual. Figure 3-43 shows the enabling of the recovery agent and key archival in AD CS.

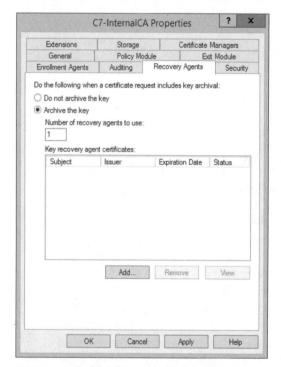

FIGURE 3-43 Enabling key archival in Windows Active Directory Certificate Services

Troubleshooting failed IRM protection

If you have set up RMS protection with AD RMS server and configured Exchange Server to communicate with the RMS server, there are a number of things that you might need to check over to ensure that it is working.

First, ensure that when you set the Super Users group that it already contains the Federation system mailbox as a member of that group. When you add the group to the RMS server, the group membership is checked once every 24 hours; therefore, if you have not added the user at the time of creating the Super Users group, you will need to wait a whole day. This is true even if you add and then remove and re-add the group again.

If you have set up RMS before, maybe for a test environment, and then remove it and add it back again, Exchange Server will have cached certificates. If they are the wrong certificates, you will not be able to encrypt and decrypt content on behalf of your users. Use Set-IRMConfiguration -RefreshServerCertificates to refresh the certificates that the server has cached.

Finally, the output from Test-IRMConfiguration should be checked for any clue to why RMS is not working.

Microsoft has published a troubleshooting guide for AD RMS that can be downloaded from *http://social.technet.microsoft.com/wiki/contents/articles/13130.ad-rms-troubleshooting-guide.aspx*.

This guide ensures that you can do the following:

- Verify that you can get to the pipeline URLs from an AD RMS client computer.
- Make sure that the user at the AD RMS client computer has an email address configured in Active Directory.
- Make sure that the SCP for AD RMS does not have a port specified for it.
- Verify that when using SSL the certificate is trusted by the AD RMS client.
- Verify that the DRM cache is cleared of any failed installation or configuration changes.
- Verify that there are not multiple .GIC or .CLC files installed on the AD RMS client.
- Verify that the IIS application pool is started.

Troubleshooting RBAC

The best way to troubleshoot RBAC issues is to have an account that is not affected by any change you are about to do. You want to ensure that after any change, that same account has the same rights it had before the change.

Remember that RBAC allows both granular and broad control to all aspects of Exchange Server administration and what users can do. If you change an RBAC setting for some users or administrators, it should not affect others and so you always have a way into Exchange to reverse the changes if you need to. (The exception is in the case of *exclusive scope settings* which require you to be in the group or the user with the exclusive settings applied.) Also, for role groups, these are expressed through actual security groups created in the Microsoft Exchange Security Groups OU. If a role group (also known as a security group) is configured to the point where it does not work, you can always remove users from this group or delete the group in the Active Directory tools to resolve the issue. Be careful not to delete the built-in role groups!

EXAM TIP

Get to know the names of the built-in role groups. These built-in role groups are listed at *http://technet.microsoft.com/en-us/library/dd351266.aspx*.

Apart from troubleshooting RBAC permissions, the other consideration is to ensure that you have a good understanding of the RBAC permission model and that there is no requirement to modify access control lists (ACLs) on the Active Directory. In fact, modifying the ACL will not solve any issues because all Exchange and Active Directory interaction happens under the Exchange Trusted Subsystem account and not the user account that is logged in. Exchange Server determines the user's permissions based on the RBAC settings that would be applied to them. Therefore, to troubleshoot RBAC you need to determine three things: the where, the what, and the who. To troubleshoot, make sure you know the what, where, and who that you are expecting RBAC to work with and check the cmdlets, target object, and source user against these settings.

In addition to ensuring the correct permissions, if permissions have been applied, they can be removed by taking away the role assignment. The role assignment is the one-to-one mapping between the scope, the role entry, and the role group. Therefore, there will be assignments for every unique combination of roles; in Exchange Server 2013 CU5, this count was at 195 different role assignments out of the box.

Thought experiment
Granting human resources staff mailbox rights

In this thought experiment, apply what you've learned about this objective. You can find answers to these questions in the "Answers" section at the end of this chapter.

You are the network administrator of Coho Vineyard and your HR department needs to update personal information on users in Active Directory that is also visible in Exchange Control Panel. Because the HR department has mailboxes on Exchange Server 2013, you decide it will be easier to give them access to the attributes they need to change via RBAC.

1. What will your general plan for configuring this requirement be?

2. How will you tell the HR department to make the required changes?

3. Who else could make the same changes?

Objective summary

- Certificates are considered valid if the receiver of the certificate trusts the issuer (that is, has the issuer's public key in their trusted issuer's store), that the current date and time is within the range of the valid dates, that the certificate is not revoked, and that the name on the certificate (subject or alternative subject name) matches the name of the sender.

- Exchange Server uses opportunistic TLS by default and this uses only the certificate public key. It ignores the issuer, date, and subject, and even the revocation status of the certificate.

- CRLs contain the thumbprint of certificates that have been cancelled, or revoked, before their validity period. Each certificate should be checked against a current copy of a CRL.

- Private keys are required to read data encrypted by the public key and to sign data that will be read using your public key. Therefore loss of private key means these two things cannot be done. Therefore having a backup of your digital certificate containing your private key is very important.

- Rights Management Protection is more than NTFS and S/MIME, etc. encryption as it is encryption and policy. It controls whether or not you can see the data you have and what you can do with it.

- RBAC controls the user and administrator's rights within Exchange Server 2010 and later, and unlike access control lists used in Exchange 2007 and earlier, the rights are valid across objects and versions that an ACL may not be.

Objective review

Answer the following questions to test your knowledge of the information in this objective. You can find the answers to these questions and explanations of why each answer choice is correct or incorrect in the "Answers" section at the end of this chapter.

1. You need to restore a certificate to a server and you have the PFX file but do not have a copy of the password. What do you need to do?

    A. You need to export the certificate again from any server that holds the private key and this time set a password and or group membership that can import the certificate.

    B. You can do this by being a member of the local administrators group without requiring the password.

    C. You can do this by being a member of the domain Enterprise Admins group without requiring the password.

    D. You need to export the certificate again from any server that holds the private key and where exports are allowed of that key. This time set a password and or group membership that can import the certificate.

2. You enable AD RMS and integrate it with Exchange Server. You find that running Test-IRMConfiguration fails. You suspect that it is down to it previously working on this server but against a different RMS installation. What should you do?

    A. Run the Super User Wizard on the RMS server and ensure the Exchange Servers group is added here.

    B. Run Test-IRMConfiguration -RefreshServerCertificates

    C. Run Set-IRMConfiguration -RefreshServerCertificates

    D. Run the Super User Wizard on the RMS server and ensure the Federation arbitration mailbox is added here.

3. In what order do you need to create a new RBAC policy and apply it to a user or group?

   A. Remove-ManagementRoleEntry

   B. Add-ManagementRoleEntry

   C. New-ManagementScope

   D. New-RoleGroup

   E. New-ManagementRole

Answers

This section contains the solutions to the thought experiments and answers to the objective review questions in this chapter.

Objective 3.1: Thought experiment

1. The different options that you could evaluate include BitLocker, smart cards, IRM for File Shares.

2. To ensure your Exchange Servers are physically secure you would enable BitLocker using the TPM chip on the motherboard to store the keys. You would also enable AD key recovery should you need to recover keys in the event of disks moving servers and needing to be recovered. You would also want to ensure physical security of the site and visit the hosting company often to ensure this is taking place.

3. You can ensure that your communications with the packaging company are secure by using TlsAuthLevel on a send connector for their domain. Use DomainValidation for TlsAuthLevel. Ensure that they have a send connector back to you that is the same, or a receive connector that requires TLS so that if they start to do clear text communications this would cause the messages to queue.

Objective 3.1: Review

1. **Correct answers:** A, B, D, and F

   A. **Correct:** You need the private key to sign emails.

   B. **Correct:** You need the private key to encrypt a copy of the email that is placed in Sent Items by Outlook, therefore if you do not have a private key you cannot encrypt messages to others as the copy to yourself cannot be created.

   C. **Incorrect:** To read a signed email you need the sender's public key.

   D. **Correct:** You need your private key, which is part of your certificate, to read encrypted emails sent to you by others.

   E. **Incorrect:** You will be able to read signed emails because they are not encrypted.

   F. **Correct:** To open previously encrypted emails that you have sent to others, you need your private key.

2. **Correct answers:** D and F

   A. **Incorrect:** You will be able to sign emails using the new certificate.

   B. **Incorrect:** You will be able to encrypt emails using the new certificate.

   C. **Incorrect:** You will be able to read signed emails from others that use the new certificate.

   D. **Correct:** You do not have your previous private key and so cannot open encrypted emails that use your previous public key.

E.   **Incorrect**: Signed emails are not encrypted and so can still be read.

F.   **Correct**: You need the previous private key to decrypt emails that you previously sent using it. Since you do not have this, you cannot read these emails.

3.   **Correct answer:** D

A.   **Incorrect**: S/MIME is user driven and so is not guaranteed to encrypt all communications to the bank.

B.   **Incorrect**: Domain Secure requires direct Exchange Server mailbox role to Exchange Server mailbox role access using MX records and this does not exist in this case.

C.   **Incorrect**: Opportunistic TLS will encrypt if a certificate is available, but if it is not it will go in clear text. Therefore this answer is not going to guarantee encryption.

D.   **Correct:** Setting TlsAuthLevel to DomainValidation and TlsDomain to the name of the certificate that the hosting company is using.

Objective 3.2: Thought experiment

1.   To secure email between known individuals you should use RMS and optionally Outlook Protection Rules. You could use transport rules to protect content automatically based on the keywords and the sender and recipient as well as educating the users about how to protect messages in Outlook and OWA. Other options include:

   ▪ S/MIME and third-party encryption options (not covered in this book) such as PGP

   ▪ If any communications go offsite, HTTPS for user connectivity along with complex (un-guessable) passwords and maybe remote access to email via a VPN with two factor authentication

   ▪ If email is sent offsite to other servers outside the Exchange organization, to require TLS on communications to these domains and cross-forest RMS or Azure RMS to protect the content at the end point

2.   You would ensure that the RMS transport decryption option is enabled.

3.   You know your business better than we do. Each has a place and it is your role as the messaging administrator to provide the best of service for your company's messaging requirements.

Objective 3.2: Review

1.   **Correct answers:** B and D

A.   **Incorrect:** This is not the name of the cmdlet. The cmdlet for getting RMS configuration is Get-IRMConfiguration.

B.   **Correct:** This cmdlet will tell you the IRM configuration in your Exchange organization.

C. **Incorrect:** The cmdlet is not correct. The cmdlet for testing RMS is Test-IRMConfiguration.

D. **Correct:** This is a valid cmdlet and answer for testing IRM.

E. **Incorrect:** The RMS cmdlet is not the correct name.

F. **Incorrect:** The IRM cmdlet uses -Sender for testing and not –Mailbox.

2. **Correct answer:** D

A. **Incorrect:** The SentToScope parameter is invalid on this answer.

B. **Incorrect:** This is an invalid cmdlet.

C. **Incorrect:** The cmdlet name here is invalid.

D. **Correct:** This cmdlet is correct.

3. **Correct answer:** B

A. **Incorrect:** This is a valid arbitration mailbox but is not the Federation mailbox.

B. **Correct:** This is the federation mailbox and so is the one needed for RMS super user rights. Full details of the steps to configure RMS for Exchange Server 2013 can be found at *http://technet.microsoft.com/en-us/library/dd351212(v=exchg.150).aspx.*

C. **Incorrect:** This is a valid arbitration mailbox but is not the Federation mailbox.

D. **Incorrect:** This is a valid arbitration mailbox but is not the Federation mailbox.

Objective 3.3: Thought experiment

1. To audit the possible changes in configuration, you would use administrator audit reports to view for who removed the eop@ mailbox on the assumption that it existed and now does not. If the mailbox was deleted in Active Directory, by the deletion of the user account, it would not be audited. You would use the same technique to view the audit log of Exchange Online Protection (EOP) via Remote PowerShell to EOP.

Objective 3.3: Review

1. **Correct answers:** C and D

A. **Incorrect:** You can receive audit reports in OWA without changing your mailbox policy. You will not be able to view XML files though, and the policy for XML files would need to be set for this policy, and that is covered in a different answer.

B. **Incorrect:** This is not a valid thing to do.

C. **Correct:** This change allows the OWA policy used by the compliance offer to view XML files in OWA if used in conjunction with answer D.

D. **Correct:** This change allows the OWA policy used by the compliance offer to view XML files in OWA if used in conjunction with answer C.

2. **Correct answer:** B

A. **Incorrect:** This is a valid arbitration mailbox but is not the mailbox audit reports are stored in.

B. **Correct:** This is the mailbox used for administrator audit reports and so is the one that must be migrated to Exchange 2013.

C. **Incorrect:** This is a valid arbitration mailbox but is not the mailbox audit reports are stored in.

D. **Incorrect:** This is a valid arbitration mailbox but is not the mailbox audit reports are stored in.

Objective 3.4: Thought experiment

1. In general, you would create a management scope for all mailboxes or a subset if that were required. Then, you would create a management role based on the Mail Recipients existing role, from which you would remove the cmdlets not needed and leave any in that are still required. Finally, you would create a role group and add the HR staff to it.

2. You would get them to use OWA and then change to ECP using the cog icon or directly to the ECP URL.

3. The users will have the rights to make the same changes, as would anyone else in the role group or with rights allocated via other management role assignments.

Objective 3.4: Review

1. **Correct answer:** D

   A. **Incorrect:** You will need to export the certificate and private key again, but this can only be done from servers where the key is exportable.

   B. **Incorrect:** You will need the password or this PFX file is not readable.

   C. **Incorrect:** You will need the password or this PFX file is not readable.

   D. **Correct:** You can only export the key from a server where it was marked as exportable from when it was imported.

2. **Correct answer:** C

   A. **Incorrect:** Checking super user will not fix this.

   B. **Incorrect:** This is not a valid cmdlet.

   C. **Correct:** This cmdlet will refresh the certificates on the Exchange Server and should replace older certificates.

   D. **Incorrect:** Checking super user will not fix this.

3. **Correct answer:** The correct sequence for these steps is C, E, A, B, and then D.

## CHAPTER 4

Configure and manage compliance, archiving, and discovery solutions

In this chapter you will look at managing compliance, archiving, and discovery solutions. Specifically we will look at Exchange Server archiving, which is not to be confused with journaling. Sometimes these two terms are used to describe each other. You will also look at the new data loss prevention product in Exchange Server and Exchange Online, and also the Message Records Management (MRM) feature set. With the MRM feature set, you will only look at the newer aspects of this, which are known as retention policies. You will then finish the chapter with a review on how eDiscovery is performed, and how the individual compliance features can be set up. Begin by taking a look at archiving.

Objectives in this chapter:

- Objective 4.1: Configure and manage an archiving solution
- Objective 4.2: Design and configure Data Loss Prevention (DLP) solutions
- Objective 4.3: Configure and administer Message Records Management (MRM)
- Objective 4.4: Perform eDiscovery
- Objective 4.5: Implement a compliance solution

Objective 4.1: Configure and manage an archiving solution

In Exchange Server 2010, a new feature was added called the archive mailbox. The idea behind the archive mailbox came about because Exchange storage on a disk is designed to use just a bunch of disks (JBOD) disk configurations, and replicate the data for redundancy across a Database Availability Group (DAG), and not to require the use of a storage area network (SAN) or a redundant array of independent disks (RAID). This means that the cost of implementing the storage for Exchange Server can be considerably reduced compared to Exchange Server 2007 or 2003. Also, due to changes in the database structure for Exchange, the size of the mailboxes can be increased. This increase in possible mailbox size means more storage is required, and with more data being transferred electronically, and the desire of users to keep more content for longer, this also means more storage is being consumed.

But this is contrary to a common mailbox configuration of small quotas, which typically come about either historically because of small (a few GBs) mailbox size in older versions of Exchange, or because Exchange is hosted on expensive storage. Therefore, users typically take content out of Exchange Server and store them in .pst files all over the network. The network is a place that is not designed to hold .pst files because they are not designed to be accessed over the network.

Therefore, how do you keep the data in Exchange, and keep a business requirement of small quotas because disk storage is probably still too expensive for large mailboxes? In the timeframe of the release of Exchange 2010, the solution was to have an archive mailbox. It was not until Service Pack 1 for Exchange 2010 that the archive mailbox could be located on a different database than the primary mailbox, or even for the archive to be stored in the cloud in Exchange Online.

With storage of the archive being on a different disk from the storage of the mailbox, it became possible to hold current data on the expensive, fast storage that Exchange was running on, to move the older data to an archive, which was running on cheaper storage or where less copies were kept on the DAG or even online, and so the cost of holding a large mailbox was becoming realized. Additionally, the added advantage of removing .pst files came to the fore. Instead of holding the .pst files on some network storage somewhere (and taking up space there), it could be held on Exchange and accessed from Outlook anywhere, not just on the LAN, and replicated and subject to eDiscovery searches in Exchange, rather than being isolated silos of information that could not easily be discovered.

To that end, this section of the chapter will look at some aspects of configuring the archive mailbox in Exchange 2013. The exam objective domain covers the following four items in the order given, though this is not really the best way to consider them from a practical use scenario.

This objective covers how to:

- Set up online archiving (Office 365)
- Create archive policies
- Set up on-premises archiving
- Plan storage for an archiving solution

Setting up online archiving (Office 365)

As mentioned above, it is possible to store your archive mailbox in Office 365. Before you look at setting this up, it is important to note that you can have the following mailbox configurations:

- Mailbox on-premises, no archive.
- Mailbox on-premises, archive on-premises.
- Mailbox on-premises, with the archive mailbox in Office 365.
- Mailbox in Office 365, no archive.
- Mailbox in Office 365, with the archive mailbox also in Office 365.

Note that the combination of a mailbox in Office 365 and archive on-premises is not possible. You can have the mailbox on-premises and the archive with it, or in the cloud, but if you have a cloud mailbox in Office 365, the archive needs to be in Office 365 with your mailbox.

To have an Exchange Online archive that is your mailbox archive in Office 365, you need to have purchased a license for online archiving. There are many Exchange Online licenses, or SKU (stock keeping unit), but not all of them provide an Exchange Online archive. The simplest way is to purchase the Exchange Online Archiving SKU, which is, at the time of writing, $3 USD per user per month. The details of this product can be found at *http://products.office.com/en-us/exchange/microsoft-exchange-online-archiving-archiving-email*, and a local price rather than US dollars can be found by changing the country/region option at the top right. Exchange Online Archiving is also available for a 30-day trial for 25 users. This product is the archive only and nothing else.

Other ways to purchase an online archive is to purchase either of the two Exchange Online products. Exchange Online is the product that provides mailboxes in Office 365. For Exchange Online there are two license options (or plans) known as P1 and P2. These Exchange Online plans are described *at http://products.office.com/en-us/exchange/compare-microsoft-exchange-online-plans*. It can be seen from this page that both the P1 and P2 plan contains Online Archive, but that the P2 license allows for unlimited storage for that archive. That is, the P1 plan allows for 50 GB of storage across both the mailbox and online archive, and you cannot store more than 50 GB. The P2 plan allows for a 50 GB mailbox and an unlimited archive.

In comparison to Exchange Online licenses, Office 365 licenses are typically packages of licenses from other products that can be bought separately, such as Exchange Online, Lync Online, and SharePoint Online, and a full copy of Microsoft Office Business, or Microsoft Office Professional Plus. Therefore, if you buy an Office 365 license that contains an Exchange Online P2 license, you get archiving and unlimited storage, whereas if you purchase an Office 365 license that contains an Exchange Online P1 plan, you get 50 GB mailbox storage. Examples of Office 365 licenses that include the P2 Exchange Online SKU are the E3 and E4 (the "E" stands for Enterprise) licenses, or the Academic E1 for Faculty licenses.

If you have an existing Office 365 subscription you can check if you have the ability to create online archives by logging *into http://portal.office.com* (as Global Admin or Billing

Admin) and clicking Purchase Services on the left-hand menu, and then clicking View Current Subscriptions on the right. This can be seen in Figure 4-1.

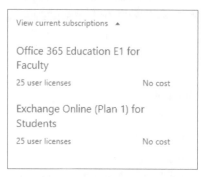

FIGURE 4-1 Viewing your current subscriptions in Office 365

In Figure 4-1, this organization has an academic plan that includes 25 licenses for Exchange Online (Plan 1). This is the Exchange Online P1 plan, which does not include the unlimited archive option. The other subscription in Figure 4-1 is an Office 365 subscription. To see the details of this subscription (which plans it includes), you need to look under the licenses for any user.

For existing and already licensed users, you can click on the user's name in the Office 365 portal, and then select the license's tab. This is shown for a single user in Figure 4-2. This shows that the Office 365 Education E1 for Faculty license is a group of products that contains the Exchange Online P1 license, and so from the viewpoint of online archives, is limited to a shared storage maximum of 50 GB across both the mailbox and archive.

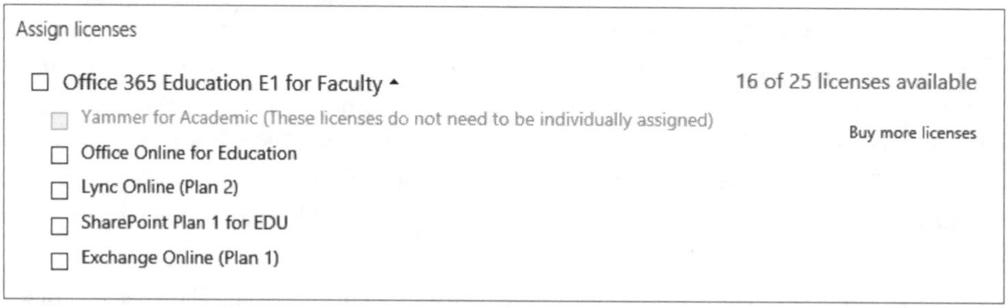

FIGURE 4-2 Viewing individual licenses assigned to users

When you create a user in Office 365 you get the option to set the license as part of the creation process. This can be seen in Figure 4-3. If users are created on-premises and synced to Office 365 using DirSync, licensing needs to be done via remote Windows PowerShell (for bulk updates), or individually in the Office 365 portal before an archive can be created.

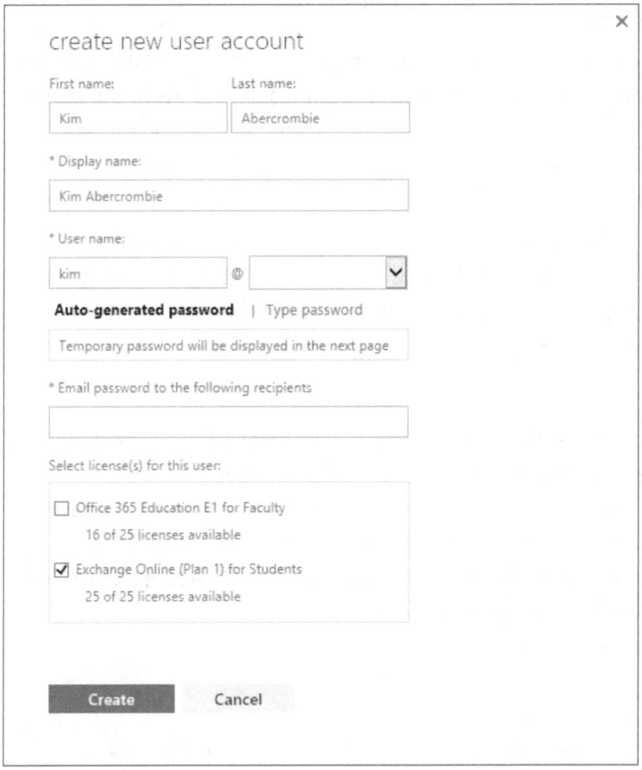

FIGURE 4-3 Creating a user and assigning a license at the same time

---

NOTE **READING USER'S LICENSES**

You can also read a user's licenses with Remote PowerShell.

Once you have a license or a trial subscription with the online archive feature included in it, you can go about setting up the online archive. How you do this depends upon where the user's mailbox is. It is easier to set up the online archive when the user's mailbox is a cloud-based mailbox, rather than an on-premises mailbox. If there is an on-premises Exchange organization with hybrid mode enabled, but the mailbox is stored in the cloud, then this adds a bit of extra configuration to the online archive setup process. Therefore, you will look at setting up the archive from these three different viewpoints separately. Later in the book you will look at archives stored on the on-premises Exchange Server.

Archives for cloud mailboxes

A cloud mailbox is one that was created using the Office 365 portal, or New-MSOLUser in Remote PowerShell. It is not a user account that is created on-premises, and exists in the Office 365 by way of DirSync. Users that exist in the cloud by way of DirSync need to be modified on-premises, but cloud users and mailboxes are modified in the cloud. Therefore, to create an archive for a cloud user you complete the following steps:

1. Add an Exchange Online Archiving license if you need an unlimited archive and the current license does not include the rights to an unlimited archive. If you want just a 50 GB mailbox + archive maximum then you do not need to purchase new licenses.

2. Enable the archive in the Office 365 portal or via Remote PowerShell.

3. Use the archive.

Step 2 is the step where the actual configuration of the archive takes place. If you are using Remote PowerShell to administer Office 365, start a PowerShell session and either type the following cmdlets to connect to Exchange Online, or save the following cmdlets in Notepad to a .ps1 file Connect-ExchangeOnline.ps1 and then run the script by typing **Connect-ExchangeOnline.ps1**. This code will connect you to Exchange Online and Azure Active Directory, which is the directory where your cloud users are kept.

```
#Script to connect to Exchange Online
$cred = Get-Credential
Write-Host "Username: " $cred.username
$host.ui.RawUI.WindowTitle = "Azure AD and Exchange Online - " + $cred.username
Connect-MsolService -Credential $cred
Write-Host "...connected to Office 365 Azure Active Directory"
$ExchangeSession = New-PSSession -ConfigurationName Microsoft.Exchange -ConnectionUri
https://ps.outlook.com/powershell -Credential $cred -Authentication Basic
-AllowRedirection
$ExchangeSessionResults = Import-PSSession $ExchangeSession
Write-Host "...connected to Exchange Online"
```

Note that in this code, the $ExchangeSession line, which prints to three lines, is all one line of code.

To run the code you need to install the Office 365 remote administration PowerShell cmdlets. The latest version of these can be downloaded from *http://aka.ms/aadposh*. These also require the Microsoft Online Services Sign-In Assistant for IT Professionals to be installed. The download page for that is also reachable from *http://aka.ms/aadposh*.

Once you run the script you will need to enter your global admin credentials and password, and then you will be connected to Exchange Online and Azure Active Directory. The above script shows you the username in the title bar of the window as well. This is shown in Figure 4-4, and is useful if you are a consultant and have different windows open that are connected to different Office 365 tenants at the same time.

FIGURE 4-4 Remote PowerShell connected to Azure Active Directory and Exchange Online

You do not need to install any software for the Exchange Online cmdlets to work because they are all remote, and are downloaded on the fly when you connect.

Once you are connected over Remote PowerShell type **Get-MsolUser** to list all of your users and type **Get-Mailbox** to list all of your mailboxes. Cloud mailboxes with not have the LastDirSyncTime property set, so they can be found with Get-MsolUser | ft UserPrincipalName ,LastDirSyncTime.

To enable an existing mailbox to have an archive you run Enable-Mailbox <name> -Archive. For <name> you can use their user principal name (UPN) from Get-MsolUser, or other naming info that Exchange can use, such as email address, display name, or alias.

To see who has an archive already, run Get-Mailbox -Archive. To see info about the archive, try a cmdlet such as Get-Mailbox <name> | Format-List Name,*archive*, which will return all of the archive information for the mailbox. You should see values such as ArchiveStatus being Active and ArchiveState being Local. Figure 4-5 shows some of the same information.

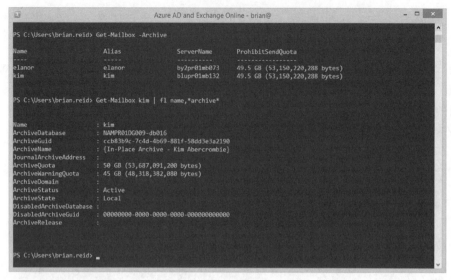

FIGURE 4-5 Remote PowerShell to Exchange Online showing archive mailboxes and further info

To configure an online archive in the Office 365 portal you still need the licenses as discussed above, and you still need to have Global Admin rights. You login using a web browser to *http://portal.office.com*, but unlike Remote PowerShell, you do not need to install any software.

To enable an archive for a user, locate the user from the Users sidebar menu, and then locate Active Users, and select the row for the user of interest. The row for the user should read "In cloud" under the Status column. Do not click the user's name because that will take you into licensing. On the right, click Edit Exchange Properties, as shown at the bottom of the figure in Figure 4-6.

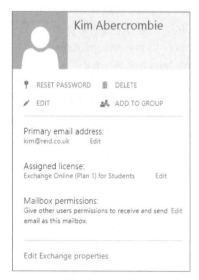

FIGURE 4-6 Viewing a user's properties in the Office 365 portal

Clicking Edit Exchange Properties will take you to the recipient details for that user in Exchange Control Panel (ECP) for Exchange Online (*https://outlook.office365.com/ecp/*). This info can also be accessed via ECP directly, rather than via the Office 365 portal.

Click the Mailbox Features menu item, and scroll down to the Archiving section. Here you will see an entry saying Archiving: Disabled, and a link underneath it to enable it. To turn on an online archive for a user, click Enable Here.

To bulk enable the archive for a lot of users, use Remote PowerShell. For example, if you wanted to enable the archive for all users who have an Oxford office, you would run the following.

```
Get-User | where {$_.City -eq "Oxford"} | Enable-Mailbox -Archive
```

This is where some of the power of PowerShell can be seen.

Archives for remote mailboxes in hybrid mode

When you have users in Exchange on-premises, and have hybrid mode already enabled so that you have linked your on-premises deployment to your Office 365 tenant, you can move your on-premises mailboxes to Office 365. The steps for doing this are covered in the next section because you are going through this process in order of increasing complexity.

Any user account that exists in Office 365 because the user properties were synced from the on-premises Active Directory to the Azure Active Directory is still modified by making changes to the on-premises object. Therefore, for users who's mailbox is stored in Office 365 but are in hybrid mode, the user object is still managed from the local on-premises Active Directory. Therefore, to enable an online archive for these users, you need to update the local Active Directory and have those changes synced to the cloud. Only when those changes are synced to the cloud does the archive get created.

Just like cloud users, both PowerShell and ECP can be used to make these changes to the Active Directory, but unlike the cloud users, it is Exchange Management Shell in the on-premises environment, or ECP for the on-premises environment. Start with PowerShell, or specifically start Exchange Management Shell on an Exchange 2010 or 2013 on-premises server.

Like the remote PowerShell cmdlets looked at above, you can use similar cmdlets here. To see which mailboxes in the cloud have an archive already, run Get-RemoteMailbox -Archive, and to see info about the archive, try a cmdlet such as Get-RemoteMailbox <name> | Format-List Name,*archive*, which will return all of the archive information for the mailbox. You should see values such as ArchiveStatus showing as Active and ArchiveState being HostedProvisioned. Figure 4-7 shows some of the same information.

FIGURE 4-7 Viewing a remote mailbox from Exchange on-premises

Figure 4-7 shows that the user already has an archive that is both hosted and provisioned. When you first set up an archive for a user (by using Enable-RemoteMailbox -Archive) it can take up to six hours to appear in this state of HostedProvisioned. This is because the setting to enable the archive is made where the user's account exists, which is on-premises. Azure DirSync will replicate these changes to your Azure Active Directory tenant that you get with Office 365 once every three hours. When the change reaches Azure AD it is replicated almost immediately to the directory used by Exchange Online. Once the change is in this directory, it is picked up by processes in Exchange Online, and the archive is provisioned.

Once the archive is provisioned, the changes to the user's properties (such as the ArchiveState and the ArchiveDatabase) are updated and written back to Azure Active Directory (these can be seen via Remote PowerShell to Exchange Online). Three hours later, at the next scheduled DirSync interval, some of these changes are written back to the on-premises Active Directory, and can be seen in Exchange PowerShell on the on-premises Exchange Control Panel. The user can use the archive once it is provisioned and before information about it is synced back to the on-premises Exchange server. However, it cannot be further administered until this information is synced back to the on-premises Active Directory.

The process for creating an archive in Exchange Control Panel has the exact same behind-the-scenes process as described earlier because the Exchange Control Panel runs Enable-RemoteMailbox -Archive for you when you enable an archive for a mailbox that is already in the cloud. To enable an archive for a mailbox in Office 365, when in hybrid mode, open

Exchange Control Panel on-premises and click on Recipients. Then select the remote mailbox (they will have "Office 365" as their mailbox type) and click Enable, under In-Place Archive on the right. This is shown for a user in Figure 4-8. Notice there is no option to create an archive in the on-premises deployment. The only supported location for a remote mailbox to have an archive is also remote in Office 365.

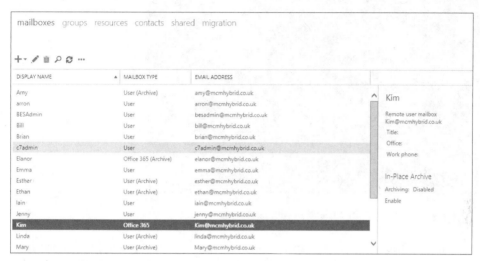

FIGURE 4-8 Enabling archives for remote mailboxes in Exchange Server on-premises

Archives in Office 365 for on-premises mailboxes

The final option to look at for creating an archive in Office 365 is for users with on-premises mailboxes. For this configuration you need to configure hybrid mode, and this is discussed in detail in the next chapter. Once you have a working hybrid configuration, you create the archives in a similar way to the cloud user, but like the remote mailbox you do the work on-premises.

From the Exchange Management Shell, to see who has an archive already, run Get-Mailbox -Archive. To see info about the archive, try a cmdlet such as Get-Mailbox <name> | Format-List Name,*archive*, which will return all of the archive info for the mailbox. You should see values such as ArchiveStatus indicating if the archive exists or not, and if it has already been provisioned in the cloud, and ArchiveState being Local. Figure 4-9 shows some of the same information.

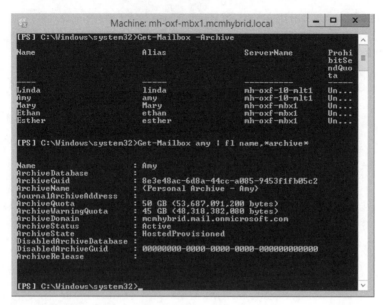

FIGURE 4-9 Viewing on-premises mailboxes with hosted archives

To enable a mailbox to have a remote archive, the cmdlet is slightly different than the ear-lier examples because here it is possible to have an archive on-premises or in Office 365. To create an archive in Office 365 for an on-premises mailbox you use Enable-Mailbox <name> -RemoteArchive -ArchiveDomain *tenant.mail.onmicrosoft.com*. The ArchiveDomain value is the Office 365 tenant email routing domain, which will be your tenant's name followed by mail.onmicrosoft.com. You can get the tenant mail routing domain from Get-RemoteDomain.

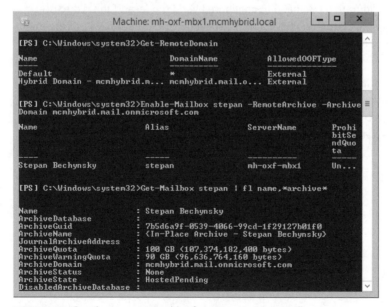

FIGURE 4-10 Creating a remote archive for an on-premises mailbox

Again, you need to wait for the archive settings to synchronize to Office 365, for the archive to be provisioned, and for the new settings to sync back to the on-premises Active Directory, which on a normal DirSync schedule is somewhere between three and six hours before the user can see and use the archive. The creation process via Exchange Management Shell can be seen in Figure 4-10. In this figure you can see the output of Get-RemoteDomain to show you the tenant routing domain, the Enable-Mailbox -RemoteArchive cmdlet, and the archive settings on the mailbox when this is complete, but before the three to six hours (if DirSync is working) have gone by, notice that the ArchiveState is HostedPending, and the ArchiveStatus is None. The user will not see an archive in Outlook or OWA until ArchiveStatus reads Active.

> **NOTE ARCHIVE NAMES**
>
> The name of the Online Archive product set has changed over the years since its launch. Depending upon when the archive was created, it could have a different name. For example, in Figure 4-10, the archive name is In-Place Archive - Display Name, after its current branding, but in Figure 4-9, on an archive created in 2013, it is called Personal Archive - Display Name. It has also been called Online Archive, if you go back a few years. In Exchange 2013, its correct name is the In-Place Archive, and if the archive is in the cloud and the mailbox on-premises, this is Exchange Online Archiving.

To create an archive in Office 365 for an on-premises mailbox using Exchange Control Panel, you first need to login to Office 365 from ECP using the Office 365 link in the blue banner at the top of the page. In Internet Explorer, this requires that both the Exchange Online portal at *https://outlook.office365.com,* and the ECP URL be added to the Trusted Sites zone.

Once you have logged into Office 365, you can create archives both on-premises or in Office 365 for on-premises mailboxes. Figure 4-11 shows the archive creation dialog box.

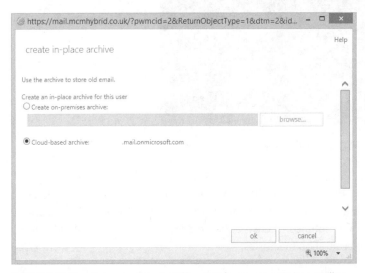

FIGURE 4-11 Creating an archive in Office 365 for an on-premises mailbox

When you already have an existing archive for an on-premises mailbox, you can move it to Office 365 from ECP using the move mailbox process and selecting to move the archive mailbox only.

> **IMPORTANT   RESTORING FUNCTIONALITY IN CU6**
>
> If you are running Cumulative Update 6 for Exchange Server 2013, you need to run the script that can be downloaded from *http://www.microsoft.com/en-us/download/details.aspx?id=44050* to restore the Exchange Online functionality.

Creating archive policies

When you enable an archive for a mailbox, as well as the archive configuration, a retention policy called the Default MRM Policy is configured on the mailbox. This can be seen in Figure 4-12, where the cmdlet Get-Mailbox brian | fl RetentionPolicy is run. It shows no retention policy on the mailbox, followed by enabling a remote archive, followed by querying the user's retention policy again. The second time, immediately after the archive is requested, the retention policy can be seen as Set.

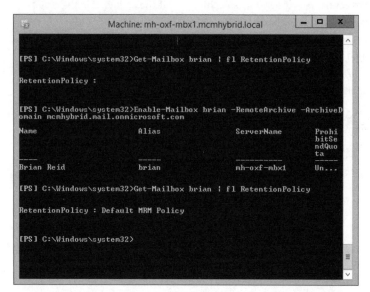

FIGURE 4-12 Seeing a retention policy applied after the archive is enabled

This policy is the default policy for Exchange Server 2013, and is applied automatically when an archive is provisioned. In Exchange 2010, the default policy was called the Default Archive and Retention Policy. Both the Default MRM Policy and the 2010 default policy are identical and contain the name settings. There is a third hidden retention policy (hidden in ECP) that sets retention on arbitration mailboxes.

If you want to apply different archive policies to users, you either modify the Default MRM Policy by changing the different retention tags that it includes, or you create a new retention policy and customize the tags found inside that policy. Later in this chapter you will look at creating and customizing retention policies and retention tags, but the exam objective domain covers the creating and customizing of archive policies, and archive tags before it covers retention policies.

This order is worth considering because an archive policy is a retention policy, just one that moves items to the archive rather than deleting them. To see your archive policies in Exchange Management Shell along with some useful information, run the following one line cmdlet.

```
Get-RetentionPolicyTag | where {$_.RetentionAction -eq "MoveToArchive"} | FL
Name,Type,AgeLimitForRetention,RetentionAction
```

This returns all of the MoveToArchive retention tags. As can be seen from Figure 4-13, there are five retention tags that move items to the archive.

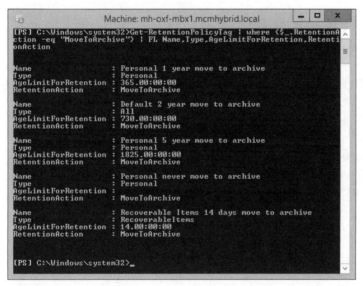

FIGURE 4-13 Archive policies

You can see from the output of these archive policies tags, one retention tag has the type value as All. This retention tag will apply automatically to all messages in a mailbox, and only one retention tag of type All exists by default.

It is worth at this point discussing the terminology used here. A retention tag is a setting that controls how long content is held for before being deleted or archived. A tag can be a default tag (Type=All) and applies to all items in a mailbox, or applies to a specific folder, or be Type=Personal, which is available for the user to use themselves and is not applied by default. In comparison, a retention policy (and not a retention tag) is a collection of tags. The collection of tags that make the policy can be applied to a mailbox. Therefore, the Default

MRM Policy, which is applied to mailboxes when the archive is enabled, is just a collection of tags. It is the tags that control the archiving or deleting.

Because a retention policy consists of a series of retention tags, if you want to customize the options available to the user, you create new tags and add them to the user's policy. A single policy can only have one tag of type All that deletes content, and one tag of type All that archives content. The policy can have one tag that applies to a given folder (that is you could have two tags that archive the Conversation History folder at 30 days and 120 days, but only one of these tags could belong to one policy). The other could belong to a different policy. A policy can contain as many personal tags as you need.

To create new MoveToArchive tags you can either use PowerShell (New-RetentionPolicyTag <name> -Type All|Personal|<FolderName> -RetentionAction MoveToArchive -AgeLimitFor Retention XX [in days]), or use Exchange Control Panel, as shown in Figure 4-14.

In Exchange Control Panel, click on the Compliance Management menu, and then click Retention Tags. From the new icon, choose the type of tag you want to create from the following list:

- Applied Automatically To Entire Mailbox (Default) [Type=All]
- Applied Automatically To A Default Folder [Type= Calendar, Contacts, DeletedItems, Drafts, Inbox, JunkEmail, Journal, Notes, Outbox, SentItems, Tasks, ManagedCustom-Folder, RssSubscriptions, SyncIssues, ConversationHistory, Personal, RecoverableItems, NonIpmRoot, LegacyArchiveJournals]
- Applied By Users To Items And Folders (Personal) [Type=Personal]

Each of the dialog boxes for each of the above options are slightly different. For example, a default folder tag cannot be used for archiving, and personal tags come with the note that you need an Enterprise Client Access License, the Exchange Online Archiving License. The P2 Exchange Online plan includes the Exchange Online Archiving License, but the standard Exchange CAL for on-premises mailboxes does not cover this functionality.

FIGURE 4-14 Creating an archiving retention tag

Once the tag is created it can be added to a retention policy. If you made a default dele-tion tag, it can only be added to a new policy because each policy can only have one default deletion tag and one default archiving tag (or you remove the existing default tags and add your new one). You can add any number of personal tags as you require, though as they are for users to select from, don't have too many because it will confuse the user interface and the user's ability to select them sensibly.

To add a new retention policy, or a tag to an existing policy, go to the Retention Policies tab on ECP. Figure 4-15 shows the error when you try to add two or more default retention tags to the same retention policy.

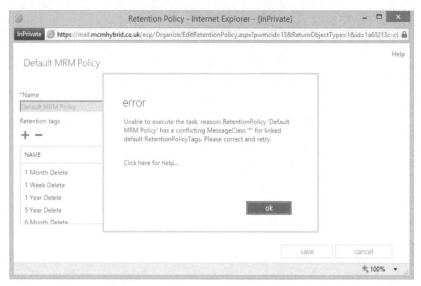

FIGURE 4-15 Error on adding more than one default retention tag to a retention policy

Setting up on-premises archiving

Planning archive storage is covered in the next section, but once you have done that, you enable an on-premises archive for an on-premises mailbox with Enable-Mailbox <name> -Archive for random database distribution (a database in the site that you run the cmdlet in will be chosen), or Enable-Mailbox <name> -Archive -Database <db_name> to select a specific database.

To complete the task of creating an archive for a user using ECP you select the user, and click Enable, under In-Place Archive.

Planning storage for an archiving solution

Since the release of Exchange Server 2010 Service Pack 1, the database that you store the archive mailbox in has not needed to be the same database as the primary mailbox. Other than that, the database that stores archive mailboxes is just a mailbox database and has nothing different about it compared to any other mailbox database. Therefore, the following statements are all valid with regard to archive mailboxes:

- Archive mailboxes can be protected with Database Availability Groups (DAGs).
- Archive mailboxes can be stored on the same database as the mailbox.
- Archive mailboxes can be stored on a different database as the mailbox.
- The mailbox database and archive mailbox database can be on different servers within the same Exchange organization.

What needs to be taken into consideration though is the impact on storage. Just like a mailbox database, the archive mailbox will grow, but how soon will depend upon the archive policies in place. If the rate of email arriving in a user's mailbox is stable over time, it will mean that eventually the archive policy will be archiving the same amount of email that is arriving into the primary mailbox database. Therefore, it is more likely that the archive database will grow, and the primary database will stay the same size, or grow at a lower rate (given mail flow staying the same). This should be taken into consideration on database sizing, and therefore it is usually recommended to distribute archive mailboxes across the same databases as primary mailboxes to spread the load evenly, unless different storage profiles on hardware of DAG replication are required for the archive mailbox.

Thought experiment
Planning an archive migration to Office 365

In this thought experiment, apply what you've learned about this objective. You can find answers to these questions in the "Answers" section at the end of this chapter.

As the School of Fine Art's storage administrator, you want to investigate the requirements for setting up Exchange Online Archiving so that the large mailbox storage, which contains a fair share of old emails, can be moved to the cloud.

1. You currently have an Exchange Standard CAL and Enterprise CAL for each faculty member, and a standard CAL for each student. What different options could you evaluate that are already included with your Exchange Server license?

2. What do you need to put in place to integrate Exchange Server and Exchange Online Archive?

3. You decide to move your students' email that is more than one semester old to the Exchange Online Archive. How will you achieve this?

Objective summary

- Archiving in Exchange Server requires an Enterprise CAL for on-premises archives, or an Exchange Online Archive license per user for an archive stored in Office 365.
- The Exchange P1 and P2 plans in Office 365 contain the rights to do archives, but the P2 plan is an unlimited archive.
- Cloud mailboxes can have an archive in Office 365, but not on-premises.
- On-premises mailboxes can have an archive on-premises or in the cloud.
- Hybrid mode and DirSync are prerequisites for archiving in Office 365 with on-premises mailboxes.
- Retention policies and retention tags with the MoveToArchive action are used to automate the moving of messages to the archive based on their original arrival date.

Objective review

Answer the following questions to test your knowledge of the information in this objective. You can find the answers to these questions and explanations of why each answer choice is correct or incorrect in the "Answers" section at the end of this chapter.

1. Which of the following retention tag actions can place emails in the archive?

   A. MoveToArchive

   B. Archive

   C. CopyToArchiveAndDeleteFromSource

   D. All

2. What will the Exchange Management Shell cmdlet Enable-Mailbox <name> -Remote-Archive -ArchiveDomain tenant.mail.onmicrosoft.com do?

   A. It will create an In-Place Archive on Office 365 for a mailbox in Office 365

   B. It will create an In-Place Archive on Office 365 for a mailbox on-premises

   C. It will create an In-Place Archive on-premises for a mailbox in Office 365

   D. It will create an In-Place Archive on-premises for a mailbox on-premises

3. What is the default retention policy that is applied?

   A. Default Archive Policy

   B. Default Archive and Retention Policy

   C. Default MRM Policy

Objective 4.2: Design and configure Data Loss Prevention (DLP) solutions

One of the new features in Exchange Server 2013 is the Data Loss Prevention (DLP) feature. This is a feature that examines the subject and body of messages to look for patterns and sequences of data that could be considered to be the sort of data that you would not want to send (or receive) by email. For example, an email containing a number of credit cards (or even one), or an email with multiple names and addresses on it. You wouldn't want to send the first of these emails because it's probably not encrypted, and you wouldn't want to send the second email because it might be an accidental or even malicious privacy leak. For both examples, email is not the way to send this information.

Before Exchange Server 2013, this information inspection and then restriction of the message could be done with transport rules and regular expression (RegEx) filtering, but it is complex to write, and with a slight variation in the RegEx or in the data, it might get through.

In Exchange Server 2013, there is a new component known as the deep text extraction engine, and a new set of transport rule predicates that can react to the results of the text extraction engine. These predicates, or conditions, then have the option to fire an action to reject or require approval of the message, or do anything else a transport rule can do.

The DLP feature also comes with the ability to monitor, but not act upon, the findings of the deep text extraction engine, which is auditing rather than enforcing, as well as alerting the user in Outlook 2013 (or OWA after Service Pack 1). Creating DLP rules from templates, custom rules, and reporting are also facets of the feature.

> **This objective covers how to:**
> - Set up pre-built rules
> - Set up custom rules
> - Design a DLP solution to meet business requirements
> - Set up custom policies

Setting up pre-built rules

There are almost fifty DLP templates that ship with Exchange Server 2013, and these will cover health, finance, and PII (personally identifiable information), as well as a handful of other scenarios specific to certain legal requirements and laws in different parts of the world. As these templates already exist, and just require enabling in Exchange, these are the best ways to get a start on the DLP feature set.

The templates are available in both Exchange Online and Exchange 2013 on-premises and are accessible from both ECP and PowerShell, but in this scenario ECP is much easier to use for the setting up and configuring of the DLP templates and resulting rules.

To create a new set of DLP rules (which is typically five new transport rules with a related DLP function), you navigate to Compliance Management, and then the Data Loss Prevention tab. On this screen you can customize the text shown in Outlook/OWA for the user when they add text to their emails that hits the DLP criteria (policy tips). If you are using Exchange Server 2013 Service Pack 1 or later you can upload a standard document format and have Exchange look for the sending of the text of that document (the document fingerprints feature). Finally, on this screen you will see a list of the DLP policies that are configured. If you are using Exchange Online (as shown in Figure 4-16) it will give you some on screen figures and reports for DLP matches and false positives.

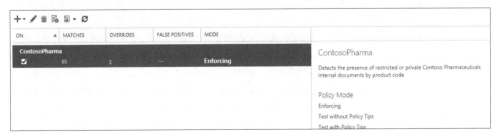

FIGURE 4-16 DLP policies and reporting as shown in Exchange Online

The example shown in Figure 4-16 is a custom example, which you will look at later because by default there are no DLP policies in the list.

To add a new DLP policy, and the transport rules that comprise that policy, you click the + icon, and choose New DLP Policy From Template. From here you can pick from the approximately 50 templates to choose from. Figure 4-17 shows you the setting up of a template to find French financial data. The default template allows users to override the rules as well as warning the user about the content of the message if between 1 and 10 matches are found in an email. The default rule also blocks the message if 10 or more matches are discovered in a single email, though of course the user can override this. These actions and count values can all be changed.

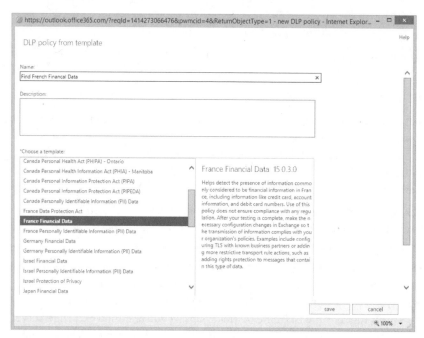

FIGURE 4-17 Creating a DLP policy from a template

In the example in Figure 4-17, the description reads as follows (this will give you a good idea of the purpose of the template):

Helps detect the presence of information commonly considered to be financial information in France, including information like credit card, account information, and debit card numbers. Use of this policy does not ensure compliance with any regulation. After your testing is complete, make the necessary configuration changes in Exchange so the transmission of information complies with your organization's policies. Examples include configuring TLS with known business partners or adding more restrictive transport rule actions, such as adding rights protection to messages that contain this type of data.

When you have selected the correct template, and have given the policy a name, you click Save, and then wait while the policy and related transport rules for the DLP template are created.

Upon creation of the policy, the first thing you will see is that the policy starts in a mode called Testing Without Policy Tips. A Policy Tip is a notification to a user of Outlook 2013 (via Exchange Web Services) that their email contains content that might be against policy. These tips are also present in OWA from Service Pack 1 and later. So note that by default there is no notification to the user. The "testing" part of this mode indicates that the policy is being tested and that if violations of the rules are found, they will not be enforced. Thus, the policy is running but no user will be affected by it. Administrators can use this state to audit the impact of this policy and see if it has any matches. If so, to whom, and therefore the sort of business impact this will generate if Policy Tips or enforcement of the policy was enabled.

FIGURE 4-18 A newly added policy in mode

Before you enforce the policy, it is worth making it clear here that the policy is now working and scanning all emails. Because the policy is written to the Active Directory for storage, in Exchange on-premises you will need to wait for replication to complete around your entire Exchange organization before all Exchange Servers will pick up this change from the Active Directory and start examining emails. Just because you are not yet blocking content does not mean the policy is not being run against current messages being sent.

Before you enforce a policy, you will look at what the parts are so that we can customize it if your business requirements mandate it. In Exchange Control Panel, change to the Mail Flow section, and the Rules tab. Here you will see one or more transport rules for each policy. Typically, you will see five transport rules for each policy as described above. Each rule here can be customized and enabled or disabled. Back on the Compliance Management/Data Loss Prevention page, you can enable all of the rules in the policy (or disable them) in one go rather than enabling or disabling on a per transport rule basis. The individual transport rules for the Find French Financial Data policy created above can be found in Figure 4-19.

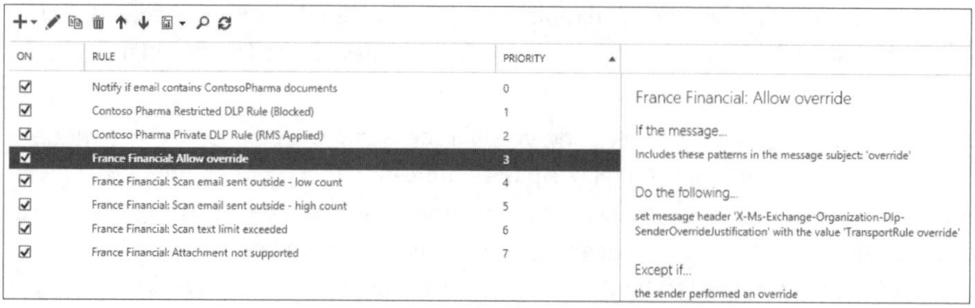

FIGURE 4-19 The Transport Rules page with the DLP policy rules shown

In Figure 4-19, the transport rules #3 to #7 are the five rules created by the new DLP policy. Any other transport rules that were already configured will have a higher priority number and remain in place.

You can see from Figure 4-19 that the transport rules look for the following:

1. Has the user overridden the fact that a DLP hit was found? This is a scenario that can occur once Testing With Policy Tips or Enforcing mode are enabled. In Outlook or OWA, the user is alerted that they are in violation of a DLP policy by way of a Policy Tip, or in any other email client by way of an NDR message back when they sent the message that contained the data that was to be blocked. If the user is allowed to override the decision in the third rule (the High Count rule), this first rule allows for that, and allows the message to skip further DLP processing by way of adding a message header.

2. Notify the user that DLP violations were found, but less than 10 of them (Low Count), and allow the user to send the message.

3. Notify the user that DLP violations were found, but 10 or more of them were found (High Count), and block the user from sending the message, but allow the user to override this decision. The word "override" is added to the subject in any email client, or the user is allowed to select the override option if they are using Outlook 2013/ OWA.

4. The fourth rule is what to do if the message is too large. This is important as any content in violation of the DLP rules might be at the bottom of the large email and thus not scanned.

5. The final rule is what to do if the message contains attachments that Exchange Server cannot scan. This is important because any content in violation of the DLP rules might be in the attachment that Exchange Server does not have an indexing filter for, and thus not scanned.

Any of these rules can be modified, such as not allowing overrides (in which case the first transport rule for the policy can be deleted), or changing the count values, or encrypting with Rights Management Services (RMS), or moderating emails that are too large or with attachments that cannot be scanned. Figure 4-20 shows changing the last rule in the policy to have the message moderated by the user's manager in the Active Directory if it cannot be indexed.

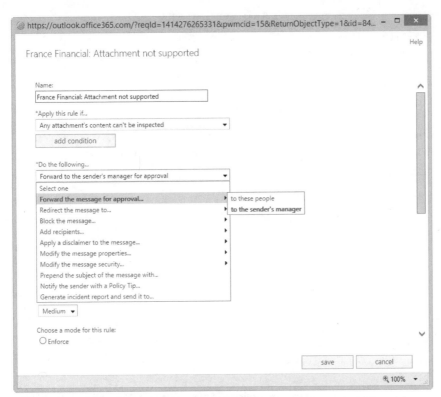

FIGURE 4-20 Enabling moderation on the Attachment Not Supported DLP policy rule

Setting up custom rules

Because DLP policies are just a collection of rules that act on the results of the deep text extraction engine, it is possible to modify the existing rules and create new ones.

If this is the case, what then is the DLP Policy? The DLP Policy is a collection of the transport rules that you work on, enable, and disable as a single unit. Therefore, if you created a policy for US financial data, there would be five transport rules that are not being enforced (testing without Policy Tips). You could change each of the five rules to either of the two enforcing options (testing with Policy Tips, or enforced) individually, but it would be done one at a time and you could end up configuring one differently from the others. Therefore, the place to enable a DLP Policy is in the Data Loss Prevention area of ECP, as all the related rules would be enabled together. Also, the best place to modify individual DLP rules, and add or remove rules, is also via the compliance management area of ECP because then you add or remove the rules from the policy.

To add or remove a rule, navigate to Exchange Control Panel, Compliance Management, Data Loss Prevention, highlight the policy, and click the Edit icon. The resulting dialog box is shown in Figure 4-21.

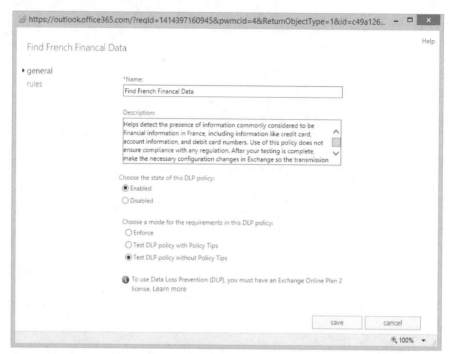

FIGURE 4-21 The DLP Policy editing dialog box

From the General tab you can change the policy to Enforce or Test DLP Policy With Policy Tips. Enforcing the policy will result in all of the rules in the policy being set to this level. From this point onward, any email that is found to match the policy will be rejected if the rule action is Notify The Sender With A Policy Tip, and the setting for this action includes Block The Message. Typically, on the built-in DLP templates, this action and property is found on the High Count rule.

If the policy is changed to Test DLP Policy With Policy Tips, users in Outlook 2013 and OWA (with Exchange 2013 SP1 or later) will be told their email contains DLP content, but they will not be blocked from sending it. This enforcement level can be looked at as a user education feature.

> **NOTE GETTING DLP WORKING IN OUTLOOK**
>
> The exam objective domain does not cover how to get DLP working in Outlook, and so it is not covered in detail in this book. In brief, Outlook learns about DLP Policies via Exchange Web Services. So AutoDiscover needs to be working and it will download policy updates once every 24 hours, and only on opening a new email in Outlook. Therefore, changes to the policy on the server might not appear on the client immediately. To force the change to the client, look up the PolicyNudges registry key online or in KB2823261.

On the Rules tab of the Policy Edit dialog box (Figure 4-22) you can edit the DLP rules as well as remove them, or add new ones. Though the resulting dialog box that appears for a new rule or an edit looks the same as the dialog box for transport rules in general, it is keeping the relationship between the rule and the DLP Policy so that actions that are policy wide will affect this rule. Create the rule in the transport rules area unrelated from the policy, and it will have the same effects and actions, but will not appear as a rule related to the policy, and will not be managed by the policy (and if running Exchange Online, will not show additional reporting for the policy on matches, overrides, and false positives).

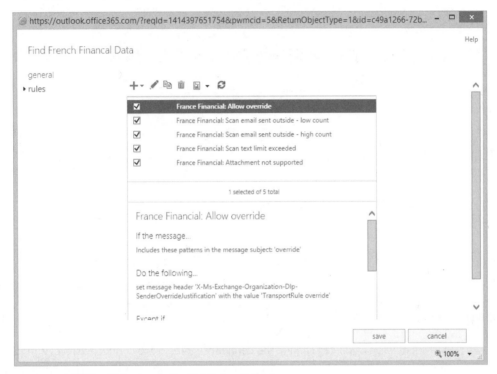

FIGURE 4-22 Editing DLP rules via the DLP Policy dialog box

For example, to remove the override function from the DLP Policy, you would disable or remove the first rule in the set, and then edit the High Count rule to Block The Message, but not to give the option to allow overrides. You would change the NDR text as well because that says that you can override the message, but if the override rule (the first one in the policy typically) is disabled, then you cannot override the rule.

Another common modification to DLP rules is to change the count value. The default rule in the template of a low count rule is set to fire the rule if less than 10 matches are found in an individual email. A high count rule exceeds 10 matches. Figure 4-23 shows the count value being modified. This can be reached by editing the high or low count rule, and then clicking The Message Contains Sensitive Information property in the rule.

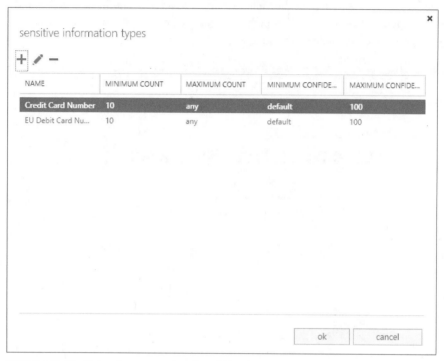

FIGURE 4-23 Modifying the count values for a DLP rule

As well as count values, you can change the confidence level. If the confidence level is reduced, more emails will be found meeting the policy, but more false positives will be found as well. Confidence is the DLP engines ability to say if a match is really a match. For example the number 4111-1111-1111-1111 in an email may look like a credit card number, but if the word "expiry" was found near it as well as the brand name of a credit card company, then the server's DLP engine would have a higher confidence that the match was found. The rule will only fire if the confidence level determined by the DLP engine that the text was a match exceeds the confidence level of the rule. The default confidence level takes the confidence coded into the DLP engine. If the DLP engine thinks something is a match then the rule will fire.

Designing a DLP solution to meet business requirements

To design a DLP solution for your business, you need to know what your business requirements are with regards to sending and receiving information, and to determine what information, if sent, would be considered a potential loss of data. For some businesses, this data loss could be an act that would be illegal, or face considerable financial penalties, or loss of customer confidence. A search on the Internet for loss of confidence keywords and the names of some well-known retailers in your country/region that this has happened to, will show you just what we are talking about.

As well as deciding what templates to use to make up your policy, you also need to consider the enforcement level. You should always start with Testing Without Policy Tips to get an idea if enforcing the policy will actually block any data. You should also consider the languages used by your users, and then to customize the Policy Tips that will be displayed. The Outlook client will display a language appropriate tip, if one is available.

Finally, you need to consider the actions to take for the rules that you are enforcing. The default actions in the template of warning via Policy Tips for less than 10 matches, and blocking for more than 10, might not be appropriate.

In Exchange Server 2013 Service Pack 1 and later, as well as in Exchange Online, there is a DLP action called Generate Incident Report And Send It To. This will generate an email with the information that the rule found, and why the rule fired on this email, and send it to the mailbox of choice. This is a good way to audit DLP incidents on-premises (where there is no reporting without installing third-party software or trawling the message tracking logs). For an incident report you can also choose what to include in the report.

Setting up custom policies

As well as setting up a DLP Policy via the templates, you can add DLP actions to a standard transport rule. Table 4-1 details the different transport rule conditions, and Table 4-2 details the actions that are related to DLP. In the Apply This Rule If column, the PowerShell cmdlet is listed for reference as well.

EXAM TIP

As settings can be changed in Exchange Server and Exchange Online using both Exchange Control Panel and Exchange Management Shell (on-premises) or Remote PowerShell (Exchange Online), it is important to be aware of the cmdlets used to configure settings, as well as the way to complete the task in ECP.

TABLE 4-1 Transport rule conditions for Data Loss Prevention

Apply This Rule If	Parameters	Description
The recipient is located [SentToScope]	Inside or outside of the organization or partner organization if using Exchange Online.	Typically, DLP is used to block or limit mail flow outside the organization, and so this transport rule condition is commonly used, but removing or changing it will allow you to have DLP rules that work inside the organization as well, if required.
The message contains sensitive information [MessageContainsDataClassifications]	The different sensitive information classifications in Exchange can be added here. This allows you to take a country/region specific template and add more country/region rules to it for example. You can also upload your own document fingerprints and select them from here, or import custom-made data classifications or templates, and use them here.	This is the main feature of the DLP rule. This is the rule action that looks for the existence of content that should be restricted. If the transport rule does not contain this condition, it is not a DLP transport rule.

TABLE 4-2 Transport rule actions for Data Loss Prevention

Apply This Rule If	Parameters	Description
Notify the sender with a Policy Tip [SenderNotificationType]	Nofity but allow to send. Block the message. Block unless a false positive. Block but allow override. Block, but allow override with justification of the override. If blocked, you can also set the default Policy Tip text.	This is the action that causes Outlook 2013 and OWA to alert the user before the message is sent. In the case of Outlook it happens while the message is being composed, in the case of OWA as it is being sent but before the send actually occurs.
Generate incident report and send it to [IncidentReportContent], [GenerateIncidentReport] and [IncidentReportOriginalMail]	The recipients of the incident report and the message properties to include in the report.	This allows a report to be sent to a selected user or users on every rule that matches. This can include the original email, as well as a description of the rule that fired and the reason why the rule fired. Even if the message is blocked and the user did not successfully send the message, the incident report will be generated.

Thought experiment
Blocking credit cards in email

In this thought experiment, apply what you've learned about this objective. You can find answers to these questions in the "Answers" section at the end of this chapter.

You manage the Exchange Online service for Margie's Travel, and have previously enabled a financial DLP Policy suitable for your country/region. As per recommendations, you enabled the policy, but left it in Test DLP Policy Without Policy Tips so that it was auditing matches to the policy without notifying users. After a few weeks you noticed a trend that showed a number of emails per day contained credit card numbers being sent from your organization to the Internet.

1. How do you enable the DLP rules to start to notify users that their actions are not appropriate for the content that they are sending?

2. What considerations do you need to take before you enable a full block of sending emails that match policy?

3. How would you enable a pilot or test phase for the impact of this data on your business before enabling it for all users?

Objective summary

- The Exchange Server Data Loss Prevention (DLP) feature uses text analysis and transport rules to audit or enforce restrictions to sending email.

- Because it is based on transport rules, any rule condition, action, or exception can be utilized in addition to the DLP conditions and actions. For example, you could moderate messages rather than block them.

- DLP rules should be modified via the DLP Policy dialog box, and not via Transport Rules directly.

- Incident reports became available with all of the headers and options in Exchange 2013 Service Pack 1.

- Use the default template settings for testing DLP, but for real world usage, customize the rules, actions, and properties to suit your business requirements.

Objective review

Answer the following questions to test your knowledge of the information in this objective. You can find the answers to these questions and explanations of why each answer choice is correct or incorrect in the "Answers" section at the end of this chapter.

1. Which transport rule condition is required for a DLP rule?

   A. HasClassification

   B. SentToScope

   C. Description

   D. MessageContainsDataClassifications

   E. UseLegacyRegex

2. Why should you modify DLP rules via the compliance management pages in ECP, and not the mail flow pages?

   A. Changing a rule in the mail flow pages will not take effect

   B. Changing a rule in the mail flow pages will take longer and might result in simple errors, such as missing a setting on a rule

Objective 4.3: Configure and administer Message Records Management (MRM)

In an earlier section of this chapter, you looked at archiving policies and described them as retention policies with a specific action. In this section, you will look at the other actions that make up retention policies, and how to create them and apply them to other users.

> **This objective covers how to:**
> - Design retention policies
> - Configure retention policies
> - Create and configure custom tags
> - Assign policies to users
> - Configure the Managed Folder Assistant
> - Remove and delete tags

Designing retention policies

Retention policies are used to ensure that data is kept only for a certain length of time. To ensure that data is held regardless of a user's action to delete the data, you need to look at the legal/litigation hold or In-Place Hold features of Exchange Server, and these are covered in the next objective of this chapter.

When a retention policy is applied to a mailbox, all messages are affected with the settings of the policy. When the message is older than the duration set by the policy, the action on the message takes effect. To achieve this, the policy is made up of the following:

- **Retention policy**   This is a collection of retention tags. There are two retention polices in Exchange 2013 by default, the Default MRM Policy that can be applied to user's mailboxes, and the ArbitrationMailbox policy that is only visible in PowerShell and used to keep the content of arbitration mailboxes manageable.

- **Retention tag**   These are the parts of retention policies that control the duration of the retention. To make a retention policy, you need to have the retention tags made first.

To design a retention policy, you need to make a retention tag for each duration, as well as a folder and action that you want to manage data for. You can have as many retention policies as you need, and you can place a retention tag into multiple retention policies, but a tag can only affect a user or be selected by a user, if it is in the policy that is applied to the user's mailbox.

NOTE **THE EFFECT OF REMOVING RETENTION TAGS FROM THE POLICY**

In the event that a user actively tags messages with a retention tag, and then that tag is removed from the policy, the messages are still affected by this retention tag but no more messages can be tagged with that retention tag.

It is worth at this point discussing the terminology used here. A retention tag is a setting that controls how long content is held for before being deleted or archived. A tag can be a default tag (Type=All) and apply to all items in a mailbox, or apply to a specific folder, or be Type=Personal, which is available for the user to use themselves, and is not applied by default. In comparison, a retention policy (and not a retention tag) is a collection of tags, and the collection of tags that make the policy can be applied to a mailbox. Therefore, the Default MRM Policy, which is applied to mailboxes when the archive is enabled, is just a collection of tags, and it is the tags that control the archiving or deleting.

To create a retention tag, you need to decide the scope of the tag. A tag can apply to all items in a mailbox, all items in a folder, or any item that a user wants it to apply to. The more specific tags take effect over the more general tags. That is, if a mailbox retention tag (of Type=All) is applied to a policy to delete email after five years, and a user applies a personal tag (Type=Personal) specifically to an individual message that will never delete that message, this message will not be deleted while the tag is applied to it, even if the message arrived in the mailbox over five years ago.

The retention tag that applies to all of the items in a mailbox is known as a default tag, and only one default tag can be added to a retention policy. Therefore, the number of different default durations you need for your organization will typically determine the number of retention policies that you create.

A retention tag that applies to a given folder can be added to a retention policy in addition to the one default tag added, but you can only add one tag for each folder. That means if you want a policy to delete the Lync Conversation History folder after six months, you could create a default folder tag for the Conversation History folder for 180 days, but you could not add any more retention tags for the same folder to the same retention policy. Figure 4-24 shows the error you get if you add two folder tags for the same folder to the same policy.

error

Unable to execute the task, reason: RetentionPolicy 'mcmhybrid.onmicrosoft.com\Executives Retention Policy' has multiple tags with Type 'ConversationHistory'. Only a single tag is allowed for a specific system folder type.

Click here for help...

ok

FIGURE 4-24 Adding two retention tags for the same folder to a policy

The final retention tag that you can have is the personal tag. This requires an Exchange Enterprise CAL or Exchange Online P2 plan to be used because it can apply to any message anywhere, and not just those in standard folders. Users apply personal tags when they need to so that they can override the default tags. If there are no personal tags in a policy (for example if the user is not licensed to have personal tags, or if overriding the policy is not allowed), the user cannot apply their own tags, and therefore are subject to the retention policy of the organization as applied to their mailbox.

For each tag you have an action that can be applied. The Move To Archive action was covered earlier in this book, and this section covers the rest. These are Delete, Allow Recovery (DeleteAndAllowRecovery in the shell), and Permanently Delete (PermanentlyDelete in the shell). In Exchange Management Shell you will also see the following values for RetentionAction: MoveToDeletedItems, MoveToFolder, MarkAsPastRetentionLimit, and MoveToArchive. MarkAsPastRetentionLimit cannot be set in ECP, but will cross out messages in Outlook 2007 and label them as expired in later versions of Outlook. The MarkAsPastRetentionLimit property will not delete or archive them.

Configuring retention policies

The exam objective domain discusses creating policies before creating tags, but this is not the way that it works because a retention policy is just a collection of tags. But as this book follows the exam objective domain, it is written in this order, though you would create the tags first.

Once you have designed your policy, preferably on paper or a whiteboard because creating it on the server and applying it could result in unexpected message loss, you can proceed with the creation of the retention tags, and then the policy. You will probably create one policy for the overall default retention period that you need (or you would customize the Default MRM Policy), and then additional policies for every group of mailboxes that the default policy is not suitable for. The only value you set for a retention policy is a name, and this is displayed to the Exchange Administrator only. The remaining settings are adding the retention tags to this policy. Figure 4-25 shows a retention policy that will ultimately be applied to the executive mailboxes being created.

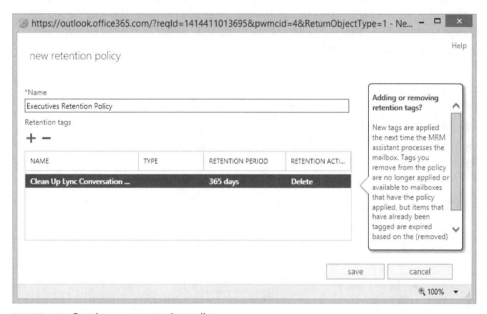

FIGURE 4-25 Creating a new retention policy

Creating and configuring custom tags

The majority of the work in creating a retention policy goes into the retention tag creation process. You only really need to create one default tag that applies to all items in the mailbox. All the other retention tags are additional to this default policy. Typically, Exchange administrators will create a retention policy tag for the deleted items and junk email folders, as well as sent items. For companies with more complex rules of retention, further folders are added to the policy. Remember that if the default policy tag is the same as any folder policy in terms of age and action, a specific folder policy tag is not required.

Finally, you would create the personal tags if you have the licenses to do this, and the business need to allow users to override administrator defaults.

Previously this chapter discussed the Type setting for the policy tag, and that we can only have one of the same type in a given retention policy, but if you are creating more than one policy, you might have more than one retention tag of the same type. Retention tags can be used in more than one policy. For example, imagine a scenario where you have two policies: general staff and executive staff. The design of the system calls for a seven-year retention period, but you decide that only executive staff can have the option to override this. Therefore, you would need two retention policies, but the mailbox default retention tag of Permanent-lyDelete at 2557 days can be applied to both policies. The executive policy would then get extra personal tags added.

If you add retention tags to a policy that deletes content, and you allow personal tags, you should consider whether or not you have a retention tag of type personal that has no action or duration (see Figure 4-26). Users can set this tag on emails that they know they need to keep beyond the default time and action of the folder they are located in. By default there is a personal tag already created in Exchange Server called Never Delete, which covers this exact scenario.

NOTE **TAGGING MESSAGES IN A TAGGED FOLDER**

When a message is tagged with a retention tag, it overrides the settings of the folder it resides in. You need to remove the tag from the message (or apply a different tag) to change the action on the message.

FIGURE 4-26 The Never Delete personal retention tag

The Delete And Allow Recovery tag will move messages into the Recovery Deleted Items folder. This is the same action as the user performs when they empty the Deleted Items folder. If the system is configured to allow the recovery of deleted items (and typically this is set to 14 days per database), the user has a second chance to recover these items. Note that items that this retention policy applies to, does not need to be in the Deleted Items folder to be deleted. The item will go from whatever folder it is in, to the Recover Deleted Items folder directly.

The Permanently Delete tag action will purge the message from the mailbox, and so it cannot be recovered. Therefore, if you are testing this tag out and you apply a six-month PermanentlyDelete tag to a policy as the mailbox default, any item older than this period of time will be purged from the mailbox. Use this tag with care.

Typically, the time of the action of the retention policy is based on when the item arrived in the mailbox because most items in your mailbox arrived there as an inbound email. For items such as calendar items, they are based on the date the item was created.

The default mailbox tag will apply to the Calendar folder (and calendar and tasks items in other folders) by default. So if you wish to maintain a calendar or tasks folder for a different duration than the mailbox default, you need to create and add to the retention policy a folder policy for the calendar and tasks folders.

EXAM TIP

Know what you can add to a retention policy. Know that you can add one mailbox retention tag that deletes messages (or deletes and allows recovery) and one default that allows archiving. Understand that if you have added both to a policy, the archive tag should have a lower age limit than the deletion tag, otherwise the message will be deleted on that number of days since creation/arrival in mailbox, and therefore cannot be archived to the In-Place Archive on a later number of days because it has already been deleted.

Assigning policies to users

Once you have the retention tags created and the correct tags applied to your policies, you can assign polices to users. Take care when doing this because unrecoverable changes to the mailbox could occur with regards to the removal of messages and other data.

You can apply a retention policy to a mailbox in two ways. The first way is via the Exchange Control Panel, and the second is via PowerShell. Let's look at both.

To set a single mailbox to use a retention policy in ECP, select the mailbox on the recipient's page, and click the Edit icon. From the dialog box, select the Mailbox Features page, and then apply a retention policy to the mailbox. This is shown in Figure 4-27.

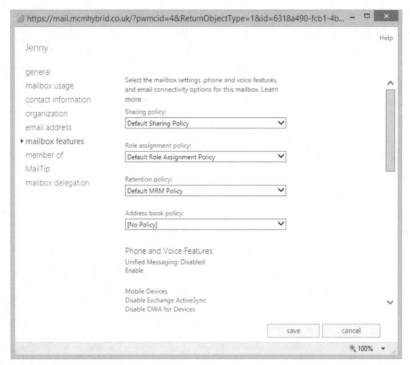

FIGURE 4-27 Applying a retention policy to a mailbox in Exchange Control Panel

To add a policy to one or more users in PowerShell, start Exchange Management Shell for on-premises mailboxes, or Remote PowerShell connected to Exchange Online for mailboxes in Office 365, and use Set-Mailbox <name> -RetentionPolicy <PolicyName> to do a single mailbox. Use any PowerShell query to return more than one mailbox, and pipe that into the Set-Mailbox -RetentionPolicy <PolicyName> cmdlet.

One retention policy is the default retention policy, and by default this is the Default MRM Policy. This is applied automatically to all Exchange Online mailboxes on creation, and to all on-premises mailboxes when an archive is assigned to them. You can change this default retention policy using Set-RetentionPolicy <PolicyName> -IsDefault $true.

Configuring the Managed Folder Assistant

Once a user is assigned a policy (or they get an archive) then the Managed Folder Assistant will begin to process the messages in their mailboxes. This processing will happen once a day, and never more frequently. At the time of processing, each message is evaluated against the current policy of the mailbox, or any folder policy or personal policy on the item. Messages that are ready for archiving are moved to the In-Place Archive (if one exists), and messages that are ready to be deleted or purged based on their creation or arrival dates, are deleted or moved to the recover deleted items folder.

Therefore, you do not need to schedule the Managed Folder Assistant, nor start it manually, as was needed in Exchange 2010. You can use the Start-ManagedFolderAssistant against selected mailboxes to add the mailbox to the processing list for the assistant rather than waiting for it to be picked up by the assistant automatically. This is ideal for testing scenarios, but should not be needed for mailboxes in a normal working environment, unless you want to force the assistant to reprocess a mailbox because the wrong policy was applied!

The default policy in Exchange Online is the Default MRM Policy. This policy contains only a two-year archive tag, and some personal tags, as well as a 30-day deleted items folder tag. Therefore, although the mailboxes in Exchange Online get the default retention policy automatically, the only immediate impact is that the deleted items folder is a 30-day folder by default. Therefore, take caution at moving users to the cloud who use their deleted items folder for archiving content.

Figure 4-28 shows the notice at the top of any email that was in the Deleted Items folder after your mailbox was moved to Office 365 (unless you set a different DeletedItems folder policy, or applied a different retention policy to the mailbox).

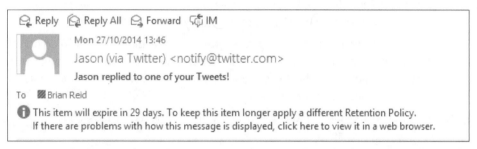

FIGURE 4-28 The headers of an Exchange Online message in Outlook when the message is in Deleted Items

The Managed Folder Assistant runs once every day and will check all mailboxes automatically. This can be changed using Set-MailboxServer and the ManagedFolderWorkCycle property. By default it is daily, and so all mailboxes should get processed once a day and will get added to the processing list within the day that they have a retention policy applied or updated.

You can use the following to report on the ManagedFolderWorkCycle setting for all of your mailbox servers in your organization. You cannot view or change this setting in Exchange Online.

```
Get-MailboxServer | Format-Table Name,ManagedFolderWorkCycle* -Auto
```

Removing and deleting tags

The tags that are available to users are controlled by what is in the policy that is applied to the user's mailbox. As an Exchange administrator, you have two options to control tags after a policy has been applied. You can either change the tags in the user's policy, or apply a new policy. Both options will result in a new set of tags being available that are different than the earlier set. There could be some overlap if some tags are left in the existing policy, or if the newly assigned policy has some of the tags that where in the old policy. In the case where the tag remains in the policy and therefore is available to the user, it will still affect the user's content as it did before, and if it is a personal tag, the user can still assign it to their content.

If users have the ability to apply personal tags to their content, they have ultimate control over the retention settings on content. If you remove a personal tag from a user's policy, that user is not able to apply that tag any more, but the content that is already tagged with the now unavailable tag remains with that tag until it has a new tag assigned. Also, because the tag has been removed from the policy, but is still stored in the Active Directory, the Managed Folder Assistant knows what the tag's properties are and will process the message based on this information.

If a tag is deleted from the Active Directory, as well as being removed from all of the policies it was allocated to, the Managed Folder Assistant now does not have information regarding what the tag should do, and so will actively remove that tag from the mailbox items during the processing cycle. This is considerably more resource intensive than just removing a tag from a policy because removing a tag does not actually affect items.

Finally, for removing and deleting tags, there is a scenario to consider where you do not remove or delete the tag, but you move the item from folder to folder, where sometimes these folders are tagged or where the items themselves are tagged. There are three simple rules for retention tags when items are moved:

- If a mailbox item moved from one folder to another, it inherits any tags applied to the folder into which it's moved.

- If an item is moved to a folder that doesn't have a tag assigned, the default policy tag is applied to it.

- If the item has a tag explicitly assigned to it, the tag always takes precedence over any folder-level tags, or the default tag.

A good example of this last example exists in Exchange Online. If an item is deleted it goes into the deleted items folder, where it gains the retention tag applied to Deleted Items from the default policy. If the item is then moved back into another folder it will keep its 30-day deletion tag because there are no other default deletion tags in the default retention policy in Exchange Online.

Objective summary

- Retention policies ensure that messages are removed or archived from Exchange after a given duration.

- Retention policies do not ensure that data is held for a given duration.

- Retention policies contain retention tags. There are two types of retention tag, the archive tag and the deletion tag.

- Archive tags move content to the users In-Place Archive if one exists. If there is no In-Place Archive, the tag has no effect

- Deletion tags delete content. The tag setting allows for permanent deletion (no recovery), or a recovery period where the content can be recovered from the Recover Deleted Items folder in Outlook or OWA.

- You can have retention policies that apply to the mailbox or to folders. Archive tags and deletion tags can apply to the mailbox, but only deletion tags can apply to folders. Personal tags (both archive and deletion) can be at the user's discretion to assign.

- Only one mailbox level archive tag, and one mailbox level deletion tag can be applied to a retention policy. Only one folder level deletion tag can be applied, per folder, to a retention policy. As many personal tags as you require can be added to a policy.

- Archiving and deletion of messages is run by the Managed Folder Assistant based on the time of item creation or arrival in the mailbox. Therefore, you need to have archive policies of a shorter duration than deletion policies, or the item will be deleted before it is archived.

Objective review

Answer the following questions to test your knowledge of the information in this objective. You can find the answers to these questions and explanations of why each answer choice is correct or incorrect in the "Answers" section at the end of this chapter.

1. You have the following retention tags. You need to create a policy that will ensure that messages in the Deleted Items folder are kept for two weeks, and messages over two years old are archived. You also need to ensure that the mailbox and archive do not hold messages that are over five years old. Which of the following tags do you add to your policy? (Choose all that apply.)

   A. Name: "Keep Deleted Items for 2 Weeks"; AgeLimitForRetention:2; RetentionAction: DeleteAndAllowRecovery;Type=DeletedItems

   B. Name: "Keep Deleted Items for 2 Weeks"; AgeLimitForRetention:14; RetentionAction: DeleteAndAllowRecovery;Type=DeletedItems

   C. Name: "Archive After Two Years"; AgeLimitForRetention:730; RetentionAction: MoveToArchive;Type=All

   D. Name: "Archive After Two Years"; AgeLimitForRetention:730; RetentionAction: MoveToArchive;Type=Mailbox

   E. Name: "Delete After Five Years"; AgeLimitForRetention:1826; RetentionAction: PermanentlyDelete;Type=All

   F. Name: "Delete After Five Years"; AgeLimitForRetention:1095; RetentionAction: PermanentlyDelete;Type=All

2. How many retention policies can you apply to a mailbox?

   A. One

   B. Two, one archive policy and one delete policy

   C. Three, one archive and two delete

   D. As many as your business requirement needs

Objective 4.4: Perform eDiscovery

Exchange Server eDiscovery is a set of features that allow the discovery manager class of user to find, and if required, remove content from some, or all of the user's mailboxes. At its core is the search functionality, which uses the indexing functions of Exchange Server. The same functions that help the user locate the contents in their mailbox are used to help the discovery managers locate content they need to find.

In this objective you will look at configuring eDiscovery, as well as some of the associated features that enable holding data so that it is not deleted from the mailbox database until a configured time period has gone by. You will also look at journaling to ensure that a copy of all messages, sent and received, are copied to separate storage.

This objective covers how to:

- Plan and delegate RBAC roles for eDiscovery
- Enable a legal/litigation hold
- Perform a query-based In-Place Hold
- Design and configure journaling
- Perform multi-mailbox searches in Exchange Administration Center (EAC)
- Evaluate how to integrate In-Place federated searches with Microsoft SharePoint

Planning and delegating RBAC roles for eDiscovery

To enable eDiscovery searches, permissions must be granted to allow users to have the rights to search other user's mailboxes for discovery purposes. By default, no users or admins have the right to do eDiscovery, and so therefore users can only search mailboxes that they can open. An eDiscovery manager does not get permission to open a mailbox, but will get permission to search the mailbox using the eDiscovery tools in Exchange Control Panel.

Though the administrator is not able to do eDiscovery by default, they are able to add users or their own account if required to the RBAC role group that provides eDiscovery. This group is called Discovery Management. Members of this group get two roles. The first role is to perform eDiscovery (the Mailbox Search role), and the second role grants the rights to enable Legal Hold on a mailbox (Legal Hold role).

> *IMPORTANT* **EDISCOVERY SECURITY CONSIDERATIONS**
>
> Members of the Discovery Management role group can access sensitive message content. Specifically, these members can use In-Place eDiscovery to search all mailboxes in your Exchange organization, preview messages (and other mailbox items), copy them to a Discovery mailbox, and export the copied messages to a .pst file. In most organizations, this permission is granted to legal, compliance, or Human Resources personnel.

If you have a limited scope of mailboxes that you want to allow search and Legal Hold to be performed against, you can create a custom management scope for either or both roles mentioned above. Creating a custom scope is covered in the RBAC objective in chapter 3.

Regardless of whether you use the default role group, or a custom role group with a custom scope, once it is enabled you need to add the users who will get these roles. This is done from EAC or PowerShell for Exchange Server on-premises, or Exchange Online. When you are using Exchange on-premises you can also directly add users to the role group in Active Directory. In ECP the user is added to the role group via Permissions, and then Admin Roles. In Exchange Management Shell, or Remote PowerShell to Exchange Online, you would use the following cmdlet.

```
Add-RoleGroupMember -Identity "Discovery Management" -Member <mailbox_alias>
```

Enabling a legal/litigation hold

In an earlier objective you looked at retention hold. That is a technology to ensure that content does not stay too long in a mailbox, but it does not stop a user actively deleting content. The legal hold features in Exchange Server 2013 and Exchange Online ensure that the content is kept in the mailbox database until the In-Place Hold policy expires, or if the mailbox is using Legal Hold, the content is kept forever (Exchange Online) or until the mailbox is deleted (Exchange on-premises). Note that if the user who is subject to Legal Hold deletes content, the item remains in the mailbox database even though the user now cannot access it as they think it has been deleted. For users that edit content, the hold process keeps previous copies of the item in immutable storage.

> *NOTE* **OWA, LEGAL HOLD AND DELEGATES**
>
> Ensure that you are running Exchange Server 2013 Cumulative Update 7 to cover an issue with Outlook Web App and mailboxes that are on hold where the mailbox is delegated to users who are not on hold.

To enable a user to be on Legal Hold (which was known as Litigation Hold in Exchange 2010), you need to have an Enterprise CAL for that user in Exchange on-premises, or a P2 plan mailbox in Exchange Online. Once you have the correct license, a hold can be enabled with Set-Mailbox or Exchange Control Panel. To enable Legal Hold using PowerShell, run the following cmdlet. This cmdlet also sets a time limit to the hold of two years.

```
Set-Mailbox elanor -LitigationHoldEnabled $true -LitigationHoldDuration 730
```

If you use LitigationHoldEnabled without LitigationHoldDuration being set, you enable a permanent legal hold that means all content in the mailbox is kept forever.

To enable Legal Hold in Exchange Control Panel, select your user in the recipients page and view the In-Place Hold value on the properties pane to the right. To then enable, or disable, hold for a mailbox, click the Edit icon when the user is highlighted, and change to the mailbox features tab and scroll down to click Enable under Litigation Hold.

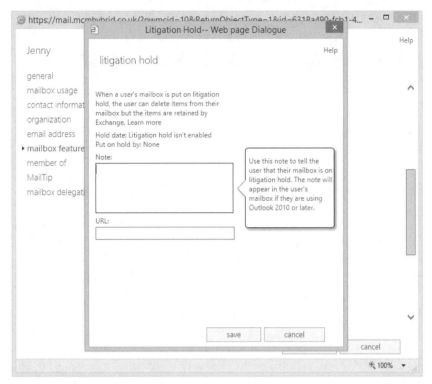

FIGURE 4-29 Enabling Legal Hold on a mailbox

Performing a query-based In-Place Hold

With the ability to search mailboxes via eDiscovery for ad-hoc queries, it is also possible to place mailboxes on hold for certain content and keywords. This allows you to have a Legal Hold scenario where the contents of the mailbox in its entirety are not placed on hold, but only where the keywords that are specified are placed on hold. Then when a user deletes or modifies an item in their mailbox, the item is inspected for the hold keyword. If present, the item is preserved for the hold duration. If the keyword is not present, the item is purged from the mailbox. If the user is subject to more than five keyword-based In-Place Holds, all items are held because that is less resource hungry than searching out many keywords and holding them.

To perform an In-Place Hold, you login as a discovery manager and navigate to the In-Place eDiscovery & Hold page of the compliance management section of Exchange Control Panel. Exchange Management Shell can also be used to do this using New-MailboxSearch.

The first step for a query-based In-Place Hold is to start a Filter Based On Criteria search from Compliance Management, In-Place eDiscovery & Hold. To place mailboxes on hold for an In-Place Hold, you need to specify the mailboxes, and you cannot do an In-Place Hold for all mailboxes. You also need to run this hold wizard as a member of the Discovery Management role group.

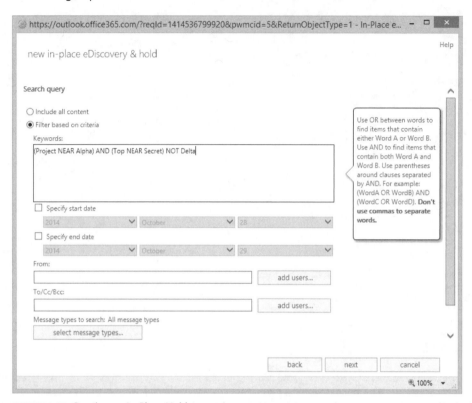

FIGURE 4-30 Creating an In-Place Hold

As you can see from Figure 4-30, when you choose to create a keyword in the In-Place Hold search, you can use keywords such as And, Or, Not, and Near. As you are searching as part of the hold wizard, you can set start and end dates for the search, as well as the sender, recipients, and message classes.

Once the search query is complete, you move onto the next screen of the wizard where you set the hold period. This is either indefinitely, or for a specific period of time. For example, you would use the time-based hold if your organization requires that all messages be retained for at least seven years. You can use a time-based In-Place Hold, along with a retention policy to make sure items are deleted in seven years.

When you click Finish, you are returned with an estimate of the search results. From the main search and eDiscovery page you can preview the search results. They appear in an OWA style view similar to Figure 4-31.

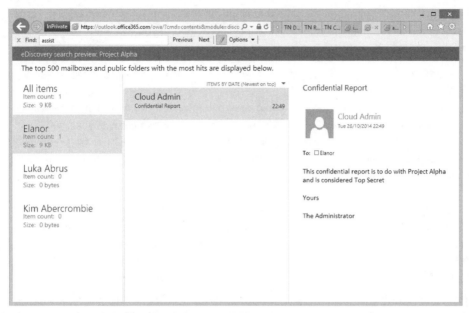

FIGURE 4-31 Preview search results for In-Place Hold queries

If a full search is run from this hold search estimate, the content is copied to the discovery mailbox, and other features of the search, such as the folder that the item is held in, are visible.

Designing and configuring journaling

Up until now in this objective, you have been looking at the In-Place compliance features. That is, where the items are held in the user's mailbox, and the search looks for items across that, and potentially other mailboxes, as required. Journaling is not In-Place compliance because the messages are copied to another mailbox with additional information stored on them for compliance reasons.

There are two types of journaling in Exchange Server on-premises, and one type in Exchange Online. On-premises Exchange Server can have journaling set up at the mailbox database level, and then every item that is sent or received from that mailbox database is copied to the journal target. Exchange Online and Exchange on-premises also support rules-based journaling. Rules-based journaling is a transport agent that copies all messages to the journal target when the sender or the recipient of the message falls into the scope of the rule.

Regardless of the method of the journaling, the final result is the same. A journal report is created that is sent to the journal target, and this report contains a list of the recipients, expanded from any distribution list, as well as the sender, and a copy of the message attached. If the message is RMS protected, optionally, a clear text copy of the message can be attached to the journal report as well. This is based on the state of the JournalReportDecryptionEnabled setting in Set-IRMConfiguration.

The journal report is an email message that is sent to the journal target address. The target address is either a local mailbox or an SMTP address provided to you by a third-party journaling service.

> **IMPORTANT** **OFFICE 365 AND JOURNALING RESTRICTIONS**
>
> You can't designate an Office 365 mailbox as a journaling mailbox for on-premises mailboxes or mailboxes in Office 365. If you're running a hybrid deployment with your mailboxes split between on-premises servers and Office 365, you can designate an on-premises mailbox as the journaling mailbox for your Office 365, and on-premises mailboxes, or use a third-party service.

Journaling is useful for compliance because it will tell you not just the message sent, but who sent and received the message, and specifically it will expand the recipients into individual addresses. For example, imagine an email was sent to the sales department distribution list. This list contained 100 mailboxes. If you use eDiscovery search, you will see that the message was sent to *sales@contoso.com*, but not who was a member of that group at the time the message was sent. Because journaling covers the typical compliance requirement of who sent/received what, to where and when, it is a common scenario for Exchange Server deployments.

Journal reports will also record the Bcc addresses that the email was sent to. To see what a journal report looks like, take a look at Figure 4-32. This shows a journal report open in Outlook Web App. The report shows the message sender that it was sent to a single recipient and Cc'd to a distribution list, and this list is expanded to its members.

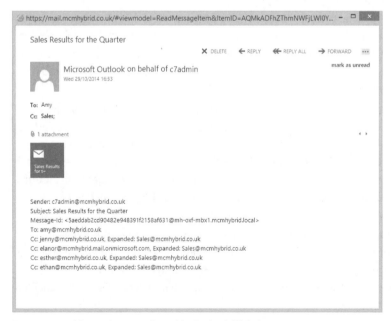

FIGURE 4-32 A journal report viewed in Outlook Web App

To configure journaling you need an Exchange Standard CAL for database level journaling, and to do journal rules, you need an Enterprise CAL. Journaling in Exchange Online requires a P2 license.

To set up database journaling, you use the Set-MailboxDatabase Exchange Management Shell cmdlet, and the JournalRecipient parameter. For example, to journal all messages sent and received from all databases in an Exchange organization (2007, 2010 and 2013), from an Exchange 2013 Exchange Management Shell prompt you would use the following.

```
Get-MailboxDatabase -IncludePreExchange2013 | Set-MailboxDatabase -JournalRecipient
<target_email_address>
```

To configure a journal rule (or rules) you need to decide the name of the rule, the target of the journal report, and the scope of the messages to journal. The scope is either internal emails, external emails, or both. Internal emails are those who's accepted domains are listed in Exchange, or those domains where there is a Remote Domain setting stating that the domain's internal property is set to true. The journal rule scope can also be Global, which means both internal and external emails are journaled.

In addition to the name, target, and scope of the journal rule, you need to decide who is covered by the rule. This is the most complex bit of journal rules. If you set the Recipient property to a single mailbox, only that mailbox is journaled. However, if you set the Recipient property to a distribution list, all of the members of the list are subject to journaling, but not just emails to the distribution list. Emails to that distribution list will be journaled, but only because they have been sent to people on this distribution list.

The following Exchange Management Shell cmdlet will journal all emails (scope is global) sent to or from members of the *sales@contoso.com* distribution list, and then send the journal report to a third-party journaling service.

```
New-JournalRule -Name "Sales Journal" -Recipient sales@contoso.com -JournalEmailAddress
contoso@relecloud.com -Scope Global -Enabled $True
```

To configure a journal rule in ECP, you would navigate to Compliance Management, Journal Rules, and then click Add Icon. In the journal rule, provide a name for the journal rule, and then complete the following text boxes.

- **Send Journal Reports To**   Type the address of the journaling mailbox that will receive all of the journal reports.

- **If The Message Is Sent To Or Received From**   Specify the recipient that the rule will target. You can either select a specific recipient, or apply the rule to all messages.

- **Journal The Following Messages**   Specify the scope of the journal rule. You can journal only the internal messages, only the external messages, or all messages regardless of origin or destination.

Then finally, you click Save to create the journal rule. This is shown in Figure 4-33, and in Figure 4-34, you can see where to enable database journaling.

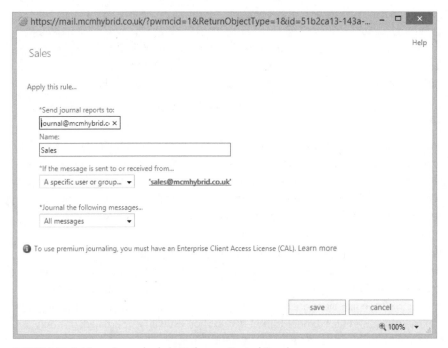

FIGURE 4-33 Setting a journal rule in Exchange Control Panel

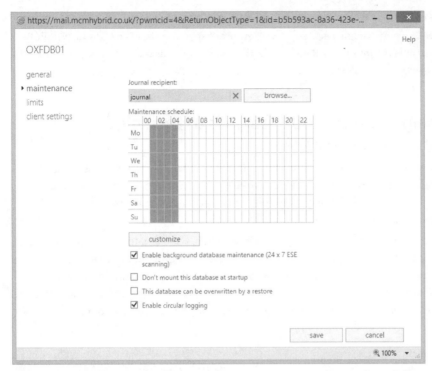

FIGURE 4-34 Setting the mailbox database journal value on the mailbox database properties maintenance page

In addition to setting up journaling, either by rules or by database journaling, it is important to configure the mailbox that will receive NDR messages from the journal. As journaling is important for compliance reasons, it is very important to be sure that if a journal report recipient starts to reject messages, there is some record of this. To enable this, create a recipient that is used for receiving these reports, and ensure that this mailbox is not subject to journaling. If you do set this mailbox to be covered by a journal rule, or place it in a database that is journaled, this mailbox will not be journaled. Then, when you have this journal report NDR mailbox in place, you configure the transport config settings of the Exchange organization to use this mailbox to receive journal report NDR messages. You should then ensure that this mailbox is frequently checked to make sure it has no content in it.

To set the transport configuration to know which mailbox to use for journal report NDRs, run the following cmdlet.

```
Set-TransportConfig -JournalingReportNdrTo journalndr@mcmhybrid.co.uk
```

Performing multi-mailbox searches in Exchange Administration Center (EAC)

To perform a search across many mailboxes using ECP, you need to be a member of the Discovery Management role group, or a custom role group with the Mailbox Search role assigned to that group. If you have a custom role, you can only search the mailboxes that fall into the scope of your role.

To access the user interface for multiple mailbox search, you need to browse to the /ecp URL and you will see the Compliance Management page. Any other pages that you see will be due to other access roles and permissions that you have. If you are a member of the Discovery Management role group you can also enable litigation hold, and so will be able to see the recipients and public folder screens, as well as allow this activity to take place. You can see the user interface in Figure 4-35.

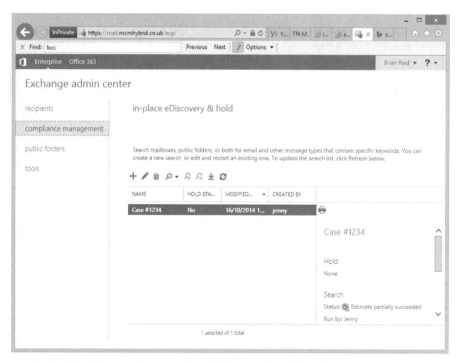

FIGURE 4-35 The Discovery Manager view of Exchange Control Panel

To create a new search you would follow the instructions listed above under In-Place Hold, apart from not selecting the In-Place Hold setting on the fourth screen of the search wizard. If you do a search of all mailboxes, you cannot select any hold settings anyway.

Upon finishing the search, it will queue for processing, and then an estimate of the search results will be returned. If the Exchange organization is a 2010/2013 co-existence organization, the search will remain queued if the federation arbitration mailbox has not been moved to Exchange Server 2013.

Once the search estimate is returned, you can decide if your keywords and scope of search are correct based on the number of hits. If that does not help, you can preview the results, as shown in Figure 4-31, earlier in this chapter. If you are happy with the estimate and the preview, you should proceed to completing the entire search. This is completed from the search icon, and then Copy Search Results. You will see the dialog on Figure 4-36.

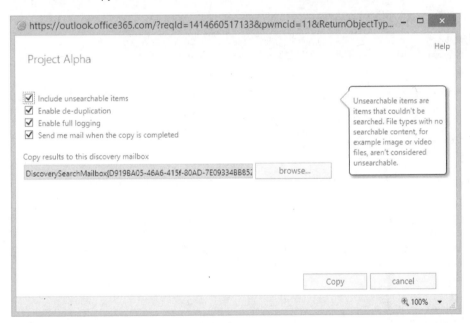

FIGURE 4-36 Search, Copy search results dialog box

There are four options to choose from, and the option to select which discovery mailbox to copy the result to. There is one discovery mailbox created when Exchange Server 2010 or 2013 is first installed, but additional discovery mailboxes can be created with the New-Mailbox <name> -Discovery cmdlet. You might want to have multiple discovery mailboxes to allow search results to be copied from mailboxes to a local discovery mailbox, rather than the default one, which might be across a distant WAN link.

Because the search is based on what Exchange Server search tools find, if there are items that Exchange Server cannot search, you can choose to include them in the results. This is the Unsearchable Items option. If you are expecting a large result, enable deduplication to keep the size of the search results as small as possible without adjusting the search keywords. The full logging option will add a log file of the actions the search took, to the discovery mailbox.

Once the search is complete, you can opt to be notified by email, and if not, you need to login to ECP to view the state of the search, which you will see on the right-hand side once the search results are selected. This will allow you to view the discovery mailbox where the search results will be stored in a folder named after the search name, and the date and time the search was conducted. Therefore, if you run the search multiple times you will get multiple date/time folders under the same search name. Other searches performed against the discovery mailbox will also be visible. An example result set is shown in Figure 4-37, which also shows an RMS protected email being rendered visible in the results set, as IRM for eDiscovery was enabled.

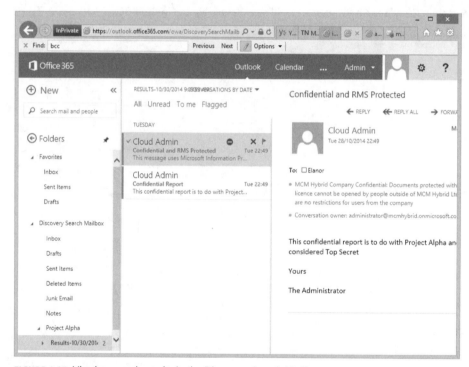

FIGURE 4-37 Viewing search results in the Discovery Search Mailbox

Other options for the eDiscovery search include stopping the search and resuming it at a later time. Once the search is finished, the results can be exported to an Outlook Data File, which is also called a PST file, for shipping to anyone outside of the scope of the Exchange environment who needs to see the results. PST files can be opened in Outlook, and also in third-party eDiscovery and reporting applications.

The export process does not require a local installation of Outlook on the machine on which the PST export is performed, but needs to be Windows 7, Windows 8 or Windows 8.1, be running Microsoft .NET Framework 4.5 and Internet Explorer 8 or later. The latest versions of the Mozilla and Chrome browsers are also supported. The software needed to do the export is installed via Click To Run technology, so there is no upfront software installation needed. The export dialog box looks like the one shown in Figure 4-38.

In addition to the PST files that contain the search results, two other files are also exported:

- A configuration file (.txt file format) that contains information about the PST export request, such as the name of the eDiscovery search that was exported, the date and time of the export, whether deduplication and unsearchable items were enabled, the search query, and the source mailboxes that were searched.

- A search results log (.csv file format) that contains an entry for each message returned in the search results. Each entry identifies the source mailbox where the message is located. If you've enabled de-duplication, this helps you identify all mailboxes that contain a duplicate message.

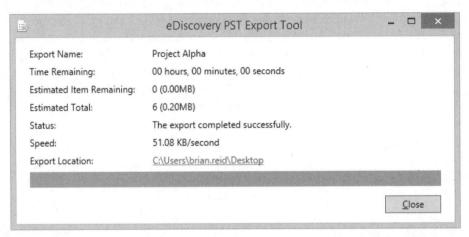

FIGURE 4-38 The PST export process for eDiscovery

Evaluating how to integrate in-place federated searches with Microsoft SharePoint

The ability to search for and successfully find content is the core of any eDiscovery product. To be able to use one product across a number of different data sources makes the search process easier and means that there are less products to install to cover the scope of documents within a given organization.

When Exchange Server 2013 is installed, it can be configured to integrate with both Lync Server 2013 and SharePoint Server 2013. From a compliance viewpoint, all Lync Server does is to save conversations to the Conversation History folder in the user's mailbox from the Lync Server to the Exchange Server. Once it is stored in Exchange, Exchange eDiscovery can be used to query Lync conversations.

Underlying Exchange's search engine is a technology called FAST that Microsoft acquired a number of years ago, and was first used in Exchange in the 2013 product. The SharePoint product has used it for a number of versions, but as they both use the same underlying search it is now possible to allow SharePoint to run searches both against its content and Exchange Server, and therefore also against Lync Server's content that has been placed in the user's Exchange mailbox.

> **MORE INFO**   **INTEGRATION FUNCTIONALITY**
>
> This is not the full scope of the integration functionality between Lync 2013, SharePoint 2013, and Exchange 2013 Servers. For more information, view the Exchange Server TechNet documentation at *http://technet.microsoft.com/en-us/library/jj150480.aspx*.

To integrate Exchange and SharePoint searches, the Exchange for SharePoint eDiscovery Center needs to be set up and configured. The full steps in PowerShell, and the command prompt for doing this, can be found in the Exchange Server documentation. In summary, the steps that need to be performed include configuring the server to server authentication, so that Exchange and SharePoint can be configured as partner applications to each other. This is done using OAuth, an authentication mechanism that is present in the 2013 versions of these two products. If you have an earlier version of either of these products, this will not work because the authentication protocol required is not available.

The SharePoint eDiscovery Center can be configured in Office 365 as well. The instructions for doing this can be found at *https://support.office.com/Article/Set-up-an-eDiscovery-Center-in-SharePoint-Online-a18f8975-aa7f-43b4-a7d6-001d14744d8e*.

Thought experiment
Configuring eDiscovery Across Exchange, Lync and SharePoint

In this thought experiment, apply what you've learned about this objective. You can find answers to these questions in the "Answers" section at the end of this chapter.

You are the CIO for Contoso Pharmaceuticals. Your company keeps data on both SharePoint and Exchange, and a Lync deployment is currently taking place. You need to ensure that each product has the ability to be searched for eDiscovery purposes.

1. What features in the three products are you going to be interested in getting your team to look at further?

2. Why would you choose to use a retention policy and a hold policy at the same time?

Objective summary

- RBAC is the only way in Exchange Server 2013 to assign both user and administrator rights that are not in the product by default. Though the Discovery Management role exists by default, it gives eDiscovery rights to all mailboxes in your organization, and so custom scopes in RBAC may be required to limit the scope of the eDiscovery user.

- Retention holds ensure that data is removed once it reaches a certain age. Legal holds ensure that it is persisted in the database until it reaches a certain age.

- Litigation Hold was the name of the feature in Exchange 2010, and though now called In-Place Hold, the cmdlets to modify the setting remain as they were in 2010.

- Exchange Server 2013 allows time based holds as well as holding content for ever

- Exchange Server 2013 has the ability to hold all data (Legal Hold) or keyword-based data (eDiscovery Search and In-Place Hold).

- Journaling is copying messages that are sent and received to an alternative storage location. In Exchange on-premises this can be a dedicated mailbox database, but in Exchange Online it needs to be either on-premises or a third-party service.

- Journaling stores the recipient information at the time of sending. Prior to Cumulative Update 7, eDiscovery searches would not be able to tell you this information, and so you would typically need to be able to do both a search and have a journal to get the recipients at the time of sending. Starting with Cumulative Update 7, you may be able to solve your compliance needs without a journal.

Objective review

Answer the following questions to test your knowledge of the information in this objective. You can find the answers to these questions and explanations of why each answer choice is correct or incorrect in the "Answers" section at the end of this chapter.

1. You need to enable journaling and Legal Hold to ensure your compliance scenario. Why is this?

   A. Because Legal Hold only tracks items in Exchange that are not delivered as messages, and journaling keeps a copy of all messages.

   B. Because Legal Hold will show you all of the messages, but not the actual recipients at the time the message was sent.

   C. Journaling only works to external third-party storage, and so eDiscovery searches allow you to query Exchange Server before you query the third-party service.

   D. Because journaling only stores the data on a single mailbox database, and therefore the performance of searching this mailbox is poor.

2. How would you ensure that the trusted members of your help desk that deal with the company executives are able to do eDiscovery searches on those mailboxes, and other help desk members are not?

A. You cannot segregate these roles.

B. You would deny membership of the Discovery Management role group to those members of the Executives group.

C. You would place the executives on Office 365, and the remaining mailboxes on-premises because you cannot search across both environments.

D. You would create a custom exclusive scope for discovery searches, and add the trusted employees to the role group that uses this exclusive scope.

3. What will the "(alpha NEAR beta NOT gamma) AND (alpha NEAR omega)" search keyword find? (Choose two.)

A. Alpha Beta Gamma Omega

B. Alpha Beta

C. Alpha Omega

D. Alpha Beta Omega

E. Alpha Omega Beta Zeta

Objective 4.5: Implement a compliance solution

The final objective of this chapter looks at tying together some of the other pieces of compliance, and user assistance features in Exchange Server. As with a lot of what has been covered in this chapter, these features work in exactly the same way in Exchange Online.

This objective looks at transport rules for compliance, mail tips to notify the user of anything you need to notify them about the recipient of when sending messages, and the use of message classifications to help inform users how they should treat the contents of a message they receive.

> **This objective covers how to:**
> - Design and configure transport rules for ethical walls
> - Configure MailTips
> - Create, configure, and deploy message classifications
> - Design and configure transport rules to meet specified compliance requirements

Designing and configuring transport rules for ethical walls

Ethical walls in Exchange Server are a way to ensure one group of users cannot communicate with another within the same organization, or occasionally between partner organizations, or those that have some association that requires that the two parties cannot communicate, but all the while to allow communication with any other party.

A few examples that are commonly used to describe ethical walls are banking, and stock and share trading organizations. There will be parts of the organization who will be able to be aware of future information that if they use this in a trading capacity in advance of that information becoming publically available, are breaking laws of insider trading. Within organizations that do both the preparatory work for future deals, and can also trade publically in these companies, there ought to be a way to ensure that the two teams cannot communicate. In some countries/regions and financial jurisdictions, these requirements may be enshrined in law.

Therefore, in Exchange Server, apart from journaling and other compliance features to audit communications, the use of transport rules will allow for the creation of ethical walls. Transport rules make ethical walls easy to achieve with minimal administrative overhead, but it must always be remembered that the rules work in one direction, and so you may require two rules for each ethical wall to stop the sender on one side communicating with a recipient on the other, and vice versa.

To create an ethical wall you need to start with some property that will allow you to identify the sender. In Exchange Server or Exchange Online, the properties can be based on anything in Active Directory (or Azure Active Directory for Exchange Online), or they can be based on group membership. Therefore, create a group, or set a property, in the directory that applies to all of the users who would be senders on one side of the wall. Create a second group, or apply a different value, to the same property or use a different property in the directory to identify the user population on the other side of the wall. From a management perspective, using the same property on both sides, with different values, or two different groups with a common naming convention, is probably the easiest to manage. Creating a wall with senders identified by a directory property and the recipients, by say, group membership, will work but could be harder to manage the maintenance of.

In Figure 4-39, you can see the properties from Active Directory of a user where the Company field has been set to Contoso Research.

FIGURE 4-39 The Company text box of the Active Directory user account populated

Once you have determined a way to identify both groups of users, you can create a transport rule. One rule will block emails from one group of users to the other, and a second rule will do the reverse. There may be scenarios where a rule is needed in a single direction only.

Figure 4-40 shows a transport rule that generates a custom non-deliverable message when users who's company is Contoso Research, emails someone who's title is Futures Trader. The custom non-deliverable error was created using the New-SystemMessage Exchange Management Shell cmdlet. If you have an Exchange hybrid organization, you need to create the custom message and transport rule in both Exchange on-premises and in Exchange Online. The PowerShell is the same for both, so create it on one and copy and paste the cmdlet code to the second environment.

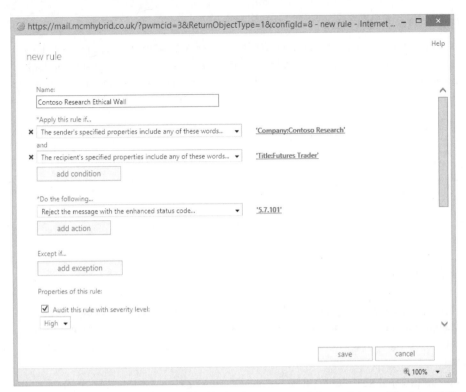

FIGURE 4-40 A transport rule for an ethical wall using a custom delivery status notification (DSN)

Some examples of New-SystemMessage for ethical rules can be found in the following:

```
# Create a system message with a unique code 5.7.101 that has both English and French replies. Returned reply is
based upon the users language settings in Active Directory
New-SystemMessage -Internal $true -Language En -DSNCode 5.7.101 -Text "Contoso Research
employees are not allowed to email future trading floor staff"
New-SystemMessage -Internal $true -Language Fr -DSNCode 5.7.101 -Text "Employés Contoso
recherche ne sont pas autorisés à envoyer un courriel à l'avenir personnel de salle des
marchés"
```

The organizations IT services help desk knowledge base tool should be updated with the error code used (5.7.101 in the above example) so that if a user queries why they received an NDR then valid knowledge on the issue relevant to the company can be obtained. The NDR that the sender receives will read "Remote Server returned '550 5.7.101 TRANSPORT.RULES. RejectMessage; the message was rejected by organization policy'" where the error code is the same as the New-SystemMessage created.

Configuring MailTips

MailTips are messages that appear at the top of the Outlook 2010 or 2013 compose window based on the recipients that have been added to an email as it is being composed. Outlook Web App in Exchange Server 2010 and 2013 also show these messages during the composing of a new message. Figure 4-41 shows a custom MailTips in Outlook Web Access.

FIGURE 4-41 Outlook Web App showing a custom MailTip

MailTips are automatically generated for a few different scenarios, and can be manually set, in multiple languages if required, on certain mailboxes. The following are the automatic MailTips that you can see, though note that MailTips can be disabled and some are disabled by default.

- **Invalid Internal Recipient** If the recipient cannot be resolved to a valid object in the directory. Typically shown when mailboxes are migrated to different Exchange organizations and the user sends an email to a previously existing user who either has not been migrated to the new environment, or when they were migrated their LegacyExchangeDN attribute was not populated with a value related to their old LegacyExchageDN. OWA does not display this MailTip.

- **Mailbox Full** Recipient is over quota, so there is no point emailing them as they will not get it and you will just get an error back.

- **Automatic Replies** You see the recipient's Out Of Office notification.

- **Restricted Recipient** You cannot email this recipient because they have a restriction on their mailbox permissions, which means that you are not able to email them. Note that you cannot get this MailTip for transport rules, just mailbox permissions.

- **External Recipients** This is disabled by default, but if enabled will tell you that the recipient is outside of your organization. This is useful for a reminder to indicate that the email may be more public than you may intend. This is especially useful when an internal distribution group contains external recipients. You enter the distribution list name, but you are told of the possible data exposure that might occur due to the list containing external recipients. To set external recipients in partner organizations to appear as internal recipients, use the Set-RemoteDomain –IsInternal $true value for the partner domain.

- **Large Audience** Each night at 13:00, the Group Metrics feature of Exchange Server (running on the server that generates the offline address book) calculates the size of each distribution group. This information is used for the next 24 hours to tell users if they are emailing a group that exceeds 25 users. Set-TransportConfig can be used to change this value to a number suitable to identifying large groups in your organization. The change takes place the next time the group metrics process is run.

- **Moderated Recipient** This tells you the recipient is subject to a moderation rule or property, and that the user may not see your message, as it will go to the moderators first.

- **Reply All On Bcc** This occurs when you reply all to an email that you received via Bcc. The other recipients of the message in the To and Cc fields will not know that you received the message, but if you reply all then they will know. This MailTip alerts you to this possible revealing of information.

- **Oversize Message** This is shown when the contents of the message exceed the allowed external send size limit, or the default receive size limit. If the sender or recipient has individual size limits, these will be used instead.

- **Custom MailTip** Will display a message set by the administrator when the recipient is being sent to. Custom MailTips can have multiple languages, and if the client Outlook or OWA language matches a MailTip translation, that language is shown, otherwise the default MailTip is displayed.

MailTips are generated via the Exchange Web Services and so both AutoDiscover and the correct InternalURL or ExternalURL for EWS is needed to ensure the user can reach the EWS endpoint and download the MailTip. The request for the MailTip happens after the user enters the recipient address into Outlook or OWA, and the request is valid for ten seconds. If the server cannot be reached in 10 seconds, or there is no response, the client stops the request and does not display the MailTip. If an email is left in a composing/drafts state for over two hours, the MailTip will be refreshed after two hours.

To set a custom MailTip you can either use the following example Exchange cmdlets, or Exchange Control Panel. In ECP, only the default MailTip can be edited, specific language tips need to be added in the shell.

```
Set-Mailbox <name> -MailTip "text to display" -MailTipTranslations @{Add="XX: Text in
the XX language","YY:Text in the YY language where XX and YY are two letter language
codes"
Set-DistributionGroup <group_name> -MailTip "text to display" -MailTipTranslations @
{Add="XX: Text in the XX language","YY:Text in the YY language where XX and YY are two
letter language codes";
```

EXAM TIP

MailTips can be set for mailboxes, groups, resource mailboxes, contacts, or shared mailboxes.

Creating, configuring, and deploying message classifications

Outlook and OWA allow users to set a property on a message called the message classification. This classification is stored on the message as a message header, and this header stays with the message while it is sent internal to the organization. Upon receipt of the message, the user is shown the text of the classification at the top of the email. The text can be customized to suit the organization into which Exchange is installed, and language specific versions can be generated. Outlook and OWA will show the default classification text if they cannot show a language specific version.

Because the classification is stored on the message as a header, it can be read by transport rules as well, and additional actions can be performed. For example, if you create an Internal Only classification, you can use transport rules to generate an NDR if the recipient is external.

Other examples might be to add certain disclaimers, or to encrypt the message at Exchange, or to use the Office 365 Message Encryption feature in Office 365. Setting a message header by way of transport rules, and then forwarding the message outbound via Exchange Online Protection enable Office 365 Message Encryption (OME). The user could set a message classification called Encrypt For External Recipients, and then a transport rule sees this classification, and then sets the OME headers so that the message gets encryption applied at send time. OME is part of the E3 subscription in Office 365.

To create a message classification, you use Exchange Management Shell and the New-MessageClassification cmdlet. You need to provide a name for the classification and a display name. The display name is what users see in Outlook or OWA. The name is what you use to refer to the classification within Exchange administration. If you set a Locale parameter to the classification, you can add multiple languages to the classification, and have Outlook or OWA display the version of the clients default language, or the default text if the specific locale is not present. The following is an example cmdlet for creating the message classification discussed above.

```
New-MessageClassification -Name EncryptForExternalRecipients -DisplayName "Encrypt for
External Recipients" -SenderDescription "The external recipient will be required to
login to a secure website to view this message"
```

When you create a message classification it is given a unique ID called a ClassificationID. This ClassificationID is the value that is stamped on the message header when the classification is added to a message. If you have two Exchange forests and need to share the same classification across the forests, you need to make the classification in one forest, then use Get-MessageClassification to retrieve the ClassificationID, and then make the classification in the second forest by setting the ClassificationID in the New-MessageClassification cmdlet, rather than allowing a new ClassificationID to be set. This means that the classification created in the second forest can display the same text for the same classification. If you have Exchange Online and on-premises in a hybrid environment, you need to create your classifications in this way so that the ClassificationID for the classification matches at both locations. If you move to Exchange Online a while after creating a message classification, you need to export the classifications and create them in Exchange Online to match the GUID used. Any transport rules used that act on that classification can then be created as well.

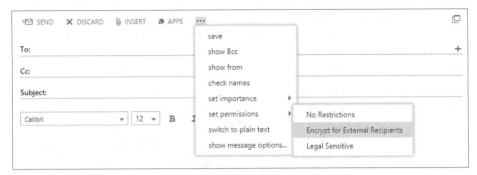

FIGURE 4-42 OWA showing the classification of the message to the sender

After you create a new message classification, you can specify the message classification as a transport rule predicate. Before Microsoft Outlook users can apply the message classification to messages, you must update the user systems with the message classification XML file created by the Export-OutlookClassification.ps1 script. This export is not needed for OWA users because the classifications appear in OWA automatically.

The Export-OutlookClassification.ps1 script file is located in the %ExchangeInstallPath%Scripts directory on an Exchange Server. To export from Exchange Online you need to copy this script from an on-premises installation, and run it in your Remote PowerShell window connected to Exchange Online. The export creates an XML file that needs to be copied to each Outlook client so that Outlook knows what classifications to display in the user interface. The XML file needs to be copied to a folder that Outlook can access, and the easiest way to do this is to use Group Policy preferences as that you can move files around the network to your domain joined machines. For non-domain joined machines, you need to copy the file using another method of your choice. Once you have the file available to Outlook, you need to set some registry keys at HKEY_CURRENT_USER\Software\Microsoft\Office\15.0\Common\Policy (where 15.0 means Outlook 2013, other version numbers can be used too):

- "AdminClassificationPath"="c:\\temp\\temp\\classifications.xml"
- "EnableClassifications"=dword:00000001
- "TrustClassifications"=dword:00000001

The sender, using Outlook or OWA, can set the message classification. In Outlook, the user clicks the File tab when composing a new message, and selects the classification from the Set Permissions button. In OWA, the user clicks the ellipsis button, and chooses the classification from the list shown under Permissions. Note that the RMS templates appear in the same place; so do not name a template and a classification with the same (or similar) names, to avoid confusion.

Designing and configuring transport rules to meet specified compliance requirements

Each organization will have specific requirements that they need to meet for legal compliance. As an exchange administrator of that organization, it is your responsibility with your legal department to ensure that you are doing what is required by the laws of the country/region that you trade in, and possibly other countries/regions that you do business in.

From the viewpoint of transport rules, you can use these to enforce a considerable amount of restrictions on email, and to audit on the actions of these transport rules. Because there are a considerable number of rules, they are not covered here (they are detailed in the product documentation), but you will look at the process of designing a rule for compliance reasons.

First, in terms of rules, there is a priority to the rule. Rules will be processed in this order. Therefore, if a rule with a higher priority (lower number) deletes a message, it will not be processed by a later rule. Equally, if a rule causes a message to be moderated, it will be sent to the moderators at that time, and will not have later rules processed on it. If the moderator approves the message, it will return to the message flow pipeline, and the later runs will be run against the message.

New to Exchange Server 2013 is a rule action to stop further processing of messages. This allows you to have rules to ensure later rules are skipped. With any rule, the version number of the rule matches the lowest version of Exchange that the rule will run on. Versioned rules came with Exchange Server 2010 (version 14), and are also valid in Exchange Server 2013 (version 15). Though the stop processing further rules is a feature that is only available in Exchange Server 2013, if you add this property to a rule that is already a version 14 rule, it will remain version 14. This is because Exchange Server 2010 Service Pack 3 can process this rule and honor its requirement, even though you cannot set this rule property from the Exchange Server 2010 shell. Other rules though are valid in Exchange Server 2013 only, and cannot be processed by a 2010 server. These rules are version 15 rules.

If you have an Exchange Server installation that has 2007, 2010, and 2013 installed (you cannot have 2003 and 2013 in the same organization), you will have 2007 rules (no version) and versioned rules that run on 2010/2013. The non-versioned rules from 2007 are copied to the first 2010 hub transport role server, or 2013 mailbox role server that is installed. After this time changes to 2007, rules are not copied to 2010/2013 servers, and 2010/2013 versioned rules are not copied to 2007 servers. The actual rules are stored in the Active Directory and the 2007 rules occupy a different location within the directory than the 2010/2013 versioned rules. Therefore, if you have multiple versions of Exchange Server installed, be aware that though rules run on the first 2010 hub transport server or 2013 mailbox server, the message goes through, rules can be executed on other machines if the rule has not yet run against that message. Therefore, rules will run on 2007 as well as 2010/2013 if the message goes through 2007 and 2010 (or later) servers. If a rule is version 14, it will run on either 2010 or 2013 servers, but if it is a version 15 rule it will only run on a 2013 server.

When you create a rule, you need to provide a condition or predicate that determines on what conditions or events the rule will fire. A rule can be written to fire on all messages, but also on specific conditions of the message, such as sender or sender property, like the one from the ethical walls example above. When a single rule has more than one condition listed, the rule will only fire if all the conditions are true. If a condition is a multiple property condition (such as word in Active Directory property), any of the words need to be valid for the condition to fire.

After you have set the conditions, you can set the actions. These are the things that happen if the rule conditions all evaluate to true. Like conditions, you can have more than one. If you do, all of the actions will fire.

Finally, for a rule you can have exceptions. This controls the times when, though the condition might be true, if the exception is also true, the rule does not fire. Unlike conditions where every predicate needs to be true for the rule to fire, with exceptions, if any one exception is true, the rule will not fire at all.

Figure 4-43 shows a rule being created where it has multiple predicates, actions, and a single exception. The rule shows that a disclaimer is added (the action) if both conditions are true, though only one of the two words in the first condition need to be found in the subject for the condition to be true. The rule in the figure also has a single exception shown. Note that to create a rule as shown in the figure, you need to create a new blank rule and select More Options to ensure that all of the options for the rule are visible. In the initial rule creation dialog box, not every action is shown.

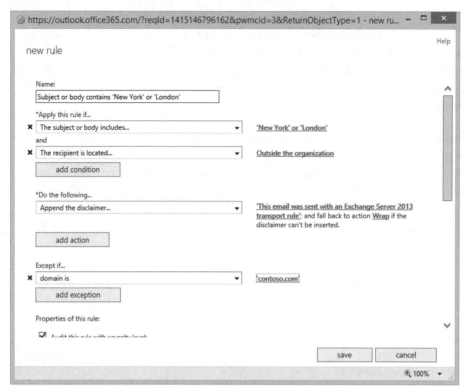

FIGURE 4-43 Creating a transport rule in Exchange Server 2013

Thought experiment
Compliance for Exchange Server

In this thought experiment, apply what you've learned about this objective. You can find answers to these questions in the "Answers" section at the end of this chapter.

You manage the Exchange infrastructure for City Power & Light. You need to ensure that users are not able to send information about individual customers out of the company.

1. What technologies in Exchange Server can you use to do this?

2. Your organization works closely with Litware, Inc. to provide your legal services. How can you ensure that your legal classifications placed on messages appear at Litware, Inc?

3. You need to move the OAB generating mailbox to a different server. What impact will this have on the Group Metrics feature?

Objective summary

- Ethical walls are ways to ensure groups of users cannot email each other.
- MailTips provide informational messages to Outlook and OWA users based on times when they might receive a non-deliverable email in response to sending their message, and optionally, when the sender needs to know additional information about the recipient.
- Message classification is a way for users to tag messages so that the internal recipient can see a predetermined property of the message, and hopefully act on that message.
- Because the server can read message classifications, transport rules can be used to enable certain restrictions and properties on the message.
- Transport rules are version specific and will only run on servers that are that version or later.

Objective review

Answer the following questions to test your knowledge of the information in this objective. You can find the answers to these questions and explanations of why each answer choice is correct or incorrect in the "Answers" section at the end of this chapter.

1. Which of the following object types support MailTips? (Choose all that apply.)

   A. Mailboxes

   B. Security Groups (not mail enabled)

   C. Dynamic Distribution Groups

   D. Mail Users

   E. Public Folders

   F. Servers

2. How do you ensure that a partner organization can make use of the message classifications that you have set? (Choose two.)

   A. They cannot use your message classifications.

   B. They work without any configuration because the email message contains the required information to display the text of the classification.

   C. They need to take an export of your classifications, and import them into their Exchange environment to ensure the display text and GUID match.

   D. They need to ensure that the internal Exchange Server message headers that store message classifications are not stripped off by the header firewall.

3. You have an Exchange Server 2007 and 2013 co-existence organization. This will remain in co-existence for a while due to the number of mailboxes that need to be moved. How will you manage transport rules during this time?

   A. Ensure all mail flow goes through a 2013 server.

B. Ensure that you do not create any transport rules on Exchange Server 2013, and instead only make them on a 2007 server.

C. Ensure that you do not create any transport rules on Exchange Server 2013, and instead only make them on a 2007 server. Then when you have made them, export them from 2007, and import them to 2013 again.

D. Ensure all mail flow goes through a 2007 server.

Answers

This section contains the solutions to the thought experiments and answers to the objective review questions in this chapter.

Objective 4.1: Thought experiment

1. The Enterprise additional CAL that you have for faculty members allows you to archive mailboxes on-premises, or in Office 365 without additional licenses. Students with just a standard CAL will need at least an Exchange Online Archive license per student.

2. Before you can implement Exchange In-Place Archiving, you need to configure a full hybrid configuration. This requires an Office 365 tenant with at least the EOA license allocated to it, DirSync enabled, and the Hybrid Configuration Wizard ran in Exchange on-premises.

3. You would create a retention tag for the duration of your semester in days, and set the action of this tag to MoveToArchive. The tag would apply to the entire mailbox (Type=All). You would then create a School of Fine Art - Students retention policy, and add the new retention tag to this policy. You would apply the policy to all student mailboxes before you give them an archive. This means that the Default MRM Policy archive would not be applied because the students already have one.

Objective 4.1: Review

1. **Correct answer:** A

    A. **Correct:** The MoveToArchive is the correct action to use.

    B. **Incorrect:** This is not a valid action.

    C. **Incorrect:** This is not a valid action.

    D. **Incorrect:** The All property is a type and not an action.

2. **Correct answer:** B

    A. **Incorrect:** The cmdlet needed for this answer to be correct would be Enable-Mailbox <name> -Archive.

    B. **Correct:** This cmdlet creates an archive in Office 365 for an on-premises mailbox.

    C. **Incorrect:** You cannot have this option.

    D. **Incorrect:** The cmdlet needed for this answer to be correct would be Enable-Mailbox <name> -Archive.

3. **Correct answer:** C

    A. **Incorrect**: This is not a valid default policy name.

    B. **Incorrect**: This is the default policy in Exchange 2010.

    C. **Correct**: This is the default archive and retention policy in Exchange 2013.

Objective 4.2: Thought experiment

1. To change the DLP policy from testing without Policy Tips, to testing with Policy Tips, you would edit the settings of the policy from ECP, Compliance Management, Data Loss Prevention, and then edit the policy. It is not recommended to change the rules at the Mail Flow, rules area of ECP (though you could make the individual changes at that location).

2. You would want to be sure that any change did not affect a valid business process. For example, if credit card numbers are being sent via email, it might be that there is already an Enforced TLS send connector in place, or that you are sending them to some internal application with an address space outside of Exchange Server (so they appear to be going outside). The DLP Policy would impact this or other legitimate business processes, and before enforcing the rule and stopping the business process, you would need to have a valid and secure alternative process, or an exception made for the current process.

3. You would add a second DLP Policy to Exchange for the same template, and then you would edit the rules of the policy to fire only for the pilot group. Then you would enforce this DLP Policy. Then it will only affect users in your pilot group.

Objective 4.2: Review

1. **Correct answer:** D

   A. **Incorrect:** The HasClassification transport rule condition is looking for message classifications and not data classifications.

   B. **Incorrect:** The SentToScope transport rule condition is typically used in DLP rules, but it is not the rule type that makes a DLP rule. SentToScope is where the message is sent to, and is typically set to NotInOrganization.

   C. **Incorrect:** The Description parameter of the transport rule outlines what the rule does, but does not actually cause the rule to do anything.

   D. **Correct:** This is the cmdlet used in a transport rule to look up the data classifications contained in the email, and to act upon certain data classifications.

   E. **Incorrect:** LegacyRegEx is a transport rule type from Exchange 2010. RegEx is used in custom DLP rules, but only when creating your own data classifications, which is not in the exam's objective domain, and so knowing how to create your own classifications is beyond the scope of this book.

2. **Correct answer:** B

   A. **Incorrect:** The two views of the transport rules are showing the same rules. Changes can be made anywhere, but to change in the compliance management pages is recommended.

   B. **Correct:** The two views of the transport rules are showing the same rules. Changes can be made anywhere, but to change in the compliance management pages is recommended.

Objective 4.3: Thought experiment

1. To ensure short periods of storage of email for temporary employees, you would use a retention tag that deletes content after the time period, with the possible consideration of permanent delete, or delete and allow recovery depending upon the needs to be able to recover data. You also need to ensure mailbox quotas are in use because without a quota, a user could still store too much info within the retention period.

2. You would need to create the following policy, with the tags listed being part of this policy, and then apply this policy to all temporary employees. In this example you have an employee naming convention where login names that start with "T-" are temporary employees.

   A. Retention Policy: Temporary Seasonal Staff Retention Policy

   B. Default deletion retention tag of two months applied to the mailbox (Type=All)

   C. Optional Junk Email folder tag for a shorter time period

   D. No personal tags in this retention policy

   E. No archive tags in this retention policy

   F. Apply to all temporary staff with Get-Mailbox -ResultSize Unlimited | Where {$_.SamAccountName -ilike "T-*"} | Set-Mailbox -RetentionPolicy "Temporary Seasonal Staff Retention Policy"

Objective 4.3: Review

1. **Correct answers:** B, C, and E

   A. **Incorrect:** The AgeLimitForRetention is a counter set in days, therefore two days is not sufficient for this solution.

   B. **Correct:** These are the correct settings for the Deleted Items requirement.

   C. **Correct:** These are the correct settings for the Archive requirement.

   D. **Incorrect:** This tag uses an incorrect Type value.

   E. **Correct:** These are the correct settings for the Delete After Five Years (1826 days) requirement.

   F. **Incorrect:** This retention policy value of 1095 days is only for three years. The two-year move to archive is independent of the five-year delete, and is not added together to get a five-year delete.

2. **Correct answer:** A

   A. **Correct:** Each mailbox can only have one retention policy.

   B. **Incorrect:** You can create one archive tag that applies to a mailbox, and one deletion tag that applies to the same, but these are tags and not policies as asked by the question.

C. **Incorrect:** Do not mix up retention tags and retention policies. You can have one policy with the number of tags that you need in it.

D. **Incorrect:** Do not mix up retention tags and retention policies. You can have one policy with the number of tags that you need in it.

Objective 4.4: Thought experiment

1. You will need to look at the eDiscovery search functionality in Exchange Server, as well as the ability to hold data with the In-Place Hold functionality using retention policies and legal hold or In-Place search holds. You will need to ensure OAuth is configured between Exchange Server 2013 and Lync Server 2013 so that Lync conversations are persisted in the Exchange Mailbox, and finally you will need to look into the Exchange for SharePoint eDiscovery Center, as well as any SharePoint compliance features needed for that product.

2. You would choose to use a retention policy and hold policy at the same time because they are different, but complementary, things. The retention policy ensures that email is deleted once it exceeds a given age. The hold policy ensures that everything is persisted in the mailbox until it reaches a given age. With both policies in place, you can be sure that content that you may be best not keeping (as it is beyond any legal requirement to hold), is removed and so that any legal case against you that requires providing matching data that you hold will not return this old data (because you do not hold it anymore), but also ensuring that newer data is kept for the legally required duration if one exists.

Objective 4.4: Review

1. **Correct answer:** B

   A. **Incorrect:** Both journaling and Legal Hold are able to copy all items.

   B. **Correct:** Prior to CU7 (the IT Pro exam is not based on this later release) the only way to do recipients at time of message is journaling.

   C. **Incorrect:** Both can store data in Exchange on-premises.

   D. **Incorrect:** Search is based on the Exchange indexes, so performance is not based on the size of the database. Though a large mailbox is more likely to return extra results and take longer to export, the fact that journaling can be split across many databases means performance can be improved if required.

2. **Correct answer:** D

   A. **Incorrect:** You can segregate these roles. Custom scopes in RBAC will allow this.

   B. **Incorrect:** You cannot deny someone membership of a group to block their access to what the group can do.

   C. **Incorrect:** eDiscovery searches in Exchange Hybrid are cross-forest, and so a search on-premises can include Office 365 mailboxes, and visa versa.

D. Correct: The exclusive scope would ensure that only the executive help desk team could manage the executives, including discovery searches.

3. **Correct answers:** D and E

   A. Incorrect: This "message" contains "gamma" and the search says not to include "gamma."

   B. Incorrect: This search does not include "omega" and the query requires "omega" near "alpha."

   C. Incorrect: This search does not include "beta" and the query requires "beta" near "alpha."

   D. Correct: This search includes the required keywords.

   E. Correct: This search includes the required keywords. The additional words do not take away from the result set.

Objective 4.5: Thought experiment

1. There are a number of valid answers to this question, but DLP, RMS, Rules, and MailTips are valid answers to this question. DLP fingerprinting of standard forms, RMS so that the content cannot be read outside the organization, transport rules to look for key worlds, and then automate the applying of actions such as RMS to the email. MailTips can be used to notify the user of a potential issue in advance of the user clicking Send.

2. You need to ensure that your message classifications are exported to an XML file and that classification is imported into the new organization.

3. The OAB generating mailbox server is used to calculate the number of users in a group each evening. This information is used for the following 24 hours until group metrics is regenerated.

Objective 4.5: Review

1. **Correct answers:** A, C, and D

   A. Correct: Mailboxes (user mailboxes, resource mailboxes, and room mailboxes) can have MailTips.

   B. Incorrect: Security groups are not mailbox recipients and so cannot have MailTips enabled for them. You can make a security group be an object in the address book by mail enabling it, and then you can set a MailTip on it.

   C. Correct: Dynamic Distribution Groups support MailTips.

   D. Correct: MailTips can be set on mail user objects.

2. **Correct answers:** C and D

   A. Incorrect: They can use your classifications if they import your classifications and ensure that the Send and Receive connectors between your organization and theirs do not remove the Exchange Server internal forest, and organization headers.

B. **Incorrect:** The classification is an internal header on Exchange, and so the other organization, without specific configuration, will not see the message header.

C. **Correct:** The header in the message contains a GUID. Therefore, the display name of the classification needs to be added to the Active Directory of the recipient organization, and the GUID of the classification needs to match.

D. **Correct:** Because the header that contains the GUID is an internal header, it will be removed by the header firewall. Therefore, the send connector outbound from your organization, and the receive connector at the inbound organization need to ensure these internal headers are not stripped off. Hybrid mode to Exchange Online does this as part of the connectors, and so would need to be done for all other cross-forest partner organizations.

3. **Correct answer:** C

A. **Incorrect:** When two mailboxes are on the same 2007 server the mail flow will not go through a 2013 mailbox server, and so 2013 rules will never be applied.

B. **Incorrect:** This will partly work, though any changes made to the rules after the first 2013 server is installed will not be automatically replicated to the area of the Active Directory that 2013 uses to store rules.

C. **Correct:** The rules made on 2007 will work in 2013, but only if exported and imported again after each change. This ensures that any 2013 rule changes that might have occurred are removed upon this importing of the 2007 rules.

D. **Incorrect:** Mail flow between two mailboxes in the same 2013 DAG or Active Directory site will not ever go via a 2007 hub transport server.

## CHAPTER 5

Implement and manage coexistence, hybrid scenarios, migration, and federation

This final chapter of the book looks in more detail at a number of features of Exchange Server that were mentioned in the other chapters. While other chapters focus on specific features and how they operate in Exchange Online or on-premises, this chapter looks at setting up coexistence between Exchange 2013 on-premises and Exchange Online, which is part of Office 365.

Note that it is possible to migrate to Exchange Online without any coexistence and this is known as a *cutover migration*. All of the mailboxes are moved to the cloud and mail flow is redirected to Exchange Online rather than on-premises, typically overnight or over a weekend, and can be suitable for some small companies. There is generally little complexity in doing a cutover migration, but it is not the best solution for moving email to Exchange Online for a lot of companies that are considering this type of migration. Therefore, this chapter covers the more complex scenarios for migrations to Exchange Online, and other coexistence scenarios with other companies.

Objectives in this chapter:

- Objective 5.1: Establish coexistence with Exchange Online
- Objective 5.2: Deploy and manage Exchange federation
- Objective 5.3: Implement on-premises coexistence with legacy systems
- Objective 5.4: Set up a cross-forest coexistence solution
- Objective 5.5: Migrate legacy systems
- Objective 5.6: Troubleshoot issues associated with hybrid scenarios, coexistence, migration, and federation

Objective 5.1: Establish coexistence with Exchange Online

The hosted Exchange Server 2013 deployment from Microsoft is Exchange Online. It exists as part of Office 365 with SharePoint Online and Lync Online, as well as a directory (called Azure Active Directory) and numerous other features such as Azure RMS and Office 365 Message Encryption, to mention a few.

This objective will look at how to coexist your Exchange on-premises organization with Exchange Online. This is known as hybrid coexistence and uses the Hybrid Coexistence Wizard to set the pieces up. The Hybrid Coexistence Wizard exists in both Exchange 2010 and 2013. We will look at it from the viewpoint of 2013 only. Even though they look different, they do similar things.

> **This objective covers how to:**
> - Deploy and manage hybrid configuration
> - Evaluate limitations of the Hybrid Configuration Wizard
> - Configure requirements for single sign-on (SSO)
> - Design and configure Active Directory Federation Services (AD FS)

Deploying and managing hybrid configuration

Hybrid coexistence is linking Exchange Online to Exchange on-premises, and vice versa. This coexistence configuration changes and sets a number of settings including send connectors, remote domains, and digital certificates. The configuration is also stored in an object called the Hybrid-Configuration, and so cmdlets like New-HybridConfiguration and Get-HybridConfiguration can be run, as well as the wizard that you will concentrate on here.

To be able to run the Hybrid Coexistence Wizard and set up hybrid coexistence, you need to have an Exchange on-premises organization that is running Exchange Server 2007 and/or Exchange Server 2010 and/or Exchange Server 2013. To run the hybrid wizard for an Exchange on-premises organization that contains Exchange Server 2003 servers, you need to use the Exchange Server 2010 Hybrid Wizard. When enabling Exchange Server in a hybrid configuration, every server in the organization need to meet certain prerequisites. For Exchange Server 2007 on-premises, the minimum version is 2007 SP3 RU10, and for Exchange Server 2010 on-premises, the minimum supported version is Service Pack 3.

For Exchange Server 2013 on-premises, the minimum supported version to support hybrid is the previous cumulative update. By the time this book goes to press, the latest CU will be CU7, which means the Exchange Server 2013 on-premises will need to be CU6 or CU7 only. Once later CUs are released, this will change with them.

Hybrid deployments are supported in all Office 365 plans that support Windows Azure Active Directory synchronization. All Office 365 Enterprise, Government, Academic, Business, and Midsize plans support hybrid deployments. Office 365 Small Business, Office 365 Business and Home plans don't support hybrid deployments. The Business Premium and Business plans are new as of October 1, 2014 and are therefore not covered in the exam. The Midsize plan will cease to exist from October 1, 2015 by which time the current users of it will have transitioned their users to a different license. Midsize cannot be configured as a new Office 365 tenant from October 1, 2014.

The remaining requirements for hybrid is that you own the domain name that you are using for Exchange Server, install some software to sync directories, and use a digital certificate that Exchange Online trusts. For the domain ownership requirement, all accepted domains in Exchange will need to be registered in Office 365 with the exception of any internal only domain, such as .local domains. Any domains that you cannot register in Office 365 must not exist on users's mailboxes as email addresses. There is typically a bit of email and directory cleaning up to do for most organizations when they move to the cloud. Also, for each domain that you register in Office 365, you need to ensure that the AutoDiscover records for that domain point to an on-premises Exchange Server 2013 Client Access Server (CAS) role. If you do not have external AutoDiscover, you need to put this in place correctly. Tools such as *http://exrca.com* can be used to check that this is working correctly.

To configure hybrid configuration, you need to complete the following steps once you have the above prerequisites in place:

■ Sign up for a new Office 365 subscription with a license that supports directory synchronization. If you already have an Office 365 subscription (also known as an Office 365 tenant), sign into that tenant as the Global Administrator. The user you create during sign-up is the first global administrator. Other users can be added and assigned this role after you sign in.

■ Add your on-premises domains to the Office 365 portal. The domains will require verification, which will require you to add a record to the public DNS server for that domain. You cannot use any domain that you cannot verify. At the end of the verification wizard, the Office 365 portal will tell you a few DNS record values to change. You should not do this DNS modification at this time because these DNS records probably already exist and point to your on-premises infrastructure. These DNS records that you are required to add are for tenants that do not already exist and are not being migrated in from an existing system.

■ Activate the Directory Synchronization option on the user's page. This happens typically after you have added your custom domains and before you enable the optional single sign-on (AD FS) feature.

■ Ensure that all of your users in the on-premises Active Directory have a user principle name (UPN) that has an Internet routable domain name associated with it. That is, if your Active Directory is contoso.local, this will default to the user principle name domain value. This can be changed in bulk with tools such as IDFix, ADModify.NET, and PowerShell. It can also be changed on a user-by-user basis in the Active Directory tools, but this is time consuming and not recommended. If you cannot change the UPN suffix because it is in use with other on-premises software, or populated with inconsistent data, see *http://blogs.office.com/2014/05/06/alternate-login-id-for-office-365-reduces-dependence-on-upn/* for information on using a different attribute from Active Directory for users to log in to Office 365 with.

- Look for other configurations within your Active Directory such as multiple forests or non-Microsoft directories. Also be aware that bad data will not sync to the cloud, and it needs to be fixed in a similar way to updating an object's UPN attribute in the previous bullet. A blog post on preparing to install DirSync can be found at *http://blogs.office.com/2014/04/15/synchronizing-your-directory-with-office-365-is-easy/*, though this was written before the Azure Active Directory Synchronization software (AADSync) was released, and so some of the information with regard to multiple forests is inaccurate.

- Once your directory is cleaned up, duplicate users are removed, and no objects remain with .local UPN suffixes, you can then install the DirSync software. At the time of writing there are two options for this. There is the AADSync software or the Azure Directory Synchronization software (DirSync). The newer of these two, AADSync, is what you will see in screen shots in this book because it is about to replace the DirSync software. It now has all of the same features as this software and more (such as support for multiple forests), and therefore using DirSync ongoing is not recommended. Instructions for installing AADSync can be found at *http://msdn.microsoft.com/en-us/library/azure/dn757602.aspx* and the software can be downloaded from *http://aka.ms/aadsyncdownload*. Instructions for the older DirSync software can be found at *http://technet.microsoft.com/en-us/library/jj151800.aspx* and it can be downloaded from *http://go.microsoft.com/fwlink/?LinkID=278924*.

EXAM TIP

The exam questions will refer to the DirSync software for a while, but apart from a few PowerShell cmdlets and the setup program, DirSync and AADSync function in much the same way.

Once the domains are verified in Office 365, and one of the two DirSync software options has been installed on an on-premises server, and is syncing to Office 365 successfully, it is time to prepare for the hybrid configuration. The full steps for completing the above can be found via links on the admin portal at Office 365 (*http://portal.office.com*). The detailed steps are not written in this book because they change over time. An example of this is the release of AADSync as this software is in the process of replacing DirSync.

Preparing for hybrid configuration

Once the on-premises Active Directory has synced to Azure Active Directory, the Users page of the Office 365 portal will list both the original administrator account, and each of the users synced from the on-premises directory. If any users are missing from here, they failed to sync, and the issue will need to be resolved on-premises in Active Directory.

Hybrid configuration provides the following options to integrate your Exchange Servers on-premises with Exchange Online in Office 365:

- Mail routing between on-premises and cloud-based organizations.

- Mail routing with a shared domain namespace. For example, both on-premises and cloud-based organizations use the @contoso.com SMTP domain.

- A unified global address list, also called a *shared address book*.

- Free/busy and calendar sharing between on-premises and cloud-based organizations.

- Centralized control of mail flow. The on-premises organization can control mail flow for the on-premises and cloud-based organizations.

- The ability to move existing on-premises mailboxes to the cloud-based organization and back again to on-premises as required.

- Centralized mailbox management using the on-premises Exchange Management Console (EMC) or the Exchange Control Panel in Exchange Server 2010, or by using the Exchange Admin Center (EAC) in Exchange Server 2013. Both versions will do centralized mailbox management using Exchange Management Shell (EMC)

- Message tracking, MailTips, and multi-mailbox search between on-premises and cloud-based organizations.

To create a hybrid configuration to link your Exchange Servers on-premises to your Exchange Online tenant, you need to configure a hybrid server. This is an Exchange Server 2013 server that does not store any mailboxes, but is used as the target for AutoDiscover, and optionally other protocols such as OWA and SMTP. You can build a hybrid server on Exchange 2010, but this will not be covered in this book. The main reason for using Exchange 2010 is that you have Exchange 2003 installed, and therefore cannot install Exchange Server 2013. If you have the choice between 2010 and 2013, choose 2013 as the server version to install.

> *NOTE* **HYBRID SERVER LICENSE**
>
> The hybrid server is provided license free, and the license key needed for the server can be obtained from *http://aka.ms/hybridkey*. The license key is available after you to login with your Office 365 global administrator account. The operating system license is not free, and Windows needs to be licensed on this server.

The hybrid server is the link for mail flow and free/busy. It is also the source server for mailbox moves to and from Office 365. Advanced hybrid configurations can be built where mailbox moves do not start from the hybrid server, and are sometimes used in multi-site Exchange deployments where you do not want a hybrid server installed in each location, but do not want to move all mailboxes via the one hybrid server location. Typically the hybrid server is installed as a pair, and accessed via a load balancer. This helps ensure high availability of the hybrid server during maintenance and unexpected outages.

You do not need to dedicate a server to the hybrid role, and an existing server can be used, but it is recommended to use dedicated servers for the role.

All of the steps to complete the Hybrid Configuration Wizard are started from the Exchange Control Panel website on-premises, but a connection from the machine that you run the wizard on to both Exchange Online and Exchange Server on-premises is required. It is recommended that if you are using Internet Explorer, do not use In-Private Browsing mode.

1. Ensure that you are running the latest version of Exchange Server on the server that you will connect to. At the time of writing, this is Exchange Server 2013 CU6. There is an issue in CU5 that means the Hybrid Configuration Wizard will fail, so do not use CU5. If you are using CU6, you need to run the fix it at *http://support.microsoft.com/kb/2997355/en-us* to ensure the wizard will work.

2. Login to Exchange Control Panel (*https://servername/ecp*) as an Exchange administrator.

3. Click the Office 365 link to the top right and login to the correct Office 365 tenant. You are now logged into both the on-premises server, and Office 365 from the same browser session. Note that if you are using Internet Explorer, you need to add your ECP URL and ***.office365.com** to your trusted sites list for this to work. Figure 5-1 shows the single browser tab connected to Office 365, and also shows the Exchange Online administration console, with a link to Enterprise on the top left, which is not present if you are administering Office 365 directly via *http://portal.office.com*.

FIGURE 5-1 ECP and Office 365 connected in one administration webpage

When you have the connection made to both on-premises and Office 365, you can start to run the Hybrid Configuration Wizard. The Hybrid Configuration Wizard performs the following steps:

1. Creates a federation trust.

2. Configures the Client Access Servers for hybrid.

3. Configures send and receive connectors for mail flow on-premises.

4. Configures inbound and outbound connectors for mail flow in Exchange Online.

5. Configures the MRS proxy settings for remote mailbox moves.

6. Configures OAuth between Exchange on-premises and Exchange Online (if you are running CU5 or later and running the wizard on the Exchange Server that is being configured for hybrid mode). If you are not running the wizard on the server, you can configure OAuth from the instructions found at *http://technet.microsoft.com/library /dn594521.aspx*.

Creating a federation trust

Creating a federation trust is setting up an authenticated connection for each of your domains between your on-premises server and Exchange Online. It is used for sharing information between Exchange organizations, and so you might have done this already for your Exchange organization. In Exchange Server 2013, this step can be run in advance of the Hybrid Configuration Wizard from the Sharing tabl on the Organization in ECP. This is shown in Figure 5-2 and Figure 5-3. If you do not have a trust in place, you will see the Enable button, but if you do, you will see the details of the trust as shown. The federation trust that will be created will be for your tenant domain, *tenant.mail.onmicrosoft.com*. A federation trust for your domains will be created in Office 365 as part of the process the wizard goes through.

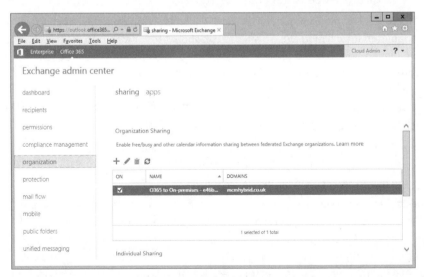

FIGURE 5-2 The federation trust shown on the Office 365 side of the administration console after it has been completed

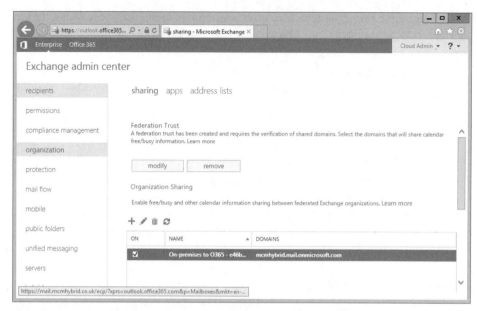

FIGURE 5-3 Federation trust as viewed from the on-premises administration page

The federation trust requires that you can prove ownership of the domain. Adding a record to the public DNS server that hosts the domain does this. The Hybrid Configuration Wizard will first verify the domain ownership, if this has not been completed. This is covered in more detail in Objective 5.2 of this chapter, which looks at federation as a stand-alone concept.

Configuring the Client Access Servers for hybrid

One of the first steps the Hybrid Configuration Wizard will do is configure a selected CAS server as the endpoint that Exchange Online will use to connect to for free/busy. This involves the setting up of a federation trust if one does not exist already, and an organization relationship between your tenant in Exchange Online and Exchange on-premises.

Configuring send and receive connectors for mail flow on-premises and inbound and outbound connectors in Exchange Online

Mail flow between Exchange on-premises and Exchange Online (and in the opposite direction) is direct between the two endpoints. It is not supported to have any SMTP gateway device between the hybrid servers and Exchange Online.

The mail flow is always encrypted with TLS. The send and receive connectors in Exchange on-premises, the Inbound connector into Exchange Online, and the Outbound connector from Exchange Online back to on-premises are configured to reject email that is not encrypted or comes from the wrong source. In Exchange 2013, the send and receive connectors can coexist with normal Internet mail flow connectors because email is always being sent to the tenant address space (*tenantname.mail.onmicrosoft.com*), or received from a server that holds the Microsoft digital certificate. Email from servers with different certificate names or address spaces will be rejected. Therefore, changes in certificates on your hybrid server can stop mail flow, and repeating the Hybrid Configuration Wizard, or modifying the connectors by hand to the new certificate details is required.

Configuring the MRS proxy settings for remote mailbox moves

One of the final steps that the Hybrid Configuration Wizard will do is enable the MRSProxy setting on all CAS servers with an ExternalURL set for Exchange Web Services. Therefore, when you run the Hybrid Configuration Wizard, all of the CAS servers in Internet-facing sites (those that have an ExternalURL set for the Exchange WebServicesVirtualDirectory) need to be online and reachable from the server that is running the Hybrid Configuration Wizard. If some servers are across a WAN from the server on which you are running the Hybrid Configuration Wizard, you might find that the wizard can take an hour or more per virtual directory, and that multiple hours for running the wizard can be expected. Figure 5-4 shows the error message you get in the Hybrid Configuration Wizard when a CAS server is offline or otherwise unreachable from the server running the wizard.

FIGURE 5-4 An error in the Hybrid Configuration Wizard

Errors in the Hybrid Configuration Wizard are recorded to a log file and a verbose .extra file. It is worth running the hybrid wizard and looking at the latest log files in the Exchange Server installation folder /V15/Logging/Update-HybridConfiguration to get an idea of the process that is performed.

Configuring OAuth between Exchange on-premises and Exchange Online

The exam will not cover OAuth between Exchange on-premises and Exchange Online because this is a new feature that first arrived in CU5. OAuth can be configured from the instructions at *http://technet.microsoft.com/library/dn594521.aspx*, or automatically at the end of the Hybrid Configuration Wizard if you are running the Hybrid Configuration Wizard on the hybrid server.

OAuth is used to authenticate communications between two entities without the need for knowledge of user names or passwords. An example of OAuth in the real world would be logging into a website (not Facebook) with your Facebook login details. You authenticate to Facebook successfully and it tells the other website that you are authenticated and allowed to access the third-party site. In Exchange Server as of CU5, OAuth is used to do cross-forest eDiscovery search. This is when a user runs a search in one forest (say Exchange Online), but wants to query mailboxes in another forest (for example Exchange on-premises).

OAuth does not replace federation trusts, though both of them authenticate servers across the hybrid configuration. If you have any Exchange 2010 servers publically available, do not enable OAuth until CU7 is available because OAuth, if configured, will attempt to connect to 2010 using OAuth and fail, when it should use the federation trust.

Using the Hybrid Configuration Wizard

The wizard starts with the Setup page shown in Figure 5-5, and continues through the process. Some of the screens are shown for information.

FIGURE 5-5 Starting the Hybrid Configuration Wizard

After you start the wizard, and it has confirmed that you are logged into Office 365, as well as on-premises Exchange Server, you will be asked if you want to set up Exchange hybrid. If you have run the wizard already, you will be asked if you want to update it. When updating, all of the previous settings are maintained.

Figure 5-6 shows the choice of whether to use Client Access and Mailbox servers, or Edge Servers for secure email transport. As an option, you can route all outbound email from Office 365 out via the on-premises servers. By default, outbound email from Office 365 leaves the Internet direct from Office 365.

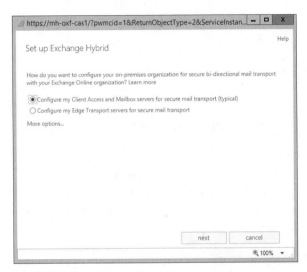

FIGURE 5-6 Choosing mail flow options

Next in the process, choose the Exchange Servers on-premises that you will receive connections from Exchange Online Protection for inbound mail flow. Then choose the sending Mailbox servers.

Every Exchange Server on-premises that you selected in the mail flow screens need to have the same digital certificate installed. The certificate will have a display name (also the same), and Figure 5-7 shows the screen where you select the certificate. This certificate needs to be issued by a trusted third-party certificate authority and be valid at the current date and time. That is, the certificate has a valid from date and an expiry date, and the current date must be within this timeframe.

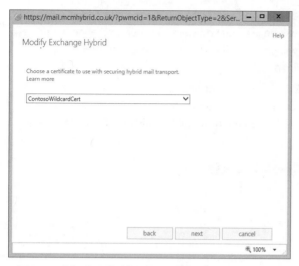

FIGURE 5-7 Selecting the digital certificate for the Hybrid Configuration Wizard

The on-premises Exchange Server (CAS) that will receive email from Exchange Online Protection (EOP) needs to be accessible from EOP, and ideally by way of an MX or A record. This is not your normal MX record for mail flow though because this is used exclusively for mail flow between EOP and on-premises. The value of this A or MX record in the form of an FQDN is entered into the wizard (and shown in Figure 5-8).

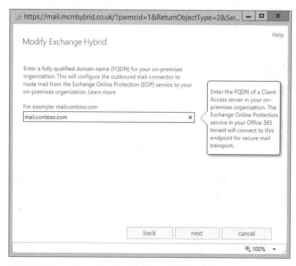

FIGURE 5-8 Setting the inbound mail flow address

Finally, you need to provide the username of an on-premises Exchange administrator and a Global Administrator for Office 365. The Hybrid Configuration Wizard will connect to both Exchange on-premises and Exchange Online as these users, and configure hybrid Exchange for you. Figure 5-9 shows this configuration process as it proceeds.

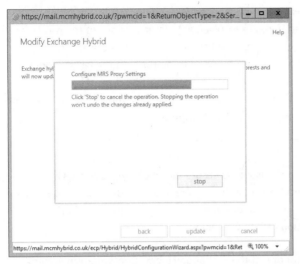

FIGURE 5-9 The Hybrid Configuration Wizard process completing

Once the Hybrid Configuration Wizard is complete, you will be presented with Figure 5-10, showing that the entire process has completed successfully.

FIGURE 5-10 The end of the Hybrid Configuration Wizard with the process being successful

Evaluating limitations of the Hybrid Configuration Wizard

The Microsoft Certified Professional exam that you are reading this book to study for is based, at the time of writing, on the RTM (release to manufacturing) version of Exchange Server 2013 Service Pack 1. It does not take into consideration any of the changes made in later cumulative updates to Exchange Server 2013, which at the time of writing (Nov 2014), cumulative update 7 is expected to be released within a month. Therefore, some of the limitations of the Hybrid Configuration Wizard described here are resolved with later versions of the product, but some of the limitations are not. It is important to point out that there are support requirements for hybrid Exchange in that you are required to be running the latest, or n-1 version of the cumulative update for support reasons. Therefore, at the time of writing, only CU6 and CU5 (the one previous version) are supported. Note that Exchange 2013 Service Pack 1 is CU4, and so it is no longer supported for hybrid Exchange.

> **IMPORTANT** **SUPPORTABILITY**
>
> Microsoft requires that hybrid Exchange customers ensure that their hybrid servers are running the latest version of Exchange Server, or the one previous release of Exchange Server (known as n-1). Therefore, upon cumulative update 7 being released, all hybrid Exchange customers should be running CU7 or CU6 only.

The following are some of the limitations of the Exchange Hybrid Configuration Wizard that need to be considered when setting up hybrid Exchange.

- **Proxy servers** Connectivity to Exchange Online is required from each of the hybrid Exchange Servers. If any network traffic to or from these servers over the HTTPS protocol goes via a web proxy server, there is no guarantee that the functions of hybrid will work. Therefore, ensure that the hybrid Exchange Servers can reach the URLs and IP addresses listed at *http://technet.microsoft.com/en-us/library/hh373144.aspx*.

- **Firewalls** As with the proxy servers, connectivity is required to Exchange Online Protection for mail flow (TCP port 25), and both MRS and free/busy (TCP port 443). The Hybrid Configuration Wizard will set up connectors to EOP and expect to be able to reach Exchange Online for free/busy, but it will not test that it actually can do that. Therefore, the URLs and IP addresses listed at *http://technet.microsoft.com/en-us/library/hh373144.aspx* must be reachable from the hybrid servers.

- **Multi-forest** The hybrid wizard does not configure hybrid if you have multiple forests connecting to the same Office 365 tenant, or single forests split across multiple tenants. The DirSync software had the same limitations, but the recently released AADSync software solves these issues, though you will need to manually configure the mail flow connectors to reach multiple tenants, if you have one forest to multiple Exchange Online tenants.

- **Service checking** The Hybrid Configuration Wizard will build the pieces needed, but will not check that they are working apart from the validity of the digital certificate. Therefore, although the wizard completed, there is no guarantee that pieces such as AutoDiscover, federation, and mail flow are working.

- **Policies** The Hybrid Configuration Wizard does not copy policies and other Exchange on-premises configuration such as transport rules, message classification, OWA policies, and settings to Exchange Online. So upon finishing hybrid, you need to duplicate any of these settings in Exchange Online if you still want them to apply to migrated mailboxes.

- **Authentication** OAuth is not configured at the end of the Hybrid Configuration Wizard unless you are using the latest versions. But OAuth did not exist for the product in the RTM timeframe, and so would not be covered in the exam. OAuth was introduced in CU4 (Service Pack 1), and the automation of OAuth came in the CU5 update to the Hybrid Configuration Wizard.

- **MRSProxy** The wizard does not configure the MRSProxy endpoints. Prior to CU4, the MRSProxy endpoint was not enabled for remote moves. The latest version of the wizard resolves this issue about enabling the endpoint for remote moves, but still requires the creation of, and checking, that the MRSProxy endpoint is actually reachable.

Configuring requirements for single sign-on (SSO)

To login to Office 365, and therefore Exchange Online, requires a username and password. Office 365 allows for three different configurations of user accounts, each with their own advantages and disadvantages. The following list summarizes the user account type, and the impact this has on logging into Office 365.

- **Cloud Identity** This user account is created in Office 365, and exists only in Azure Active Directory. It is not related to any user account that may exist for the user in any other system, and it has a password that is associated with this account only. This type of user is the easiest to set up because it requires no extra hardware or software installation on-premises. It does require the user to remember multiple usernames and passwords because their login to Office 365 is not the same as their login to anything they may have on-premises. The username and password could be set to be the same, but they will have different expiry dates, and need changing at different times. So, setting them the same will cause user confusion.

- **Synchronized Identity** This user account exists on-premises and the editable copy of this account is within the Active Directory on-premises. Using either the DirSync or AADSync software, this user is replicated to Azure Active Directory, and the user's password is hashed twice, and replicated to the cloud as well. When the user logs into Office 365, the entered password is hashed twice using the same hash, and if the entered and now hashed information is the same as that replicated from on-premises, the user is logged in. Note that Office 365 does not see, or can determine the user's password, but uses a hash of the user's password to determine if the password is correct. This user type requires DirSync or AADSync installed on a single machine on-premises, and every three hours user changes are replicated to the cloud. Within two seconds of the user changing their password on-premises, the password hash is replicated to Azure Active Directory. On-premises the user requires a UPN that is Internet routable (that is, it looks like a valid email address), and a server to run the DirSync software.

- **Federated Identity** This is the same user account as in the synchronized identity. It is created on-premises and replicated to the cloud, but this time the password is not hashed and replicated to the cloud (or if it is, it is not used for login). When the user enters their username, the domain portion of the name is read, and the user directed to the publically available AD FS server infrastructure created on-premises. The on-premises AD FS server authenticates the user and tells Microsoft Online (Office 365, Azure, Intune) that the user can login. Therefore, Microsoft is not responsible for user authentication, but the on-premises Active Directory, via the AD FS servers are. For this configuration, you need to have the pieces listed in the rest of this section in place. This is the most complex of the three user authentication options to set up, but the user is logging in with the same username and password, and also from the same source authentication system that they logged into their PC with. Therefore, they are already signed in, and do not require a second login for Office 365.

To implement AD FS, and therefore single sign-on, you require the following:

- Active Directory Federation Services (AD FS) installed on-premises.

- A Web Application Proxy (WAP) installed on-premises (usually in the perimeter network). The WAP server is the AD FS proxy server that comes with Windows Server 2012 R2. If you are using Windows Server 2012 or 2008 R2, you will have an AD FS proxy server installation instead of a WAP installation. WAP acts as an AD FS proxy for inbound connections from the Internet to the AD FS server (rather than publishing the AD FS server direct to the Internet). It also provides other web proxy services that are not needed for single sign-on, and so are not discussed here. Therefore, the WAP server role feature and earlier AD FS proxy roles are to be considered analogous for the purposes of single sign-on.

- A digital certificate issued for the namespace of the AD FS server. This certificate needs to be trusted by Office 365, and so must be issued by a trusted third-party certificate authority. The name on the certificate can be a subject alternative name, and so the name can be included on your existing Exchange certificate, or by using a wildcard certificate.

- A load balancer is recommended because it is highly recommended to have more than one AD FS server, and more than one WAP/AD FS Proxy server. If either the single WAP, or AD FS server should go offline, the users will not be able to login to Office 365 because the AD FS system is required for login. Therefore, a load balancer in front of the WAP/AD FS proxy server in the perimeter, and a second load balancer in front of the AD FS servers, is highly recommended.

- The final requirement is to enable single sign-on in Office 365. This is done from the Users, Active Users area of the admin portal. The steps to complete this process require installing the Windows Azure Active Directory Module for Windows PowerShell, and using PowerShell to connect to the AD FS server and to Office 365, and then to change the domains you want to use from a managed domain to a federated domain. Federated domains use an AD FS server for login, managed domains rely on the Microsoft Online authentication system.

Designing and configuring Active Directory Federation Services (AD FS)

To design and configure AD FS for single sign-on with Office 365, you need to install the AD FS server, and the WAP or AD FS proxy server. The AD FS servers need access to the Active Directory domain controllers. They can be installed as a role on a domain controller for use in lab or test environments. Installing AD FS on a domain controller can also reduce server count and operating system licenses when installing AD FS in a small organization, but that limits the AD FS server to using Active Directory only from the local domain controller, and not from all of the domain controllers installed in the current site, thus reducing availability of AD FS. The WAP/AD FS proxy server cannot be installed on a domain controller, nor can it be installed on the AD FS server itself. You have a minimum server requirement for AD FS of at least two servers, and for high availability, at least two more because you should have at least two WAP/AD FS proxy servers, and two AD FS servers.

AD FS design

Typically the WAP/AD FS proxy server is installed in the perimeter network. This means there will be a firewall between it and the Internet, and between the proxy and the AD FS server as well. The AD FS system communicates over HTTPS, so only TCP port 443 needs to be open from the WAP/AD FS proxy to the AD FS server (or more typically to the load balancer in front of the AD FS servers), and also TCP port 443 open from the Internet to the WAP/AD FS proxy. A suggestion of a network topology for AD FS is shown in Figure 5-11.

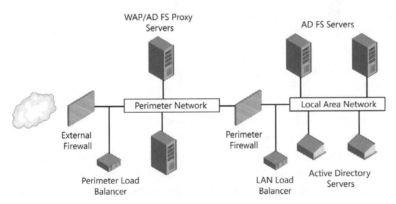

FIGURE 5-11 A suggested AD FS network diagram

In addition to the TCP port 443 (HTTPS) rules on the firewalls, you would probably include rules for server management and remote access from the LAN to the perimeter network as per your requirements. But all you need for AD FS is HTTPS published from the WAP/AD FS proxy (or perimeter network load balancer) to the Internet, and the same published from the AD FS server (or LAN network load balancer) to the WAP/AD FS proxy on the perimeter network. The return traffic to these network paths needs to traverse the firewalls as well.

Users will access AD FS by way of connecting to the service that they need to authenticate on to. Users do not start by browsing to the AD FS server. The user will connect in this case to Office 365 and attempt to login. When they enter their login name, the domain they enter will be seen as a federated domain, and the user will be redirected to the AD FS server. If the user is on the Internet, or on the LAN, they will be directed to the same URL. Therefore, the AD FS server needs to be reachable via that same URL (configured during the set up of AD FS) from both the LAN and the Internet. This is done via DNS.

In public DNS you will add an A record for the external IP address of the WAP/AD FS proxy server, and in internal DNS you will add a record for the IP address of the AD FS server on the LAN. When you have load balancers, you will use the virtual IP address that they host that is load balancing the AD FS infrastructure. For example, in Figure 5-12 you can see a similar network to Figure 5-11, but this time, example IP addresses are shown. For example, you would use 192.168.10.10 as the A record value for the AD FS server in internal DNS (this IP is on the LAN load balancer), and 131.107.2.200 as the A record for the same server name but in public DNS (this IP is on the external firewall, publishing the perimeter load balancer).

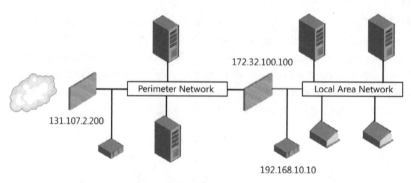

FIGURE 5-12 IP address examples in AD FS

The WAP/AD FS proxy servers need to be able to resolve the AD FS server name to the AD FS servers, or the load balancer in front of the AD FS servers. Therefore, if the perimeter network can do DNS resolution to the internal DNS servers, this will work fine. If the perimeter network cannot resolve internal DNS, a HOSTS entry will be required on each WAP/AD FS proxy server for the IP address that the AD FS servers are published into the perimeter on. In the example in Figure 5-12, this would be 172.32.100.100, which is on the perimeter network and publishes the load balancer on the LAN.

A common name for AD FS servers in DNS is sts.domain.com. The *sts* portion stands for "secure token service," which is what an AD FS server is providing. You are not restricted to using this name though, and other names that are typically used are login.domain.com, or adfs.domain.com. Whatever name you use that value needs to be resolvable from the LAN, the perimeter, and the Internet. It is the same name that you need on your digital certificate. Therefore, the A record in DNS in all of the preceding examples, and the subject name or alternative subject name on the certificate, needs to use this name. In the example in the "AD FS server configuration" section below, you are going to use *sts.contosochemists.co.uk*.

AD FS server configuration

This section summarizes the steps to install the AD FS server on a Windows Server 2012 R2 server (sometimes unofficially known as AD FS 3.0), and a Web Application Proxy server, also on a different Windows Server 2012 R2 server. Once installed, the WAP server will be configured to connect to the AD FS server.

Before you begin, it is a good idea to install the digital certificate that contains the AD FS server FQDN onto both the AD FS server and the WAP/AD FS proxy server. The same certificate is used in all cases, and the private key needs to be available for these services to use. You can install the certificate into the personal store by importing the PFX file that contains the digital certificate and private key using the MMC certificates snap in. Make sure you use the local computer account certificate snap in and not the current user, which is the default. AD FS 3.0 has no requirement on IIS, and so IIS is not installed on these servers.

The AD FS server needs to be joined to a domain in the forest that it will authenticate against. The AD FS server role can be installed from Server Manager. The first few dialog boxes of the installation are self-explanatory, and common to all role installations. Once the role is installed, you can start the AD FS server configuration. The WAP/AD FS proxy server does not need to be joined to the domain. The WAP feature of Windows Server 2012 R2 is part of the Remote Access role.

To install the AD FS server role, start Server Manager, and add the Active Directory Federation Services role, as shown in Figure 5-13.

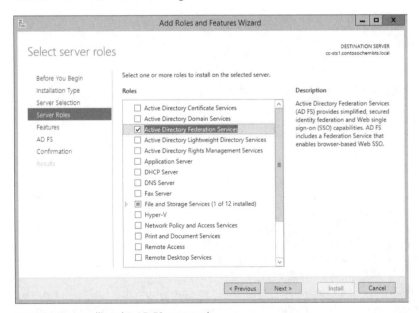

FIGURE 5-13 Installing the AD FS server role

Once the role is installed, the configuration of the service can take place. The requirements for completing the installation are a domain admin account, and a publically trusted digital certificate that is already installed on the server. If you were creating a new AD FS server environment, you would choose the option to create the first federation server in a federation server farm. If you were adding the second or third server, you would add these to the farm.

> **NOTE STANDALONE SERVER FARMS**
>
> If you are installing AD FS server on Windows 2012 or earlier, you can create a standalone server farm. This allows only one server in the farm, and does not provide any redundancy or options for high availability. You will see from the above choices that this is not an option in Windows Server 2012 R2.
>
> Therefore, even if you are just creating a lab environment, you should always create a server farm because you have the ability to add more servers if you want, or need to. Avoid creating standalone AD FS server deployments.

On the Specify Service Properties page, select your trusted digital certificate (or import it if you have not installed it already), and then select the correct service name from the second drop-down list. Finally, add a display name, which users will see at login. This is shown in Figure 5-14.

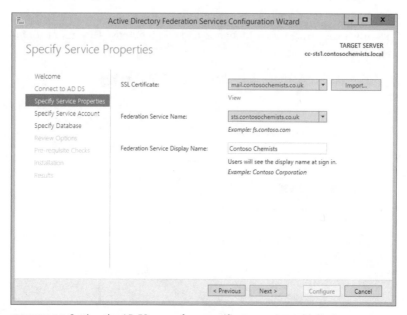

FIGURE 5-14 Setting the AD FS server farm certificate, service, and display name

If you have a wildcard certificate, you will be allowed to enter your choice of service name. Remember the service name is the value in DNS that resolves to both the WAP server from the Internet, and the AD FS server from the LAN.

On the Specify Service Account page, you might get a warning about group managed service accounts, and needing to run the PowerShell Add-KdsRootKey -EffectiveTime (Get-Date).

AddHours(-10). This is only possible with a Windows Server 2012 R2 Active Directory schema. If you do not have this schema level, you can use an existing domain user account. This account needs to be a domain user (not administrator), and have a non-expiring password. This user account would be similar in concept to most service accounts that you create in Active Directory.

For your configuration database, most deployments can use Windows Internal Database, but if your AD FS sizing requires SQL Server, or you want to use other features of SQL Server such as database mirroring, you can select the database here. The wizard needs the rights to create and configure the database on the SQL Server. To size your AD FS deployment, use the Excel spreadsheet at *http://download.microsoft.com/download/3/1/3/31312F45-4AB3-4B54-8E23-6326BAF4F5BC/ADFS-capacity-planning-sizing-spreadsheet-DLC.xlsx*, and for sizing in terms of CPU and memory, view the table at *http://msdn.microsoft.com/en-us/library/azure/jj151831.aspx*.

The remaining screens of the wizard are just summary pages and configuration checks. On confirming these, the service will be configured. Once AD FS is installed, you can check that it is operational by browsing to *https://sts.domain.com/AD FS/ls/idpinitiatedsignon.htm*, where sts.domain.com is the URL for the AD FS server from a browser on the LAN. DNS updates should already have been completed to ensure that sts.domain.com resolves to the AD FS Server correctly. If DNS is correct, and the server installation is successful, you should see the view shown in Figure 5-15.

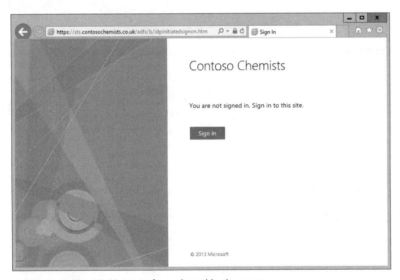

FIGURE 5-15 The AD FS server forms based login screen

On the LAN, the AD FS server FQDN should be added to the Local Intranet zone in Internet Explorer, and once it is, clicking the Sign In button will result in automatic sign in when browsed from a domain joined client PC.

Web Application Proxy configuration

To install the WAP server, install the Remote Access role on the server (as shown in Figure 5-16). On the role services page, select the Web Application Proxy (Figure 5-17). You will be shown the features required for the WAP role service, which you need to confirm to complete the selection of the role service.

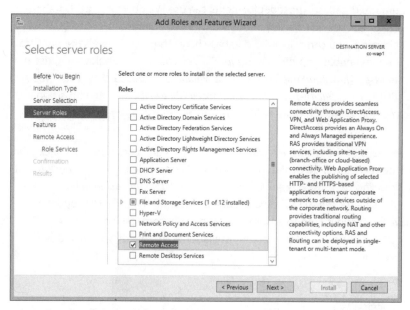

FIGURE 5-16 Installing the Web Application Proxy by way of the Remote Access role

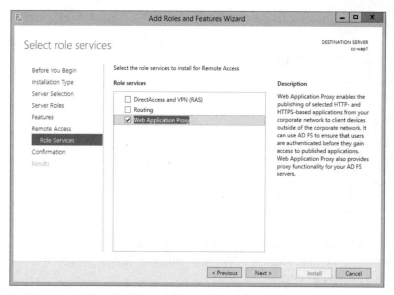

FIGURE 5-17 Installing the Web Application Proxy role service

Once the WAP role service is installed, and the AD FS server is also installed, make sure that you can browse to the AD FS server. This will check that you have the correct firewall ports open (TCP 443), and that name resolution is working. You should be able to browse the URL *https://sts.domain.com/AD FS/ls/idpinitiatedsignon.htm* where *sts.domain.com* is the URL for the AD FS server. You should see the same login page as when testing the AD FS server was working. It is a blue graphic to the left, and a sign-in form to the right. This is shown earlier in Figure 5-15.

If the WAP server can reach the AD FS server login page, you can continue the WAP configuration. This is started from Server Manager. It requires three pieces of information. The first piece of information is the service name, for example sts.domain.com. It also requires a username and password of an administrator account on the AD FS servers. If the service name and credentials are correct, select the AD FS proxy certificate that you have already installed on the WAP server. Then on the final screen of the wizard, you will be shown the PowerShell that you could use to do this again, should you want to install multiple servers. Configuring the AD FS proxy takes a minute or two, and then you should be able to browse the same URL as used earlier, but this time from the Internet, through the external firewall to the WAP server. The WAP server is proxying the connection to the AD FS server, and not completing the authentication itself.

Configuring Office 365 to use single sign-on

The final step in configuring single sign-on to Office 365 is to change the domain that you have already added to Office 365 so that it requires federated sign-on. This involves connecting with PowerShell to both Office 365, and the AD FS server. The PowerShell cmdlets are the Windows Azure Active Directory Module for Windows PowerShell, and these can be downloaded from the Office 365 administration portal. To run them on Windows Server, you need the 64-bit version, though at the time of writing, the 32-bit version had reached end of life and was not getting any further updates. Therefore, the 64-bit version should be the version you always install. The installation of the PowerShell cmdlets might have a few additional requirements based on the version of Windows you are running them on, such as specific .NET Framework versions, or the Microsoft Online Services Sign-In Assistant, but the installation will prompt you through these requirements as you complete the installation.

When you have the Windows Azure Active Directory Module for Windows PowerShell installed, you can start PowerShell, and run the following cmdlets. The first set of these cmdlets are useful to keep saved to a PS1 file because connecting to Office 365 via remote PowerShell is a frequent administration task when you have a service in the cloud.

```
$cred = Get-Credential
Write-Host "Username: " $cred.username
Connect-MsolService -Credential $cred
Write-Host "...connected to Office 365 Azure Active Directory"
```

This code results in a prompt asking you for your Office 365 administrator credentials. It then uses these credentials (stored in the $cred variable) to connect you to Office 365. The code also writes this information to the screen so that you can tell whom you are logged in as because you can open multiple PowerShell windows, and each could be logged in as a different user!

Once you are logged in, you should run Get-MsolDomain to check that you have added all of the domains that you want to have federated users under (Figure 5-18 shows this output). A federated user is one whose login is federated to the AD FS server on-premises. All of the users in a given federated domain will use single sign-on, and you cannot have some users in a domain using AD FS, and the others in the same domain not using AD FS. Federated users also require that their login name contain the federated domain. For example, if you own *contoso.com*, and you register *contoso.com* as a domain in Office 365, it will work for users either created in the service, or users created on-premises and synced with DirSync/AADSync. If they are created on-premises, the user needs the user principal name (UPN) value to contain this domain, so a user *bill@contoso.com* would be a correct UPN value, but *bill@contoso.local*, or another value, would either not be valid (.local is not Internet routable, so not valid for Office 365), or if not registered in Office 365, could not be synced to the cloud.

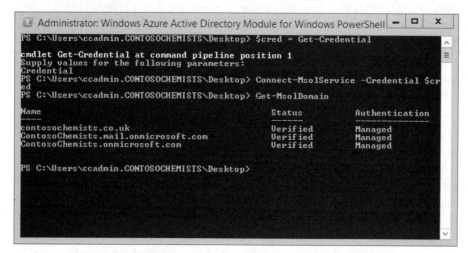

FIGURE 5-18 Get-MsolDomain shown in a Remote PowerShell session to Office 365

Once you have verified that Get-MsolDomain returns all of your required domains for single sign-on, and your users have synced to the cloud with one of the listed domains, you are ready to change the domain from managed to federated.

To change the domain, first ensure that the PowerShell session is connected to the AD FS server. You do this with the Set-MsolADFSContext PowerShell cmdlet. The full cmdlet is shown here.

```
Set-MsolADFSContext -Computer <AD FS server FQDN>
```

Once you have made a connection to the AD FS server, and even if you are running the cmdlets on the AD FS server, you need to run the above cmdlet. Then you are ready to change your domains from managed to federated. The cmdlet for doing this is Convert-MsolDomain-ToFederated, and the name of the domain. If you have more than one domain, you must run the cmdlet with the -SupportMultipleDomain switch as well. An example of running this in PowerShell for a company with a .com, a .co.uk, and a .fr domain would be as follows.

```
Convert-MsolDomainToFederated -DomainName contoso.com -SupportMultipleDomain
Convert-MsolDomainToFederated -DomainName contoso.co.uk -SupportMultipleDomain
Convert-MsolDomainToFederated -DomainName contoso.fr -SupportMultipleDomain
```

This process (shown in Figure 5-19) will connect to both the primary AD FS server and Office 365, and generate self-signed certificates for encrypting and sharing the token information, and then swap the certificates with the other party. As part of Office 365, you need to ensure that you know the expiry date of the certificate, and using the above cmdlet to update the AD FS token signing certificates before they expire. Alternatively, you can download the Microsoft Office 365 Federation Metadata Update Automation Installation Tool (*http://gallery.technet.microsoft.com/scriptcenter/Office-365-Federation-27410bdc*). This tool is a Windows PowerShell script that you run on your AD FS server to keep the certificates in sync between Office 365 and AD FS server.

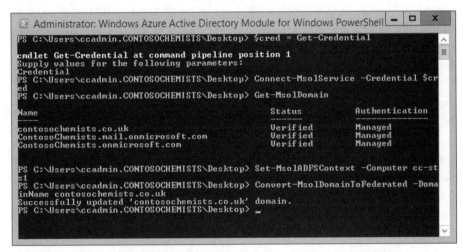

FIGURE 5-19 Converting a domain to federated

Once the domain has been changed to federated and confirmed with Get-MsolDomain, you should be able to visit *http://portal.office.com*, and login as a user with this domain. Upon entering the username (and before entering the password), you will be redirect to the AD FS server URL. If you are running Internet Explorer on a domain joined PC on the LAN, you will automatically be logged in (if the AD FS server URL is in the Local Sites zone). If you watch the address bar in the browser, you should see it redirecting to the AD FS server, and back to Microsoft Online to log you in.

Thought experiment

Evaluating sign-in options

In this thought experiment, apply what you've learned about this objective. You can find answers to these questions in the "Answers" section at the end of this chapter.

You manage Exchange Server for a large organization and you have a hybrid configuration in place for a small pilot of 100 users. Some of the pilot users are reporting back that the need to login to each Office 365 service separately is considered reduced functionality and recommend changes if the company went beyond the pilot into production.

1. How can you tell what authentication scheme you are currently using?

2. You want to pilot AD FS. What do you need to put together to make this pilot work?

Objective summary

- The Hybrid Configuration Wizard is a feature of Exchange on-premises that allows the on-premises organization and an Office 365 Exchange Online tenant to appear as a single organization.

- Hybrid configuration will set up secure mail flow between the on-premises organization and the Exchange Online tenant, as well as federated free/busy sharing.

- Support for hybrid configuration requires that Exchange on-premises remains within the current or previous version of Exchange Server 2013.

- The hybrid wizard only links mail flow and free/busy. Features of Exchange, such as rules and policies, need to be added to Exchange on-premises, and Exchange Online manually.

- AD FS allows for single sign-on. It is not a requirement of hybrid to have AD FS and federated logins.

Objective review

Answer the following questions to test your knowledge of the information in this objective. You can find the answers to these questions and explanations of why each answer choice is correct or incorrect in the "Answers" section at the end of this chapter.

1. You run the Hybrid Configuration Wizard and it fails during the MRSProxy stage. What is the likely reason?

    A. You are running Exchange Server 2010 and Exchange Server 2013 client access servers.

B. You are running Exchange Server 2003 and Exchange Server 2013 client access servers.

C. Not all of your client access servers are online or reachable from the hybrid server.

D. AutoDiscover is not implemented correctly, and the client access servers cannot be located.

2. You want to ensure that all of your emails to the Internet from your Exchange Online users go via the on-premises infrastructure. What do you need to set up?

A. You need to select centralized mail flow during the Hybrid Configuration Wizard.

B. You need to delete the connectors made by the Hybrid Configuration Wizard, and replace them with manually created connectors.

C. You cannot do this feature with Exchange Online.

D. You need to have your MX records pointing at your on-premises infrastructure.

3. You had a working AD FS server that has been working for one year, and today it stopped authenticating users. Which of the following would be your first consideration given that it has been installed for one year?

A. The token signing certificate has expired.

B. The Windows Server is not activated and has shut down.

C. Your third-party digital certificate has expired.

D. Your user accounts passwords have expired.

Objective 5.2: Deploy and manage Exchange federation

Federation is the configuration in Exchange Server that allows the sharing of information between different Exchange organizations. It is also used between the on-premises organization and Exchange Online to share the same information when Exchange Online is running in hybrid mode with Exchange on-premises.

To set up this sharing, and allow different domains to share free/busy, message tracking, and other features such as contacts, you need to first create a federation trust, and then an organization relationship to connect two organizations to allow sharing.

> **This objective covers how to:**
> - Manage federation trusts with Microsoft federation gateways
> - Manage sharing policies
> - Design certificate and firewall requirements
> - Manage organization relationships

Managing federation trusts with Microsoft federation gateway

The federation trust is a configuration of Exchange Server that allows two or more external organizations, also running Exchange Server, to securely communicate to share free/busy information (also known as *calendar availability*). The sharing of this information can only happen between two parties by prior arrangement, and the federation trust is the underlying connection that brokers the communications between the parties involved.

To create a federation trust to allow for calendar, and other sharing between Exchange organizations, involves proving ownership of your domain names, and then creating a trust between your on-premises server and the Microsoft authentication platform called Azure Active Directory. Later, when you want to share information with another Exchange organization, you both swap information via Azure Active Directory that acts as a broker for your communications. If a sharing request is received by your organization, it must have come from one of your partner organizations, and the request must contain proof within it of whom it came from. That proof is cryptographically signed, and is only available via the other organization's federation trust with Azure Active Directory. Therefore, a spoofed sharing request will not contain the correct proofs, and so will fail to elicit any information.

> *NOTE* **CHANGE OF NAME**
>
> The objective domain for the exam, and therefore the title of this section, refers to the authentication broker as the Microsoft federation gateway. This has recently been named the Azure Active Directory (or Azure AD) after the actual product that hosts the authentication system.

To create a federation trust in Exchange Control Panel, follow these steps:

1. On an Exchange 2013 server in your on-premises organization, navigate to Organization, Sharing.

2. Click Enable to start the Enable Federation Trust Wizard.

3. After the wizard completes, click Close.

4. In the Federation Trust section of the Sharing tab, click Modify.

5. In Sharing-Enabled Domains, next to Step 1, click Browse.

6. In Select Accepted Domains, select the primary shared domain from the list, and then click OK. This will present the Edit Sharing Domains dialog box, as shown in Figure 5-20.

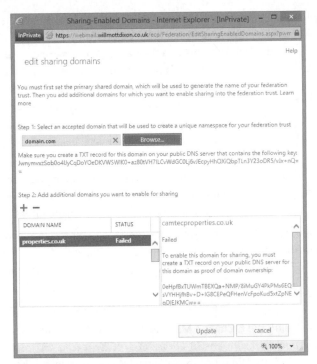

FIGURE 5-20 Adding domains to a federation trust

The domain you select for Step 1 is used to configure the OrgID for the federation trust. The value used in Exchange 2013 is uniquely generated. In Exchange 2010, you needed to create a subdomain of your accepted domain, and then create a federation trust with this name. Therefore, if you specify the federated domain *contoso.com* as your organization's primary SMTP domain, the account namespace FYDIBOHF25SPDLT.contoso.com will be automatically created as the OrgID for the federation trust, if you are doing this for the first time on an Exchange 2013 server. If an OrgID already exists, having been created in Exchange 2010, it is probably in the form of *service.contoso.com* where *contoso.com* is one of your accepted domains and "service" is a value for a subdomain you are not already using, or likely to use.

1. Make a note of the federated domain proof that's generated for the primary shared domain. You'll use this string to create a TXT record on your public DNS server. It is recommended that you copy this long text string directly from the Exchange Server into your DNS console to avoid typographical errors because the string value needs to match in DNS that which Exchange Server asks you to use. If the TXT record is created by using an incorrect federated domain proof string, the Windows Azure AD authentication system won't be able to verify proof of domain ownership, and you won't be able to add it to the federated organization identifier.

2. Click Add to add additional domains to the federated trust for email addresses that will be used by users in your organization that require federated sharing features. For example, if you have users that use a subdomain in their email address, such as *sales. contoso.com*, you would add the *sales.contoso.com* domain to the federation trust. A federated domain proof string will be created for each additional domain selected. You must create separate TXT records on your public DNS for each additional domain.

3. Using the federated domain proof strings provided for each domain (use Get-Federated-DomainProof -DomainName <fqdn> to retrieve this from the shell), create TXT records for each of these domains on your public DNS server. Wait for your DNS providers up-date schedule to pass before moving onto the next step. Depending upon your provider, this could take up to 24 or more hours if they make the changes for you, or just a few minutes if you enter the records directly into a service that does immediate updates.

4. After the TXT records are created and replicated, click the Modify button in Exchange Control Panel, Organization. This time you will be able to click OK, and Microsoft will check each DNS proof string against the public DNS server. The federation trust will be created if all of the proof strings are found in DNS.

5. Once the trust is created, you can remove the proof strings from DNS if you want.

It is possible to do the above using the Exchange Management Shell. For the instructions on doing this see *http://technet.microsoft.com/en-GB/library/jj657462(v=exchg.150).aspx*. If you need to retrieve the federated domain proof that is shown in the console, but have closed the console, it is possible to retrieve this information using Get-FederatedDomainProof in the shell.

Once you have a federation trust in place, and the self-signed certificate that it uses for the trust has replicated around all of your Exchange Servers, you can modify the trust. Modify-ing the trust is similar to creating it if you add new domains because you need to prove your ownership of them. If you remove a federated domain, and then choose to add it later, you will need to go through the proof of ownership process via public DNS again.

In Exchange 2010 RTM federation trusts were created using a public certificate, and against the Microsoft Live ID authentication platform, and not the Azure Active Directory au-thentication platform. Therefore, it is recommended that organizations that created a federa-tion trust back when Exchange 2010 was released, and before Exchange 2010 Service Pack 1 was installed, should delete and recreate their federation trust. When two organizations need to share information, and the authentication of this is via federation trusts, they both need to use the same authentication platform.

> **IMPORTANT   REFRESHING FEDERATION METADATA**
>
> There have been issues recorded where the federation data stored in the Azure Active Directory authentication platform has become stale and out of date. If sharing via a federa-tion trust was working and now is not, it is recommended to run Get-FederationTrust | Set-FederationTrust -RefreshMetadata $True.

If you have a web proxy enabled in your organization, Exchange Server will need to either bypass the proxy server, or the proxy server will need to transparently allow requests from the Exchange Server without authentication requests. If the web proxy requires authentication, the error shown in Figure 5-21 will appear in Exchange Control Panel as you configure the federation trust.

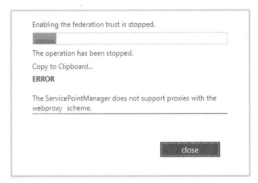

Enabling the federation trust is stopped.

The operation has been stopped.
Copy to Clipboard...
ERROR

The ServicePointManager does not support proxies with the webproxy scheme.

close

FIGURE 5-21 Authenticating proxy error when creating a federation trust

To create a federation trust and bypass the proxy, ensure that Exchange Server has a direct route to the Internet, or that the proxy server that it has to use, will not require authentication when connections come from the Exchange Server. The Exchange Server proxy setting for federation trusts is set using Set-ExchangeServer <server_name> -InternetWebProxy <proxy_url>, and not via Internet Explorer or netsh where most applications' proxy settings are configured.

Managing sharing policies

Sharing policies are configurations in Exchange Server that allow other organizations and individuals to access some of your information in your mailbox (chiefly calendars and contacts). By having access to this information, they can collaborate with you in their business, or manage schedules on a personal level.

Exchange Server supports sharing of calendars from either the personal level, which requires sharing policies, or at a corporate level (multiple users in the organization to the partner organization), which requires organization relationships. Therefore, the easiest way to see if you need to set up a federation trust and an organizational relationship is a factor of the number of users at each end. If you want to share one or two users' calendars to individual users on the Internet, you can use a sharing policy, and no federation trust is required. If you want to share some or all of the user's calendars in your organization, to some or all of the users in a different Exchange organization, it is easier to complete with a federation trust and an organization relationship.

A federation trust, as previously described, configures settings in Azure AD for your domains. Then, when users need to access your users free/busy or calendar information, they can be authenticated via the federation trust. To control which users can access what level of free/busy information within a domain, you create an organization relationship. Organization relationships, though similar in final result to a sharing policy, are different and are covered later in this chapter.

In summary, the following outlines whether you need a sharing policy or an organization relationship:

An organization relationship is required when:

- A federation trust is needed.
- You do anything that recommends the external domain needs to be federated.
- Sharing free/busy information (including subject and location) with external organizations for a set of many users.

A sharing policy is needed when:

- Sharing calendar folders with free/busy or free/busy information and subject and location.
- Sending sharing invitations to external recipients.
- The sharing applies to all external domains.

Sharing policies are assigned to mailboxes, and the settings in the policy control what the user can do. There are two sharing policies by default. These are called Default Sharing Policy and Anonymous Calendar Sharing. Both allow the sharing on a one-to-one basis, or your free/busy information, but only the free/busy state, and not the subject of the meeting or the location of the meeting. The Default Sharing Policy is assigned to all domains and requires a federation trust between the parties to be used. The Anonymous Calendar Sharing policy does not require any authentication, so does not require a federation trust, but on Exchange on-premises requires the creation of a /owa/calendar URL that the recipients of the calendar sharing invitations can go to.

So with either or both of the above options, the prerequisites required for a federation trust or /owa/calendar URL require the user that is assigned one of the two previous policies so that they can share their calendar or free/busy information. By default, all mailboxes are assigned the Default Sharing Policy, and so can share their calendar with other federated Exchange organizations.

You will need to create additional sharing policies if you want to share more than just free/busy information (that is, subject and location), and if you have specific requirements for different domains. This is because the default policy is simple free/busy information and all domains. In the default policy, this can be seen on the Domains value, which reads "*:CalendarSharingFreeBusySimple", if you view the sharing policy with Get-SharingPolicy | Format-List.

EXAM TIP

A given mailbox can only have one policy assigned. If you want different policies for different domains, you need to create all of the domains and combinations of sharing restrictions in the same policy.

The steps to create a sharing policy are to login to ECP, select an organization, and then select the sharing tab (which you are on by default). From here, click the Add icon in the Individual Sharing area. The top area of the page is for organizations with federation trusts, and an organization relationship between them. When you create a new policy, you need a name and one or more sharing rules for the policy. A sharing rule is a combination of a domain (or all domains) and the level of sharing you want to allow. That is if you want to share free/busy, free/busy time and subject and location, or the entire calendar appointment information. You can also share your contacts folder as well. This is shown in Figure 5-22.

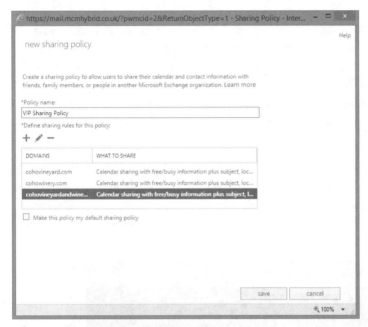

FIGURE 5-22 The New Sharing Policy dialog box

Modifying sharing policies and deleting sharing policies (if they have been removed from all mailboxes) are simple tasks to complete. When you have the sharing policy the way you want it configured, you need to assign it to one or more mailboxes. For example, to use Exchange Management Shell to assign the previously created policy to all users with VIP in their job description, you would use the following.

```
Get-User | Where {$_.Title -ilike "*VIP*"} | Set-Mailbox -SharingPolicy "VIP Sharing Policy"
```

If the remote domain in the sharing policy is an Exchange organization, a federation trust needs to be put in place. Following this trust, the sharing policy can be used. If the remote domain is running a version of version of Exchange Server before 2010 on-premises, a 2013 server will need to be installed as well because cross-forest sharing via federation trusts only works between two Exchange 2013 or 2010 CAS servers.

For sharing policies to anonymous users on the Internet, you could assign the mailbox the Anonymous Calendar Sharing Policy, but federated sharing will fail. Instead, you need to create a new policy that allows both federated sharing to your selected remote domains and anonymous sharing. To create a new sharing policy to allow calendar sharing with anonymous Internet users and specific domains via a federation trust, you can use a cmdlet similar to the following:

```
New-SharingPolicy -Name "Anonymous and Contoso" -Domains 'Anonymous:
CalendarSharingFreeBusySimple', 'contoso.com: CalendarSharingFreeBusySimple' -Enabled
$true
```

This policy allows free/busy (but not subject and location) sharing with *contoso.com* via a federation trust if they are an Exchange Server organization. It also allows the same level of free/busy sharing to anonymous domains (those without a federation trust—that is, those running Exchange Server 2003 and earlier, or non-Exchange Server email domains).

When you create an anonymous sharing policy, you are told to check that you have created the calendar URL in OWA. The cmdlet to do this is on all of your Exchange CAS servers is as follows.

```
Get-OwaVirtualDirectory | Set-OwaVirtualDirectory -AnonymousFeaturesEnabled $true
```

The Anonymous Features setting of OWA enables the /owa/calendar URL and needs to be run against each OWA virtual directory in the site that contains mailboxes that have anonymous sharing policies. The cmdlets to create this policy assign it to a single mailbox, and set the OWA virtual directory policy, as shown in Figure 5-23.

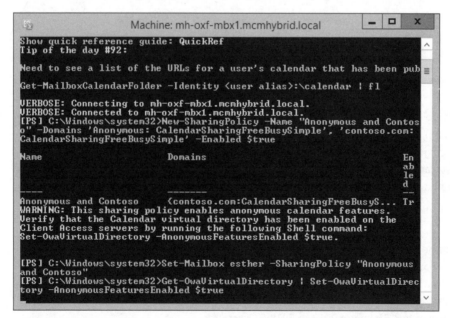

FIGURE 5-23 Cmdlets to create an anonymous sharing policy, assign the policy to one user and set the OWA virtual directory AnonymousFeaturesEnabled setting to True

To share a calendar or free/busy information from the user's perspective, once the required policies (that is, a federated trust and sharing policy, or if anonymous, a sharing policy) are in place, they need to share their calendar or grant free/busy permissions to the specific user. By default, calendars include the Anonymous permission, but do not grant any rights to it. If you share to Internet users with an anonymous policy, you need to ensure that Anonymous has permissions to access your calendar. The Outlook view of default calendar permissions can be seen in Figure 5-24.

FIGURE 5-24 Outlook calendar permissions

The default permissions are authenticated users (shown in the dialog box as Default), and have free/busy permissions, and Anonymous users have no permissions. If a user clicks the Share Calendar button on the Outlook toolbar, they see Figure 5-25.

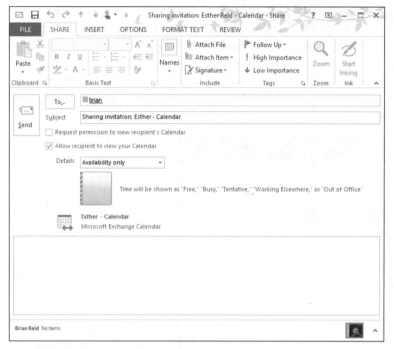

FIGURE 5-25 Sharing a calendar to an Internet user

If permission is not available for the level of access desired (for example free/busy), you will see an error message like the one in Figure 5-26, and a prompt about publishing your calendar.

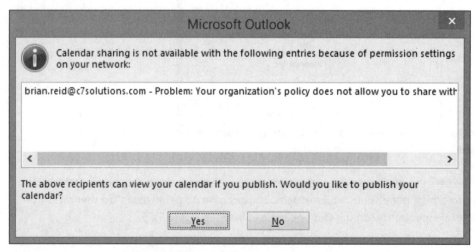

FIGURE 5-26 Error when calendar sharing is not possible

When calendar publishing is available, the Yes button takes you to your OWA URL, and also the Calendar Publishing options (you can use the Publish Online button in Outlook to go directly here). Here you choose the time window you want to publish, the level of details to be published, and whether or not it is restricted to a set of users or public. Public sharing means the calendar URL can be searched for. Restricted means the user has to receive the URL to use the calendar, but this does not stop them from sharing the same URL with others! There will be two URLs displayed once you start publishing, one for subscribing to the calendar (viewing the changes as they are made), which is an .ics file, and one for viewing a static view of the calendar in a web browser (an .html link). For example, you can open the .ics file in Outlook and view the user's calendar, as well as any update within your normal calendar in Outlook. You will see that the URL to the .ics file and the .html file is the OWA URL for the site the user is in, and the /Calendar/ subfolder. A redacted view of this information can be seen in Figure 5-27, where some of the calendar URL has been removed so that it cannot be subscribed to.

FIGURE 5-27 Publishing a calendar anonymously to individual users

The default sharing policy in Exchange Online is to allow anonymous sharing of calendars and to allow free/busy, as well as the subject and location. The AnonymousCalendarFeatures setting is already enabled on all OWA virtual directories in Exchange Online because virtual directory administration by the tenant administrator is not possible. If you do not want to allow users to publish calendars with external users, create a new sharing policy without anonymous rights, and assign it as required.

Designing certificate and firewall requirements

Federated sharing features require that the Client Access servers in your organization have outbound access to the Internet by using HTTPS. You must allow outbound HTTPS access (port 443 for TCP) to all Exchange 2013 Client Access servers in the organization.

For an external organization to access your organization's free/busy information, you must publish at least one Client Access server to the Internet. This requires inbound HTTPS access from the Internet to the Client Access server. Client Access servers in Active Directory sites that don't have a Client Access server published to the Internet can use Client Access servers in other Active Directory sites that are accessible from the Internet. The Client Access servers that aren't published to the Internet must have the external URL of the virtual directory of the Exchange Web Service set with the URL that's visible to external organizations.

As users external to your organization need to connect to your Internet published CAS server over HTTPS to complete a sharing connection, the certificate on the Internet facing CAS server needs to be a valid certificate from a trusted issuer and in date. The subject name of the certificate needs to match the URL used to reach the server. The name of the server that the external party will need to connect to will be listed in the calendar sharing invite that is sent to that user. This invitation will contain the external URL for the Exchange Web Services virtual directory in the site that the user's mailbox is located.

Managing organization relationships

Once the federation trust is completed, that is once the federation trust is enabled, the DNS proof values obtained and added to external DNS, and the federation trust completed, you can create organization relationships. An organization relationship is used to create a relationship with an external Exchange Server 2010 or Exchange Server 2013 organization, or an organization in Exchange Online, for the purposes of accessing calendar and free/busy. When you configure hybrid mode, an organization relationship is created between the on-premises organization and the Exchange Online organization for the same company as part of the Hybrid Configuration Wizard.

The organization relationships can be created, modified, and deleted in both ECP and the shell. Figure 5-28 shows the New Organization Relationship dialog box, which is the same as running New-OrganizationRelationship from the shell. In Figure 5-28, everyone in the company is allowed to share their free/busy info with users at Woodgrove Bank.

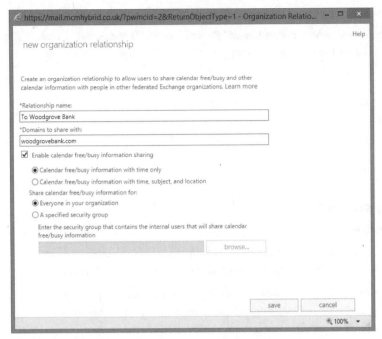

FIGURE 5-28 Configuring an organization relationship

Woodgrove Bank would have needed to create an organization relationship as well before this will work because the request for the free/busy information comes from a CAS server at Woodgrove Bank, and is authenticated by the Azure Active Directory by way of their federation trust. That server is granted a token to use when accessing a CAS server belonging to the organization that is shown in the screen shot. Therefore, any organization with a federation trust cannot access your free/busy or calendar information unless you have a federation trust and have created an organization relationship for that organization. The token Woodgrove Bank obtained from Azure Active Directory can only be read by the recipient organization, and the request for free/busy or calendar info comes direct from Woodgrove Bank encrypted via the token. Only the recipient organization can read the data encrypted with this token, and so the recipient organization will only grant the request if the information is cryptographically valid.

As well as allowing everyone in an organization to share free/busy and/or calendar information with a remote organization, you can restrict it to members of a security group if you wish. Then only the free/busy of the mailboxes in that group will be seen by the other party in the organization relationship.

As well as obtaining a token from Azure Active Directory, the remote organization will access a CAS on your organization via AutoDiscover. Therefore, if AutoDiscover is not working, you will find that organization relationships do not work either.

The "On-premises to O365 - *guid*" organization relationship that you might see in your organization is the one created as part of the Hybrid Configuration Wizard. This organization relationship should not be modified, and if deleted, should be recreated via the Hybrid Configuration Wizard.

Thought experiment

Sharing calendars

In this thought experiment, apply what you've learned about this objective. You can find answers to these questions in the "Answers" section at the end of this chapter.

You manage Exchange for a group of organizations that have three independent forests and Exchange Server organizations on-premises. You have been tasked with ensuring that the three Exchange organizations, which all run Exchange Server 2013, are able to share calendar information with each other.

1. What do you need to configure in each Exchange organization?

Objective summary

- A federation trust is used to obtain tokens to authenticate to remote Exchange Server 2010 and higher forests for the purpose of retrieving free/busy, calendar, MailTips, mailbox delivery reports, and other settings.

- An organizational relationship controls the specific sharing settings between two federated Exchange organizations.

- A sharing policy allows users to publish their calendars to other users. Do not confuse publishing calendars and sharing calendars in Outlook. Sharing a calendar is just setting permissions on your calendar and asking another user to do the same, either within the organization or over a federation trust. A sharing policy is for publishing calendars.

- The Hybrid Configuration Wizard creates a federation trust between the on-premises Exchange organization and the Exchange online organization.

Objective review

Answer the following questions to test your knowledge of the information in this objective. You can find the answers to these questions and explanations of why each answer choice is correct or incorrect in the "Answers" section at the end of this chapter.

1. What Exchange Management Shell cmdlet do you use to get the TXT string you need to enter into public DNS for a federation trust if you have closed the Federation Trust Wizard?

   A. Get-HybridConfiguration -GetFederationTrustString AllDomains

   B. Get-FederationTrustString -DomainName <fqdn>

   C. Get-TXTRecord -FQDN <fqdn>

   D. Get-FederatedDomainProof -DomainName <fqdn>

2. An Office 365 administrator wants to allow users to publish their calendars online. What do they need to do in Exchange Online?

   A. Nothing is required because anonymous sharing is the default.

   B. They need to create a new sharing policy for anonymous usage and update the OWA virtual directories for their tenant in the cloud.

   C. They need to create a new sharing policy and assign it to the users who need it.

   D. This feature is not available in Exchange Online.

3. You need to restrict calendar sharing between a remote organization to a select group of users. How would you do this?

   A. Ensure that the allowed users share their calendar with the remote domain and the others do not.

   B. Create an organization relationship that is restricted to members of a security group.

   C. You cannot restrict organization relationships more specifically than to the entire domain.

   D. Use Add-MailboxFolderPermission to change the permissions on calendar of the recipient mailbox to publish it to the Internet.

Objective 5.3: Implement on-premises coexistence with legacy systems

When you install a new version of Exchange Server into an organization, it is highly likely that you will keep both the old and new version in place for at least a short while. Keep both versions even if this is just the short period of time between installing, moving some users as a pilot program, and then moving the rest of the users before the old system is decommissioned. This should cover the period of time when users will expect to be able to communicate with those mailboxes that have been migrated, and those migrated users will expect to be able to communicate with those that have not yet been migrated.

And coexistence is not just for the users. During the period of coexistence, you need to ensure that:

- Emails are delivered to the correct users.

- When a user logs in to Exchange, the user reaches the correct mailbox on the correct version.

- All of the users' existing devices continue to work while their mailbox is moved between versions of Exchange Server.

This objective will look at the considerations to make in Exchange Server to support migrating from Exchange 2007 or Exchange Server 2010, to Exchange Server 2013. You cannot directly migrate from Exchange 2003 to Exchange 2013, and so this scenario (which is migrating to Exchange Server 2010 and decommission 2003, and then migrating to 2013) is not covered as a separate topic.

> **This objective covers how to:**
> - Plan namespaces for coexistence
> - Configure proxy redirect
> - Plan firewall configuration for coexistence
> - Plan for mail flow requirements

Planning namespaces for coexistence

For users and devices to be able to access their mailboxes, they need to be able to login to the correct location. It is generally correct to say that, if a user logs into the later version of Exchange, then Exchange will know whether the correct configuration is in place and how to route the user to their mailbox on the older or legacy version of Exchange Server. But if the user who has been migrated to the newer version logs into the older version, they will not be able to access their mailbox.

Therefore, to ensure that users can access their mailbox regardless of whether it has been migrated to the latest version, users always need to login to the latest version. The URL that the user uses to login, especially to services such as Outlook Web App, is usually pretty ingrained, and if you change the URL, the user can accidently use the old one. Therefore, it is common that the URL used to access the service is moved to the new version once initial testing on the new version shows that it is working fine.

This URL used by the user, or the URL entered into the device, is known as the *namespace*. For coexistence with Exchange Server 2007, an additional namespace is required. Coexistence between Exchange Server 2013 and 2010 does not require any additions to the namespace. If you coexist with 2007, 2010, and 2013, as you have 2007, you need the additional namespace to support coexistence.

Take a look at an example. Contoso has two offices, one in Oxford and one in Nuneaton. Users in the head office at Oxford are accustomed to using *oxford-mail.contoso.com* to reach their mailbox, and users in Nuneaton expect to access their mailbox via *nuneaton-mail.contoso.com*. When they login, they see their 2007 mailbox. Exchange 2013 is installed in Oxford and the "oxford-mail" DNS entry is changed to point to the Exchange 2013 endpoint. The user browses to *oxford-mail.contoso.com/owa* and gets the 2013 style login page. They enter their credentials, and Exchange queries Active Directory for the right to login and access their mailbox settings. Exchange Server 2013 sees that this user is on 2007 in the Oxford office, and so redirects the browser to a new namespace specifically for the 2007 mailboxes. An example for this namespace, which must be resolved by DNS to the Exchange 2007 endpoint in the correct site, could be *oxford-legacy.contoso.com*. The user does not need to remember this URL because they are redirected automatically. Equally, a namespace such as *nuneaton-legacy.contoso.com* will need to be created and used for the 2007 servers in Nuneaton when 2013 is installed in that site. All of these names will need to be on a digital certificate as well as *autodiscover.contoso.com* (which always is pointed at the latest version of Exchange, and so does not need a legacy namespace).

You can see from this example that when you have mailboxes in a site on Exchange 2007, you require a second namespace to be able to reach those servers and mailboxes before you migrate them to Exchange 2013. If you took the same example with Exchange 2010, you would not need an additional legacy namespace. The reason is that Exchange 2013 is able to connect directly to Exchange 2010 Client Access Servers in the same site, and does not require the user to be redirected to the legacy server version. That is, when a user on an Exchange 2010 server browses to *oxford-mail.contoso.com*, the Exchange 2013 Server proxies the connection to the Exchange 2010 Server in the same site, and the user sees their mailbox. If the user's Exchange 2010 mailbox is in a remote site, Exchange 2013 will either proxy or redirect the connection depending upon the protocol. Table 5-1 outlines how Exchange 2013 connects to a mailbox on a legacy version of Exchange Server.

TABLE 5-1 How different Exchange protocols and services connect to legacy Exchange Servers

Protocol / Service	Exchange 2007	Exchange 2010
Outlook Web App	Redirect to legacy namespace. The legacy namespace is set as the ExternalURL on the Exchange 2007 OWA virtual directory.	Proxy if there is no ExternalURL. If there is an ExternalURL set then redirect to that URL.
Exchange Control Panel	N/A	As for OWA for Exchange 2010 above, unless ?ExchClientVer=15 is appended to the URL. Appending this value to the URL forces the connection to Exchange 2013 ECP.
POP/IMAP	Proxy	Proxy
ActiveSync	Proxy	Proxy
AutoDiscover	Proxy to Exchange 2013 mailbox. Exchange 2013 does not connect to user's mailbox on Exchange 2007.	Proxy to users mailbox server.
Outlook Anywhere	Proxy	Proxy
Exchange Web Services	AutoDiscover to 2013, which returns the ExternalURL of the legacy namespace. Application connects to 2007 namespace.	Proxy

A few of the above can be clarified further:

- Before you migrate mailboxes to 2013, you will need to update the digital certificate on 2007 to contain the current URL and the legacy URL. Then when you are ready to have users connect initially to 2013, you need to change the ExternalURL for Outlook Web App (OWA) and Exchange Web Services (EWS) on all of the Exchange 2007 servers that are affected by this change to 2013. For example, in the earlier scenario of *oxford-mail.contoso.com* and *oxford-legacy.contoso.com*, if you had not yet installed Exchange 2013 in Nuneaton, users of *nuneaton-mail.contoso.com* are still hitting a 2007 server first, and so there is no requirement to change their ExternalURL.

- The AutoDiscover SCP should point to the 2013 namespace for all servers. The servers that return the best AutoDiscover information are those running the latest version of Exchange Server.

- Because Exchange Server 2013 will redirect to Exchange Server 2007 for OWA and never proxy the connection, all Exchange Server 2007 Client Access Servers need to be Internet reachable for Internet users, and LAN reachable for LAN users.

Full details of all the different options can be found online at *http://blogs.technet. com/b/exchange/archive/2014/03/12/client-connectivity-in-an-exchange-2013-coexistence-environment.aspx*.

In summary, coexistence with Exchange 2013 is considerably easier than it was with Exchange 2003 because a lot of the service and protocol connections are proxied and not redirected to legacy namespaces.

Configuring proxy redirect

The exam objective domain contains the title, "Configure proxy redirect." Proxy and redirect are different things, and of them, only redirection needs configuring because proxy works automatically. As seen in Table 5-1 in the previous section, most protocols use proxy to connect from Exchange 2013 to the legacy version. Redirect is only used for OWA 2007 and only OWA 2010 when there is an ExternalURL in place. So you will look at just these two scenarios.

For OWA access for 2007 mailboxes the user will have a URL that they enter into their browser or a bookmark/favorite that they have saved. Therefore, keeping the same URL is highly recommended. To ensure a valid redirect back to Exchange 2007 once the URL they use is pointed to Exchange 2013, you need to change the ExternalURL on OWA on all the Exchange 2007 CAS servers in the site to the same value. This value would be the chosen legacy namespace value, which in most documentation is called *legacy.domain.com*, but does not need to actually have the word legacy in it at all. It just needs to be a unique value that DNS can resolve and that the chosen value is in the digital certificate that is bound to the Default Web Site in IIS on the 2007 server. This certificate should ideally contain both the legacy namespace and the primary namespace (*oxford-mail.contoso.com* and *oxford-legacy. contoso.com* in the ongoing example in the previous section). Containing both names allows you to update the certificate before you change the ExternalURL, and swap the endpoint from 2007 to 2013, thus reducing the work needed to change the endpoint location.

For Exchange 2010 mailboxes, an OWA login to 2013 will redirect to the ExternalURL of the OWA virtual directory in the site that the user's mailbox is located in. If the user is located in the same site as the Exchange 2013 server (that is the ExternalURL for 2013 is the same as the ExternalURL for 2010), the user's mailbox will be accessed via a proxy from Exchange 2013.

Planning firewall configuration for coexistence

For users to be able to access Exchange Server from the Internet, you will need to publish one or more Exchange Client Access Servers to the Internet. This publishing is either direct (via a network address translation (NAT) firewall) to the IP address of the Exchange CAS Server, or by publishing a load balancer that is forwarding the data to an array of Exchange Client Access Servers.

If the protocol that you are connecting over is proxied to the legacy server, there are no additional ports to open in the external firewall. Exchange Server 2013 and the legacy Exchange Server on the LAN must have no blocked ports between them because Exchange Server is not supported with firewalls between Exchange Servers on the internal network.

If the protocol you are connecting over is redirected, you need to publish the legacy server to an external IP address that is resolved to the legacy namespace. Figure 5-29 shows this example.

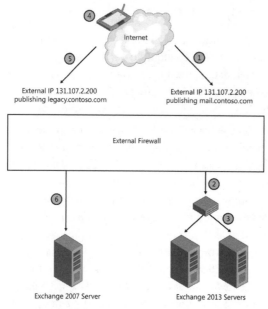

FIGURE 5-29 Publishing Exchange Server for redirection

In Figure 5-29, you can see the following sequence of events where a user is redirected to OWA on Exchange 2007.

1. The user enters *https://mail.contoso.com/owa* into a browser on their device on the Internet. The name is resolved to the external IP address 131.107.2.100.

2. The external firewall is publishing the load balancer that distributes load across the Exchange 2013 servers on TCP 443. The connection from the user traverses the firewall to the load balancer.

3. The load balancer sends the data to one of the Exchange 2013 servers. The server authenticates the user and sees that they have a mailbox on Exchange 2007. The ExternalURL for Exchange 2007 in the user's site is *legacy.contoso.com* and the user is connecting to OWA. The server then redirects the user via a 302 browser redirect to go instead to *https://legacy.contoso.com/owa*.

4. The device is told to go to *https://legacy.contoso.com/owa*, and so DNS is queried for the IP address of this URL and it resolves to 131.107.2.200.

5. The device connects to 131.107.2.200, and the firewall is publishing the Exchange 2007 Client Access server on this IP address, and also over TCP port 443.

6. The connection for *https://legacy.contoso.com/owa* is passed through to the Exchange Server, and the user can access their email.

Planning for mail flow requirements

The previous few sections have not discussed transport and SMTP coexistence. That is because, even though mail flow is very important, it does not need to change when the user changes endpoints, nor does it typically involve a new namespace. Typically you either change your firewall to publish TCP 25 from the old servers to the new servers, and so there are no changes to your MX records or the settings at your anti-spam cloud vendor, or you update your firewall to a second IP address (which is recommended to allow you to test the changeover). Then when you are ready to change the SMTP endpoint, you update the A record that the MX record points to, or update your settings at your anti-spam cloud vendor to use the new IP address. The old publishing rule and IP address on the firewall can typically be closed a few days later.

Other changes that you often need to make for mail flow coexistence are for internal mail flow. You will probably have some applications or printers/scanners that send email. These applications and devices will need to use the 2013 servers, and stop using the old servers. To do this you will typically need to create receive connectors on Exchange Server 2013 Client Access Servers bound to the Frontend Transport service that treats emails from these devices or applications differently. If the device or application sends anonymous email to Exchange for users within the Exchange organization, you need to do nothing extra because Exchange 2013 will receive anonymous emails for its accepted domains automatically (unlike Exchange 2010, which needed configuring). But when the application or device needs to send email to the Internet, it either needs to authenticate to the Client Access Server (on TCP port 587), or you need to create a new receive connector that allows relay to the Internet, and is restricted to the IP range of the application and devices that will use it. The following is an Exchange Management Shell cmdlet that will create a connector and set relay permissions against it so that an application or device on 192.168.10.10 or 192.168.10.11 can send email to the Internet. Relay permissions are granted by the connector authentication being ExternallyAuthoritative.

```
New-ReceiveConnector "Relay Connector" -TransportRole Frontend -Server EXCHCAS1
-Bindings 0.0.0.0:25
-RemoteIPRanges 192.168.10.10,192.168.10.11 -Banner "220 Contoso Relay Enabled SMTP
Server on EXCHCAS1"
-PermissionGroups Anonymous -AuthMechanism Tls,ExternalAuthoritative.
```

ExternallyAuthoritative means anything running on those servers can email the Internet. If you want to restrict it further, you would want the application to authenticate with a username and password. Then only that application on that server would be able to send emails externally. In this cmdlet, the Banner property is useful for testing purposes. If you connect to the Exchange Server that the cmdlet was run on from the application server whose IP address was listed over TCP port 25, you should see the banner returned to you as shown in Figure 5-30. If you have connected to the wrong Exchange Server, or the application or device IP was different, you would not see the banner and would know you had connected to the wrong receive connector. The connector also offers TLS as defined in the cmdlet, and which can be seen with the STARTTLS verb in Figure 5-30.

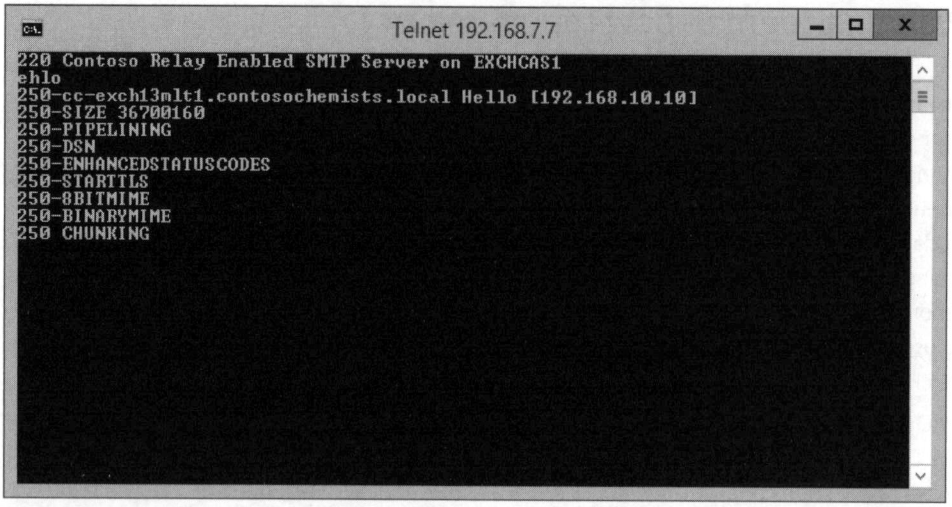

```
Telnet 192.168.7.7                    _  □  X

220 Contoso Relay Enabled SMTP Server on EXCHCAS1
ehlo
250-cc-exch13mlt1.contosochemists.local Hello [192.168.10.10]
250-SIZE 36700160
250-PIPELINING
250-DSN
250-ENHANCEDSTATUSCODES
250-STARTTLS
250-8BITMIME
250-BINARYMIME
250 CHUNKING
```

FIGURE 5-30 A banner being shown when connecting from the application server to the Exchange Server and the correct relay connector being verified

Thought experiment

Upgrading Exchange Server

In this thought experiment, apply what you've learned about this objective. You can find answers to these questions in the "Answers" section at the end of this chapter.

You manage an Exchange Server 2010 organization and want to install an Exchange Server 2013 server so that you can test the new version with only your mailbox being migrated. You want to ensure that the installation of Exchange Server 2013 does not impact the existing Exchange Server 2010 users.

1. How will you ensure that you can move your mailbox to Exchange Server 2013?

2. How will you ensure that other users' mailboxes are not impacted by this change?

Objective summary

- Exchange Server 2007 coexistence with Exchange Server 2013 for Outlook Web App requires a legacy namespace.
- Exchange Server 2010 coexistence with Exchange Server 2013 does not require a legacy namespace, unless Exchange Server 2010 is in a remote site and proxying connections from Exchange Server 2013 will not work and redirection to the legacy namespace is required.

- Exchange Web Services for Exchange Server 2007 coexistence will return the External-URL of the EWS endpoint suitable for the 2007 mailbox (the legacy namespace) if the AutoDiscover endpoint is correctly connected to Exchange 2013.

- All other protocols will proxy through Exchange 2013 and not require the client to change the endpoint.

- Firewall changes are needed for scenarios where redirection occurs but not where proxy occurs.

Objective review

Answer the following questions to test your knowledge of the information in this objective. You can find the answers to these questions and explanations of why each answer choice is correct or incorrect in the "Answers" section at the end of this chapter.

1. Which of the following subject and subject alternative names would be needed on a digital certificate for a 2007 to 2013 migration?

   A. legacy.contoso.com; mail.contoso.com; legacy-autodiscover.contoso.com; autodiscover.contoso.com.

   B. legacy.contoso.com; mail.contoso.com; legacy.mail.contoso.com; autodiscover.contoso.com

   C. mail.contoso.com; autodiscover.contoso.com

   D. legacy.contoso.com; mail.contoso.com; autodiscover.contoso.com

2. Do you need a legacy namespace for an ActiveSync client with a mailbox on Exchange 2007 when the URL that is registered in the device points to Exchange 2013 endpoint?

   A. Yes

   B. No

3. What is the TCP port on the server recommended for client SMTP connections?

   A. 25

   B. 475

   C. 587

   D. 2525

Objective 5.4: Set up a cross-forest coexistence solution

With Exchange Server being the typical email server product installed in most organizations, there may be requirements to link or merge Exchange Server when installed in multiple forests. This is especially the case when different companies merge or are involved in takeovers, but is useful when partner organizations want to share information. It is also useful when an organization needs to create a new Active Directory forest, and to migrate services to the new forest. This objective looks at the things you need to be aware of from the viewpoint of coexisting multiple forests.

> **This objective covers how to:**
>
> - Set up cross-forest availability
> - Design certificate and firewall requirements
> - Set up cross-forest mail flow
> - Design and configure AutoDiscover
> - Set up shared namespaces

Setting up cross-forest availability

Previously in this book, you looked at free/busy between different organizations and on-premises and Office 365 when using federation trusts. Availability between any Exchange 2010 or 2013 organization can be provided by way of a federation trust. If the organization only has Exchange Server 2007 in use, or both forests use the same domain name, or there is no Internet connectivity to Azure Active Directory to get a federation trust token, you need to configure the availability service for cross-forest topologies.

There are two types of cross-forest topologies. The first is where the source and target forests are trusted at an Active Directory level, and so that users in one forest can access resources in the other forest with their username and password from the source forest. The second type of topology is one where there is no forest trust in place.

With a forest trust in place, it is possible to grant availability to the user level. That is a user can share their calendar for free/busy (or free/busy, subject, and location) for a given user in the remote forest. When the forests are not trusted, you need to set up a configuration that allows the source forest to query the target forest for availability, but you cannot restrict it down to which users you want to grant availability for. All users are accessible to the source forest.

EXAM TIP

If you want to implement bi-directional availability, that is Forest A can query free/busy in Forest B, and Forest B can query free/busy in Forest A, you need to run the below cmdlets in both directions because the availability cmdlets work in a single direction.

If Forest A can retrieve availability from Forest B, and Forest B can retrieve availability from Forest C, this does not mean Forest A can see availability for Forest C. To do this, cross-forest availability between A and C will need to be put in place (and probably between C and A in reverse to allow availability in the opposite direction).

The cmdlets used to configure cross-forest availability differ depending upon whether the forests are trusted or not. To link two trusted forests for cross-forest availability, use the following single line of PowerShell to set up the initial permissions in Forest A, with a service account from Forest B.

```
Get-MailboxServer | Add-ADPermission -Accessrights Extendedright -Extendedrights "ms-Exch-EPI-Token-Serialization" -User "<Remote Forest B>\Mailbox servers"
```

Then run the following cmdlet in Forest A to link the forests.

```
Add-AvailabilityAddressSpace -Forestname ForestB.com -AccessMethod PerUserFB -UseServiceAccount:$true
```

AutoDiscover must be working so that a mailbox server in Forest A can find the correct endpoint for *ForestB.com*.

To configure bidirectional cross-forest availability, repeat these steps in the target forest.

When the two forests are not trusted, it is only possible to query availability in the target forest and return the free/busy setting that is applied to the default account. Figure 5-24 earlier in this book shows the calendar properties dialog box and the permissions applied to the default user. When the forests are not trusted, the only free/busy that can be retrieved is that assigned to the default user. Specific settings for specific users in the other forest cannot be assigned. To configure cross-forest availability when the two forests are not trusted at an Active Directory level, use the following cmdlets. The first cmdlet runs in the target forest.

```
Set-AvailabilityConfig -OrgWideAccount "ForestB.com\User"
```

The second and third cmdlets run in the source forest. The output from these cmdlets can be seen in Figure 5-31.

```
$fbUser = Get-Credential (Enter the credentials for organization-wide user in Contoso.com domain)
Add-AvailabilityAddressspace -Forestname ForestB.com -Accessmethod OrgWideFB -Credential:$fbUser
```

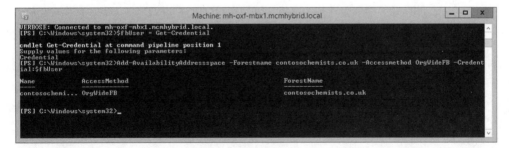

FIGURE 5-31 Configuring untrusted cross-forest availability lookups from the source forest

As previously mentioned, AutoDiscover must be working for cross-forest availability to work. Availability has a time out of 10 seconds. Therefore, AutoDiscover, and then the availability lookup, must complete in less than 10 seconds or the lookup to the remote forest may fail. If the two forests are trusted, an SCP can be exported from the target forest and installed into the source forest. This is done using Export-AutoDiscoverConfig, and more details on this can be found at *http://technet.microsoft.com/en-us/library/aa996849.aspx.*

Finally, to do cross-forest availability, there must be a contact object in the source forest for each mailbox in the remote forest that could be queried. In a lab environment, it is possible to manually create these contacts to prove that the concept works; in a production environment, a tool such as Forefront Identity Manager will be needed to maintain contact objects in the source forest for each change of mailbox in the target forest.

> **NOTE** **CROSS-FOREST AVAILABILITY WHITE PAPER**
>
> A paper describing the steps to configure and troubleshoot cross-forest availability is available at *http://blogs.technet.com/b/exchange/archive/2011/03/04/3412075.aspx.*

Designing certificate and firewall requirements

Like a lot of Exchange Server, there are certificate and firewall implementation considerations when crossing forests. This, for availability, is similar to previously described requirements. Regarding certificates on CAS servers in the target, they must be valid and trusted by the source mailbox servers. That is they must have the EWS ExternalURL on the certificate because the subject, or subject alternative name, and the certificate, must be issued by a provider that the source Exchange Server trusts.

Availability is a web service, and so for firewalls, any firewall between the forests will need to allow TCP 443 access from all of the source mailbox servers to the CAS server in the target that is returned by the AutoDiscover lookup.

Setting up cross-forest mail flow

Mail flow between two forests can be as simple as mail flow between two different organizations on the Internet. That is, you just configure MX records in the DNS server that the source forest queries, which points to the destination forest. If the MX records you use are the public MX records for the remote forest, your mail flow will follow the path of Internet outbound email when leaving your organization, and will be seen as part of the general Internet inbound email entering the other organization.

Using features such as TLS, and knowledge of the source IP address, it is possible to distinguish the inbound email from one organization and consider it apart from the general flow of Internet email, and thus treat it differently. For example, if you know the source IP address of Forest A, you can create a transport rule in Forest B to say that email sourced from the IP address that is Forest A's outbound email, or source IP address is to automatically get a Spam Confidence Level (SCL) of -1. Therefore, the email from Forest A will never end up in the user's Junk Email folder. Other techniques you could use include.

- **Specific receive connectors** In the target forest, you create a receive connector where the RemoteIPRanges value is set to the source forests outbound IP address. As long as that organization connects directly to you, and you see the SMTP data coming from this IP range, your receiving Exchange Server in the target forest will receive it via the new connector. The permissions on this new connector can include settings such as how the email is authenticated (ExternalAuthoritative), or has a permission assigned to the connector so that the messages are not checked for spam.

- **Direct delivery** If the two forests can reach each other for SMTP traffic without going via the Internet, you can create receive connectors on servers that they can reach that are not your normal inbound from the Internet receive connectors. To route messages to these servers specifically, you need to create a send connector on the source organization using the name or IP address of the receiving transport server at the target forest. This receiving server needs to run the CAS role in Exchange Server 2013 because this role contains the Frontend Transport service, which is designed to accept and route messages to the correct mailbox role server. This CAS server will need to have a receive connector created on it with the correct RemoteIPRange setting if you want to distinguish inbound messages by source IP address.

- **Office 365** If the remote company uses Office 365, the tenant administrator of that organization can create inbound connectors of type Partner to receive emails from the source IP address of that other forest into the target forest, and allow them to be treated as emails of a specific type, and not be candidates for spam checking.

In summary, cross-forest mail flow is nothing more than the correct combination of send and receive connectors on-premises, and inbound and outbound connectors in Office 365.

Designing and configuring AutoDiscover

Clients and Exchange Servers, as well as Exchange Online, use AutoDiscover to find endpoints to connect to for finding and connecting to mailboxes. This has previously been mentioned in context with federation trusts, moving mailboxes to Office 365 (as part of the hybrid wizard), and in this section on doing cross-forest free/busy.

To design and configure AutoDiscover for any of these services, and for basic client connectivity to Exchange functionality, which it is used for most of all, requires a few things to be set up. These are:

- An A record in public DNS (and if using split DNS, in private DNS as well is recommended)

- A digital certificate with the value of the A record as its subject, or more often, subject alternative name on it

- TCP port 443 published on an external firewall

- And usually a load balancer

The AutoDiscover service is a web service that runs on all Exchange Client Access Servers. It is available from the /Autodiscover/Autodiscover.xml endpoint on the Default Web Site (it is also available from /Autodiscover/Autodiscover.svc, but this is primarily used by the Lync client). In addition to the URL of the service, AutoDiscover is available on a few well known DNS namespaces, and also can be queried from the Active Directory for domain joined PCs. The exact behavior of the client depends upon the individual client and version because some clients (iPhone) will do AutoDiscover once on account setup and never again, and others (Outlook) will do it frequently. Some versions of clients will work differently too. Outlook 2010 domain joined will look up the Active Directory service connection point (SCP), whereas some versions of Outlook 2013 will query the SCP and DNS at the same time.

The well-known endpoints for AutoDiscover are as follows, and should be queried in the following order.

1. Domain joined clients query the SCP to determine the location of the AutoDiscover endpoint. If not domain joined, the client should only do the rest of the list until it gets a valid response.

2. *https://domain.com/autodiscover/autodiscover.xml* (where domain.com is the SMTP domain in the user's email address).

3. *https://autodiscover.domain.com/autodiscover/autodiscover.xml.*

4. HTTP redirection. This goes to the two URLs above, but over the HTTP protocol and not HTTPS, and looks to see if they are being redirected to a different website. The client should prompt if this is the case, though there are known redirections that the client does not prompt for, such as redirections to Office 365.

5. DNS SRV query.

6. An XML file on the local machine. The path is configured by a registry key.

7. Cached URL in the Outlook profile (an Outlook 2013 feature).

AutoDiscover stops when a valid response is received. A valid response is one where the client connects to the above URLs (in order) and sees if they need to login. Upon successful login, they post data that should elicit a response in the form of XML. The XML contains the settings that the client needs to located services on the Exchange Server.

The SCP value in the Active Directory defaults to *https://client_access_server_name/ autodiscover/autodiscover.xml,* and is added during the Client Access Server installation. The domain joined client will search the Active Directory for the SCP and list them by the Active Directory site that the client is located in. They will then connect to the first re-turned value from the Active Directory, which is usually the oldest server (first installed). It is recommended that Set-ClientAccessServer cmdlet is run to update all of the values in the Active Directory (or per site) to point to a load balancer in front of an array of CAS servers to provide high availability for AutoDiscover. An example of the cmdlet that can be run to do this is as follows (one for the Exchange 2010 servers in your organization, and one for the Exchange 2013 servers).

```
Get-ExchangeServer | Where {($_.AdminDisplayVersion -Like "Version 14*")
-And ($_.ServerRole -Like "*ClientAccess*")} | Set-ClientAccessServer
-AutoDiscoverServiceInternalUri https://autodiscover.contoso.com/Autodiscover/
Autodiscover.xml
```

[Run from 2013 PowerShell]

```
Get-ExchangeServer | Where {($_.AdminDisplayVersion -Like "Version 15*")
-And ($_.ServerRole -Like "*ClientAccess*")} | Set-ClientAccessServer
-AutoDiscoverServiceInternalUri https://autodiscover.contoso.com/Autodiscover/
Autodiscover.xml
```

The URL to use needs to point to a CAS server, or preferably a load balancer in front of a CAS server farm. The URL does not need to match the URLs that AutoDiscover uses when doing a DNS lookup, rather than an SCP lookup, but can be the same as shown here.

For non-domain joined clients, or clients that are domain joined but are not currently on a network where the domain is reachable, you need to provide the DNS lookup method to find AutoDiscover. The best solution is to offer the *autodiscover.domain.com* A record pointing to a firewall that is publishing the Exchange Client Access Servers. The firewall rule that publishes OWA is typically used because the servers that offer OWA also offer AutoDiscover. There are other scenarios, such as the SRV record and HTTP redirects, that are typically not needed for a simple AutoDiscover deployment, and so these can be read about further in the AutoDiscover Whitepaper at *http://technet.microsoft.com/en-us/library/jj591328.aspx* (this refers to Exchange 2010, but the concept is the same for Exchange 2013).

Setting up shared namespaces

Finally, for this objective you will look at shared namespaces. With shared namespaces, more than one Exchange organization shares the email domain. When there is a shared email domain, the users at two different Exchange organization have email addresses that end with the same domain extension. For example, one Exchange organization has users with email addresses that end @contoso.com, and a second Exchange organization has the same domain extension. These are typically required in company mergers and acquisitions, as well as when two separate organizations have a shared parent company name.

Shared namespaces are in contrast to MX records for mail flow delivery. An MX record will point to a defined location, and so all email for the domain will go to where the MX record is pointing. If a domain is shared between two or more organizations, the following needs to be considered:

- Email from the first SMTP environment where the MX record delivers the email needs to be able to get to the second location, if there is not a valid mailbox for it in the first.

- Once email reaches the last SMTP environment, it should not route back to the first environment if no mailbox was located for the user. This will cause mail loops for unresolved recipients.

- Users in the first location should be able to look up users in both their, and the other locations, in their address book.

- Users in the second (or other) locations must be able to send email back to the first location.

In terms of Exchange Server, this has been the same since Exchange Server 2007. In Exchange Server, you create an accepted domain. This tells Exchange that it can accept email for this domain and deliver it to any mailbox with that email address stamped on it within the organization. Also, Exchange Server has the concept of different types of accepted domains. These types are authoritative, internal relay, and external relay. They behave as follows:

Authoritative accepted domains   This accepted domain type can be added to an email address policy, and Exchange can automatically stamp email addresses on mailboxes based on this policy. This domain type also says that the recipient must exist within the Active Directory or the email is considered invalid. Therefore if a mailbox exists in this forest for *kim@contoso.com* and an email arrives for that address, it will be delivered. But if there is no mailbox or other recipient type (contact, distribution group), it will be rejected.

Internal relay accepted domains   This type of accepted domain can also be added to email address policies, but there is no requirement for there to be an object with any given recipient address in the Active Directory that the Exchange organization is part of. That means that if an email arrives in an Exchange organization for *kim@contoso.com*, and there is no mailbox for *kim@contoso.com*, the Exchange Server will attempt to deliver it to another SMTP server. To deliver to another system, there must be an explicit send connector for that domain going to the other SMTP server, or the email will loop back to the current organization's MX record endpoint. If the mailbox exists though, the message will be delivered. That means you cannot have two *kim@contoso.com* mailboxes, one in each forest, and expect delivery to both. That still requires a distribution group, and multiple unique mailboxes.

External relay accepted domains   This type of accepted domain, unlike the other two, cannot be added to an email address policy. You can, however, add email addresses with the domain name of this accepted domain type to recipients manually. If an email arrives in an organization that has contoso.com as an external relay accepted domain addressed to *kim@contoso.com*, and if the object exists locally, it will be delivered. If not, the Edge Server on the network edge will deliver the message to the next organization via a send connector on the Edge Server. The email does not need to enter the actual organization to be delivered onward. In an internal relay accepted domain (the previous example), the message is always forwarded by the receiving mailbox server, and so even if you have an Edge Server in front of an organization with internal relay domains, the message will traverse the Edge Server to the internal servers, and be redirected from the Internal servers.

Therefore, you need to pick your accepted domain type to ensure valid onward routing. The final organization in the chain of email systems should always be authoritative (or the equivalent for that SMTP system) so that unresolved recipients at the end of the chain do not get routed around to the start of the chain again. But all the other email systems on the route are going to be either internal relay, where you do not need to create mail contacts for each valid object in the next or later hops, or authoritative accepted domains where all users in the later hops must be listed in the first organization.

Figure 5-32 and Figure 5-33 show two organizations, both *contoso.com* for their email address space, but separate Active Directory forests and Exchange organizations. Also shown are the objects that are needed to make mail flow work. Note that AutoDiscover will not work for these organizations unless the contact in the first organization routes to a separate address space in the second, and not the same address space.

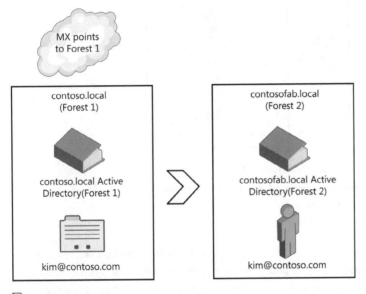

The chevron is a send connector for contoso.com

contoso.com is an authoritative accepted domain in both Exchange organizations

FIGURE 5-32 Authoritative accepted domains

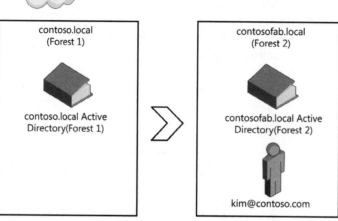

The chevron is a send connector for contoso.com

contoso.com is an internal relay accepted domain in Forest 1, and authoritative in Forest 2

FIGURE 5-33 Internal relay accepted domains

Without a contact the use of the same SMTP domain in both organizations will result in failures when querying AutoDiscover to find mailboxes in the second forest. With a contact object, AutoDiscover will connect to the second forest when the first forest returns a redirection based on the SMTP address of the contact (in Figure 5-32). In Figure 5-33, there is no contact, so no redirection is returned and AutoDiscover will fail in this scenario. Therefore, if both Forest 1 and Forest 2 are Exchange 2007 or later forests where AutoDiscover is needed, the domain type can be either authoritative or internal relay, but the contact or mail user object in the first forest needs to have the email addresses stamped on the object (*kim@contoso.com* in our example). But the target of the contact (the external address) should be a different domain so that AutoDiscover information can be queried additionally. For example, the contact should have the external address as *kim@contoso-fabrikam.com*, and *kim@contoso.com* as an additional email address. Email will arrive in Forest 1 and be rerouted to *kim@contoso-fabrikam.com*. Kim in the second forest needs *kim@contoso-fabrikam.com* as an additional email address, but *kim@contoso.com* as her primary address. Therefore, all email that she sends comes from the primary address, and the secondary address is just for mail routing between the organizations. AutoDiscover will query the *contoso.com* domain and find a mail contact for Kim with an external address of *kim@contoso-fabrikam.com*. AutoDiscover will now repeat its steps, but for the *contoso-fabrikam.com* domain, and thus successfully located Kim's mailbox in Forest 2.

Thought experiment
Shared free/busy

In this thought experiment, apply what you've learned about this objective. You can find answers to these questions in the "Answers" section at the end of this chapter.

You manage Exchange for a few different companies as their messaging consultant. You want IT staff in those companies to be able to see your calendar free/busy so they can book your time for consultancy.

1. What Exchange free/busy sharing options do you have available to you?

2. Which is the easiest to set up?

Objective summary

- Free/busy can be queried in remote Exchange organizations by way of AvailabilityAddressSpace or organizational relationships.

- AutoDiscover is very important for cross-forest scenarios, and so needs to be working.

- Considerations need to be made for mail flow cross-forest because the email typically must be considered internal, not rejected, or spam filtered, and often guaranteed encrypted.

- Different accepted domain settings control how messages are delivered or rejected based on the existence, or lack of, mail recipient objects in the Active Directory.

Objective review

Answer the following questions to test your knowledge of the information in this objective. You can find the answers to these questions and explanations of why each answer choice is correct or incorrect in the "Answers" section at the end of this chapter.

1. Which types of accepted domain will always forward messages if they are not resolved to local recipients?

   A. Authoritative

   B. Internal Relay

   C. External Relay

   D. Edge Server Relay

2. What cmdlet is used to update the AutoDiscover SCP value for a given Exchange Server?

    A. Set-ClientAccessServer

    B. Set-ExchangeServer

    C. Set-MailboxServer

    D. Set-AutoDiscoverVirtualDirectory

Objective 5.5: Migrate legacy systems

This exam objective looks at the migration from Exchange Server 2007 and Exchange Server 2010 to Exchange Server 2013. It is also possible to migrate other email products into Exchange Server, and Exchange contains tools to migrate from a PST file into a mailbox. There is a large partner market for tools to migrate from outside of Exchange Server into Exchange, both from archiving products, PST files, and other email systems (typically IMAP and POP-based systems).

This objective looks at the parts of the migration that have not been covered in depth in other sections. Where a migration is actually a feature covered elsewhere, you will see a pointer back to that content.

This objective covers how to:
- Determine transition paths to Exchange
- Migrate public folders
- Migrate mailboxes
- Upgrade policies
- Plan to account for discontinued features
- Transition and decommission server roles

Determining transition paths to Exchange

Exchange Server 2013 can be migrated to from Exchange Server 2007 and Exchange Server 2010. There is no support to install Exchange Server 2013 and Exchange Server 2003 in the same Exchange organization. This is because Microsoft supports n-2 (that is the current version and the two previous versions) for upgrading and Exchange Server 2003 is n-3. It is also out of its support period as well. That does not mean you cannot migrate from Exchange 2003 to Exchange 2013, it is just that there is not a direct path to this with the built-in Exchange Server 2013 migration tools.

Migrating from Exchange Server 2007 and Exchange Server 2010 to Exchange Server 2013 can happen in the same Active Directory forest and therefore the same Exchange organization. You can install Exchange Server 2013 servers as long as Exchange Server 2007 is at Update Rollup 10 for Exchange Server 2007 Service Pack 3 on all Exchange 2007 servers in the organization. Any Exchange Server 2010 servers need to be at least Service Pack 3 on all servers. Exchange 2013 installation will check that this prerequisite is met. If you have any Edge role Exchange servers, they need to be at the minimum versions as well.

> **IMPORTANT   EDGE ROLE VERSIONS**
>
> Be aware that updates to the version of the Edge role server are not written back to the Active Directory apart from the time EdgeSync is created. Therefore, an Edge role server could be equal to, or in excess of, the minimum version required. But if EdgeSync was not recreated, the version of the installation as recorded in the Active Directory will be wrong, and Exchange 2013 will not install.

Exchange 2007 SP3 Update Rollup 13 or later on the Exchange 2007 Hub Transport server is required if you want EdgeSync to work with an Exchange Server 2013 Service Pack 1 or later Edge role.

Because Exchange Server 2003 cannot be installed in the same Exchange organization as Exchange Server 2013, the only upgrade path with the built-in migration tools in Exchange Server is to upgrade to a supported version of Exchange Server (2010 SP3 is recommended), and decommission Exchange Server 2003 before starting the 2010 to 2013 migration. These are two separate migrations. If you use a third-party migration service or software to do this for you direct from 2003 to 2013, they will do this by creating a second Active Directory forest for Exchange Server 2013, implementing cross-forest coexistence for mail flow as described earlier, and then use their own mailbox migration software to migrate the mailbox data and public folder data. At the end of a 2003 to 2013 direct migration, you will have more than one Active Directory forest to manage and additional hardware for new Active Directory domain controllers. This needs to be kept in mind compared to the double-hop migration.

Migrating from PST files can be done using the New-MailboxImportRequest cmdlet, and this can be a way to migrate from an email system that has local PST file storage, or where the data can be exported to a PST file.

Finally, most other email systems support IMAP or POP for mailboxes. Exchange 2013 does not contain an IMAP or POP inbound migration product. The IMAP toolset in Exchange is Exchange Online, and for migrating to Office 365. Therefore, to migrate from IMAP or POP (or a web-based email product such as Gmail), a third-party migration tool is required.

Migrating public folders

In previous versions of Exchange Server, a public folder migration was simple. You ensured that your public folders where replicated to a public folder database on the new version of Exchange, and you removed the replica from the old version. Once replication was complete (which happened in the background automatically), you could decommission the public folder database on the old version of Exchange.

With Exchange Server 2013, it is nowhere near as simple! The single change that caused the complexity with the migration is that there are no more public folder databases. Public folders are now kept in mailboxes. This allows the public folders to benefit from DAG replication and high availability just by ensuring the public folder mailbox is replicated in a DAG, but there is now no support for multiple copies of a replica that can all be independently accessed. This change requires that public folder migration is now a cutover migration.

A public folder cutover migration involves scaling and sizing for the amount of data you need to migrate, and this may require waiting for cumulative update 7 or later, if you have a very large public folder databases because this version of Exchange 2013 has much better public folder scaling support. The cutover involves making one or more public folder mailboxes in 2013, creating a CSV file of the folder to mailbox mapping (that is, /Sales/Oxford public folder goes to pfMailbox1 but /Sales/Nuneaton goes to pfMailbox2). A mailbox should not exceed 50 GB and room for growth should be allowed, so the mapping ensures that you keep busy public folders away from each other to spread the performance impact. Large public folders can be distributed to different public folder mailboxes to distribute the content. Once the mapping file is done, the public folder move request can be started. Once this finishes, it can be refreshed to update just the latest changes to the folders. Finally, the cutover happens, and users are locked out of the legacy folders. A final migration occurs to grab the latest changes, and the new public folder mailboxes are live. Users with mailboxes on Exchange Server 2013 can access the modern public folders, users with mailboxes on older versions of Exchange Server cannot. Therefore, migrating to public folders on Exchange Server 2013 requires that the mailboxes are migrated first.

Whilst you still have mailboxes on Exchange 2007 or Exchange 2010, you have two options regarding public folders and migration. The first option is to decommission public folders. If this is the desire of the company, make sure that the Offline Address Book is distributed via the OAB URL on the Client Access Server, and not stored in a public folder, and that organization forms are no longer in use. Outlook 2003 does not work with Exchange 2013, so the requirement of Outlook 2003 to connect to a public folder on startup is not an issue because you will already have migrated away from this client. The second option is to maintain an Exchange Server 2010 or 2007 infrastructure to host the public folders on, and ensure that users on 2013 have access to the legacy public folders. This legacy access has changed since the release of Exchange Server 2013. In Exchange Server 2013 Cumulative Update 7 and later legacy public folder access is going to work the same way Exchange Online mailboxes can access legacy on-premises public folders.

From the release of Exchange Server 2013 CU1, legacy access to public folders was done in the client (Outlook), and the client connected to the public folders directly on the legacy version of Exchange in the same way they did in previous versions. In Exchange 2013 CU5 and later, support exists to provide an AutoDiscover response to the client for a proxy mailbox on the legacy server. The client then repeats the AutoDiscover query, this time for the proxy mailbox, and gets back a connection method to the legacy public folder, and then is able to connect to it. Exchange Server 2013 CU7 and later will not support the direct connect method, though it may remain working for a while. From CU7 and later the supported method of connectivity from a 2013 mailbox to legacy public folders is via the AutoDiscover route. Steps for configuring Exchange Server 2013 CU5 and later for legacy public folder access can be seen at *http://blogs.technet.com/b/exchange/archive/2014/11/07/on-premises-legacy-public-folder-coexistence-for-exchange-2013-cumulative-update-7-and-beyond.aspx*.

Migrating mailboxes

When you move a mailbox, you're moving it from a source mailbox database to a target mailbox database. The target mailbox database can be on the same server, on a different server, in a different domain, in a different Active Directory site, or in another forest. From the viewpoint of Exchange 2013, the source mailbox must be Exchange 2007 or 2010, or Exchange Online (where you can migrate mailboxes away from Office 365).

For a migration, Exchange Server 2013 migration tools are to be used. You would not use the 2007 or 2010 migration tools to move to Exchange 2013, but only the Exchange 2013 tools to pull the mailbox to Exchange Server 2013. In a single forest, this migration does not change the Active Directory object. Cross-forest migrations require that the new Active Directory object be created in the new forest using a provisioning tool. Microsoft supports Forefront Identity Manager to do this, and Prepare-MoveRequest.ps1 script.

Once the Active Directory object is provisioned (in a cross-forest migration), or if staying in the same forest, you are ready to migrate, there are two ways to do a migration in Exchange Server 2013. The first way is in ECP where you create migration batches (shown in Figure 5-34) that allow you to add a group of users to a migration, to either a different database (2007, or 2010, or 2013 migrations on-premises are just migrations from one database to another), or from another forest (if migrating cross-forest from 2007, 2010, or 2013). Remember you cannot migrate from 2003 to 2013 even cross-forest, without third-party migration tools. You can move users via a CSV file, which contains a single column called EmailAddress, and contains the SMTP address of each user, one per row, that you want to migrate. In ECP you can add the users you want to migrate directly in the dialog box if you do not have a CSV file to import.

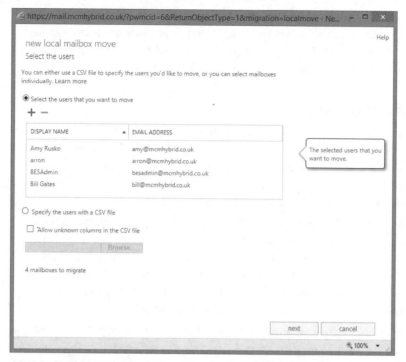

FIGURE 5-34 The local mailbox move dialog box in Exchange Control Panel

Once the CSV or users are added, the following screens in the wizard will ask the migration batch name (which is used to start and stop the migration for all of the users in the batch in a single action), control whether or not to move the archive mailbox, and optionally the database for the mailbox and the archive. If the databases are not set, Exchange Server will move the mailbox and/or archive to any database in the current site of the Exchange Server the move is being run on. You can stop databases being selected during move requests with Set-MailboxDatabase db_name -IsExcludedFromProvisioning $True. A migration batch will then allow you to set start and completion times, for example to start manually at a later date, or straight away and to complete automatically or manually, as well as email a report to the administrator running the batch.

The second way to do a migration into Exchange 2013 is using Exchange Management Shell. Here there are two cmdlets that can be used, the first being New-MigrationBatch, which does the same as discussed above, though it requires a list of users from a CSV file. Additionally, it allows for incremental syncs every 24 hours to be enabled or not, as well as other options not available in ECP. An example migration batch cmdlet for a local move, as used in a migration, could be as follows.

```
New-MigrationBatch -Name PilotUsersGroup2 -Local -CSVData ([System.
IO.File]::ReadAllBytes("C:\ExchangeMigrations\MCMHybrid-NewMigrationBatch.csv"))
-AllowIncrementalSyncs $true -AutoComplete:$false -NotificationEmails brian@mcmhybrid.co.uk
```

Cmdlets such as Start-MigrationBatch and Complete-MigrationBatch are used to start and finish batches that use -AutoComplete set to $False.

> **NOTE MIGRATING TO EXCHANGE ONLINE**
>
> The same cmdlet is used to perform migrations to and from Exchange Online.

Also available for migrations is the New-MoveRequest cmdlet introduced in Exchange 2010. This cmdlet can use the BatchName property to allow you to manage a number of individual moves in one group, similar to a MigrationBatch. Unlike the migration batch, it is not used for moves to Exchange Online, nor does it generate an email report when complete.

To move cross-forest and to Exchange Online, one or more migration endpoints need to be created. These use AutoDiscover to locate the settings they offer, and are specified during a remote move. They are not needed for local moves.

Once the move is in progress, it can be managed from both the web console and the shell. Controls that can be placed on moves include suspending a move and resuming a suspended move, for example when you are doing moves over the night or weekend, and you want to pause them during the business day due to network and server load. You can also report on the state of the move with Get-MigrationUserStatistics for batch moves, or Get-MoveRequest-Statistics for move requests.

Upgrading policies

When you migrate Exchange between versions, some objects that where created in previous versions will need to be updated. This was required for an Exchange 2003 to 2007, or 2010 migration, but apart from the Offline Address Book and a federation mailbox, there is nothing that needs to be upgraded during a 2007, or 2010 to Exchange Server 2013 migration. It is worth noting that transport and journal rule migrations from 2007 will happen automatically, but will be updated to version specific rules, which will therefore require rule administration on specific versions of Exchange Server from that point onward. This is the same consideration that needed to be made for an Exchange 2010 upgrade.

You might find that when migrating to Exchange Server 2013, the email address policies are not correctly upgraded, as they should have been when migrating to 2007 or 2010 during that project. The same is true for routing group connectors that still exist, and should have been deleted during the 2007 or 2010 migration. These address policies can be upgraded as per the instructions for Exchange Server 2007. You will need to use the previous version of Exchange Server before it is removed to delete the routing group connectors.

Planning to account for discontinued features

There are some features that are discontinued in Exchange 2013, and so if you use these features you need to mitigate, or migrate as required. There is a sizable list, some of which are items removed in the architecture, such as Hub Transport and UM roles because these have been built into the Mailbox and CAS roles. But other features and options are removed, such as the Microsoft Management Console for administering the server, and support for Outlook 2003.

The full list can be found at *http://technet.microsoft.com/en-GB/library/jj619283.aspx*.

Transitioning and decommissioning server roles

Once you have Exchange Server 2013 sized correctly for your organization, and then installed, you can transition to the new servers. This is done by updating DNS internally, and updating firewall rules and/or DNS externally so that user's connections are made to Exchange Server 2013 first. Exchange Server will then proxy or redirect the user's connections as appropriate for the protocol, and the location of the user's mailbox as previously covered. Once the user's mailbox is migrated to Exchange Server 2013, the user's connection will be proxied from the Client Access Server that receives the connection to the mailbox server that holds the users active mailbox.

Once all of the mailboxes, and if applicable, public folders, are migrated off of the legacy version of Exchange, you can start the decommissioning process. This ends with the uninstallation of the server using Control Panel Add/Remove Programs so that the legacy software is cleanly uninstalled from both the server and the Active Directory. But before the server is uninstalled, it is best to log traffic to the server looking for valid connection attempts. It is likely that some applications, especially SMTP and other clients that do not use AutoDiscover, will still be connecting to the server. Legacy versions of Exchange Server do a considerable amount of logging, and these logs can be used to look for connection attempts.

If an attempt is found in the logs, it will typically contain the mailbox name or the source IP address. This will allow the cause of the connection to be mitigated. Eventually, you can get to a point in time where you suspect no connectivity. At this time it is recommended to turn the server off for a few weeks and see if anything breaks! You can always turn on a server that is off quite quickly, quicker than reinstalling it anyway.

> **IMPORTANT   KEEPING LEGACY EXCHANGE AROUND?**
>
> Once you have uninstalled all of a given version of Exchange Server from an Exchange organization, you cannot install more of that version again. Therefore, keep an Exchange Server 2007 and/or 2010 server, all roles installed on it, until you are sure you do not need to reinstall a server of the same version. This server with all of the roles on it will allow future installs of that version if needed.

Finally you can uninstall the server, which must be uninstalled from the computer, and this process removes its settings from the Active Directory as well. Just turning off an Exchange Server will cause problems later on.

Objective summary

- Exchange Server 2013 cannot be installed in the same Exchange organization (that is, the same Active Directory forest) as Exchange Server 2003.

- Exchange Server can move mailboxes from other supported versions of Exchange Server and via PST files. Third-party products are used for migrating from other sources.

- Public folders for Exchange Server 2013 are stored in one or more mailboxes, known as public folder mailboxes. These mailboxes require a cutover migration from public folder databases of previous versions.

- Mailbox moves are always from the higher version of Exchange using either the console or shell to start the move.

- Ensure that all decommissioned servers are correctly uninstalled at the end of their life.

Objective review

Answer the following questions to test your knowledge of the information in this objective. You can find the answers to these questions and explanations of why each answer choice is correct or incorrect in the "Answers" section at the end of this chapter.

1. From what versions of Exchange Server can you upgrade to Exchange Server 2013 directly?

   A. Exchange Server 2000

   B. Exchange Server 2003

   C. Exchange Server 2007

   D. Exchange Server 2010

2. You want to distribute your mailboxes randomly across all of your Exchange Server 2013 databases, so that load and performance are randomly distributed, but you want

to exclude selected databases on which you will store the mailboxes of employees that have left. Which of the following will configure a database to be excluded in this way?

A. Set-Mailbox db_name -IsExcludedFromProvisioning $True

B. Set-MailboxDatabase db_name -IsExcludedFromProvisioning

C. Set-Mailbox db_name -IsExcludedFromProvisioning $True

D. Set-MailboxDatabase db_name -IsExcludedFromProvisioning $True

3. Which of the following New-MigrationBatch cmdlets are valid?

A. New-MigrationBatch -Name PilotUsersGroup2 -Online -CSVData ([System. IO.File]::ReadAllBytes("C:\ExchangeMigrations\NewMigrationBatch.csv")) -AllowIncrementalSyncs $true -AutoComplete:$false -NotificationEmails brian@mcmhybrid.co.uk

B. New-MigrationBatch -Name PilotUsersGroup2 -Local -CSVData ([System. IO.File]::ReadAllBytes("C:\ExchangeMigrations\MCMHybrid-NewMigrationBatch. csv")) -AllowIncrementalSyncs $true -AutoComplete:$false -NotificationEmails brian@mcmhybrid.co.uk

C. New-MigrationBatch -Name PilotUsersGroup2 -Remote -TXTData ([System. IO.File]::ReadAllBytes("C:\ExchangeMigrations\NewMigrationBatch.txt")) -AllowIncrementalSyncs $true -AutoComplete:$false -NotificationEmails brian@mcmhybrid.co.uk

D. New-MoveRequest -Name PilotUsersGroup2 -Online -CSVData ([System. IO.File]::ReadAllBytes("C:\ExchangeMigrations\NewMigrationBatch.csv")) -AutoComplete:$false -NotificationEmails brian@mcmhybrid.co.uk

Objective 5.6: Troubleshoot issues associated with hybrid scenarios, coexistence, migration, and federation

This last objective looks at how you can troubleshoot the various features of Exchange Server that you have looked at in the rest of this chapter.

This objective covers how to:

- Troubleshoot transport
- Troubleshoot Exchange federation trust and organization relationships
- Troubleshoot client access
- Troubleshoot SSO/AD FS
- Troubleshoot DirSync
- Troubleshoot cross-forest availability

Troubleshooting transport

To understand SMTP, mail flow and transport is the best place to start so that you can have a grip on being able to troubleshoot it. If you are having mail flow issues, the best steps are to isolate the issue to the area where the problem is occurring. For example, does the message arrive with your server, or is the problem in mail flow happening within your organization?

The best way to troubleshoot mail flow is to enable all of the mail flow logging that you can. In Exchange Server 2013, there are log files for every transport service, some of which are enabled, and some of which are not. Typically, those that generate a small amount of logging are enabled, and the more verbose log generators are disabled. Exchange transport will delete logs when they exceed a period of typically 30 days, or 1 GB per log folder, whichever comes first. These sizes can be changed using Set-TransportService should you exist in an organization with such massive mail flow that the logging size is not sufficient, or the duration not long enough for your needs.

Individual transport services, such a Frontend Transport, or Mailbox Transport can have their verbose logging enabled to assist with troubleshooting. This is done with the Set- cmdlet for the service name, for example Set-FrontEndTransportService, and the Set-MailboxTransportService as two examples, and then using the protocol logging level cmdlet. This changes per protocol, for example MailboxDeliveryConnectorProtocolLoggingLevel (Mailbox Transport service) and IntraOrgConnectorProtocolLoggingLevel (Frontend Transport service). To work out which property to set, you can use Get-FrontendTransportService server_name | FL *logginglevel*. This will return all of the properties containing LoggingLevel because the protocol logging always contains logging level. The logging level is "none" by default, and can be changed to "verbose." Note that this will generate a lot of logs, and so testing the issue on a lab environment is recommended.

Message tracking logs are also a good friend for troubleshooting, as are agent logs because both of these logs, as well as the connectivity logs, can help you track down message locations.

Apart from message logging, the other place that transport is best looked at for troubleshooting is back pressure (*http://technet.microsoft.com/en-us/library/bb201658.aspx*). This is when the server runs out of resources, or close to runs out, and the server will stop sending and receiving, typically anonymous emails first (those from the Internet and applications that do not log in). If the issue does not go away, the server will stop message flow for authenticated messages as well. The most common reason for back pressure is disk space, though available memory can often play a part. Releasing disk space and adding more memory will solve the issue for a while, or full time depending upon the scope of the initial issue. If you are going into back pressure frequently, and you resolve it and it happens again, your server is typically undersized, or you do not have enough servers for the load of email you are sending.

Troubleshooting Exchange federation trust and organization relationships

Earlier in this chapter you looked at federation trusts and organization relationships. As you saw then, the federation trust is a connection that is made to the Microsoft federation gateways (now known as the Azure Active Directory) to retrieve a token for the endpoint Exchange Server that they are attempting to reach. This source Exchange Server needs to have set up its own federation trust first before it can do this. To set up a trust you need to add to external DNS the TXT record that Exchange Server tells you to use. Do not delete and recreate the federation trust, otherwise you will need to repeat the DNS configuration.

Once the trust is made it is okay to keep in place, unless it was made during the Exchange Server 2010 RTM timeframe, in which case it should be recreated because these were made and stored in the Microsoft Live ID authentication system, and not Azure Active Directory. You can use Get-FederationInformation -DomainName domain.com to retrieve information from the authentication authority. If the TokenIssuerURIs reads "urn:federation:MicrosoftOnline," that domain is stored in Azure Active Directory.

When you have hybrid mode running, and an organization email address space, say contoso.com, is located in two locations, online and on-premises, the federation trust will only return a token to access on-premises. The users in the cloud cannot have their free/busy viewed by remote organizations unless they lookup the tenant routing address space (that is *user@contoso.onmicrosoft.com*). This is a limitation of federation trusts.

A federation trust can be tested using the Test-FederationTrust cmdlet. This, like a lot of the Test- cmdlets, requires that the test mailbox has been created. To create the test mailbox, change to the $exscripts folder and run New-TestCasConnectivityUser.ps1. You need to enter a password. This PowerShell script needs to be run once per Active Directory site. This creates a mailbox called extest_<randomdigits>@domain, and permissions it needs are granted to it.

Federation trusts require access to the Microsoft Online datacenters to set up and retrieve the trust information. Therefore, the Exchange Servers in your organization either need access to the Internet, or if there is a proxy server before the Internet, it cannot require authentication.

The federation trust is created on one Exchange Server, and the self-signed certificate that is created is replicated to the other servers. Therefore, if the replication fails, or a new server is installed and replication has not completed, you may have federation trust issues with that particular server. Get-ExchangeCertificate will return the certificates Exchange Server is aware of on a particular server.

Finally, AutoDiscover is used to locate the EWS endpoint for connecting to partner organizations. Therefore, if you cannot look up external DNS, or connect over TCP 443 to the Internet, you will fail to reach the endpoint that you need to reach for federation trusts to be used.

Troubleshooting SSO/AD FS

Active Directory Federation Services (AD FS) is a complex product and justice to troubleshooting it cannot be done here. However, the topics you need to look at to cover most of the issues you might see are:

- **Firewalls** You need inbound TCP port 443 connectivity to the WAP server, and from that to the AD FS server. This connectivity needs to be on the address published for the federation name in DNS (the federation name is something like sts.domain.com).

- **Certificates** The AD FS server and the WAP server need to be loaded with the trusted third-party certificate that the other party in the federation relationship trusts, and that is also trusted by the clients and devices that will use this AD FS farm. Microsoft will trust certificates issued by the list on *http://support.microsoft.com/kb/929395*.

- **Connectivity**   It is important to check that connectivity to both the AD FS server on the LAN, and via the Internet, is available at all times. Depending upon the product used and the type of authentication in place, different endpoints are connected to. For example, a web browser will connect to the nearest endpoint, but Outlook via Exchange Online will always connect to the WAP server, and then through that to the AD FS server (this will change from Feb 2015 with the multifactor authentication updates to Office 365 (*http://blogs.office.com/2014/11/12/office-2013-updated-authentication-enabling-multi-factor-authentication-saml-identity-providers/*). You can use the Remote Connectivity Analyzer to check AD FS, as well as numerous other settings, such as AutoDiscover, from the Internet. The Remote Connectivity Analyzer instructions can be found at *http://support.microsoft.com/kb/2650717*.

- **Login failure** The AD FS application event logs on the AD FS server (when using AD FS on Windows Server 2012 R2) will record information about a failure to issue a token for a user, and thus the user's inability to login. The logs will record a lot of known information about the user, and why the token was not issued (for example, invalid password). Earlier versions of AD FS required debugging enabled to get this information.

Troubleshooting DirSync

The Azure Directory Synchronization tool is best considered an appliance. That is, you install it and forget about it. The Miisclient.exe tool, found in the Syncbus folder on the installation path, can be used to see if it is failing to sync users, though the first indication of that is usually failing to find the user in Office 365, or that the user's settings in Office 365 are incorrect.

Because DirSync is just an appliance, it will take the information in the Active Directory, ensure it is valid, and push it to the cloud. Therefore, if the data is not valid, that is the most likely time for it to fail. The most common reasons for objects in the Active Directory not being valid are duplicates or invalid settings, such as UPN being set to something like domain. local (when domain.local is the Active Directory forest name).

Therefore, the steps to install DirSync include a series of steps for tidying up your directory. IDFix is the recommended tool to use for this. Once you have a successful sync, failure to sync later on is usually due again to duplicate entries, or invalid data being added. If users in Exchange Online cannot find users in the global address list when in hybrid mode, this is a good source of the issue.

The DirSync tool also syncs password hashes to Azure, and troubleshooting this is covered in *http://support.microsoft.com/kb/2855271*.

Finally, if the synchronization stops working, it is often due to a password expiring. On-premises, the DirSync tool is run with an Enterprise admin account, but all this does is to create its own account that has the permissions it needed. The account needed for Office 365 though needs to be made before the software is installed, and it needs to be a Global Admin. Ideally it will not have an expiring password. If the DirSync software stops after 90 days that is the most likely reason that synchronization stops working. Via Remote PowerShell to Office 365, you can run "Set-MsolUser -UserPrincipalName sync-account@tenant.onmicrosoft.com -PasswordNeverExpires $true," as shown in Figure 5-35.

FIGURE 5-35 Disabling required password change for the account used for DirSync

Troubleshooting cross-forest availability

There is a considerable amount of things that can go wrong with cross-forest availability, not least AutoDiscover, firewalls, certificates, namespaces, permissions, users, and contacts! Therefore, this book just points you in the direction of the troubleshooting whitepaper at *http://blogs.technet.com/b/exchange/archive/2011/03/04/3412075.aspx*.

Objective summary

- The best resources for troubleshooting are knowing the product or feature very well and then using sensible resources online.

Objective review

Answer the following questions to test your knowledge of the information in this objective. You can find the answers to these questions and explanations of why each answer choice is correct or incorrect in the "Answers" section at the end of this chapter.

1. Which of the following are the correct URLs for the tool used to check remote connectivity to Office 365, and Exchange, Lync, and AD FS on-premises?

    A. *http://exrca.com/*

    B. *http://testconnectivity.microsoft.com/*

    C. *http://testexchangeconnectivity.microsoft.com/*

    D. *http://exrca.onmicrosoft.com*

Answers

This section contains the solutions to the thought experiments and answers to the objective review questions in this chapter.

Objective 5.1: Thought experiment

1. To tell what authentication scheme you are currently using, you could login to remote PowerShell for Office 365 and run Get-MsolDomain. If any domain is listed as federated, and users have usernames in that domain, you are using AD FS. If a domain is listed as managed, you need to see from the Users page in the Office 365 administrators portal if you are syncing users for that domain from an on-premises AD. If you are, you are probably using DirSync with Password Sync, though you could have separate passwords and manage them separately in the Office 365 portal. If users are logging into the pilot with an onmicrosoft.com username, you are not using AD FS or password sync.

2. To put together a working pilot with AD FS server, you need an available public IP address, firewall, and DNS changes, a number of servers installed with Windows Server, and then AD FS and WAP/AD FS proxy. Optionally, but highly recommended, are load balancers and multiple AD FS and WAP servers. Finally, you need to ensure that your users log in with a domain name that you will change to federated.

Objective 5.1: Review

1. **Correct answer:** C

   A. **Incorrect:** You can run mixed versions of Exchange Server with Exchange Server 2013, as long as they are 2007 SP3 RU12 or Exchange Server 2010 SP3 or higher.

   B. **Incorrect:** You can run mixed versions of Exchange Server with Exchange Server 2013, as long as they are 2007 SP3 RU12 or Exchange Server 2010 SP3 or higher.

   C. **Correct:** All of your servers need to be online and reachable before you run the Hybrid Configuration Wizard.

   D. **Incorrect:** AutoDiscover is not used to locate servers for administration purposes, but used for users to locate their mailbox settings.

2. **Correct answer:** A

   A. **Correct:** The Hybrid Configuration Wizard centralized mail flow is required for this feature.

   B. **Incorrect:** Though you could delete the connectors and make your own, this would not be the correct way to achieve this aim.

   C. **Incorrect:** This is not correct. You can do this with centralized mail flow.

   D. **Incorrect:** Your MX records are for inbound mail flow and not outbound, as this question is asking.

3. **Correct answers:** A and C

   A. **Correct**: The token signing certificate is valid for one year.

   B. **Incorrect**: Non-activated servers will not shut down after one year.

   C. **Correct**: This might be the answer, though you might have a multi-year certificate, but it is a good step to check.

   D. **Incorrect:** This would not stop AD FS from working. AD FS would tell you your password had expired and would need changing.

Objective 5.2: Thought experiment

1. Each Exchange organization will need the following done to ensure that they are able to share calendar information between them:

   A. Ensure AutoDiscover is operational for each organization and for each domain that could be used to access a user's calendar. AutoDiscover should resolve to a 2013 CAS role server.

   B. Create a federation trust in each Exchange organization. Ensure that there are no authenticating web proxies between the Exchange Server and the Internet, and that the Exchange Server has unfiltered access to HTTPS on the Internet.

   C. Get the domain proof text with Get-FederatedDomainProof for each domain.

   D. Add a TXT record to public DNS that has the proof string for each domain as the value of the TXT record.

   E. Wait until DNS changes are published, and complete the federation trust. Select the primary domain and add any additional domains to the trust.

   F. Create an organizational relationship in each Exchange organization for the other two Exchange organizations. Allow calendar sharing and do not restrict permissions.

   G. Test the federation trust and organization relationship by viewing a calendar of a user in a different forest. Repeat the test for all of the forests.

Objective 5.2: Review

1. **Correct answer:** D

   A. **Incorrect:** Even though the Hybrid Configuration Wizard configures federation trusts, it only does it for the on-premises to Exchange Online domains. Therefore, you do not change the federation trust with the HybridConfiguration cmdlets.

   B. **Incorrect:** This is not a valid cmdlet.

   C. **Incorrect:** Even though this would appear to be a valid cmdlet becaue the TXT record is required, the value is not obtained via this invalid cmdlet.

   D. **Correct:** This cmdlet will retrieve the TXT record value required.

2. **Correct answer:** A

   A. **Correct:** The default behavior in Exchange Online is to allow anonymous calendar sharing.

   B. **Incorrect:** The default sharing policy is already configured for anonymous and the tenant administrator does not have access to the OWA virtual directories in Exchange Online.

   C. **Incorrect:** The default sharing policy is already configured for anonymous access.

   D. **Incorrect:** This is not correct. Anonymous sharing is available in Exchange Online.

3. **Correct answer:** B

   A. **Incorrect:** Organization relationships are used to set this sharing in place and not permissions on calendars.

   B. **Correct:** A security group is used to restrict the right to access calendar or free/busy information on the organization relationship.

   C. **Incorrect:** This is not true. You can restrict to the membership of a single group.

   D. **Incorrect:** Organization relationships are used to set this sharing in place and not permissions on calendars.

Objective 5.3: Thought experiment

1. To move your mailbox you can either install Exchange Server 2013 in the same organization as Exchange Server 2010 and use the 2013 tools to move the mailbox, or you can export your mailbox to a PST and import again into a new forest. If using a new forest you need to configure shared namespace mail flow routing. You will need to ensure that Exchange Server 2010 is running Service Pack 3 or later for coexistence to work.

2. If using the same forest, you will not update the endpoints for mail and AutoDiscover etc. to point to Exchange Server 2013, as you will use a different namespace to connect to your mailbox. For AutoDiscover, editing the HOSTS file on your computer will direct your client alone to the correct Exchange Server endpoint.

Objective 5.3: Review

1. **Correct answer:** D

   A. **Incorrect:** This digital certificate contains a legacy namespace for AutoDiscover, which is not required.

   B. **Incorrect:** This digital certificate contains two legacy namespaces, *legacy.contoso.com* and *legacy.mail.contoso.com*. Only one is required and either one would do, but *legacy.contoso.com* requires less configuration on DNS (it is not a subzone) and so is recommended.

C. Incorrect: This digital certificate does not contain a legacy namespace as required for Exchange 2007 coexistence.

D. Correct: This is a correct example for a 2007 coexistence digital certificate.

2. **Correct answer:** B

   A. Incorrect: You do not need a legacy namespace because Exchange 2013 will proxy the connection to the Exchange 2007 server.

   B. Correct: Legacy namespaces are required for OWA 2007 only because this is the only protocol that redirects. The rest proxy, and so do not require additional namespaces.

3. **Correct answer:** C

   A. Incorrect: Though port 25 can receive authenticated client connections, port 587 is recommended for client-to-server communications because 25 is reserved for SMTP server to SMTP server communications.

   B. Incorrect: Port 475 is the Mailbox Transport Delivery service port for Exchange Transport delivering to the mailbox, and is not for client communications.

   C. Correct: TCP port 587 is recommended for mail user agents (MUA) connecting to mail transport agents (MTA). An MUA is SMTP speak for an SMTP client and an MTA is an SMTP server, such as Exchange Server.

   D. Incorrect: Port 2525 is used by Exchange Server 2013 transport service when both the CAS and Mailbox role are installed on the same server.

Objective 5.4: Thought experiment

1. You can make use of calendar sharing (anonymous, via the Internet), organizational relationships via federation trusts, and availability address space sharing.

2. All things being equal, federated trusts and organizational relationships are the easiest to set up and maintain. They also allow your partner organization to share their calendars or free/busy with other organizations if they set up relationships as well.

Objective 5.4: Review

1. **Correct answers:** B and C

   A. Incorrect: Authoritative accepted domains will deliver to a valid recipient or reject the message.

   B. Correct: Internal relay accepted domains will forward the message to the MX record or preferably a send connector that routes to the next hop when a message address cannot be resolved locally.

   C. Correct: External relay accepted domains are the same as internal relay accepted domains (answer B) with regard to delivering to a valid recipient, or forwarding onward to the next hop.

    D. **Incorrect:** This is not a valid domain type.

  2. **Correct answer:** A

    A. **Correct:** "Set-ClientAccessServer -AutoDiscoverServiceInternalUri https://autodiscover.contoso.com/Autodiscover/Autodiscover.xml" is an example of this cmdlet.

    B. **Incorrect:** Set-ExchangeServer does not set the SCP.

    C. **Incorrect:** Set-MailboxServer does not set the SCP.

    D. **Incorrect:** Set-AutoDiscoverVirtualDirectory does not set the SCP.

Objective 5.5: Thought experiment

  1. You can install an Exchange Server 2003 server using the RecoverServer installation switch and then uninstall it correctly. This will clean up the Active Directory. It is possible to remove servers from Active Directory with AdsiEdit, but this is not supported. Ideally you would look in the Exchange Server 2013 installation log file for the cause of the failure and you might get further information in the log as to the reason why it has failed to install.

  2. You would need to check the version of all your Exchange 2010 servers that are installed. Pay particular attention to any Edge Servers because they may have been SP1 at time of install and when EdgeSync was implemented, but are now the correct version. Also, incorrectly uninstalled (that is, turned off and not uninstalled) servers remain in the Active Directory and need to be removed properly or recovered and uninstalled.

Objective 5.5: Review

  1. **Correct answers:** C and D

    A. **Incorrect:** Exchange Server 2000 needs to be migrated to a separate forest and with either PST migration or third-party tools. It can be migrated via Exchange Server 2007 or Exchange Server 2010.

    B. **Incorrect:** Exchange Server 2003 needs to be migrated to a separate forest and with either PST migration or third-party tools. It can be migrated via Exchange Server 2007 or Exchange Server 2010.

    C. **Correct:** This upgrade is allowed.

    D. **Correct:** This upgrade is allowed.

  2. **Correct answer:** D

    A. **Incorrect:** This cmdlet uses Set-Mailbox and not Set-MailboxDatabase.

    B. **Incorrect:** IsExcludedFromProvisioning requires a $True or $False switch.

    C. **Incorrect:** This cmdlet uses Set-Mailbox and not Set-MailboxDatabase.

    D. **Correct:** This cmdlet will work.

3. **Correct answer:** B

    A. **Incorrect:** Online is not a valid move type.

    B. **Correct:** This cmdlet will work.

    C. **Incorrect:** TXTData and a text file is not a valid file format or file type. It is CSV-Data and a .csv file with a single column called EmailAddress.

    D. **Incorrect:** This cmdlet uses New-MoveRequest, but all of the parameters are from New-MigrationBatch.

Objective 5.6: Thought experiment

1. You would use Exchange Server 2013 features such as Get-Queue, Get-MessageTrack-ingLog, and protocol logging for the transport service.

2. You would open the Miisclient.exe program on the DirSync server and look for errors in the sync client. Errors could be fixed using IDFix or any other Active Directory tool or script.

3. The Remote Connectivity Analyzer for remote users, and using clients and a web browser to access Office 365 from on-premises.

Objective 5.6: Review

1. **Correct answers:** A, B, and C

    A. **Correct:** This URL takes you to the Remote Connectivity Analyzer.

    B. **Correct:** This URL takes you to the Remote Connectivity Analyzer.

    C. **Correct:** This URL takes you to the Remote Connectivity Analyzer.

    D. **Incorrect:** This is not a valid URL

Index

A

O

OAuth 288, 293
Office 365 11, 90, 102, 139, 280
  Azure RMS i n 144
  cross-forest mail flow 331
  journaling restrictions and 250
  licenses 205–207
  online archiving in 205–216
  shared namespaces in 337
  single sign-on in 294, 301–303
  subscription 281
  tenant 281
Office 365 Message Encryption (OME) 266
Office ProPlus edition 145
online archiving. *See also* archives/archiving
  licenses 205–207
  setting up 205–216
Online parameter 7
on-premises mailboxes archives for 213–216, 220
opportunistic TLS 155
organization relationships 316–318
  troubleshooting 348–349
OrgID 307
outbound connectors 107, 121, 286–287
Outlook
  configuring S/MIME settings in 149–151
  message encryption 152–154
Outlook 2013 Trust Center 149–150
Outlook Address Book 93
Outlook Anywhere 91, 92, 93, 94, 322
Outlook calendar permissions 313
Outlook Protection Rules 172–174, 175
Outlook Voice Access 3–4
Outlook Web App options page 18, 19–20
Outlook Web App (OWA) 3-4, 21, 93, 94, 97, 98, 119–120, 154, 321, 322
  Anonymous Features setting 312
  configuring to support XML files 184–185
  legal hold and 246
  S/MIME and 145, 154–155
  virtual directory policy 312
Oversize Message 265

P

passwords 143
PB4S-Configuration-user@domain.com.xml file 173
Permanently Delete tag 239
permissions 134–135, 195–196
PIN numbers 29, 36, 143
PKI. *See* Private Key Infrastructure (PKI)
poison queues 111
policy migration 343
Policy Tips 225
POP/IMAP 322
port 587 115
port 5060 6, 10
port 5061 10
port 64327 124
Port parameter 6
port TCP 475 114
PowerShell 6
  cmdlets 4
  configuration of call answering rules via 20–21
  creating dial plan using 25
  disabling Unified Messaging via 32
  enabling Unified Messaging via 31
preferred architecture (PA) 22
pre-licensing 177
Primary Active Manager (PAM) 74, 87
priority values 103
privacy
  digital signatures and 148
  S/MIME and 148
Private Key Infrastructure (PKI) 146–147
private keys 142, 146–147, 148, 152, 155, 192–194
protected voice mail 2–3, 33–35, 41
  settings 34–35
  setup using Exchange Admin Center 34–35
  setup using Exchange Management Shell 35
protocol layer 96
proxy layer 89. *See also* Client Access Server (CAS) role
proxy redirect 323–324
proxy servers 118-119, 292, 295, 297, 309
proxy settings 287
public folder migration 339–341
public keys 142, 146–147, 148, 152–153, 155

About the authors

BRIAN REID is a freelance consultant, instructor, and author specializing in Microsoft Exchange Server. Brian has extensive experience helping customers design and integrate Exchange Server and Active Directory in the enterprise. Brian is skilled at migrating various versions of Exchange to the latest versions and to Office 365, as well as other email server products. Brian specializes in Exchange Server organization design and architecture, and problem remediation. Brian is both an MCM (Microsoft Certified Master) and MVP (Most Valuable Professional) in Exchange Server. In addition, Brian is a sought-after speaker at Exchange conferences and events. He blogs on his company website at www.c7solutions.com.

STEVE GOODMAN is a consultant for Ciber UK, focusing on Exchange, Microsoft Office 365, and Microsoft Lync. He is actively involved in the Exchange community, authoring, blogging, and hosting Exchange, Lync, and Office 365 podcasts, He speaks often at user groups and conferences. Steve holds multiple certifications and is an Exchange Server MVP.

From technical overviews to drilldowns on special topics, get
free ebooks from Microsoft Press at:

www.microsoftvirtualacademy.com/ebooks

Download your free ebooks in PDF, EPUB, and/or Mobi for
Kindle formats.

Look for other great resources at Microsoft Virtual Academy,
where you can learn new skills and help advance your career
with free Microsoft training delivered by experts.

Microsoft Press

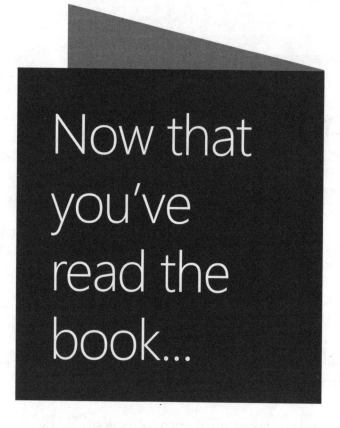

Now that you've read the book...

Tell us what you think!

Was it useful?
Did it teach you what you wanted to learn?
Was there room for improvement?

Let us know at http://aka.ms/tellpress

Your feedback goes directly to the staff at Microsoft Press,
and we read every one of your responses. Thanks in advance!

 Microsoft